"My Heart Is So *Rebellious*"

The Caldwell Letters

1861 – 1865

With Annotations By
John K. Gott,
and
John E. Divine

Introduction
By
T. Triplett Russell

Edited By
J. Michael Welton

Publication of this book has been made possible
through the sponsorship of
The Fauquier National Bank
10 Courthouse Square
P.O. Box 561
Warrenton, Virginia 22186

For

Ann Mabey Welton,

Cleland Burwell Welton II

and

Lucy Sommerville Welton

ACKNOWLEDGEMENTS

I am fortunate to be one of a number of individuals, spanning many generations, each of whom has made this book possible:

Charles Caldwell (1866-1956), son of Lycurgus and Susan Caldwell, is due a great deal of posthumous recognition for preserving, transcribing and excerpting the entire collection of letters, and distributing copies among the family. He also researched and authored an extensive family history, much of which has served as the historical authority for the book's background. Because of this thorough and diligent work late in his life, these letters became at first a treasure for the family, and are to be shared now with a larger community.

His daughter, Virginia Caldwell Gale (granddaughter of Susan and Lycurgus and also a granddaughter of Col. Charles E. Biedler, youngest of Mosby's Rangers), is current steward of the letters. She deserves a terrific vote of thanks for allowing me to peruse, for days at a time, the collection. Moreover, she graciously opened her home and gardens in New York to me, and over meals and late night ice cream, proved a most admirable hostess.

Bell Gale Chevigny, holder of the letters' copyright, has been quite generous in sharing them, as well as her research and knowledge of the history of the Caldwell and Jeffords families. Her willingness to do so is greatly appreciated; her challenge to me to recognize their significance beyond the era during which they were written cannot be measured.

The financial commitment that has made publishing this book possible implies great risk, and demands an unwavering trust in the project's editor. Those who make this kind of commitment also must be owners of a vision for success—that the past and future *can* be harnessed in the present, with the potential for outstanding results. We are fortunate in Fauquier to count among us The Fauquier National Bank, for whom this kind of vision is daily the rule, rather than the exception. More specifically, credit must be given to the bank's president, C. Hunton Tiffany, and its board of directors.

Fauquier's tradition of oral history—of stories passed from generation to generation—has come to yield over the years two results: first, much of the history here has been placed into the hands of a few individuals generally acknowledged as natural heirs to the words, deeds and icons of the community's elders; second, there exists little more than a relative handful of books on the county's history. "It used to be," John K. Gott once told me, "that people would say: 'Why don't you write that down?' And people would answer: 'Oh, only yankees write books.'" Thankfully, local historians like Nancy Baird and Mr. Gott disagreed, and have published volumes. It is through Mr. Gott's colorful annotations that many of the characters in these letters come to life, and through his generous contributions of an 1854 map of Warrenton and an 1860 census that the reader will find the raw data leading to the discovery of precisely who and what this town was about during the war years.

I am also truly grateful for the participation of John Gott's personal friend and collaborator, T. Triplett Russell, an architect and historian whose introduction and notations here help weave together history, families and architecture into one fabric. And, through Mr. Gott's efforts, the book also contains footnotes by local Civil War historian John E. Divine, whose knowledge of troop movements in Fauquier and across the nation during the war adds much to the understanding of the letters.

I am indebted also to a great number of individuals who have encouraged and assisted me as I pulled this book together. They include Lorene Head, whose secretarial service, keen eye and patience made the transcribing process a relative breeze; Irving L. Hottle and Clare Caruso of Winchester Printers, for professional guidance and publishing acumen; the staff of the Fauquier County Library; the Staten Island Academy; and the members of the Black Horse Chapter, United Daughters of the Confederacy (of which Susan Caldwell was an early member), the Warrenton Antiquarian Society, and the Fauquier Historical Society. Others in Warrenton who helped include Lynn Hopewell, Gertrude Trumbo, Burke Davis III, and Harry Wonham.

Finally, although each of the above has certainly aided me in many ways, it is important to emphasize that the ultimate responsibility for this book—including its flaws and errors—are, of course, mine alone.

J. Michael Welton

FOREWORD

It was twentieth-century poet and author James Agee who, in Lawrence Bergreen's 1984 biography, *James Agee, A Life,* observed that: "The two main facts about any letter are its immediacy and the flawlessness of its revelations," and that "in the sense that any dream is a faultless work of art, so is any letter."*

I believe Mr. Agee's thoughts are especially relevant to these letters telling the story of a Virginia family snared in an unexpectedly protracted American Civil War.

In the broadest sense, this is a story dealing with a number of themes with which each of us, as Americans alive in the last of the 20th century, is familiar today: the question of family life, extended and disrupted; the uncertainty of an unstable economy, brought on by inflation and a major national deficit; and the conundrum of slavery and race relations—present since the drafting of the Constitution, one of the causes for the war during which these letters were written, and quite possibly, the largest single question facing the American people today.

But it is primarily the story of a 19th-century woman of the middle class. It is the story of *her* war—viewed through her eyes, interpreted through her religious and emotional filters, and written by her hand to the people about whom she cared most. More significantly, it is a personal record of her conflicts arising from the repeated collision of romantic ideals with brutal realities.

Daughter of a sailmaker, Susan Emeline Jeffords Caldwell was transplanted by marriage to the town of Warrenton, Virginia from her native Charleston, South Carolina. Most of her letters here are written to her husband, Lycurgus Washington Caldwell, who, at the time of the war, was employed by the Confederacy in Richmond. Hers form the bulk of this correspondence, although there are included a number of letters from Lycurgus, his brother, their brother-in-law, and members of her family.

Her husband's correspondence, coming from Richmond, contained much of the news from the capital of the Confederacy, and, as she wrote on June 9, 1862, was considered "more satisfactory than the newspapers" in Fauquier County. The apparent result was that his letters were distributed around the county (for example, in June of 1862, she wrote of passing them on to Mr. Hunton and Mr. Love), were eagerly read, and evidently disposed of.

The story's settings include Richmond, Virginia, Charleston, South Carolina and Booneville, Missouri, but its focus is almost exclusively upon Warrenton, a small town in the foothills of the Blue Ridge Mountains. Although no battle was fought there, the town's location near Washington, D.C., the Shenandoah Valley and the Manassas Gap railroad placed it, on some days, in the hands of southern officers like General J.E.B. Stuart or Colonel John S. Mosby, and on others, in those of Generals George B. McClellan, John W. Geary, Rufus King, Ambrose E. Burnside, John Pope, James Shields, or George G. Meade.

---

*Lawrence Bergreen, *James Agee A Life,* (New York: E.P. Dutton, Inc., 1984), p. 220.

Although a fervent believer in the "Cause" she initially portrayed as glorious, Susan wrote letters that gradually reveal the agonizing impact of its cumulative harvest. She may have survived the war, but she was forced to live its daily horrors, as Warrenton was transformed into hospital and cemetery for Confederate and Federal troops alike.

Throughout this war, Susan Caldwell suffered personally. She watched in agony as soldiers, civilians and innocent children suffered. She lamented the deaths of those she knew and those she did not. And she was driven nearly to insanity at her helplessness during the sickness that led to the death of her daughter.

Separated from her husband, she also might as well have been a continent away from her family in South Carolina. She heard infrequently from them, relied upon newspaper accounts and word of mouth to learn of events affecting them, and displayed a strong imaginative awareness of their circumstances.

Her yearnings for peace and a united family—present from the war's outset—became stronger and more frequent as the war spiralled downward. By March of 1865, she had seen Warrenton and Fauquier pillaged, her own household plundered by Federal troops, two family deaths inside the home, and her husband, seemingly safe as a clerk at war's beginning, earnestly engaged in a doomed, last-ditch defense of Richmond.

These letters, then, are a tribute to a woman who is not the mythical, fire-breathing Southern plantation owner, but who possessed an almost incredible patience, faith and will—believing that she and her family, God willing, would live and love together at the end of the conflict.

Each letter is titled, since some are from Susan, some from Lycurgus, and some from other family members. Most are dated; however, those which are not have been placed, after careful consideration, into the time frame which seemed most appropriate, given the events or issues addressed.

Some will appear fragmented, where pages were missing from the original collection. Others, because of illegible handwriting, will be missing a word or two. Ellipses (...) will indicate such lapses.

To preserve the immediacy and context of the moment in which these letters were written, I have attempted to faithfully reproduce the grammar, spelling, emphasis, and punctuation used by the correspondents. Although errors by the writers may seem painfully obvious to the reader, I have chosen to resist, out of respect for the authors, the temptation to add any more 20th century editing marks than clarity demands.

For the curious, one last note: the book's title is drawn from one of Susan's final letters in this collection, dated January 15, 1865.

I believe the reader will find it meaningful on a number of levels.

J.M.W.

CAST OF CHARACTERS

James Caldwell (1794–1832)

Although he is never mentioned here, James was progenitor of much of the family around which this volume revolves, and the individual who established the Caldwells in Warrenton.

As a young man, he was employed in a printing office in Winchester. By 1817, he was publishing his own newspaper, "The Palladium of Liberty," the first for Warrenton and Fauquier County.

He died in 1832. His wife and children continued to live in the house he had completed the year before in Warrenton, and which he had already placed in the names of his three offspring.

Frances Pattie Caldwell (1803–1863)

Daughter of William Pattie, Sr., of Fauquier County, Frances was married to James Caldwell on December 24, 1818. She would bear five children in Warrenton, including:

> Francis Marion Caldwell (1819–1899)
> Lucy Ann Caldwell (1822–1911)
> Lycurgus Washington Caldwell (1823–1910)
> Patrick Henry Caldwell (1827–?)
> Susan Frances Caldwell (1832–?)

Both Patrick Henry Caldwell and Susan Frances Caldwell died in infancy. Frances is known in these letters as "Grand Ma."

Francis Marion Caldwell (1819–1899)

Known here as "Frank," Francis Marion Caldwell had established, by the time of the Civil War, a newspaper called "The Observer" in Booneville, Missouri. After siding with the Confederacy in the battle near there on June 17, 1861, Frank fled to Texas at the rebels' defeat.

At war's end, he returned to Booneville and resumed publication of his newspaper.

Lucy Ann Caldwell Finks (1822–1911)

She is referred to throughout these letters as "Sister" and "Anty." Her marriage to John W. Finks in 1840 was the first within the Caldwell home in Warrenton.

By 1850, Frank Caldwell had sold his rights to the home to Lucy's husband, leaving the ownership shared between Lucy, her husband, and Lycurgus Caldwell.

Although Lucy and John Finks had no children of their own, they did adopt Rebecca Ann Stofer, who died in 1853, and also invited others to live at home with them, apparently as wards. These were "Lutie" Finks, a niece from Waynesboro, and Sally Withers, who would later marry Warrenton businessman Albert Fletcher.

John William Finks (1818–1879)

Known here as "Mr. F.," "Uncle Will," and called "Daddy" by the Caldwell children, Mr. Finks was entrepreneur, publisher and landowner. He operated a drugstore on Main Street (said to be the first with plate glass windows in town), served as commissary for the Confederacy in Fauquier, and also published the "Warrenton Flag of '98," one of the town's earlier newspapers of record.

He was the son of Fielding (1789-1874) and Frances Botts Triplett Finks (1789-1869), who were originally from Culpeper, and who moved to Front Royal in 1850.

At the time of these letters, Mr. Finks had access to at least one farm (probably his parents' in Front Royal), which would provide those living in the Caldwell home with food to eat and fuel to burn during the war.

He is also credited with a number of improvements to the home and grounds of the house built by James Caldwell.

Lycurgus Washington Caldwell (1823–1910)

Addressed by his wife as "Papa" in these letters, Lycurgus was the youngest son of James. He was 9 years old at his father's death, but was educated in private schools. By 12, he was working in a printing office in town. By 17, he had left for Washington, to be employed by Samuel F. B. Morse, and was present later, when the first telegraphic message was sent from Washington to Baltimore.

Placed in charge of a telegraph office in Charleston, he met Susan Jeffords at the house where he boarded, and married her on October 1, 1851. He later secured a position with the U.S. Treasury Department in Washington, and moved there with his wife shortly after their marriage.

By April, 1861, at the outbreak of war, Lycurgus already had resigned his position with the U.S. Treasury, and moved with his family back to Warrenton, to the home in which he still held one-third interest.

As these letters begin, Lycurgus had departed Warrenton for Richmond only a day before, seeking a post within the Confederate government.

Susan Emeline Jeffords Caldwell (1827–1913)

The author of the majority of these letters, Susan was the daughter of John H.

Jeffords and Mary Humbert Jeffords of Charleston, South Carolina.

A devout Baptist, she was descended from the Reverend William Screven, who constituted the First Baptist Church of Charleston in 1683 and was its first pastor.

She married Lycurgus in 1851, and would bear three children before the war and one child during it. They were:

William Caldwell (1855–1903)
Frank Huntington Caldwell (1857–1946)
Jessie Caldwell (Walraven) (1859–1946)
Lucy Lee Caldwell (1861–1864)

She signs her letters here: "S.E.C." Her husband addresses her as: "Daughter."

William Caldwell (1855–1903)

The oldest son of Lycurgus and Susan, he is called "Willie" in this correspondence. Six years old when the Civil War began, he later would attend, according to his younger brother Charles' account, nearby Bethel Military Academy and the University of Virginia.

Frank Huntington Caldwell (1857–1946)

Born in Washington like his older brother, Frank lived in Warrenton as a boy, attending private school there. He would eventually serve as editor and publisher of "The True Index" in Warrenton before selling the newspaper to Thomas E. Frank, who, in 1905, renamed it "The Fauquier Democrat."

Jessie Caldwell {Walraven} (1859–1946)

Born in Warrenton just before the war, Jessie was beginning to walk and talk as these letters begin.

Much later she would marry an Edgar Walraven of Pennsylvania, and upon the dissolution of that marriage, move back to her childhood home with her two daughters, to live there most of the remainder of her life.

In her life, Jessie would become one of Warrenton's pioneers in women's rights—crusading for votes for women, and *working* (until that time, an unheard of practice in Warrenton for white, middle income women) as a legal secretary, as Warrenton's telephone switchboard operator, and as correspondent for "The True Index."

Lucy Lee Caldwell (1861–1864)

The apple of her mother's eye, Lucy Lee was the infant of the family during the war. Her brief life and personality are reflected in a number of these letters, after her birth on the tenth anniversary of Susan's and Lycurgus' wedding date—October 1, 1861.

Also among those living and working within the Caldwell home are a number of slaves, to whom Susan Caldwell refers as "servants." Among these are "Aunt" Lucy, "Aunt" Harriet, "Uncle" John, Cinda, Susa, and Alice. Unfortunately, little more than what is contained in this correspondence is known of them.

INTRODUCTION

Historians tend to base their work on the life and times of important personages who, by reason of their power and high station, are able to shape the course of events more or less to their own liking. The reader is often left wondering how the ordinary man or woman fared when left to cope with the difficulties of survival in troubled times not of their own making. We know, therefore, a great deal about the day-to-day existence of leaders, but relatively little of the rank and file.

What did he or she think of the chaos swirling about? How did he or she grapple with the everyday hardships and privations suddenly thrust upon them? What sort of life did he or she live in a world turned upside down?

The duration of the American Civil War, especially for those living in Virginia, was a time of trial and tribulation. Coming, as it did, without much warning to a peaceful and prosperous country, it caught the average individual without experience in the havoc of war and its aftermath.

Intimate knowledge of such matters can only be obtained through the careful perusal of contemporary letters written in the white heat of the moment, and in diaries written in contemplation of the day's events. When families were torn apart by war or other calamities in the 19th century or before, letters were the only means of communication. Diaries provide the only other record of day-to-day events of minor importance, and are also essential to a complete understanding of an age of internecine strife.

The letters of Susan Emeline Jeffords Caldwell to her husband, Lycurgus Washington Caldwell, and his to her, provide just such a window on an era. Essentially, they are concerned with the well-being of their families and friends in Warrenton and Richmond, Virginia, as well as in Booneville, Missouri, and Charleston, South Carolina.

To fully understand these letters, it is necessary to know something of the background of the people who wrote them. The records of Fauquier County, fortunately, are largely intact, and yield much about them. The house in which they lived is still standing in a part of Warrenton not too greatly changed since the mid-19th century. We know, in general, who was related to whom, and what their past history had been. We know also that, although they were not wealthy, they were in relatively comfortable circumstances before the war.

The pleasant little town of Warrenton, in the northern Virginia Piedmont, is about 50 miles west/southwest of Washington, D.C. It is the county seat of Fauquier County, having begun as Fauquier Court House soon after the county was created in 1759. It was not incorporated until 1810, when it was given the name Warrenton, perhaps in honor of General Joseph Warren, who was killed at Bunker Hill. More likely, however, is that the name was for the Warren Academy, established there shortly after The Revolution.

By 1810, the town was well-established, boasting, in addition to its courthouse, a boys' school, two ordinaries, one or more public houses, a jailhouse, a variety of shops, and a number of quite substantial residences.

A shop that was lacking was one for printing, and for a weekly newspaper. To Warrenton sometime before 1817, therefore, came the youthful James Caldwell, son of Joseph Caldwell, who had been a soldier in the Revolutionary War, and present at Yorktown. James Caldwell had been working in Winchester in a printing shop under the tutelage of Jonathan Foster, editor of "The Republican Constellation," Winchester's weekly news sheet. By 1817, Caldwell had set up his shop in a small building "at Jail and South Seventh Streets," now the site of the Olde Towne Texaco.

By mid-summer, he was ready to launch his newspaper, "The Palladium of Liberty." At that time, editors often reached into the classics for their banners. In ancient Greece, the Palladium was the statue of Pallas Athena, set up in Athens to protect the city; thus, Caldwell offered protection to the liberty for which his father had fought. A copy of one of the early editions, dated, August 23, 1817, may now be seen in the Library of Congress. It was Fauquier's first newspaper.

Either James Caldwell had private means, or "The Palladium of Liberty" was an instant success, because, a little more than a year later, its editor and publisher felt secure enough to marry Frances Pattie, on December 24, 1818, in Warrenton. She was the daughter of William Pattie, Sr., a Warrenton merchant.

On the 26th of November, 1826, James Caldwell bought a large lot in Warrenton from John A. Cash. It was at 106 Smith Street, and extended through to Chestnut Street. He had the deed recorded in the names of his children. It has been suggested that this unusual procedure may have been used to protect them, in the event that something should happen to him, from the consequences of any notes that he may have endorsed which might later go by default—the action of a prudent man in an age of widespread speculation and economic fluctuation.

On this lot he commenced the construction of a large fieldstone house in the then-prevailing Federal style. The design was quite simple, and it seems probable that the five-bay front wall was devoid of decoration except for the fanlight over the door, ever-present in the Federal style.

The construction of this house, one of the finest in Warrenton, indicates that James Caldwell was doing very well in the prosperous, early years of the 1830's. Conspicuously lacking, however, were the outbuildings necessary for even a townhouse at that time. Doubtless, he intended building them as required, but fate intervened. He was to live in his new house only briefly. Leaving his unfinished property in Warrenton, he went to Culpeper County, where he wanted to establish another newspaper. There he died suddenly, on July 30, 1832, before his 40th birthday. He was buried in the Episcopal Church Yard in Culpeper. His widow, Frances Pattie Caldwell, who survived him by more than 30 years, was laid beside him in November, 1863.

After his death, his widow continued to live in the Warrenton house, raising her three children. Apparently they were left in comfortable circumstances. The children were given a superior education, but we do not know much of the details of Frank's or Lucy's. Lycurgus attended a school for boys run by Captain George L. Ball, in a small brick building at 28 Smith Street, where he received a thorough grounding in English, Mathematics, Latin and Greek. He may also have attended the celebrated Warren Academy, as he was named as a pupil of a "Mr. Leary," who is known to have taught there. However, it should be noted that small private schools of the sort run by Captain Ball were quite capable of preparing boys for entrance to West Point, Princeton, or The University of Virginia, to name three favored by young southerners. He is said to have served later a brief apprenticeship in a printing shop in Warrenton operated by John Marshall. In 1840, Lycurgus, aged 17, was evidently ready to try his wings.

The marriage of his sister, Lucy, now 18, gave him the opportunity. She married, at the Caldwell house, John William Finks, aged 22, on January 8, 1840. John Finks, son of Fielding and Frances Botts Triplett Finks, was already considered one of Warrenton's most prominent young businessmen. With Dr. Luther Hamme, apothecary, he owned and operated a drug store in Warrenton. He also owned or had access to two farms, probably in Warren County. His grandfather, Daniel Triplett, of Warren County, died in 1845, leaving an immense landed estate. The farms may have been his mother's share of her father's land.

When John Finks moved with his wife into the Caldwell home, Lycurgus departed for Washington. Finks later bought Frank Caldwell's share in the home, but Lycurgus retained his interest.

In the meantime, Lycurgus found interesting employment in Washington with Samuel Finley Breese Morse, a noted artist. Morse was working on an invention—no less than an electric telegraph. Young Caldwell soon became proficient in operating the machine, and is said to have been present on May 24, 1844, when Morse, in Washington, tapped out his famous inquiry, "What Hath God Wrought," to an amazed recipient in Baltimore. Some have said that Caldwell himself tapped out the message, but the family refrains from such a claim.

John Finks started immediately making substantial improvements to the Caldwell home, and adding the outbuildings that James Caldwell had not had time to finish. A carriage house on the back lot, a stable for horses and cows, a meat house near the main house, as well as a "beehive" dairy and icehouse a short distance to the north of the dining room door were among the additions attributed to Finks.

By far, the most ambitious project was, however, the alteration and addition to the house itself. By 1851, the house, built some 20 years before, was evidently deemed in need of something to bring it up to date, and to relieve its relative austerity. The house was not so much enlarged as it was "Italianized," by the addition of an ornate portico with a "porch" room above. It was more than enough to change the architectural heritage of the house.

After his marriage, Finks was listed as the owner of the Caldwell house, tentatively, and for tax purposes. Lycurgus, still a one-third owner, continued his work for Morse.

Morse sent him as telegraph operator to Fredericksburg, and then to Charleston, South Carolina. There, at the house where he boarded, he met Susan Jeffords, whom he married on October 1, 1851. Lycurgus and his bride returned to Washington sometime before January 10, 1855, when their first child, William, was born. Lycurgus worked there as an auditor in the Treasury. At that time, if not earlier, he knew Harvel Harris Goodloe, also in the Treasury, of whose good offices he would soon be in need.

A second child, Frank H. Caldwell, was born in Washington on May 24, 1857, and a third, Jessie Caldwell, was born in Warrenton on September 2, 1859. In late 1859, Lycurgus returned with the family to his Fauquier County home.

On the 17th of June, 1861, there came a letter from his friend Goodloe, written from Richmond, suggesting that he come to Richmond and apply for a position in the Post Office or Auditor's office of the Confederate government. He was in Richmond four days later, when he received a letter—the first in this collection—from his wife, expressing the hope that he had secured a position in the "Solicitor's" Office, where the work "will not be so tedious as in the General Post Office."

He was then 38, too old, his wife reckoned, to be called upon to serve in the army, should there be a war. In all likelihood, neither he nor she could have dreamed at the time that a war could be as devastating, or last as long as this one would.

In fact, the Caldwells and Finks were fortunate. They had, at the least, a roof over their heads and food on their table. The farms in Warren County were miraculously unscathed, so they were not often without fresh fruit and vegetables, or a warm hearth.

These letters, written between June, 1861 and March, 1865, place in sharp focus the anxieties and hardships felt in Warrenton, Richmond, Missouri and South Carolina. They provide us with an unusually clear picture of strained family relationships, day-to-day struggles, and a slowly declining social system—all brought about by the American Civil War.

T. Triplett Russell

James Caldwell
(1794-1832)

Frances Pattie Caldwell
(1803-1863)

Lycurgus Washington Caldwell
(1823-1910)

Susan Emeline Jeffords Caldwell
(1827-1913)

Lucy Caldwell Finks
(1822-1911)

John William Finks
(1818-1879)

The Caldwell Family (c.1910)
Susan Caldwell is fifth from left; Lycurgus, sixth from right.

Jessie Caldwell Walraven (1859-1946)
with her two daughters, Jessie Finks Walraven (later, Mrs. Courtenay S. Welton) and
Helen Chamberlain Walraven (later Mrs. William H. Edwards).

The Caldwell Home, 12 Smith Street, Warrenton, Virginia (c. 1880)

1861

Susan Emeline Jeffords Caldwell to Lycurgus Washington Caldwell

Warrenton, Via
Sunday, June 23rd, 1861

Dearest Papa

Thinking a few lines from home will be gratifying to you, I have concluded to write to you this morning. I am all alone in my room—Sister and Mr. F. with the two boys have gone to the Methodist Church to hear the new Preacher who has arrived to take Mr Ward's place—having suffered very much all yesterday and last night with severe sick headache—and it continues to ache this morning, I was afraid to venture out in the sun—it bids fair to be a very warm day. Yesterday was pleasant all day—I was glad of it as it was more agreeable to you for travelling. Mr Richard Smith[1] informed Mr Finks of his having met with you at Gordonsville—

I hope all went well with you and you are now safely domiciled in Richmond. May the Good Lord protect you while there from all that can hurt both soul and body. We have all missed you. Jessie has inquired for Papa—but insists you are up street at Daddy's store—bring her cake. Frank tells her No—Papa gone to Richmond. Willie could not become reconciled to going without his first having seen you. I expect you will meet with Mr Brooke[2] in Richmond—he's anxious to take his seat with the members before Convention adjourns. Everything remains about the same as when you left—no news stirring.

I hope you will be successful on obtaining a situation in the Solicitor's Office—the work will not be so tedious as in General Post Office—keep up good spirits—and don't be desponding—all things will work for good. I feel very sanguine as to your success. I expect Mr Finks will join you on Tuesday—tomorrow (Monday) being

---

[1] Richard M. Smith (1819-1872), son of William Rowley and Lucy Steptoe (Blackwell) Smith of 'Alton,' near Bethel. Richard M. Smith was a distinguished educator and editor. He founded the Warren Green Academy in Warrenton and was professor of science at Randolph Macon College. He established the *Virginia Sentinel* and edited the Richmond *Enquirer*. (J.K.G.)

[2] James Vass Brooke (1824-1898): After studying law in the office of Judge R. C. L. Moncure, in his native Stafford County, he removed to Warrenton as a lad of 18 years, where he was licensed to practice his profession. He later engaged in practice with his brother-in-law, the Hon. Samuel Chilton (see pg. 189 n. 33). On May 23, 1844, he married Mary E. Norris, daughter of Thaddeus and Ann (Calvert) Norris. He was a Whig in politics, a member of the Secession Convention, and signed the Ordinance of Secession. He had been elected to this Convention to succeed Capt. John Quincy Marr (see pg. 135 n. 104), who resigned to command the Warrenton Rifles. He organized Brooke's Battery, attached to Poague's Battalion of Artillery, Jackson's Corps. During the Valley Campaign of 1862, his ankle was shattered in removing a gun from the mud. He rejoined his battery, acting as Colonel, during the battle of Fredericksburg. On the advice of surgeons, he resigned from the military and in 1863 entered the Virginia House of Delegates from Fauquier. After the close of the War he formed a partnership with Hon. R. Taylor Scott, which lasted for more than 30 years. He practiced at the Fauquier bar for 55 years, and continued to serve as a member of the House of Delegates (1871-72) and State Senate (1877-1879). Col. Brooke served many years, either as Mayor, Recorder or Councilman of Warrenton. It was largely due to his efforts, against the strong opposition of some of the leading citizens, that a water supply was secured for the town. He was for 45 years an elder in the Presbyterian Church, 25 years superintendent of the Sunday School and an active Mason and Knights Templar. (J.K.G.)

Court day[3] he cannot well leave the Store to the boys. I will send you a suit of clothes by him. If you conclude to remain longer than Mr F. send by him what soiled clothes you may have—that is shirt, drawers and socks—if you remain and you have worn your *white pants and coat dont send them home*—you must get them washed in Richmond by Mr Goodloe's[4] washer. You will need them to wear while there as the weather is so very warm—Tell Mr Goodloe to say to Mrs. G. I wrote her a letter of 6 pages on the receipt of hers and had hoped she had received it. I suppose you will write home and tell us how you are getting on. I am very anxious to hear—

Sister was sick all yesterday—but is up and about again—Grand Ma is as usual. Willie is quite well. Frank is about as you left him—Jessie has considerable cold and is very restless during the night—nothing tho of a serious character.

I must close as my eyes pain me much. All join me in much love to you. Children send a bushel of kisses. Keep up a cheerful disposition—and all will be well—my kind regards to Mr G.

Your ever affec
daughter, S.E.C.

Mr. Finks says if you will walk to Columbia Hotel tomorrow afternoon (Monday) you will find Gov. Smith.[5]

---

[3] When the Justices of the County met in Warrenton on the fourth Monday of each month, to take care of the official business brought before them, the town sprang to life. Citizens from every corner of the county gathered, not only litigants having business before the "gentlemen justices." They began to arrive early, some travelling since Sunday afternoon, and remained late—sometimes for the entire sitting of the Court for two or three days. This was especially true of "March Court," which signalled the end of winter and the isolation occasioned by winter weather and unbelievably bad roads. Court Day was a time to trade and sell farm produce, buy staples and dry goods, attend auctions of slaves, cattle and real estate at the Court House door. Horse-trading, gambling and drinking, followed by fist-fights and "free-for-alls" highlighted the social activities of the time. For weeks, merchants had advertised their goods, patent medicines, seeds, etc. and certainly "Court Day" was no time to be away from one's business. (J.K.G.)

[4] Harvel Harris Goodloe (1821-1884), a native of N.C., served in the Treasury Dept., Washington, D.C., resigned and obtained a similar position with the Confederate government, and moved to Tenn. in 1872; he was born at Louisburg, N.C. and died in Nashville, Tenn.; he married in 1848 at Mt. Pleasant, Tenn., Mary Ann Buckner of Waverly, Tenn., daughter of Anthony H. Buckner & Isabella Stewart Buckner. Paul M. Goodloe II, *Goodloe Genealogy* (Baltimore: 1982), p. C-35. (J.K.G.)

[5] Virginia Gov. William "Extra Billy" Smith (1797-1887) earned his nickname when he established a mail-coach service from Fairfax to Culpeper in 1827. Aggressively extending this service from Washington, D.C. to Milledgeville, GA, he soon obtained so many extra payments under postal contracts that he became known as "Extra Billy." He was elected to the Virginia Senate in 1836, and would remain in politics, off and on, for the next 36 years. In the early 1840's, the Smith family moved to Warrenton, buying 200 acres and building *Monte Rosa*, now known as *Neptune Lodge*, at 343 Culpeper Street. He was elected to the U.S. House of Representatives in 1841; the largely Democratic Virginia General Assembly elected him Governor in 1845. He headed west for the California Gold Rush in 1848, and returned to Warrenton in 1852—running again for the House of Representatives, where he served until 1861. Robert E. Lee commissioned him a Colonel in the Confederacy, and Smith was soon leading his men into battle, shading himself with a large blue umbrella at First Manassas and Sharpsburg. He was promoted to Brigadier General in Feb., 1863, led a successful charge at Gettysburg (bareheaded, with sword), and was promoted to Major General.

By 1864, he was again elected Governor of Virginia—at a time when Union forces held half the territory of the state, with its capital, Richmond, as their objective. He remained Governor until the fall of the Confederacy. After the war, in his 80th year, he was elected to the House of Delegates in Virginia, where he served until his death in 1887. After a service in Warrenton, he was buried in Hollywood Cemetery in Richmond; his portrait still hangs in the Old Fauquier County Courthouse. Anne Brooke Smith, *News and Notes From The Fauquier Historical Society*, Warrenton, Va., Vol. 8, No. 4 (1986), Vol. 9, No. 1 (1987). (J.M.W.)

Saturday Night

I have but few moments to write—it is now 1/2 past 10 O'clock—Children all well. I am quite well, no headache. Mr Grant will take your trunk to Richmond. I hope you will get it by Monday. Write me as soon as you can and tell me in what condition you received it as Mr Paulee informs me all trunks are searched at Culpepper—I know they cannot find any article which will be objectionable in yours. I dislike to have the things I send over looked—but I suppose I must submit.

Good night. God bless you.

Please write and send to Marcus Cooper[,][6] we will be certain to get them.

Yours affec
S. E. Caldwell

Warrenton, Via
Friday, June 28th, 1861

Dearest Papa

Your letter of yesterday was cordially welcomed by me, I was satisfied tis true to hear verbally by Mr Finks, but your familiar handwriting I much prefer to see.

I think you have been very fortunate in securing a situation so soon with so little trouble or inconvenience—Many thanks do I send to Mr Goodloe for his kindness and his true friendship manifested in your behalf—I shall ever remember him with grateful emotions. He and his wife are true friends of ours. I always believed it so when in Washington. Mrs G. wrote me a long letter and remarked that the children had been troubled with colds, but were better, that the Baby was growing finely and was very healthy. She herself was doing well—a very good account of all. I will write as soon as possible to her.

I miss you very much. I feel the responsibility of the children at night—Jessie is not well—you remember she was complaining the morning you left—well she seemed to be much better all day and was sprightly up to the morning Mr F. left for R. She seemed drooping—I became uneasy and sent for Dr. Chilton[7]—he said she *was not seriously sick*—but he would give her a little Calomel—I gave her three

---

[6] Marcus Cooper, merchant in Culpeper. (J.K.G.)

[7] John Augustine Chilton, M.D. (1812-1886) "the last descendant of that name in Fauquier, of Captain John Chilton [killed at the Battle of Brandywine during the Revolution], was a marked character. He studied medicine in Jefferson College, Philadelphia, and spent several years in New York hospitals fitting himself for his profession. He returned to Warrenton and his subsequent life was spent there. He had not had the benefit of modern scientific methods, but his intuition of disease was remarkable. He belonged to the philanthropic school of the old fashioned practitioner. To relieve suffering was the object of his life and he ministered to the poor and lowly at whatever cost of time or comfort and without thought of remuneration. He volunteered in the Civil War, but was not accepted on account of age. He devoted himself, however, to the care of the wounded brought to impromptu hospitals in Warrenton. After his death a monument was raised to his memory in the cemetery at Warrenton by the citizens of that place." Fauquier Historical Society, *Bulletin* (Richmond: 1923), p. 327. (J.K.G.)

powders and she on Wednesday seemed *herself again*. To day she was taken with something like Diarrhea and sick stomach—and I feared Cholera Infantum so I sent this afternoon for him to see her again—he said perhaps she had eaten something of fruit kind. I told him yes she had eaten pickle cherries—he said that was wrong, and must not allow her to eat such things. He has left powders for her if she continues to have sick stomach—she seems much better at present, 9 O'clock P.M., and will not give her powder unless she rouses and has a sick turn—the Dr told me I need not be uneasy about her—to keep her from fruit and hot sun and she will do very well—so you need not grow unhappy or uneasy about her. I only write you all about everything as it occurred and as it would have been if you had been at home. Sister says Jessie is doing very well and so far all she needs is to be kept in doors out of the hot sun—I will positively write you about her if she should seem more drooping—I hope she will rest well to night—and be bright in the morning. Frank said prayers for her—and he puts great faith in his asking the Good Lord for any one. Willie has gone to a Concert given at the Seminary of Dr Bacon's[8] school—we were all invited. Frank has almost run himself out of his shirt to day—came in with it almost torn off.

Mr. Finks wants you to go to Purcell L. Ladd's store and inquire the price of Linseed Oil—as he forgot to do it himself—says you must write the price when you next write—dont mention anything about it to Mr Spillman who will hand you your package.

Says he would like to purchase the Sugar, but can't raise the funds at present.

Says also if you are not suited in a Boarding House after looking around that Mrs Martha Yeatmen keeps a Boarding House on Franklin, West of the Capitol near Dr Hoge's church.

Please hand the enclosed note to Mr Brooke. Mr Finks purchased the goods for you that this suit is made of. Spillman cut them out and Sister and I have made them up for you, hoping you will be pleased with them and that they will fit you and be useful to you during your stay. Sister deserves much credit for they are made nicely. I send you a shirt—you have buttons with rings you can take out of your shirts before you send them in wash—keep your soiled clothes in bag. You better keep your cloth coat hanging up—as the trunk will press it and cause it to *wrinkle*.

I hope your health will be preserved and you become satisfied in Richmond— I am very sorry the travelling expenses are so high. Write as often as you can and say what days I must write you. All join in love.

Your affec daughter

Write word about your suit of clothes if they were a good fit.

---

[8] Joel Smith Bacon, D.D. (1802-1869) was a native of Cayuga Co., N.Y. He was a graduate of Hamilton College and Newton Theological Seminary. His life was devoted to teaching, holding only one stated pastorate during his career. He was President of Georgetown College, Ky., 1829-1831, and President of Columbian College (now George Washington University) 1843-1854. Devoting his life to female education, he taught in Georgia, Louisiana and Alabama, coming to Warrenton in 1857 to become Principal of the newly organized Fauquier Female Institute. After Dr. D.W. Thomas resigned the pastorate of the Warrenton Baptist Church, Dr. Bacon served during the war as what we know today as interim-pastor. His daughter, Josie, married Luther M. Spilman, attorney-at-law, and it was at their home in Richmond that Dr. Bacon died in November, 1869. (J.K.G.)

Warrenton, Via
Tuesday, July 2nd 1861

Dearest Papa

I had hoped to have received a line from you either yesterday or to day—but no letter has arrived. I intended writing you a long letter to night notwithstanding you are indebted to me. I am compelled tho' to write you only a note—as Mrs Tongue[9]— Sis and Mr Utterback[10] have been here all evening and it is now 10 O'clock and I am fearing Jessie will awake every moment.

I am happy to tell you that Jessie is *almost well* again—she seems to be gaining all her flesh—and has regained her appetite—her bowels are now in a good condition to night. The Lord has been good and kind to us in restoring our little darling to her wonted health so soon—for she was a sick child for a day or so.

Willie and Frank are doing very well. They want to see you. Jessie talks about you each day—Grand Ma is as usual—is anxious to hear from you. Willie has sent you a letter written just as he was standing by the Bureau—no one knew he was writing, he says Pa must excuse the writing—but he was in a hurry and he has spelt get wrong—but any how he knows how to spell it by this time.

Please write me how often I must write you, and the days you will expect letters, and when I must expect the same from you.

We have just received news of the capturing of a lot of Coffee, Ice—and other articles from the Federalists—good news is it not! Wish you had the ice in Richmond as you are in need—

I hope you are well—I dream of you frequently and sometimes my heart grows heavy and sad—and I cant tell for why. I judge it must be your being away—and the sad state of the times. I understand Tom Lunsford[11] liked to have been taken prisoner—but he succeeded in knocking the man down and getting off. How glad I was to hear of his escape. His wife is very sick—I feel sorry for her—

---

[9] Frances (Yeatman) Tongue (1819-1891) daughter of John Yeatman of Warrenton. She married, July 8, 1834, John R. Tongue, a successful tanner of Warrenton. They were the parents of Johnsie Tongue, a member of the Black Horse Cavalry and later a prominent merchant in Warrenton. Alexander Hunter, in his *Women of the Debatable Land* (Washington, D.C.: Cobden Publishing Co., 1912), pp. 40-182, incorrectly pays tribute to "Mrs. Johnsie Tongue" instead of Mrs. John R. Tongue. He says, "She was the Florence Nightingale of Mosby's Confederacy. Certainly if every good deed which she performed had been a block of granite, and had been placed over her last resting place, she would sleep beneath a column that would overtop the loftiest peak of the Blue Ridge. She was a saint to the wounded whom she tended, and an angel to those who held her hand as they entered into the 'Valley of the Shadow.' So long as the traditions of the old burg shall be handed down from father to son, from mother to daughter, will the name of that white-souled woman, Mrs. Tongue, be cherished and honored." (J.K.G.)

[10] Addison Warren Utterback (1836-1896), son of Armistead and Mary (Crump) Utterback. He was born near New Baltimore and came to live in Warrenton at the age of 17. He was employed as a clerk in the store of Spilman & James, became a partner with Messrs. Lear & Adams. Later, he was a partner with James T. Utterback, his brother. On the breaking out of the war, he entered the artillery company raised by Capt. James V. Brooke in Fauquier County. After the resignation of Capt. Brooke, Lt. Utterback was elected in his place and served through the War as Captain of the battery in Poague's Battalion. Capt. Utterback married Virginia P. Tongue, who, during the 1860 census, was a 21-year-old, daughter of John R. Tongue. Their son, John Armistead Utterback, mentioned in these letters, was born in 1861. (J.K.G.)

[11] Tom Lunsford, a resident of Warrenton at the time of the 1860 Fauquier County Census, listed himself as age 35, engaged in the occupation of "Discount Paper." (J.M.W.)

I judge you have seen Mr J. Spillman[12] [sic] in Richmond—I am glad he will make something for himself—in getting out his Patent—

I wrote to Mrs Goodloe—last week I hope she will get it—I told her to write twice a week to Mr G.—

Mr. Cooper is staying with us—he has your room—Mr. Finks is out on guard to night—I am glad on that account Mr Cooper is with us—

We have three sick soldiers in Warrenton from Manassas. The Ladies made up $150 and went to Culpepper with it to day to help the sick there, and will send bedding and other things.

Good Night. I would like to say I wish you were here but that would be wrong in me. May God bless & preserve you.

Your affec daughter,
S.E.C.

John William Finks to Lycurgus Washington Caldwell

Warrenton July 3/61

Dear Sir

I wish you to go to the Dispatch Office and have the daily sent here to E. M. Spilman[13] for the worth of a $1.00 which is inclosed. Also have B L Withers changed from twice a week to Daily—Say to R M Smith that there is great complaint about the Engine not reaching here. There has been and since Saturday last ... Susan expected a letter yesterday evening—As she will write it is useless for me to undertake to write anything concerning the family.

I have had herd [sic] direct from the fight Ashby had over in Maryland—The Dispatch's account is about true. Ashby lost two men, one a Maryland and a Fauquier man—The man from Maryland killed *six* of the Lincoln tripe before he was killed—

---

[12] John Robert Spilman (1822-1910) married Sarah Amanda Freeman (1825-1892) in Fauquier County on Sept. 28, 1846. John Spilman was a well-known contractor of Warrenton; he built the Culpeper County Court House, the Warrenton Baptist Church and it is thought he built the Scott-Keith home on Winchester Street. The Spilmans had no children but reared a relative of Mrs. Spilman, Fanny Freeman. Fanny married Stirling Jackson and had the following children: Ann, Loretta and Edward Morgan Jackson. Mr. and Mrs. Spilman are buried in the Warrenton Cemetery—their stones bear no dates, but indicate that Mr. Spilman served in the Ordnance Department, C.S.A. (J.K.G.)

[13] Edward Martin Spilman (1822-1910), a native of Culpeper County, married in 1849 Eliza Cummings Day, daughter of Baldwin and Lucretia Guthrie Day. Mr. Spilman became a lawyer and enjoyed a lucrative practice as partner of Benjamin Howard Shackleford (see pg. 142, n. 120) and was later Judge of the Fauquier County Court. According to family records, he was "turned out" of the Baptist Church as a young man for dancing. At the age of 80, he, with Gen. Eppa Hunton of the same age, was confirmed in the Episcopal Church. A portrait of Judge Spilman, painted by his daughter, Miss Lucretia Spilman, hangs in the Fauquier Court House. Malcolm L. Melville, *Spilman Papers* (Forestville, Calif.: 1965). (J.K.G.)

Capt Ashby[14] killed five. I think our men killed 22 men and captured ten horses and would have killed more if they could have caught them.

Ashby's brother[15] is badly wounded[,] two bullets in him and two sabre cuts and arm broken.

A party of Kentucky'ans went out the other night near Alex. and killed eight—one man a Sergeant belonging to the Goochland Company was with them who was killed. He was the only loss on our side.

There is no news here except everything is dull—I recd. a letter from Father[16] who says the joint worm is enjoying the wheat very much and the corn is low on account of no rain—but it is clean and looking well. He commences harvest this week.

JWF

Susan Emeline Jeffords Caldwell to Lycurgus Washington Caldwell

Warrenton, Via
Wednesday July 10th, 1861

Dearest Papa

Your letter arrived very unexpectedly—but was indeed very welcome to me. The weather has been excessively hot—we have all suffered from its effects. I have had Frank sick for two days like he was when you were with him. He had eaten too many gooseberries again—that with the hot weather made the little fellow very sick, he had burning fevers—I had to give him a Calomel powder—which made him very sick until the medicine operated—he threw off some *bile*. He is well again but rather fretful. I have to give all my attention—he dislikes being kept from fruit. He wants to see Papa very much—and would sleep with you very willingly at night. I guess Mama will say Amen to that, and be glad of the relief of the responsibility—altho he is not very troublesome. I asked him what message must I send you—he says all he wants is some nice *candy* and wants to see you—he will have it you have gone to the war and you are fighting Lincoln.

Willie keeps well—but will run all day—he says a lesson regularly ever day of his own accord—he is very anxious to make a visit to Richmond. He says tell Papa indeed I will write him a nice long letter the next time Mama writes—that he says a lesson every day—and wants to see him. Sister says Jessie is the smartest thing she has ever heard talk—she is very affectionate, perfectly devoted to Frank. I told her

---

[14] Turner Ashby (1828-1862), General (C.S.A.), was a native of Fauquier County and Captain of the "Mountain Rangers," organized in northern Fauquier in 1858. This cavalry troop became Co. A, 7th Va. Cavalry. He rose from Captain to Colonel of the regiment and was promoted Brig. Gen. on May 23, 1862. He was killed on June 6, 1862, while fighting near Harrisonburg. (J.K.G.)

[15] Richard Ashby did not survive his wounds; he was reported to have been brutally beaten, as well as shot. His death is said to have had a very melancholy effect upon Turner Ashby for the remainder of his life. (J.M.W.)

[16] Fielding Finks lived on a farm near Front Royal. (T.T.R.)

a night or so ago that if she asked me for tea during the night I would have to take a switch with me in bed—that I would give her water—on awaking that night she asked for *water* in place of tea. The second time she awoke she says tea, Mama dont whip me—I could not then refrain from giving her the tea—now wasn't that smart in her—she calls for you every day—says you have gone to Richmond—she is thin, but she is bright and well—and has good appetite. I do love the little creature, she shows so much affection for me at all times.

Sister has just returned from dentist—Dr. Bispham.[17] She has had her front tooth filled—expects to go back on Friday and have another fixed. She seems very well since her return home—

Cash Cologne[18] has joined the Warrenton R[ifles]. His mother is very unhappy about his going—he left last week, was in good spirits when he left.

Mr. Finks thinks of going to Manassas tomorrow—I will send some pillow cases, I think, to the Sick. I will send your coat and telegraph fixin as opportunity offers—don't get impatient about them. Please take good care of yourself and try and keep well—then I will be happy during our separation. Be particular about your bed—have all the *bugs* kept away. My washer woman charges me $4 per month. I cant do better. I have tried. Mr F. says you should have traded off your $5 long ago. I must close. Mr F. wants to write.

God bless and protect you,

affec daughter,

S.E.C.

Francis Marion Caldwell to Lycurgus Washington Caldwell and Lucy Caldwell Finks

Bank of La.

Danville, Rusk Co., Texas
July 14, 1861

Dear Brother & Sister—Having somewhat recovered from the exhaustion of a tedious and prostrating journey, and the depressing mental anguish of the gloomy state of affairs surrounding me, I now attempt to give you a history of circumstances

---

[17] William Newbold Bispham, D.D.S. (1814-1869) was born in Philadelphia, son of Stacey Budd Bispham and Ann Newbold, his wife. He married Mary Ann Vandewall Clopton, daughter of Dr. Nathaniel V. Clopton and Sarah Susan Grant (Skinker), near Remington. After his marriage, Dr. and Mrs. Bispham moved to Warrenton, where he practiced his profession until his death. Mr. Joseph A. Jeffries recorded in the *Warrenton Virginian* (c. 1904 "Memory Sketches Grave and Gay,") under the pseudonym "AITOCS": "He was a tall handsome polished gentleman, a superb talker, hence an attractive feature of all assemblies of which he was a component part." (J.K.G.)

[18] John A. Cash Cologne (1840-1903), son of Edgar N. and Susan F. (Cash) Cologne (see pg. 138 n. 114), was born in Warrenton. He enlisted in the Warrenton Rifles (Co. K, 17th Va. Regt.) commanded by Capt. John Q. Marr. He rose to the rank of Sgt. and was captured at Bermuda Hundred on Aug. 30, 1864 while on picket duty, and sent to Camp Hamilton, Va. After the war Mr. Cologne married Fannie G. Maddux of Marshall, where he was a merchant. (J.K.G.)

connected with myself in the past four weeks. You have heard long since of the troubles in Missouri and I will not attempt in a letter to give any detailed account of them, but will at once commence and confine my remarks to that particular portion of them directly operating upon me. On Monday morning, about the hour of early breakfast, on the 17th of June, a battle was fought at Boonville, Mo., between the Federal forces and State troops, which lasted about three hours. Governor Jackson[19] had been driven from the capital of the state and had retreated to our city. The Federal troops had taken possession of the capital and appointed a military Governor, when they pursued Jackson up the river in three steamers with a force of about three thousand men. The latter was in our town only three days and had collected in our camp three and a half miles below the town on the river about six hundred men. On the morning of the 17th June, as I have before stated, this small force was attacked by about one thousand Hessians, retaining as a reserve force on the boats about two thousand men. In the engagement we lost three men, and the enemy about seventy. I had joined a company of citizens numbering about seventy, who were not regularly mustered into the State service, but were desirous of participating in the fight, and if successful, returning to our business avocations again when it was over. Our company was under arms all day Sunday preceding the fight, and at night were permitted to go to their respective homes and have their horses fed and get suppers, to meet again at two o'clock. About one o'clock on Sunday night in leaving home I kissed my wife and taking Gussy by the hand bid her be a good girl, which she with emotion, as young as she is, promptly promised to obey. I then told my wife if disaster should befal us, I could not trust myself to be taken prisoner, and enjoined it upon Louis to remain quietly at home with the family, and not participate in the fight. Arrived at the appointed place of meeting for our company, twenty men were detailed as scouts, which were divided into two companies, ten men in each. In one of those scouting parties, I was appointed. Our party traveled upon the road to Jefferson City for some distance and about day-light met a traveler from that city, who informed us that Blair and Lyon had left at the same time that he had and were doubtless close at hand. We then directed our course toward the place where our little army were encamped. But before we reached it we discovered from the smoke of the steamers the enemy were approaching just above Rockport, eleven miles below Boonville. We gave the information, and passed by on the encampment of our troops to watch their landing. A short distance below the encampment of our troops two pieces of artilery [sic] had been mounted on the river bluff, but the enemy evaded this by landing in a bend of the river some distance below and out of range of the guns, at a point called Elliott's wood yard. Just before we reached this point and discovering from no longer seeing the smoke of their steamers that they had effected a landing, we took a right hand lane road following some fresh foot tracks we discovered in the road. About one or two hundred yards after we had entered this lane, at the rise of

[19] Gov. Claiborne F. Jackson of Missouri had replied to Abraham Lincoln's request for troops on April 15: "Your requisition is illegal, unconstitutional, revolutionary, inhuman, diabolical, and cannot be complied with." Shelby Foote, *The Civil War: A Narrative; Fort Sumter to Perryville* (New York: Random House, 1958), p. 53. (J.M.W.)

a slight hill we discovered some of the enemy a short distance ahead of us. Fearful of getting entrapped we put spur to our horses and retreated a short distance upon the road we had come. We then rode back a few miles and met with the balance of our company. Informing them of what we had seen, we here took another right hand lane road, which led into a road running parallel to the one we had been travelling, and which would bring us upon the left flank of the portion of the enemy we had seen. Our intention was to surprise them and have a little brush with them. But before we had more than traveled half the distance to the road for which we had started, in looking across a wheat field which separated us from the road we had just left, we observed the enemy marching in double quick time, and as far as the eye could reach the road was black with them. Just as we observed this and called a halt, we saw our troops advancing upon the same road to meet them, and at once the battle commenced. The enemy were checked and driven back upon the road. On the brow of a hill about half a mile in rear of the point at which the fight commenced and near the river they opened upon our men with four pieces of artillery. We had one cannon which was brought forward, but it was only fired four times. The wheat field between the two roads was occupied with their infantry, well armed with Minie rifles. As the battle waxed warm we made one effort to charge them through the wheat field in flank, but our men had been ordered to retreat, and our enthusiasm brought to a sudden check, for just as we raised a shout and had put our horses in a lope, the battery saluted with a fire of grape which whistled unmusically above our heads, and an officer coming through the field of wheat bid us not to enter it or every of us would be cut off, that our men were retreating. Long after this we witnessed the slow and sullen retreat of our men. Some of our men left their horses and entered the wheat field to get shots at the enemy. In this way we lost a noble young man of our company, Dr. James Quarles, we did not commence to notice until our retreat was cut off in the direction of town, and we fell back in a direct south course. At noon we came up with the scattered fragments of several companies, at Seats' Mill, about six miles south east of Boonville. We here went to a spring some distance from the mill and the main road until this gentleman's family prepared something to eat for the men and sent it out to them. We were here informed that Gen. Parsons had reached Boonville just as the fight was over with four pieces of artillerry {sic} and four hundred men, and there was some talk of renewing the fight at Boonville, but this was not done as our men were too much scattered. A portion of them took boats at Boonville and went up the river and it was difficult to say where the rest were. Parsons retreated south to Syracuse. I with some six or eight rode all the afternoon of this day and slept that night at a house six miles from town. The next day we rode all day not knowing which course to take until about noon when toward the western boundary of the county we were met by Mr. Frank Mitchell, who was with the Governor's staff, and sent as a messenger to us. Coming up with this party, we took the road south to Syracuse and here met with the command of Gen Parsons and Governor Jackson. We remained in camp at Syracuse until Thursday morning 20th of June collecting our scattered forces. About daybreak of this morning we took up the line of march and the Federal troops, upon a forced march from Boonville, entered Syracuse. At nine o'clock of the same morning that we left it. They followed on after us about eleven miles further, as we afterwards ascertained, but we were drawn up in battle array to give them a fight—just before we reached Cole Camp, so near were they reported to be upon our rear. We travelled all that day and all the night following, reaching Warsaw, in Benton county, a distance of forty miles, at daybreak, stopping only to feed our horses and to eat ourselves. Here we crossed the Osage river on Friday morning, expecting the enemy to attack us every moment. As we passed by Cole Camp we brought along with us twenty-six prisoners which had been captured in a fight between two companies of our men and some neighborhood Dutch, the latter numbering about six hundred. We administered an oath to them at Warsaw and let them go. The Governor after crossing the river at Warsaw, put on a disguise dress and left the army to make his way into Arkansas. On the south Bank of the Osage river the army encamped near the Pumbleatak Bridge during Friday and Saturday, and moved from this point to Humansville, a short distance south, in Polk county, on Sunday the 23rd of June. I left the army Friday morning with some other gentlemen, when Governor Jackson left it. Friday night we got our suppers at a gentleman's house living near Oseola, fed our horses in the prairie and slept upon our saddle blankets. Saturday morning we went into Oseola, and were very hospitably received by the people, who did for us all they could. Our horses were shod and fed, and we remained here until Sunday morning at the hotels, free of any charge. Here I disguised myself by putting on a clean white shirt, and found it necessary to get a heavier pair of shoes to travel in, as I had left home with a thin pair of lasting shoes on that did not feel comfortable when the dew was on the grass or I had to be off my horse in the mud. Many incidents of my trip I am compelled to pass over in order to confine this letter to something like reasonable bounds. Six of us left Oseola in St. Clair County, on Sunday morning the 23rd of June, viz. Judge Tompkins, Portus Muir and Wm Collins travelling together, and Dr. Dobyns, Wm H. Howard and myself forming another party, determined to run the gauntlet and if possible make our way into Arkansas, stipulating to meet at Fayetteville, about forty miles distant from the Missouri line. We knew that Federal troops had reached Springfield, in Green county, that they were passing down our western border on the line of Kansas, and were in our rear pressing from the center of the State. They were moving toward the Arkansas line in the shape of the letter V and we were anxious to get out before they would close up the gap to our escape. The morning we left Oseola our party swam our horses over Soc river, but this was only a slight preparation to ride through a soaking rain the balance of the day, consequently our travel was not so good making only the distance of thirty miles to Cartersville, in Cedar County. The next day we rode forty miles to a point south of Mahan's Ford on Spring river at the house of a Black Republican by the name of Gattan. We were very fearful of falling into a trap at this place and being arrested. We were questioned very closely but managed to disarm their suspicions so as to escape. In this region of the State the people were very much divided, Union companies were forming and demanding to be armed. And the companies of Secessionist which had been organized and had started to join the State troops in the interior were apprised of the disastrous state of affairs and were rapidly retracing their steps and moving towards the southern border of Missouri into Arkansas. From Gattan's we reached Keatsville, a distance of fifty-eight miles, by sundown, on Tuesday, the 25th June, and while we were getting our horses fed and our suppers, a gentleman named Jarvis Barker, residing a short distance this side of Springfield, came into Keatsville and stated that a detachment of Federal troops would encamp at Cafeville that night, only eight miles in our rear, and would be in Keatsville early the next morning. Considering it unsafe to spend the night here, two of us had our horses saddled, one horse being lame that he could travel no further, our party set out with a guide to direct our course, and we traveled twelve miles, into Arkansas, before we slept, so this day and night together we did not rest until we had travelled seventy miles. As there were three of us and only two horses now, and the weather very warm, we travelled slowly to Fayetteville, in Arkansas. We remained here two nights and one day. Ascertained here that Jackson had reached Camp Walker, in Benton County, on the Arkansas and Missouri line. The news from Missouri put the people of Arkansas into a state of commotion and excitement. McCulloch was yet at Fort Smith in command of the Confederate forces, but he forthwith issued a proclamation to the people of Arkansas to arm, and set about moving his force from Fort Smith up to Camp Walker, a distance of one hundred and fifty miles. Strangers with but little money, we determined to make our way to Van Buren, upon the Arkansas river, where I fancied I should be able to get some employment. But a distance of twenty miles short of this place we were induced to stop on Saturday and Sunday the 29th and 30th of June with a kind hearted and hospitable farmer named B.F. Hale, on Lee's Creek, Crawford County. His kind wife put a new seat in my pantaloons and here I had my shirt washed. At this place young Howard prevailed upon me to accompany him to Texas, where we now are, at the house of an uncle of his, named Willis Wilson, a very wealthy planter. On Monday the 1st day of July, we bid our friend and companion Dr. Dobyns good bye and set out to make this trip, which took us nine days journey travelling forty miles every day except the two last, as our horses had become so jaded we could not make this distance. Our route you will discover by referring to a map was upon the confines of civilization, passing along the line of the Indian nation and Arkansas until we entered Texas, crossing Red river at Lanesport in the corner county of Arkansas. You can imagine our condition, having travelled between seven and eight hundred miles, under a burning sun, with only the suit of clothes we had upon our backs, with money from the sale of my revolver and Bowie knife just enough to pay our expenses, but none to spare even to buy a clean shirt. Here we are kindly treated, and will remain to recruit ourselves and horses. The fatigue I have undergone was very trying, my hands for a time were blistered by the sun, but they soon became toughened, but my lips became raw from sun blister and are not yet entirely well. We do not think of returning to Missouri by the same route we came here. Governor Jackson will make an effort to get the Southern Confederacy to give him assistance. Since he arrived at Camp Walker, we have heard that he has issued a proclamation, but we have not yet seen it. Before I left the State of Missouri I sent my wife several messages informing her of my intention to try and get into Arkansas, but there is no way now of communicating with her. Until peace is declared or the Black Republicans are driven from Missouri I cannot hope to see her again. Should there be an opportunity to return soon, we are but sixty miles from Shreveport, Louisiana, on Red river, where we can sell our horses and go down this stream to the Mississippi, and up it to Missouri. In the meantime I wish you to write to me and send me some newspapers; we will likely remain here long enough to receive them and if we should not our kind friends here will attend to all our requests relative thereto. I have some hope that McCulloch will penetrate into Missouri with his southern army, and that the citizens of that State will rally around his standard. If this is not done we believe still he will have some fighting on the border of Arkansas. But much depends upon Missouri herself. If things remain in a protracted and undecided state I will before a great while make my way to some large town where I can get employment. It is useless to bewail the misfortunes which surround me, if I am penniless in my old age, having lost all that I have saved in a long series of years of toil, and after awhile I am permitted to remain with my wife and Missouri as a State within the Southern Confederacy, I shall feel contented and happy. Having unburthened my bosom of its troubles to those who I believe will offer me their advice and commiseration I will now bring this letter to a close. That which troubles me most now is that I cannot communicate with my family. I might have endured the humiliation of swearing allegiance to Lincoln's government for their sakes, but I had no assurance that this would have purchased my security, and with my sacrifice ruin to them was inevitable. Be sure to write at once, and send me also some newspapers. With love to you all, remember me as your brother

F. M. Caldwell

John William Finks to Lycurgus Washington Caldwell (undated)

I have wrote over concerning the wheat—and will go out next week if possible and have it attended to.

I merely wished to know the price of Linseed Oil, not that I bought it—the goods have not yet reached here but suppose they are at Gordonsville.

Ashby has but one brother, Col. A. and he was in the fight. He has a cousin in Washington. Hand this dollar to the Editor of Dispatch and request him to send paper (daily) to J.P. Chase, Warrenton, Va.

I have not heard from Wheet since I wrote, but hope the worm did not ignore it. I do not like Johnson having to retire. There is getting to be great dissatisfaction through this section of the State with the Southern Confederacy—The Union man that was before she went out say that things are as they predicted. Virginians would have all the fighting in her border and would have to furnish the men to do it—I am sorry to confess the truth of it—As Rob't Scott[20] says: We have more men in the field

---

[20] Robert Taylor Scott (1834-1897), a son of Robert Eden Scott and a prominent member of the Warrenton bar. He organized, at Warrenton, April 1, 1861, a company known as "Beauregard Rifles," later Co. K, 8th Va. Regt. He was promoted Major, A.Q.M. on General George E. Pickett's staff. At the time of his death, Major Scott was Attorney General of Virginia. (J.K.G.)

than all the South put together, which is true—the other states have it seems, stopped sending troops—Davis ought to have had at least one hundred thousand troops from the South here by this time—If he had, 20 thousand would not, now, be dodging through the valley—if they do not do better they had better retire from the fight, and let Va. take single handed.

It is useless to go into this fight here on the border with less than one hundred thousand men—fifty at Manassas and fifty thousand up the valley—and unless the Southern States do better, our people will become disheartened, as they seem to be now—Gray's men leaving here had a very bad effect.

J

Susan Emeline Jeffords Caldwell to Lycurgus Washington Caldwell

Warrenton July 17th/61

Dearest Papa

I read your letter of Monday written to Mr Finks—also notes to Sister and myself—then again Mr F. received one from you by Mr Brooke. I see by your style of writing that you are again unsettled in mind as regards your stay in R. Now Mr C. I see no reason why you should leave your office in which you are serving your Country and sufficient salary given you to support your family and assist Mr F. all you can during these perilous times. I think you are wrong in so doing while I at the same time admire you for your true nobleness of soul and strong feeling of devotion you bear towards Mr F. in offering to go in his stead.[21] I must say my heart sinks within me fearing you may be influenced so to act—not by Mr F.—but by others who may talk you into it—Now from my heart I hope and pray Mr F. will not have to leave his business and family. I could not bear to see him start from home to leave us and I cannot tell why it is, but I feel as if he will be relieved—Scruggs[22] seems to think so—If you were of a hearty robust nature perhaps I would feel differently in hearing you speak of living in the Camp. I know that God is every where and your life will be preserved if in accordance to his will at any place and under all circumstances— but yet I feel as if you will be more liable to be exposed to danger and sickness, maybe even death at Manassas Junction than in Richmond.

My mind is kept too much excited for my situation—you must try and resolve upon your remaining in Richmond and allow my mind to grow quiet. I have not been

---

[21] Lycurgus had evidently offered to serve in the Confederate Army, in place of his older brother-in-law. (J.M.W.)

[22] John Emmett Scruggs, Col., 85th Regt., Va. Militia, and editor of the *Warrenton Whig*. (J.K.G.)

well for several days. If you were in Warrenton of course I could not say as much—but you are away and relieved from Military duty and that should reconcile you to remain, for you are not fitted for to undertake the hardships of a Soldier's life—Please write me a letter that will quiet my mind. All join me in love to you—Children are tolerably well.

Warrenton Via
Saturday Night, July 20th, 1861

Dearest Papa

Your letter of the 18th sent by Mr Segwick[23] [sic] was received this afternoon, and I hasten to reply to it as you remark you have not heard from home by letter since last Saturday. I am surprised that the mails are so irregular—Mr. Finks and myself both wrote to you many times last week—I remember of writing in pencil to you twice—I wrote you on last Sunday, and sent it by Mr Tavenner[24] Monday—and to my utter amazement Mr F. *returned* into my hands on Wednesday last, Mr Tavenner having forgotten through press of business to hand it to you. I then wrote a note and so did Mr F. and mailed it to you on last Thursday morning—hoping you would be fortunate enough to receive it that evening and relieve your mind from anxiety. I want you to feel free from all anxiety on our account. We feel safe in Warrenton and are willing to remain. I am willing to risk it at any rate for a time longer—for I am comfortable here—and would not be as much so any where else excepting at my own house. Sister says she is perfectly willing to remain in Warrenton now that she knows that Mr F. will leave when the Militia are called out. He has been appointed Commissary—will get a salary and will be little exposed if any to danger. The Militia expected to leave for Manassas on Monday next—Mr. F. spent $10 of his money in drugs and other things—fixed them up with useful articles from one and all and sent them to Head quarters to be used for the Militia—after making all arrangements—Col. Scrugs [sic] received orders to this effect—that the militia must remain at home until sent for. Mr Finks says he is very sorry, he wants to go since his promotion to Commissary. I know I am glad they are ordered to remain at home. I think *Capt.* Brooke is very much disappointed, he had issued his orders for his Company to erect their tents at the Grove beyond Dr Stephens[25] (Hewlitts) and encamp there to drill—he is now much chagrined at the order sent from those in Richmond—He has been

---

[23] Charles Sedwick, son of Warrenton merchant, Benjamin Sedwick, had joined Co. H, 17th Va. Regt. (Old Dominion Rifles) from which he was discharged June 3, 1862 as being underage. On April 1, 1863 he enlisted in Co. H, 4th Va. Cav. (Black Horse Cavalry). He was paroled at Winchester on May 6, 1865. (J.K.G.)

[24] Chas. H. Tavenner, of Warrenton, was a wealthy innkeeper, according to the 1860 Warrenton census, taken when he was 38. He owned real estate valued at $19,619 and personal property valued at $14,415 at that time. (J.M.W.)

[25] James H. Stephens, Warrenton's most prominent druggist, whose clerk in 1860, Joseph A. Jeffries, was to succeed Mr. Stephens in that business. Mr. Jeffries, a member of the Warrenton Rifles, became Fauquier's earliest local historian. (J.K.G.)

wearing his Uniform every day—has been down to see Gen. Beauregard[26] on special business from Col. Scruggs—has had all things ready and packed to start at a minute's warning from headquarters. I know Sis Utterback rejoices over the change.

I beg of you to make yourself perfectly happy during your stay from us in Richmond. I am glad you are there. Much prefer you to be there than here with us— I cannot believe that old Scott[27] will ever gain possession of Richmond—in case Richmond should be attacked tho', I will coincide with all your wishes. As dear as your life is to me and I feel at present as if I could not live without you I would not have you act the *Coward* you may rely upon it. I shall not reproach you for anything you may do at such times, but oh! my dear husband should Richmond be attacked my only and earnest prayer will ever be that the Arms of Almighty God may be ever around you to protect your life which is so dear to me. I long to see you. It seems as if it has been the longest 4 weeks I have ever spent and yet I know not when to look for you. May you be preserved from sickness.

Mr. F. has written you of the Battle at Bull Run[28]—Mr. and Mrs Millan with old Mrs Millan had to leave their Farm and home in Fairfax just as quickly as possible on last Thursday morning. They brought their clothing, beds and bed clothes but left all their servants but one—the *nurse* for the children. They having no home in Warrenton, Mrs Cooper's house being rented—Sister invited them all to stay here, which they did—they left this morning for Mrs Cooper's in Culpepper. They have lost almost every thing all their wheat oats and grass—But Mrs Millan seemed Cheerful under it all.

I have been suffering with sick headache for two days past—and am suffering much pain to night. the children are in their usual health.

Frank says you must bring him 2 balls of cord to fly his kite with—Willie only wants his gun—and Jessie wants to see Papa—remembers your watch—your telling it to open for her—I will send your *Coats* as soon as an opportunity offers—must I send the telegraph fixins?

Good night. Love from each one to you.

Your affec daughter

---

[26] Pierre Gustave Toutant Beauregard (C.S.A.), professional soldier, "Hero of Sumter," who comes to Virginia with high reputation easily won during the initial hostilities at Charleston, S.C. He is 43, an admirable actor in a martial role, and he displays great self-confidence on the basis of limited experience with troops. From the outset, he shows a lack of the sense of logistics and he grossly overestimates the strategical combinations possible with green troops and inexperienced staff, but he has the good fortune to rout the enemy at Manassas, July 21, 1861. The aftermath of this victory brings to light some curious mental qualities and a singular infelicity in writing. All these combine to get him into trouble with the President and the War Department. Latin in look, he is of medium height and middle weight. His soldiers call him "Old Bory" and say he has the eye of a bloodhound. Lettered admirers insist he might have been the reincarnation of one of Napoleon's marshals. Douglas Southall Freeman, *Lee's Lieutenants*, Vol. I (New York: Charles Scribners Sons, 1946), p. xxxii. (J.M.W.)

[27] Lt. Gen. Winfield Scott (1786-1866) (U.S.A.), General-in-Chief for 20 years was, at the beginning of the Civil War, far from the hero of the War of 1812 and the Mexican War. He was now 75 years of age, suffering from dropsy, gout, vertigo and practically immobile from obesity. After a running feud with his younger, former friend, Gen. George B. McClellan, Scott had little choice but to resign in November 1861. He lived to see the victory of the Federal forces, dying in 1866. A Virginian by birth, he died at West Point, N.Y. and is buried there. (J.K.G.)

[28] This letter is dated July 20th, although the battle was not fought until July 21st. She may be referring to the fight at Blackburn's Ford on the 18th—or she held the letter several days after the dateline. (J.E.D.)

John William Finks to Lycurgus Washington Caldwell

Warrenton July 21/61

Dear Sir

I suppose you have heard of the fight at Bull Run although not a true account which seems impossible to get—The Warrenton Riflemen were in the hottest of it and only two of them wounded—Young Sinclair was shot through the side a portion of the calf of the leg shot off—but the Dr thinks he will recover—Capt. Shackelford was shot in the ancle [sic] but no bone was broken—They are both here. There is one thing certain the Lincoln ites were whiped [sic]—whether they stay whiped or not—I do not know, but think they will as 20,000 men had arrived at Manassas since. I suppose Patterson has returned to Washington to reinforce McDowell, or Johnson would not have come to Manassas.

We have orders to go into Camp here on Monday and await orders.

There was some 400 malitia [sic] at Manassas when the fight commenced—at the firing of the first gun they made tracks and the last that was heard of the Green Company they had passed Culpeper C.H. The others are scattered through Prince Wm & Fauquier. Their Col.'s led—Susan will write home matters—I am in Scruggs staff.

F

P.S. Since writing Sedwick has just handed me your letter which he forgot to deliver until about Sunday—We have written three letters this week—One of them Tavenner returned—I have a good place and would like very much to spend a week or so in the Army.

The Warren Guards fought hard—They and the Alex G reached across and charged beyond and made the yankees fly—I have not heard whitter Triplett[29] was wounded or not—From the best information I think there were about 1000 killed and wounded—

Beauregard will attack it is thought to morrow and try and chase them into Washington—18000 of Johnson men have arrived.

JW Finks

---

[29] According to Triplett family records, this could be a number of individuals, including John W. Finks' uncle, Col. William Hedgman Triplett (see pg. 233 n. 43), who lived on the family estates in Warren County, or one of the Colonel's sons, Thomas H. Triplett, William Broadus Triplett (b. 1835), or James Pendleton Triplett, who, according to the 1860 census, was living in the Finks' home and was employed as "store boy," in the Hamme-Finks' drug store, age 14. It might also be James D. Triplett, who, according to the 1860 census, was a dry goods clerk, age 37. (T.T.R.)

Dear Sir

I left this morning for Manassas but the Rockaway broke down and I had to return—I was very sorry as I have heard nothing of Fielding[30] except he was in the fight.

Murray's Com.[31] the one forming when you were here, were all kill [sic] except 37 as only that no. answered to their names, but they distinguished themselves before they were—After Clay Ward was shot and every Officer with the exception of young Mitchell the 3rd Lieut, they charged Shurmans [sic], flying artillery. Killed every man and captured it. Then it was the enemy made a rally and retook it killing nearly all of the Army. Fauqr. has suffered severely—I have just seen a letter which states positively that Patterson is a prisoner.

We were badly whiped at 12 O'clock, Johnson & Beauregard seeing snached [sic] a flag a piece and riding up and down the lines call on the men to save the South & Virginia, and the same time reinforcements coming up they rallying drove the enemy back and held the advantage until the flight. We took every thing they had 60 Cannons, Flying Artillery, blankets, Haversacks, Guns, Pistols et al—This I get from a Geo. capt. who is a Ex-Member of Congress. He thinks their loss is twelve thousands and ours about 2500 all told. Two dead and 19 wounded were brought here this morning and a good number at the Junction to come.

50 pounds Cut Loaf Sugar
25　"　best Coffee
10　"　Pulverized
　6　"　best Green Teas
40　"　of Coffee
Box Adamantine Candles

For the Store

Box Candles
1 Doz　bottles Scotch Snuff
5　"　Rappee　　　"
2 Doz. boxes concentrated Lye

---

[30] According to Triplett family records, Fielding Finks (1789-1874) married Frances Botts Triplett (1792-1869) of Warren County, Va., in 1817; they had eight children, including Charles Fielding Finks, who was their youngest son, born in 1834, brother of John William Finks (1818-1879) of Warrenton. It is, presumably, the younger Fielding who is mentioned here. (J.M.W.)

[31] Edward Murray, served as Captain, Co. H (later Co. C) 49th Va. Infantry, organized May 28, 1861 at Warrenton and called "Fauquier Guards," commanded by Col. William Smith. Captain Murray was born in Maryland, August 12, 1819; graduated from U.S. Military Academy in 1841; served in U.S. Army 1841-1855; farmed in Fauquier County, 1855-1861; promoted to Lt. Col., July 19, 1861 in the 49th Va. Inf.; transferred to General R.E. Lee's staff as A.A.G. 1862-1864; died July 3, 1874 at West River and is buried in Anne Arundel County, Md. Laura Virginia Hale and Stanley S. Phillips, *History of the Forty-Ninth Virginia Infantry C.S.A., "Extra Billy Smith's Boys"* (1981), p. 320. (J.K.G.)

1 " Bakers bitters
5 " Allum
Purcell & Ladd, furnish all but candles & they may have them.

F

Warrenton July 24/61

Dear Sir

I have just returned from Manassas & found every body in good spirits and 30,000 men marching and getting ready to march in Alex.

One of Genl. Barnum's aids arrived here this evening and says our Troops are at Vienna, and will be in Alex. to night at 12 O'clock.

The Federal forces nearly all left. Carrington, Wilcox, Eli, Cochoran & others I understand was in the train as prisoners, which was to leave for Richmond. I hope they have Carrington—

It's an awful sight to go over the dead—I suppose ... five hundred ... in the field yesterday rotting.

Your letter of the 22nd did not reach here until to day coming from Manassas.

We have had no mail here from Richmond since Saturday.

The malitia [sic] are here drilling. Susan will write I presume.

Hand this memorandum to Purcell Ladd & Co.

Triplett is very anxious for his money—I send you a letter from him.

We are all well & in good spirits.

I got a Haversack which was picked up with Ezra Caldwell Compy. E No 26 on it and gave it to Will.

F....

Susan Emeline Jeffords Caldwell to Lycurgus Washington Caldwell

Warrenton, Virginia
Wednesday, July 24th, 1861

Dearest Papa

Your letter written last sabbath has been received today. I have been anxiously on the lookout for one from you but for several days there has been no connection with the Richmond train and have had neither letters or papers.

You have by this time read and heard every particular in regard to our glorious victory of Sabbath last. We certainly have gained much thus far and may the Good Lord continue to be with us in battles which are to follow as old Scott declares that he will recover at all hazards every piece taken from him by us, and I believe firmly

37

he will make the effort and that right early—I understand our troops are rapidly advancing on to Alexandria and it is supposed may arrive there at 12 O'clock to night—we will hear more particularly by morning mail.

We have several of the wounded soldiers in our town. One at Mrs Gaines[32] wounded in the foot. I think his name is Miller from Richmond belonging to Griswold's [sic] Company[33]—he is doing well. There are two at Mrs Brooks, both wounded one in foot, the other in side—Mrs. Watson[34] has one from Alabama, a Dr Todd—he has three wounds—doing well. Mrs Tongue has one from New Orleans, a Mr Kelly wounded in the hand—Mr. Boatwright[35] has one from Charleston So. Ca., a Mr Purse wounded in the foot. I called to inquire after him to day. There is a Mr Haynesworth from Sumter District So. Ca. (Cousin to Charles Haynesworth who waited on us when we were married) at Edward Spillman's, his leg has been amputated, he is in a very precarious condition, tis thought he will die, his brother is with him. I offered at both places to do any thing towards their relief at any time.

We have a gentleman by the name of Robinson from Huntsville Alabama. He was slightly wounded in his shoulder but his hat has very many bullet holes. He may return to his Company tomorrow. I must now tell you about Jessie on the arrival of the soldier in the porch, she took her rocking chair and sat close up to him and called him her soldier—after sitting awhile she jumped up and seized a cup of water from which she had been drinking and handed to the soldier—saying soldier want wata [sic]—Sister tried to check her—but Jessie said tis cean atty [sic]—meaning clean water. She was then quiet for a while, still sitting close by him when suddenly she started in his lap—and said soldier you want dinna [sic] for eat. He was very much taken with her and of course we at home thought it was extra smart—after supper she jumped in his lap and told him she loved him, pulled his beard and called him Billy White—We asked her if she was sitting in Billy White's lap—she said *no*— tis my soldier, Billy White home pointing over to the house.

Mr. Finks asked her the other day what must he tell Papa—she says *"Come home."* I think she is *extra*.

We are all glad to learn you are well and that you are content to remain in Richmond.

Mr. Finks brought Willie a haversack with the name of Caldwell on it. I wonder if he could have been *one* from the Island. It's Isam or Isham Caldwell.

---

[32] Mary F. Gaines, age 29 at the time of the 1860 census, listed her occupation as housekeeper. The former Mary Mildred Foster, she married William Gaines, Sr. on Jan. 24, 1850. (J.M.W.)

[33] Possibly Capt. Joseph Griswald's Company, "Old Dominion Guards," an element of the 1st Va. Inf., later reorganized. (J.K.G.)

[34] Mary E. (English) Watson, wife of Joseph H. Watson who came to Warrenton about 1844 when he purchased the business of John M. Jacobs and continued the latter's clock and watchmaking activities as well as the sale of jewelry and silver spoons. On April 27, 1847, he married Mary E. English. In 1850 he returned thanks to his friends and customers and reminded them that he was to be found "next door to the post office." "*Flag of '98,"* (Oct. 12, 1850). In 1847 he purchased a lot and house on Main Street "running to the centre of the alley between the silversmith shop now occupied by said Watson and a saddlery shop." George Barton Cutten, *The Silversmiths of Virginia* (Richmond: The Dietz Press, Inc., 1952), p. 179. Mrs. Watson's brothers, John and Henry English, frequently mentioned in these letters, have not been identified. (J.K.G.)

[35] William Boatwright, merchant, of Warrenton. (J.K.G.)

I am anxious to see you. You need not be anxious about us. We will remain in Warrenton. Children are as usual. I am getting on very well.

Good Night. All join me in love.

Your affec daught
S.E.C.

John William Finks to Lycurgus Washington Caldwell

Warrenton July 26/61

Dear Sir

I sent this morning by Express to Peterson & Co. a part of my Soda Fountain, which I want re-lined inside & put in good repair—I wish you would attend to having it fixed immediately and sent up by Express—Also request Purcell & Ladd to send me with other things ordered 3 doz rubber nipples

There is no news except our forces are very near Alex. Fielding nor Triplett was hurt—in the fight. Jessie is still attending to her soldiers—

Spillman promised to call and see you. He keeps under the Spottswood House. Call and see him—There is no doubt about Scott's Eppullets [sic] & sword being in the possession of our men.

Tell Peterson not to send soda ordered by Express, but by freight.

The Malitia are drilling every day and will soon make good soldiers—I expect several of the wounded will die before ... days as they are very low.

All well at home

Yours in haste
JW Finks

I send you $300 which place to my credit in the Bank of Va. Send nipples by Spilman & Purcell who have sent other goods.

Susan Emeline Jeffords Caldwell to Lycurgus Washington Caldwell

Warrenton, Virginia
Wednesday Night, 31st/61

Dearest Papa

I enclosed a letter in Mr F. on Tuesday morning thanking you for your favors of 25th and 27th and begging you to gain all the information possible from Gov. Jackson in regard to Frank. I hope you will be successful.

Mr. Spillman returned this evening and has sent your package to me. I thank

39

you kindly for my letter and truly my heart replies to your wish of being settled in life and have us all around you. Separation is hard to bear—I miss you very much and my heart yearns after you—yet I would not have you go to travelling expenses and neglect of your business to make a visit home. I will be content to abide your own good times. I know you are as anxious to come yourself. My heart longs, yearns after peace—so that families can be once again united—how much worse off are the poor soldiers' wives far away—(with their husbands wounded and many unable to leave their homes to come and nurse those whom they tenderly love) than I am—I hope I am grateful.

The children sure delighted with their books—Willie says he knows he can read his for it has easy words—Frank kept his in hand till time to go to sleep—says I must be sure to read it all to him. I told Jessie you sent her a Cake and I would give it to her—Uncle Will told her he would bring her two, she said yes two cakes and her eyes were as bright as diamonds—she is looking very well now.

I received a long letter from Mrs Goodloe. Her brother Larry had been to see her—sick some days—yet started on for Virginia. Her children are all well. Baby very fat.

Mr. Finks says please see that all the *screws* to the *fountain* are in good order—get the man to be very particular and have every part of it in good order—and then be certain to send it by *Express* as he wished it sent as soon as possible. He loses about $20 per day while without it.

Willa Neal and husband with little ones arrived in Warrenton last night from Leesburg—Mr. Neal is anxious to get back to Baltimore—he understood he could not return to Baltimore—they are much concerned about it, but I expect it is only a report and he will have no difficulty.

I will try and send your coat & Tel fixens by the first opportunity—being a large package it is not every one who would be willing to take it. I think I shall send them separate.

I have just received a letter from Sister Mrs Suares[36]—she inquires particularly after you and hopes you are not in Camp—

I did not know my letter was so much blotted. You must excuse it.

The So. Ca. are all well cared for here. I have not sent them any thing fearing those persons whose houses they are stopping at would take offense.

We expect a Charlestonian from Culpepper who is sick at our house to morrow. I have not learned his name. I shall do all in my power to do him good and make his stay pleasant. Mr Robinson is doing well. There were some 70 sick ones brought in

---

[36] Harriet Suares (1817-1891), addressed here as "Sister," was Susan's aunt, the sister of John H. Jeffords. She lived in Charleston with her husband Benjamin C. Suares (1811-1892), a tailor. They were married by the Reverend Basil Manly on January 13, 1837. (Brent H. Holcomb, *Marriage and Death Notices from the Baptist Newspapers of South Carolina, 1825-64* (1981), p. 4.) Their children, as listed in the 1860 census were Elvira, 22, teacher; Basil, 21, book-keeper; Julia, 17; Ellen, 15; Anna, 13; and Carry, 8. In the 1850 census, a Benjamin, 8, is also listed. (See note on Benjamin in Harriet Suares' letter of April 23, 1862.) Basil Suares may well have been named for the Reverend Basil Manly, who was pastor of the First Baptist Church in Charleston from 1826-1837; Susan's parents (see note to her letter of Dec. 21, 1861) appear to have named their last two sons for this same man. (B.G.C.)

from Manassas to day. Mr Finks took 2 with measles and put them in Jones'[37] room—they are doing very well to night. Sister attends to them—has been twice to day to see them. They are very grateful.

This has been the hottest day—and is certainly the hottest night. The children will be restless I know. Good Night.

All join me in love. Children send kisses. May you be preserved from sickness and danger.

Your affec daughter,

S.E.C.

Warrenton, Via

Thursday, August 8th, 1861

Dearest Papa

Your much welcome letter written on Tuesday last has been received. I was anxious to hear what you had to say in regard to Frank—You reproach me for mourning over Frank's condition—We feel proud of him for this daring adventure—yet we cant but feel for his lonesome situation in the midst of strangers and without employment and can get no word of comfort or relief to his wife who of course is anxious of his whereabouts.

Mr. Finks says you must not think of sending the $100 by the gentleman you spoke of who was in Richmond who was procuring arms for Missouri—He may never see Frank and it is too much to risk—says you better send a *check* for the amount and if Frank ever receives it he will answer of course. This is not exactly what Mr F. said about check I shall ask him when he comes in—I hope Frank will yet be able to join Jackson's army, it is the wish of Sister's—Grand Ma is troubled yet speaks of him with much pride—says she knows he will get along for he has ever done it from a youth. Sister wrote him a long letter and sent papers to him.

Willie and Frank listened to the story about the boy who captured the Yankee—Willie soon inquired if all the money belonged to the boy—he wondered what he would do with it—I hope Beauregard will never forget the boy and will raise him to honor—Mr. Roberson who is staying with us says it is all correct—he saw the boy and he belongs to his Regiment.

We have lost by death several soldiers—a gentleman from Huntsville Alabama came on to Warrenton last week to nurse a nephew who was wounded, was taken very ill the morning after his arrival—and his sickness proved to be typhoid pneumonia—he died Tuesday—persons in the room with him said it was distressing to hear him beg for his life to be spared—said he could not die—he was not prepared for death—begged to be fanned to keep breath in him as long as possible—he was an old bachelor and wealthy—how wrong for us to postpone the preparation for death—for we must all die—I feel it daily—and fear I am not ready if I were to be called suddenly away—

---

[37] Probably Elcon Jones, listed in the 1860 Census as an 18-year-old clerk living in the Finks' home. (B.G.C.)

You too my own *beloved* husband I think of and pray daily for—Let us resolve to live for Heaven—for indeed our time to leave this world will soon roll around and how delightful even the thought of our meeting in Heaven never more to part—and I trust our dear little ones will follow us too.

Separation is almost intolerable at times here below if such be true—what must the separation forever.

I have not seen any of the So. Ca. soldiers yet—I called on two but would not go into their rooms—they are badly wounded, and not knowing them personally, I did not care to intrude. I have sent some little niceties to two who were worse off than others—Would it be proper for me to call on each one—and when asked to their rooms to go—if you think so I am ready to do it. Mr Haynesworth's wife has arrived. He is not expected to live—Mr. Barton of Charleston is very ill, threatened with Lock Jaw. He is a married man with two children. How very distressing are the times with us. There is a gentleman at Mrs. Watson's named Garratte, he is very ill with Intermittent fever he says he feels as if he will die—He has only been married 14 months, has a young wife and an infant—He is from Selma, Alabama—How hard to die among strangers—The two very sick ones with us are much better, they are able to be up and about.

The weather is excessively hot—I never suffered by day or night when in Charleston—I suffer very much. I am much debilitated and suffer much pain both in my side and back—hurts me to write.

The children suffer from the heat—Willie has a severe cold—says tell Papa he loves him and thanks him for his book—will write to him when the weather grows cool. Frank too has cold—but is out doors all day. I told him you would send him card—I am going to buy it for him. He now wants a knife—says he can cut as well as Willie.

Jessie is not well—she looks thin—but is sprightly. I judge it must be the extreme heat—she talks often of you, says how much she loves you—she is very affectionate ever ready to soothe and caress the boys—she went to Frank today and put her little arms on him and called him her pet—my little pet brother.

I must close for I feel as if I shall melt away. Please take all care of yourself this hot weather. Be careful you do not take cold from sudden exposure. By all means have a good comfortable room. I received your check and will give Grand Ma $2.00. I hope you have not stinted yourself to send to me for I have some yet of what you left—I have spent some for fruit and so on for Soldiers.

I wish you could send by some one coming from Richmond to Warrenton some large ripe peaches—can't get good ones here for the sick—*don't send by Express*, send by some one you know—but dont do it unless convenient.

I will send Coat by first opportunity.

All join me in love to you. Bushel of kisses from each of little ones and Mama.

Your affec daughter
S.E.C.

Mr. Finks says you better deposit the money in bank and send a check to

Frank—Ask the Cashier when the check is returned to notify you before it is paid so you can tell if it is Frank's handwriting—

Warrenton, Va
Tuesday Night, August 13th, 1861

Dearest Papa

I received your last letter and would have answered it before but I know you would receive a note with your coat by Sunday or Monday—

You ask me if I want to come to Richmond before Frost—I cant well leave Warrenton you know before November[38]—if the Good Lord should spare my life during what I must soon pass through—I am very anxious to see you, time seems very long since you have left us. I think we never before have been separated so many weeks from each other—but I am not discontented or repine at my situation, for I am assured that you are more lonesome and suffer more privations than I do. I have every thing around me to make me happy. I am far better off than thousands who are compelled to give up their husbands perhaps never to behold them in life again—give them up to find a soldier's grave.

I think we both must content ourselves to live this way till things are in a more settled condition, your salary is limited and you will have use for every penny. I would gladly come to Richmond—but my judgement says wait till this strife between the North and South takes a turn for the better—for it would cost much expense to get us all with you and have us comfortably fixed—as for my part I think we better wait patiently.

I received a letter from Charleston saying that Cousin Samuel P. Moore, M.D.[39] was in Richmond—also that William Westmore had left Charleston for Richmond to meet Cousin Samuel—Cousin S. being his Uncle. The people at home were anxious for me to ask you to find them out—particularly the young man. I have never seen him—he has been living in New Orleans—if you feel inclined to find them out you can do so—

Mr. Finks says that the goods from Peterson has not yet arrived—wants to know why it is—that freight comes up daily from Richmond—that other persons have received goods from Richmond—please to attend to it soon as possible—he also wishes you to go to Purcell and inquire the *price of bottles* by the *gross*—bottles holding about pint and half.

A Mr McDonald from Columbia So. Ca. has been staying over at Mrs

---

[38] Susan is pregnant with the Caldwell's fourth child, due in the fall. (J.M.W.)

[39] Samuel Preston Moore, M.D., Surgeon General (C.S.A.), was a cousin of Mary Humbert Jeffords, Susan's mother. His sisters were married to a pair of brothers: Susan Moore was married to William Westmore and Ellen Moore to Westmore's brother, according to a 1928 letter of Susan's niece, Lila Jeffords Thompson, addressed to Charles Caldwell. The William Westmore and the Westcoats Susan refers to in this and subsequent letters are probably Westcotts, with names misspelled. (B.G.C.)

Brooke's[40]—has been very sick with measles—he is now better, called to see me yesterday evening. I was much pleased with him—he told me about the two Wescoats—they are now stationed at Vienna—Capt. Cuthbert's company.

The children are doing tolerably well—Jessie says tell Papa she loves him and wants him to bring her goodies—she will kiss him for nice things heap times. She talks sweetly to all around—and is excellent company for us all—she loves the soldier—and will sit in his lap quietly and talk with him—Frank says he wants to see Papa—he begs for all the bullets and wants a pistol—he prayed to night that the Good Lord would make Papa and Mama good—all of his own accord. I hope his little prayer may be answered for us both—Frank and Jessie are very fond of each other and it is amusing at night to hear them talking to Old Kriss to bring them goodies—she was rather ill natured at one time and I said Old Kriss Jessie is a bad girl, in a second she said No Old Kriss, me is good now—bring me goodies—don't bring Frank some—she understands all about it—

Willie intended to write you a letter to day but he overstaid his time up the street and felt too tired. He says tell Papa he will be sure to write tomorrow. He is very attentive to the sick soldiers and inquires if they are So. Carolinians—tells them he is from So. Ca.

Jessie has disordered bowels now very often and I am compelled to be careful in her diet. Mr F. gave her some fried apples—I told her Daddy was naughty to give her apples—she said no—Daddy good man.

I suffer almost constantly with my back and side. I feel really tired and in pain since writing thus far and must close.

Grand Ma is better—Sister is complaining—Children send kisses and love to Papa—Mama sends her share also.

Your affec daughter,
S.E.C.

John William Finks to Lycurgus Washington Caldwell

Warrenton Augt 16/61

Dear Sir

Please purchase the following articles and send by Express as soon as you can

3   of Quinine 3.50
1 ½ of Gum Opium   4
3 Drums of Morphene (Sulphur) or $10 worth
100# of Extract of or Browns Logwood if you can get it also call at Randolphs

---

[40] Mary E. (Norris) Brooke, wife of James Vass Brooke, lived across the street from Judge William H. Gaines, at what is now 74 Waterloo Street. (J.M.W.)

and get me six quires of note paper, with Flag and six bundles of note envelopes with Flag—I suppose Homer has purchased the paper, please hurry him up and request him to send *me another barrel of soda—3000 Envelopes @ 10 ct. pack—6 rms paper @ 2.50*

Call at Davenports provided Homer has not purchased at, get me a barrel of Porter, not paying over $2 per doz. Also inquire the price of them of Imperial & Gunpowder teas.

Yours
JW Finks

Send me 5 Doz ink Powders - 75cts doz
2 group of 2 oz. ... round
4 doz small vial corks assorted
If you cant get extract get Browns
You can find all at P.L. & Co.

Susan Emeline Jeffords Caldwell to Lycurgus Washington Caldwell

Warrenton, Via
Thursday, August 22nd, 1861

Dearest Papa

I expect you have wondered why you have received no letter from me this week—you will be reconciled to the disappointment if you have experienced such. I was taken quite sick on Monday last—had to give up and go to bed. I was taken similar as I have been when taken with bilious colic altho I had eaten nothing during the day that would have been hurtful. I had been suffering with sick headache. I was very much alarmed fearing it may produce sickness of another character for which as yet I am unprepared. I took as much brandy as I could with discretion, and kept very quiet. I suffered pain all day Tuesday, could not walk across the floor. I have been since relieved somewhat of the pain tho' not entirely. I came down stairs today to my meals. Sister kindly took charge of children while I was complaining. I hope soon to be myself again, if I take good care of myself which I will try to do.

The weather has been rainy for near two weeks. The earth is very damp, the children are kept with colds. I pity the poor soldiers during this long siege of damp weather. The tents are not such as will keep water out. We had two South Carolinians to dine with us to day. They called to see me and were here when the dinner bell rang. Sister invited them to stay and they seemed to enjoy their dinner—it was much better so than great preparations. I have written to the *Wescoats.* Mr McDonald promised to take one for me to them, as their company was next his.

I understand they are making preparations for another attack. We can't tell when or where, but the sick and wounded are being removed from Manassas—Oh! may the God of Battles shield those we care for from death.

I have the painful news to write you of Lieut. John R. Haynesworth's death—

he died yesterday morning of his wound after enduring untold agony for one month. His wife was with him—she came to Warrenton as soon as she could with impunity, having been in her confinement during the time of his being wounded. She left her *babe* but *one month* old at her home in Sumter—I understand she is but 18 years old—this being her *first babe*. I feel deeply for her—how sad must be her heart, for she came on hoping she would soon take her husband back to his own loved home to nurse him—and see the little one she had left behind. But alas! How mysterious are the ways of Providence—I was anxious to write her a note to have her feel in her loneliness here among strangers there were sympathizing hearts around her—but I understood she left in this morning's early train. I sent many times to inquire of him—and twice sent little niceties to him. I dont know if they ever found out my whereabouts.

I must close—I am too tired to write more at present.

The children had some ducks given them to day—and by some mismanagement all are lost—On Willie's coming to supper he was told his duck was lost—he was much grieved and commenced to cry—whereupon Jessie said dont cry Baba—duck come back again—and tried her best to quiet him. She is the sweetest little thing I ever saw. She on awaking this morning said Mama Papa come a day me see him me love him—you want see him—me nice Mama see him—I asked her what she would do when she see Papa—me kiss him and hug him—Mr. Finks remarked he would take Willie to Richmond to see you—she jumped up and said me go to Richmond see my Papa—

Frank says tell Papa I am a good boy sometimes and he must bring him a double barrelled pistol that can shoot bullets, he is big enough to shoot. Willie came home all tired down having been to see the presentation of a Flag to Taylor Scout's [sic] company—I asked what I should tell you—he said Papa had not answered his letter—loved him and was coming on to Richmond—

GrandMa is much complaining—looks badly—I wrote to Mrs Goodloe last week—I am anxious to hear from her—

Mr. Finks is anxious about his goods. Stevens has received his, and ordered them since Mr F.

I will write you another time about children's wearing apparel. You have been absent 2 months to day—Love from all.

Your affec daughter

As I have time to write more I will add more to my letter. Mr Finks has just handed me your note to him. I am glad to learn you keep your health—Don't deceive me if you are sick—I have felt anxious about you during the summer season and now that the weather is damp and rainy, you must be careful and not take cold. Change your socks when you get them wet. Many thanks to you for your purchase of the spool cotton. I wish tho' you had selected the numbers to range from No. 40 to 70. Then I should have been able to have done sewing of any material. I hope you selected *Coats'* cotton, for we cannot use any other make on the sewing machine. But if not, dont trouble yourself about it. Send it when you get the opportunity. You need not get any more just now as I have purchased a few spools myself. They sell here at 10 cents per spool—20 cents difference in the dozen, as you gave $1.00.

All of our little ones are now fast asleep. Willie & Jessie have taken some cold to day—Both are coughing since they have gone to sleep—I hope it will leave them before to morrow. Oh! How I miss you with the children. I feel sometimes as if the responsibility is more than I can stand when I feel badly. I do long and pray my dear husband for peace. Separation from you for so long a time is painful to me. I feel as if I would enjoy your company with redoubled pleasure when again permitted to be together in our own home with our little ones around us. I am comfortable and happy here but I would much prefer to be in my own home with you and children. But I know you are far more lonesome than I am and that makes me content when my thoughts turn to you all alone in Richmond.

Be sure to get some goods for one or two pair of every day winter pants for yourself—also look for Factory cloth suitable for clothes for Willie—send samples if you are doubtful of its answering—I think I can get on without buying for Frank if I use the piece you brought home to make a shirt of when connected with Lee Guard—

Mr. Finks has just told me of the death of one of the soldiers of Typhoid Fever—poor fellow many more will soon follow on.

I fear our little town will become unhealthy towards fall there are quite a number of cases of Scarlet fever in families among children, both white and colored. I dread the disease.

Every one is expecting a battle to come off soon—did I tell you that Mr Moses who was with you in office in Washington has been in Warrenton? I did not know until the day he started for Camp—he was with his Cousin—I would have been pleased to pay him some attention.

I am sorry you cant find Dr Moore—perhaps he has returned with Gov. Jackson—as he was from Missouri—

Sister has just written to Henrietta[41]—we are all very anxious to hear from Frank—poor fellow his case is pitiable.

Willie wrote you a letter but spoiled it so he was ashamed to send it—you are mistaken if you think I wrote his letter, no indeed he wrote it himself—he is very anxious to visit Richmond. I would like Frank to come too but you will not have sufficient time to leave your office to devote to his amusement—the little fellow and Jessie too wants to go to see Papa—But never mind a better day is coming when we shall be happy together by our own fireside.

Monday morning...
    Dearest Papa
    I spent an unhappy night, dreaming and thinking of you while asleep and when awake troubled—on awaking this morning, Jessie awoke and after asking for a piece of bread she says Mama, Papa sick—me sorry, Papa sick. And then in an instant she turned towards Frank and said Fanky—Papa dead—and continued to repeat. You may think me foolish and treat it slightly, but my heart feels heavy—has ever been

---

[41] Wife of Francis Marion Caldwell, in Booneville, Mo. (J.M.W.)

all summer and your letters are ever hailed with delight—I am up this morning this early only to write and *insist* as well as *beg* you to write just *one line* after the arrival of Mr F. in time to tell me if you are well and able to be out and at your business. Now please my own dear husband try and gratify me. Tomorrow will be long coming to me at best, and I hope it may please the Good Lord to permit me to learn you are restored to your usual health again—

I want you to come home if you are not able to be at your business and let me nurse you while I am up. Mr F. promises me to bring you home to me if you are sick—I sent you your trunk having the good opportunity as you can better accommodate your clothing—also a carpet bag—that when you should come you can leave your trunk and lock it up—I put the sample of Canton flannel in the trunk for you to look at. If possible, you can get 12 yds. as heavy. I gave 14 cts. for it 2 years ago for your drawers. Don't worry about it if your time is occupied.

Goodbye, would it was me starting instead of letter.

May God Bless You.

Warrenton, August 27th, 1861

Dearest Papa

I have received both your kind letters, one by mail and one by Mr Pattie—who also brought some oranges and limes with a doll for Jessie. Many thanks to you for the fruit—I gave one of the oranges to a soldier—I have inquired around if they could drink Lemonade—but most of them are given to diarrhea who are sick and cannot use it—there are four more down with Typhoid fever who may not live this night through, all young promising men, one married man—There is much distress in our midst—There is a So.Ca. soldier at Mrs Dr Ward's[42] who is seriously wounded—delirious all the time from the quantity of Laudanum they are compelled to give him to make him sleep—I would call and see him but I could gain no pleasure. I sent him some nice jelly, and intend to inquire if he can drink Lemonade. He is a married man, his wife is not aware of his critical condition—Major Hammond of Georgia (cousin to Gov. Hammond of S. Ca.)[43] took tea with us last night—He says more of his men will die since the battle of 21st than could have been killed or wounded in the battle from the effects of exposure and hard living with double quick march of 8 miles while exhausted the morning of 21st in order to gain the battlefield. He says there is much mismanagement—and the soldier's life is not looked to as it should be when first taken sick in camp. The Major has been ill of typhoid fever—He is staying at Octavia

---

[42] John Ward, M.D. (1826-1885), according to the census of 1860, was the father of three children, ages 4 to 8. He was a son of Berkeley Ward and served as surgeon in the United States and Confederate navies. (J.K.G.)

[43] For a more complete record of the Hammond family, see *The Hammonds of Redcliffe* by Carol Bleser (Oxford University Press, 1981). (J.M.W.)

White's—she kindly offered to nurse him. He is better but very weak. The Capt. of his company, Capt. Brown—is lying very ill of Typhoid fever at Mrs James Brooke dont think he'll recover.

Jessie was delighted with her doll—says she loves Papa and will kiss him heap when he comes—she will have it she is going to Rich—with Daddy and Willie she talks sweetly—I wish you could hear her. You would be surprised. She has a passion for the Soldiers—loves all—This morning Frank says Mama dont you know I love you as I love Anty—I told him he should love Mama and Papa best, for we did everything for him—he says well Papa dont do any thing for me now. I told him not now because you are away—in an instant tho' before I said a word, he said but Mama he has gone away from us to make some money to send us, that's what. I then talked with him and told him, yes that was so—but someday we would live together and you would help dress him again. He wants to see you, thinks somehow you have gone to the war to fight Lincoln—he talks right old at times.

The weather has been rainy and damp all day. The children have been as noisy as possible on account of being shut in.

I went out shopping yesterday. They are asking very high prices for flannel. I am compelled to give 50 cts. for flannel worth 25, but there is no choice—Willie, Frank and Grandma all stand in need of flannel—Mr. Utterback says it sells as high in Richmond—You had better look around for *woolen* goods for *pants* for *yourself*— see what Factory cloth can be bought for suitable *pants* for Willie—send samples—

The tea seems to be given out in town—you better buy me a couple of pounds of *good tea* for me to have during my sickness, if you have an opportunity to send it on—Rice is selling at 12 1/2 cts per pound here—

I see by the dispatch Thomas Wescoat is sick at Louisa Court house. I am sorry[—]I wrote to know all about him.

I am not feeling well to day, but nothing serious. I hope I shall see you as soon as you can get off, but I am willing to abide your time. If I should be sick I will send for you sure—but I hope all will be well with me until October. I have much to do in the sewing line before that time.

Little ones and Mama send a bushel of love and kisses to our dear Papa. We are longing to see your face in our midst.

Your own dear affec daughter,
S.E.C.

Warrenton Fauquier
Sunday, Sept. 1st, 1861

My Dearest Papa

My mind has been much troubled about you in not having received a letter from you all the week. Jessie and Frank both said Papa sick, altho it was innocently said it caused me many anxious thoughts. On the arrival of the cars this evening Mr Finks inquired for a letter. There was none at Post Office—but meeting with John

Spillman—he told him that you had been very sick, but was much better. Was able to be out again. He also received packages and letters from him which I was glad enough to get and devour the contents to learn of your sickness—I am grieved to know you have been suffering from your old complaint—Please *my own dear husband take good care of yourself* while separated from me. Separation at this time is painful to me—but the sting is greater and harder to bear when I learn you are suffering from disease. I cannot be near you to wait upon you. Now write and promise me you will not allow your feet to get damp or wet without changing socks as soon as possible— also to change your clothing with weather.

The children were delighted with their letters. I just wished you could have been near by to see how their eyes glistened at the sight of the money—All reading their letters and talking about what they would buy with their money. All three going at same time, you could not hear your ears. Willie says I'll keep mine—Frank said just see Anty what Papa sent me just like Willie's. Jessie says me buy cake, Papa send me. I love Papa. I told her, her dear papa had been sick she seemed troubled and commenced telling each one separate that Papa in Richmond was sick—she sorry Papa sick—Her dress is very pretty—It will come in as a *Birth day* present. She will be 2 years old to morrow. What did it cost? Frank screamed with delight to Willie, Oh! Willie here is a new suit for us—Mama says Papa sent for both of us—I am so glad.

Many thanks for the fruit—The oranges are in good condition—The peaches are spoiled excepting two I think.

Willie's shoes are first rate but too large. Mr F. will tell you about the change. Frank's shoes are good yet. I have had heels put to them—don't buy any more for children—they are supplied just now with clothing sufficient—

If you had time during the day to look around, I would like about 12 yds. of *Heavy unbleached Canton flannel.* You will have to pay either 14 or 16 cts. per yard, perhaps 20 cts. for extra good—If I can find a sample I will send it—don't worry about it tho' if you are not sufficiently well to walk much. I want drawers for you and myself. I have sent you a pair of pants, I bought it back from Mrs Cooper—They will suit for you on cool days. I send you a cravat—and collar and your night shirt. See that you have good warm socks—Buy them if you stand in need.

I return you the *check* you sent for $30. I wish you to keep it yourself and buy out of it a nice *overcoat. You need it now.* Be sure you do it. The $5.00 will answer for me.

I have received the spool cotton.

You will be surprised to see Mr F. & Willie. We would have sent Frank but feared you would not have time to attend to him. He will be disappointed.

I have been sick with another similar attack, but am well again. I will have to be more careful in my diet.

Be sure to buy your overcoat.

All join me in love. Please write soon and tell me how you are. Buy some Red Oak bark and make a tea like you did at the farm and cure yourself. You will grow weak if you do not.

Dearest Papa

Mr. Finks and Willie arrived safely at home to us again very unexpectedly on yesterday. Willie was very tired and looked rather worsted from his trip. The musquietoes [sic] had nigh disfigured the little fellow and the bites he complained of very much. His foot gave him some pain where he said he narrowly escaped from being run over by a horse and carriage—Providence protected him. He seemed delighted with his trip—said Richmond was far prettier than Washington, your office was much better than the Solicitor's Office—all things pleased him well. Frank looked into the trunk to see what you sent him. Mr F.'s comb and brush was wrapped in paper—Sister handed them to him—He eagerly grasped them and was much delighted—Showed them around then trotted off to my room to put them carefully away. He uses them altogether for himself. The little fellow is very anxious to see you—talks of you often. He is very much broken out with hives now, and he is fretful and restless at night. I fare badly at night when anything is the matter with Frank— His appetite is good, but he grows slowly—He is getting fond of dress and cries for a clean suit if I have none ready to hand.

Jessie seems as well as usual, but her bowels are disordered she dearly loves peaches and it is difficult to prevent her from eating them when all of us have them daily. She was charmed to meet her Dadda and Willie. She could not kiss them enough and says my Dadda come, she is the smartest child I have ever seen—She knows you are away and talks about you as well as Willie or Frank—she admires the dress you sent her and tells everybody her Papa in Rich—sent it to her—and talks about *Doll* baby—

The weather is very unsettled, it has been raining all day. Children are kept in doors—and you cant hear yourself talk, I was about to say, when they are about.

I have been trying to get my furniture varnished so as to get my room in readiness, but both Cabinet makers are kept engaged at present in making coffins for the poor unfortunate soldiers who die in our midst, and also in fixing up articles for the hospitals—I feel very anxious to have it done as the time for their need is drawing closely on—If I find I cant succeed, I will put the carpet down and retain the same furniture in room.

How were you pleased with your pants? I hope they will fit nicely—I thought they would come in nicely for cool damp days instead of your wash pants.

The *Cravat* was intended for you. I mentioned in my note. I bought the silk and made it so you would have a nice one for Sunday go to meeting days—I will send you one as soon as opportunity offers again—

I also intended for you to keep trunk and carpet bag—But perhaps I shall have another chance to send them—I expect you need a trunk to keep your clothing from dust.

Take good care of my *Bible*. I intended to write you long ago to purchase one but having failed to do so I thought I would send mine—You must buy one, and return mine. Mrs Wilson gave it to me you remember and I must not lose it.

I was much disappointed in the Canton flannel. I was anxious to get it like sample I sent you was the reason I sent to Richmond. I could have purchased from old Rinsburg[44] [sic] a better piece than you sent at 14 cts. and a first rate article for 18 cts—but yet neither compared with sample—I hardly know whether to make your drawers out of it—It will neither be warm or last. I know you did the best you could and dont mean to complain of you—The merchant cheated you surely to make you pay 20 cts. What did you pay for Willie's shoes?

Now I must beg you to look up some *Tea* for me—Mr. Finks said he could not get it by the pound—Grand Ma is much distressed and has been making inquiries at all the stores for tea—to night she had a sample sent her from Mr Boatwright's store at $2.00 per pound. Write me word if I must buy a couple of pounds to put aside for my sickness, you know I will need it then.

Sister says make inquiries if you can get it by the pound in Richmond and the price—Also coffee—The prices are exorbitant here on groceries—

Sister says if you have received a letter written by her to Mr F. asking him to purchase worsted—you need not trouble about getting it—as in choosing the shade will require daylight, and your time is too limited.

I am glad you are comfortably fixed—I would like to pay you a visit myself—when I am ready. I dont think I shall wait to be invited. I long to see you—but I am contented as long as you are well, and remain satisfied yourself—take good care of yourself.

Quite a distressing scene occurred in our neighborhood on last Monday. A Capt. Brown from Georgia was sick of typhoid fever at Mrs Brooke—he was ill when he arrived and being a married man they telegraphed his wife—He died on Saturday last—His wife did not arrive until Monday—when her heart was well nigh broken to learn the saddest of all news to her—that her loved one was buried forever from her sight. She went into spasms—and the Dr had to stay with her—poor woman, I understand her grief is intense—she never speaks a word to anyone. On yesterday she went to the Graveyard and stretched herself on her husband's grave—and on her return was as disconsolate as on the evening of her arrival—He was quite young and was married in December last—How much distress in our land.

Mr. Finks wishes *2 or 3000 Envelopes*. He will send you a check for them. Please attend to it early.

Good Night my own dear husband may Angels guard you this night, and at all times is the earnest prayer of your ever...

Devoted and affec daughter,
S.E.C.

Children & all send bushel of love.

I sent you your check back because I wished you to purchase an *Overcoat* for yourself. Please buy one at once and Mr F. will send you back the check. Now do it at once.

I am tired. It is after *10 O'clock.*

---

[44] The family of Abraham Rindsberg, from Bavaria, Germany, had settled in Warrenton. Mr. Rindsberg was a dry goods merchant. Henrietta Einstein, also a native of Bavaria, aged 21, lived in the Rindsberg home in 1860. (J.K.G.)

Dearest Papa

Your's of Friday last was duly received on yesterday. I am glad to know you are improving and are feeling well again. Do take good care of yourself; the weather is very changeable and damp this month. We have had so much rain that the earth seems saturated with dampness, which keeps the children with colds for I cannot keep them in doors, they keep such a fuss.

Willie has recovered from his journey. He talks so much about Richmond and when he shall go again.

Frank thinks he should go the next time—We would consent to his going—but he could not stand the travel and confinement in your office all day and your business is such at present as requires your undivided attention.

Uncle Will has promised Jessie she shall go see Papa and she enjoys the idea—talks about going to Rich as a matter of course. She does not keep regular in her bowels it being a hard matter to prevent her from eating peaches. Her hair grows so fast, it is very long and will only stay in curl when first arranged for she is here, there and everywhere in a short time—I am going to try and get some silk to knit her a *nett* for her head.

I am much gratified and well paid for the fixing up of your pants, as they please you and you are satisfied with my bargain—I felt as if you would need a pair during this month in place of summer pants, and those like your coat would be most too heavy. I will send you a cravat in place of the one Mr Finks brought home.

I have partly purchased a dress for myself for winter from Mr Utterback's. He asks $1.00 per yd.—the dress will cost $12.50 cts. I wished to do without it but Sister thinks I will need one. I know I will but I dont like to spend so much money. But I bargained with Mr U. I would not pay him for some time, say January, and I thought I could lay by a few dollars each month till then and the dress would not appear to cost so much.

By the bye you need not trouble yourself about purchasing *tea* or any of the articles you mentioned in your letter as all can be bought at more reasonable prices with us. I have bought some very good tea from Marion English for $1.50 per pound—and Mr Helm has some extra good at $1.75 so you see we can do much better here. Mr H. has just received his chest from Richmond. Rice is 12 1/2 cts. per pound here. Coffee—32—So you can give yourself no further concern about buying groceries in Rich—

The Washerwomen are raising their prices in washing. Soap, wood and starch sell so high—I tell you money goes fast when you are compelled to spend it out for articles that seem but little in themselves.

You say you wrote to Mother and answered all her inquiries, did she ask you anything in particular about me? If so, how did you answer her? She has put the question to me but I have avoided telling her anything about myself fearing she may grow uneasy about me. She thinks there is something ahead and wishes to be satisfied—so if you have told her—I need not be keeping the truth from her any longer.[45]

I do not expect to be sick before the 1st week in October, but I may be sooner. I feel very badly at times and it is labour for me to attend to the children at night when fretful. But I will soon be over with my troubles I hope and Oh! may the Good Lord spare my unprofitable life. I have no patience at times with the children and I am both ashamed and grieved. No one knows what I suffer at times in regard to my situation, and many a time I feel as if I am overburdened with anxiety and care and that causes me to feel annoyed at little things that others would laugh at. It hurts me to bend over even to write a letter—then again I feel wearied in waiting on the children— altho I have as much help from Sallie[46] as I would get perhaps from a larger nurse. But on the whole, I think I get on very well with Jessie—the fault lies in myself. I need to cultivate patience—but it seems to me as if I shall never gain the grace—At times I would give anything I possess if I could just act more quietly and been more amiable towards the children.

Mr. Finks says he intends sending an order for things at Pursell's soon and he will tell you then about sending the envelopes at same time.

I shall make inquiries about the cloth for your *Overcoat* for I am anxious for you to have one as soon as possible. Do you wish a *Cape* buttoned on your Coat. Write me the exact style you wish it cut if I can get the cloth. I will await your answer.

The weather has changed since dinner, it is now rainy and damp—children all in doors and kicking up a fuss—Frank cries out now and then with a bump. Jessie howls for fruit if she gets a glimpse of any.

The grapes are ripening, the white ones are very nice but not as sweet or as abundant as heretofore. Those in the garden will not amount to as many as those two years ago—

I must close—all join me in love to you.

I hope with you that your Landlady will continue to give satisfaction and you be contented.

When will Mr Goodloe pay a visit to Tennessee? I am awaiting an answer from Mrs G. to my last letter.

Mrs. Gaines has a *son* about three days old. So has Mrs Lunsford and Mrs Baggarly—Mrs. B.'s is a daughter.

Children send a bushel of kisses and love to Papa. Oh! how cordially you will be welcomed when you can get off to pay us a visit—May God bless you and preserve you my dear husband from sickness and danger.

Your devoted & affec daughter,
S.E.C.

Don't give yourself any uneasiness about me. I do not feel the least alarmed. I know no harm will befall me here. No one in town feels uneasy in regard to Lincoln. He cant get Warrenton no way.

---

[45] A reference, evidently, to Susan's pregnancy. (J.M.W.)

[46] Possibly "Sallie" Withers (see pg. 57 n. 47). (J.M.W.)

Warrenton Fauquier
Thursday Sept. 12th, 1861

Dearest Papa

Yours of the 11th has just reached me through Mr Jackson. I congratulate you on your good fortune. You richly deserve your promotion for you give all your time and attention to your business. We are all pleased knowing $200 will add much to our comfort.

I dream of you often times and sometimes I feel unhappy and low spirited from my dreams fearing you may be again suffering from sickness. You must always write me if you are sick, would much rather know all about you at all times. Be sure you do it always.

Now there is yet another thing that weighs on my mind. Several gentlemen who have seen and conversed with you—tell me you do not appear happy and contented in mind—you appear dissatisfied. Be candid with me and tell me if you are unhappy and the cause of it? Now I think you should try and make yourself happy and contented in mind. You know I and the children are well cared for and near enough to you to hear from us daily if any of us are sick you can hear in a short time and get permit to come home—then again at present you are pleasantly situated in a nice boarding house, pleasant friends, and a good situation yielding a sufficiency for your family—which has not been the case with many who have been thrown out of business from Washington. I feel as if you have made a great sacrifice in thus separating yourself from your family in order to have them comfortable—You miss many pleasures once derived from the company of your little ones in which you so much delighted—I flatter myself, you miss me for many little comforts. Yet taking all these things in consideration—you should be cheerful and happy and spend your spare time pleasantly. You need not have one uneasy thought about us in Warrenton. Mr Finks is doing first rate in his business—We have plenty of every thing that is nice and palatable—we are as comfortable in every respect as we have ever been. The Lord has blessed us all with our usual share of good health. We feel no fear for our safety we feel assured that Lincoln and his troops will never trouble Warrenton—we feel happy and secure in our own home for there is nothing to make us afraid.

Now write on the receipt of this, if the gentlemen only imagine this of you or if you are really dissatisfied in mind in regard to your absence from us all. I feel very anxious to know the state of your mind.

By the bye I received a letter from Preston Wescoat asking me to be kind enough to send him some under clothing—He had no change, lost his clothes the day of the battle—I felt as if I could not refuse him. I intend making two shirts and two pairs of drawers—if I can and send them to him. I dont feel able to get any thing expensive, as he did not mention any thing in regard to funds. Mr Wescoat is fully able to give his children all necessary articles for their comfort.

I have bought my dress from Mr Utterback I will not have to pay him for some time yet. I have been trying to get a piece of Factory cloth for your overcoat—but have not succeeded—the cloth being made at present is course and heavy for the Soldiers in camp. I will continue to try. Every article of goods of all description is scarce here—

What is here is sold at enormous prices—We will have to make out as well as we can.

Willie says a spelling and reading lesson each day and earns a penny. He puts the pennies away.

Frank has the hives again. He is full of a trip to Richmond—is anxious to be with you—loves to talk about you—Jessie says, I will kiss Papa when he come home—Papa well now, Papa send me pretty dress—ain't it nice Mama—She will surprise you in her conversation. I am tired. Good night. May God bless and preserve you. Be content, the day will soon roll around for you to get permit come to Warrenton to see us all. I want you to write a note to Dr Chilton and tell him I will require his services between this & 1st October. Beg him to be in town and pay me undivided attention. Enclose the note in my letter. Please do it at once. I feel anxious for him to know of it—as he is not as attentive to his patients as formerly.

I will expect a letter from you by Sunday. A bushel of love from all hands.

Have you ever received your black coat from Mr Horner?

Warrenton Fauquier
Wednesday Night

Dearest Papa

Your much welcome letter I received yesterday with note for Mr Finks and Dr Chilton—Sister gave Dr C.'s note to Mr F. I told her to say to him Dr C. need not call to see me before I sent for him.

I have had another severe attack of sick headache—was in bed all of yesterday. It was similar to the one I had before the birth of F. But thanks to the Good Being I am enabled to be up to day and altho my head still aches, I am trying to pen you a few lines to enclose in Mr F.'s letter he has handed me.

I am sorry you have lost your undershirts. They were very good ones—had tape sewed on the shoulders and across the hem down the front to keep them from tearing down—But please dont allow yourself to be without them this changeable weather. I priced them here and can only get them at Rinsburg at $2.00 and very indifferent— So you better buy another one like the one you have already purchased at $2.50.

I cannot get at present any factory cloth for your overcoat—Mr Sedwick told me that Crenshaw & Co. kept all such things in R—and you better go there and see, and write word if you can be supplied to suit your taste. Attend to it once and let me hear from you.

Please see if you can purchase in Richmond any good fresh *Broma*—You know what I mean—It is what Mrs Campbell use to make for Mrs Wilson during her confinement. We bought it at Coburn's for 25 cts. a package—you can get me 2 or 3 if they do not sell much higher than 25 cts. a pack. Send them with Mr F.'s articles—

Tell Mr Goodloe I wrote to Mrs G. weeks ago—ask him if she ever received it. I want to hear from her. I fear my letter never reached her as she is prompt.

I have had my furniture varnished—it will cost about $3.00—Have put my

Carpet down. It was much too large but looks very nice. Everything is now ready for me at any time I shall need to go into the room. I am at present sleeping in the middle room—I fear Sister will have most too much to do to attend to Frank and Jessie during my sickness—After a week tho' I will be able to take one back if I am not very sick—Jessie has cut one of her jaw teeth, I just found it out to day. I judge it was the cause of her disordered bowels. She is looking quite well at present. Frank is better of hives—Willie has a swollen jaw, occasioned either from cold or decayed tooth, have not found out as yet which it is—I bought Sally[47] a dress, and also a calico cover for the *lounge*. Aunt Harriet will have to sleep on it at night in my room.

Good night, cant write more, my eyes ache very much. Children send kisses and love to dearest Papa. Jessie went to sleep talking about you.

If you think you can get any *stouter* Canton flannel in R—try and send me a *Sample*—don't think of buying it until you send a piece for me to judge—I think tho you better see what these *flannel drawers*, like your *under shirts* can be bought for (colored ones are the best). Mr Finks wears them during the winter—You will need thick drawers by November.

I am glad you are well and you have a contented mind. Dont be uneasy about me. The Good Lord I feel will take care of me as He has done heretofore. It would be a source of comfort and pleasure to me if you could be near me—but as such cannot be I bear it patiently. I know you will come to me should I be very sick and that creates a contented mind within.

May God bless you my dear husband and keep you under all circumstances.

Your devoted & affec daughter,
S.E.C.

Warrenton Fauquier Co.
Saturday, Sept. 21st, 1861

Dearest Papa

Mr. Finks intending to write to you by to morrow's mail I thought I would pen you a few lines. I am hoping to hear from you this evening by the Cars.

The weather is very unpleasant and rainy today—the children all in doors and there is a constant hubbub—

Willie is much complaining. His jaw is much swollen and has a severe cold— he runs out at all times and has his feet wet oftentimes when Sister is not aware of

---

[47] This was either a domestic slave, or Sarah Alexander Withers, reared by the Finks, a daughter of Jesse Howard Withers (1804-1856) and Frances Eleanor (Carter) Withers (1822-1856). She was born in 1850, married February 15, 1872 to Albert Fletcher, a local Warrenton merchant. She died in Warrenton on November 27, 1877. Mrs. Fletcher was a sister of Samuel Melville Withers (1845-1937) who was a member of the Black Horse Cavalry. He lived on the old Withers' family home near Great Run which was called "Oak Lawn," married four times and was the father of 11 children. (J.K.G.)

it—I hope tho' with care he will soon be all right again. He will not give up—is anxious to be all about and eating.

Frank is all broken out with hives again—he did not sleep or permit me to sleep one hour all night. He seemed to be in an agony at times—and he has been fretful all day with them. Strange he is so much troubled with them. Grand Ma says he eats hearty of fruit and bread and she judges that must be the cause.

Jessie seems well—Mr Finks makes her very saucy—she is too smart for any use—she amuses us very much. I think she would know you at any time for she calls you always when she looks at your likeness—She always says I kiss my Papa when he come home see Mama. Then she will say won't that be nice Mama—

I have found a remnant of good *Canton flannel here* at 20 cts. per yard and *intend making* you *2 pair* of *drawers*, so you need not buy *flannel* ones unless you prefer them—write me word which you prefer.

Be certain to buy your Under Shirts for Rinsburg now asks $3.00—a piece—each article of goods goes up in price each day—

I have my room all nicely arranged—one great trouble off my mind. Dr Chilton promises to be punctual so now all I have to do is to sew on until the time arrives.

Dont be the least uneasy about me—All will be well with me I hope.

I cannot find any goods for your Overcoat—Have you looked at the Establishment I wrote you of—Crenshaw is one of the firm. I cant remember the first name.

Soldiers die here daily—Oh! It seems so sad to have them sicken and die from home and loved ones.

I was much elated at hearing that Lee had the federalists surrounded—but the good news has been contradicted.

Goodbye, write soon. Did you succeed in getting the Broma for me?

It is pouring down rain—All join me in love.

Your affec daughter,
S.E.C.

I will make your drawers next week if I am able.

Warrenton Via
Thursday Sept. 27th, 1861

Dearest Papa

You are very stingy with your letters to me. I had hoped to have received one from you yesterday—but did not. Mr Finks received one acknowledging the receipt of checks and other bills—

Mr. F. and Willie went over to farm on Tuesday last, will not return before Saturday. They are having charming weather.

Don't trouble yourself about housekeeping and all such like until after my sickness—I am as anxious as you are to be settled, but we must see our way clear before we attempt it. We have been separated 3 long months and I long to be united once again—but I try to bear up under all with patience—the children need your discipline and watchcare.

Did Mr Goodloe mention to Mrs G. I had written to her? I long to hear from her. Remember me kindly to him.

Mr. Thayer I expect knows Brother W.—I hope they are pleasant people.

The children are well. I could not write you all the smart sayings of Jessie—She is saying something to astonish us all the time—

Frank this morning inquired of me if Uncle Will staid [sic] any much longer if Lincoln would not come and get us. I told him no—we were able to fight him away—then he said if he does come, Mama and we treat him good, he won't trouble us—you think he will? He talks much about Lincoln.

Our town is filled with sick soldiers. Some die each day.

The weather is charming—Children are out doors all day long. Who do you think has a baby boy? Mrs Utterback—I was surprised no one knew any thing was the matter with her. She has a fine boy—Mr. U. is much pleased. It will be news for Mr F. when he returns for he had no such idea—

Mr. Lunsford is quite sick of Typhoid fever—Some think he will get better.

I will keep my letter open until the mail arrives—I could write more, but my pen is shocking bad. Goodbye take good care of yourself and come home when you can—some will say to me dont you expect him—I tell them yes, I am always expecting you for you are as anxious to see us as we are to see you—but circumstances prevent you—you cannot get leave of absence from office.

I have made one pair of drawers for you and expect to make the second pair to day—Will send them to you soon—Children send a bushel of love and lots of sweet kisses to dear Papa.

Goodbye once again. May God bless and preserve you from sickness and danger is the constant prayer of your much ...

devoted and affec daughter,
S.E.C.

No letter this P.M. I feel disappointed—please write soon.[48]

Warrenton Fauquier Co.
Wednesday, Nov. 13th, 1861

Dearest Papa

Your kind affectionate letter I received, and feel very grateful to know you keep well and are comfortably situated. I knew you would be glad of your feather bed after

---

[48] Lucy Lee Caldwell was born October 1, 1861 in Warrenton; this explains the long break in correspondence through October and part of November. (J.M.W.)

you had it fixed. Try and keep well of your *disease*, by using all the care you can in regard to damp feet and injurious food, and I shall promise you to be contented and happy. I would love to pay you a visit—but that would appear selfish in me—for all hands want to see you and be with you—now I wonder if this would not be a better plan—for me to wait until *Christmas* week and *you* come yourself and the *money* I would spend for *board* in Richmond would buy much to gratify all the little ones—It is a long time for me to wait to see you until then (should our lives be spared) but I am willing to undergo the sacrifice if you think you can spend a *couple of weeks* with us at that time—of course I know you cant come before then—What say you to it?

I feel much troubled in regard to the fight or the taking rather of the forts near Beaufort.[49] I expect it was not thought of there that an attack would be made and came upon them very unexpectedly. I am anxious to get a Charleston paper—to learn all the particulars. I do hope and pray that they will not get possession of the town of Beaufort. They will then have gained their point in sending off our Cotton—and thus the *war* be continued. Oh! May our people *burn* with double quick time all their cotton at once, so if they are outdone the Federalists will have nothing to get which will benefit them. I see Messrs. Pope and Baynard, very wealthy planters, burned all on their premises before leaving. I am sorry for the people of Beaufort and the Islands around, what consternation—*William McMillan's*[50] family and relatives are there— I know Mother is about frightened out of her wits. They can now better sympathize with us in Virginia. I wonder if any of the Regiments here from Carolina will return to the defense of their state. Capt. Cuthbert of Palmetto Guards[51] is from Beaufort, and all his family are around about there—Oh! that we will have force sufficient to drive them from our coasts and from our state.

Friday will be a Fast day. I hope true and fervent prayers will be offered up for the protecting care of Almighty God in our behalf. We need His all powerful arm to be around and about us—

The children have kept well up to this time. I have never seen them look as well and be as healthy. Jessie is as fat as she can be—Begs for you to come back every day. The other evening she was standing at my back window and the soldiers were firing into the grave of some one who they had just buried. On hearing the gun she sprung to her feet and said Lincoln killed my poor soldier—bad old Lincoln, showing she understands he is the cause of their death, for *no* one was saying a word about the soldiers.

Frank is very uneasy about Lincoln's coming here, tells me not to go out and

---

[49] In late October, 1861, Admiral Samuel F. Du Pont (U.S.A.) sailed out of Hampton Roads with a convoy of 17 cruisers conveying a force of about 12,000 under General Thomas W. Sherman; destination, Port Royal Sound. On November 7, after a bombardment, they took possession of Forts Beauregard and Walker. The civilians and Confederate soldiers at nearby Beaufort, S.C., in face of the advancing troops, burned bales of cotton stored there for shipment, to prevent them from falling into enemy hands. (J.K.G.)

[50] William D. McMillan was an old friend of Susan Caldwell's. He corresponded with her when he was a cadet at the Citadel. (B.G.C.)

[51] Palmetto Guards: Probably a reference to the Palmetto Sharpshooters of South Carolina, commanded by Col. Micah Jenkins, 26, whose conduct during the battle of Seven Pines "had been above all praise." Douglas Southall Freeman, *Lee's Lieutenants*, Vol. I (New York: Charles Scribners Sons, 1946), pp. 242-9. (J.M.W.)

leave Baby Sister at home—he asked me if Lincoln would fight the Good Lord? He says you know Mama, if the Good Lord was to come down from Heaven and be here, if the Lincoln folks were to trouble him, wouldn't we fight for him—he says you know the Good Lord loves us and takes all the care of us and he can do all he wants, and he won't let Lincoln trouble us any how—I think the little fellow is improving and growing some—he has a quantity of chestnuts put away, puts them away to save he says when he wants them to eat. He seems very fond of the baby, is distressed when it cries.

Willie is as usual—we are trying hard to make him say a lesson every day—but it seems to be a very great punishment to him to be in doors that length of time— he does not improve fast.

I have taken cold—and have not felt very well for a few days. I am now suffering from headache. I hope I will soon feel better, for I have no time to lose from my sewing at present. The baby occupies much of my time. I often wish for a nurse, but will try and do without one as long as I possibly can. You must excuse this hasty scrawl, for I am obliged to attend to the baby at the same time. Some days she will sleep the best part of the morning, but yesterday and to day she has preferred to be awake—

Horace Pattie buried his youngest child Monday. He has been much afflicted. Mr Fletcher has also buried another one of his. I hear of several grown persons having the Scarlet fever also. Little Frank Brooke[52] has it now—but is not very sick—Willie Brooke[53] has gotten quite well. Mrs Brooke says it only requires care and good nursing. Oh! may our dear ones be preserved—We must trust them in the care of the Good Being who doeth all things for the best.

Mr. Finks bought from Mr Helm's sale an extension dining room table for $25. A very nice one it is.

I wish you would get me about 4 yards of *Canton* flannel if you can get it about 20 or 25 cts. per yard. Dont go over that price because I would do without it than give more than 25 cts—Inquire how Coat's spool cotton sells by the dozen—and write me word—If you buy the Canton flannel, send it with Mr F.'s things. But dont buy it if it sells high. I can get on without it.

I wish I could hear from Mrs Goodloe. I wrote to her when the Baby was 2 weeks old but have received no answer—How is coffee selling at present?

Butter is now 30 cts. per pound with us.

Goodbye, God bless and preserve you my own dear husband, and keep you in health till we meet again. Children send a bushel of love and kisses to Papa.

Your affec & devoted
daughter
S.E.C.

---

[52] Francis C. Brooke, son of Col. James Vass and Mary (Norris) Brooke, age 5 at the time of the 1860 Warrenton Census. (J.K.G.)

[53] Willie Brooke - William Throckmorton Brooke, son of Col. James Vass and Mary (Norris) Brooke, age 14 at the time of the 1860 Warrenton Census. (J.K.G.)

Warrenton Via
Saturday, Dec. 21st, 1861

Dearest Papa

I fully intended writing you a note to send in Mr Fink's letter of yesterday, but Miss Lucy Lee was most too fussy for to allow me.

I received your letter in which you mentioned you were rather doubtful of your coming to see us during the Christmas—I wish much for you to be with us—you always enjoy the pleasure the children afford you at such times. I hope Mr Morse[54] may succeed in getting you a free ticket—but then I feel when I think of money that I care naught for it—and $12 would not be uselessly thrown away by your paying us a visit as we are compelled to be separated. I am as happy as I can be here, and feel contented—yet my heart goes out after you and I think you must be lonesome so long absent from those you love.

We are trying to arrange a Christmas tree, it is quite a difficult task to keep the children from finding out what we are about—they miss us out of the room and fly all about to find us—as yet, they have not found out but they think by the way they look around that something is going on—Sister is now arranging the *moss* and I am Sentinel. The doll's head we succeeded admirably with and have just finished dressing it. It will charm Jessie I know, for she is begging Old Kriss to bring her big doll baby—I bought several toys to dress the tree with, and with those left from last year, we will have quite enough without spending any more money. I do hope you will be able to come and enjoy the pleasure with us.

I have overlooked the names of the sufferers from the late fire in Charleston and find my dear Father's[55] name left out, also Brother Will's[56] house is safe—but there are many names of those I feel much sympathy for—I feel grateful to you for your liberality in subscribing $10 to their relief—I know full well what prompted you to do so at such times as these, it being my own dear native home.

---

[54] Possibly Samuel F. B. Morse, with whom Lycurgus previously had been employed. (J.M.W.)

[55] Susan's father, John H. Jeffords (1801-?), was son of a Charleston tailor, John Jeffords (1761-1841) *(Charleston Directory and Stranger's Guide* (1813), p. 40). His lifelong career as a sailmaker began around 1819 (Ibid. (1819), p. 35.). On Jan. 4, 1822 in Charleston he married Mary Louise Humbert (1800-1878), daughter of Sarah Gilbert and William Humbert of Charleston *(Marriage and Death Notices from the City Gazette of Charleston, S.C.,* p. 49). According to Lila Jeffords Thompson, in a 1913 letter to Charles Caldwell, Sarah Gilbert was the direct descendent of Sir Humphrey Gilbert, who came to America in William Penn's expedition, and great-granddaughter of Reverend William Screven, who in 1683 constituted the First Baptist Church of Charleston, the oldest Baptist church in the South (H.A. Tupper, *Two Centuries of the First Baptist Church of South Carolina* (1889).) Mary and John H. Jeffords' children were Samuel (1822-54), William G. (1825-1903), Susan (1827-1913), and, according to Mrs. Thompson, Basil (1829-). Mrs. Thompson's letter asserts that Basil went west in 1850 and was never heard from. As the 1850 census does not list Basil, but does list the three older children and Manly, we may surmise that Manly was a fifth child. See note on James Manly Jeffords in Susan Caldwell's letter of Feb. 14, 1862. (B.G.C.)

[56] William G. Jeffords (1825-1902), Susan's older brother, is listed in the *Charleston Directory 1852,* p. 65, as a clerk at Adger's Wharf, and in the *Charleston City Business Directory 1855,* p. 54 as a bookkeeper at Adger's Wharf. He married Annie Mary King (1834-1862) in 1851. Their children were: Elizabeth Annie (1852-1860), Victoria (1853-), Robert Adger (1855-1856) and Alice Amelia (1857-). In the family plot in Magnolia Cemetery there is also a plot for Abbie Julia (1860-1861). After Annie's death, William married her sister Elizabeth M. King (1836-1920) in 1863; their children included Elizabeth Annie (Lila) Jeffords Thompson (1864-1949), William G. (1866-), Arthur I. (1869-), John Mitchell (1874-1874), and Ernest Hart (1875-1946). (B.G.C.)

My feelings have been much worked upon in the past two days—you know I wrote you that I had become interested in the Hospital where the So. Carolinians are—well, about two weeks ago some twenty were brought in and among the number was an interesting youth of only 18 years old, Mr Paul Miller—he did not appear much sick, had the mumps, soon it was discovered he had typhoid fever, yet he was cheerful and never complained, always said he was better—I would go and take him little nourishment and inquire after him—On Monday he was taken worse and died on Thursday. Poor boy, he was surrounded by strangers, but I feel that they did all they could for him—They telegraphed for his Father, but he did not come. I sent a *green* wreath to put on his coffin and went out to the Graveyard to see him buried. I have felt since his death that I wished I had gone to his bed and talked with him, but I feel timid on entering the room and only inquire of them how they are and pass on—he was a beautiful boy, very intellectual countenance.

Willie has recovered from the mumps and is as bright and happy as a lark—talking about Christmas and what Old Kriss will bring him.

Frank has had the mumps since Monday—he was rather fretful at first, but does first rate now—he is almost well again—

Jessie seems almost herself again—She is gaining her appetite and is lively and happy—She talks much about Papa coming from Richmond to see her and bring her good things, as yet she has not taken the mumps—

Miss Lucy Lee grows some and is a good baby. Please dont forget Octavia White's shoes—I mean her gaiters, *No. 5*, *thick sole* and *heels*. If you come and have any shirts to mend, bring them along. Dont bring any clean shirts, I can get some of Mr F.'s if you are not going to stay long. Dont buy any more for children—have enough.

I would like to have 6 yards of fine bird eye diaper for aprons for the children—2 yds. of *narrow checked gingham*, blue or green for sun bonnets, 2 pair of shoes No. 5 or 5 1/2 for Jessie, and 2 pair for Lucy Lee, No. 2. If you see slippers that number for both children, then get one pair of shoes and one pair of slippers for each child. I would like a *shaker* bonnet for Lucy Lee, a *white* one No. 4 if it can be had. Also a few yards of *white* gum elastic for *garters* for Jessie. Cant get any in town. And get the 1 1/8 of poplin like my dress if it can be had and a couple of india rubber nipples.

Come if you possibly can. Goodbye.

I must write to Mother, have not written since fire.

Your affec daughter,
S.E.C.

If tea does not sell too high, bring a pound with you for Grand Ma.

Undated

Dearest Papa—

Seeing a soldier I intend asking the favor of him to drop this in some by way so you can get it—We are all peaceable—*no enemy near* and we do not know where they are—

Children are all better—Baby almost well. I long to hear from you—please be easy about us. We will be well cared for under all circumstances. Take care of your precious self—God grant we may soon see each other again, or at least have tidings one from the other—Keep up a cheerful heart, remembering altho separated—our *children* are *comfortable*, more so now than they could be *even with you in Richmond.*

God bless you my own dear one—Promise to be calm under all circumstances and take good care of your health which is precious to me.

Get Hampton's tincture and take it regularly.

Goodbye—God bless you—Children are all doing well—

Your affec daughter,
S.E.C.

No enemy near us yet. We are quiet, not the least disturbed in mind—Will be happy again when I can hear from you.

Undated

Dearest Papa

We are all well. I write in haste as the gent is ready to go. Please take care of yourself—get *Hampton's Tincture* and take it regularly.

No Yankees here yet—and *none likely* to come—Keep good heart, we shall do well—Love and kisses from all hands.

Don't be worried about us—write if possible.

We are all well.

Your aff daughter,
S.E.C.

I have bought you some *socks.*

S.

1862

Susan Emeline Jeffords Caldwell to Lycurgus Washington Caldwell

Warrenton Fauquier
Wednesday Jan. 8th 1862

Dearest Papa,

Your letter was received and perused with eager delight—was charmed to know you were well and getting on so nicely with your business. I hope you will without difficulty or overtasking your strength be able to accomplish in your business what you have proposed to do. I fear tho' you have undertaken too much.

I am sorry to have to tell you our darling Jessie has the *mumps*—poor little soul she seems to suffer more than either of the others—she is much disfigured very much swollen each side and under her throat. I hope tho—she will soon get rid of them as the boys did—and be bright and happy again as she is wont to be—May the Good Being grant my prayer in her behalf unworthy tho' I be. I am always unhappy when the little ones are complaining. I then feel your absence more keenly—She said to night on going to bed she hoped to be better in the morning. She is a dear one.

Mr. Finks has gotten quite well again. We are all much relieved for we were fearing it would prove to be Typhoid fever—he thought so himself and felt anxious to know. I gave your messages to Dr. Hamme[1] to deliver to Mr S—in regard to leather and shoe thread.

Lute has arrived. She got here Saturday evening. Sister and myself went down to meet her—she came alone from home and came nigh being put out at Manassas—her trunk was left at Gordonsville, and has just arrived in this evening's train—we were fearful of never hearing from it again—but luck was on our side this time. Lute has grown quite tall—is very pretty I think—She will start to school to morrow—We are anxious to get some *worsted* to knit her a hood for school, and can't get any here—will you inquire of Mrs. Thayer—if there is any in Richmond—if so, write us word and we will write you the colour we wish, and quantity.

Willie and Frank are well. I think Willie intends writing you a letter—he is like all boys of his age—more eager for fun and frolic than study. He has been sleighing down the hill all day—and has enjoyed the snow. He came home yesterday with feet so wet that the water could be wrung out of his stockings, and he contended he was not cold or tired from being out all day.

I am very well satisfied with my girl—she is rather inexperienced—and requires watching—but does admirably. Of course I dress and undress the baby

---

[1] Luther E. Hamme: In 1852 Mr. Hamme, a native of Berkeley Co., Virginia (now West Virginia) opened a drug store on Main Street. In 1855 Mr. Hamme took Mr. John W. Finks in as a partner; later, a Mr. Withers, possibly Jesse H., acquired Finks' interest and the firm was Withers and Hamme.

Mr. Hamme enlisted in the Warrenton Rifles; promoted to 4th Corporal, he served on "detached duty" to the Medical Department as a hospital steward to care for the wounded after First Manassas. Cpl. Hamme was discharged as "being overage" on Aug. 13, 1862. He survived the War, but very little is known of his life thereafter. It was a custom at the time, as it often is today, to refer to a druggist as "doctor," which Mrs. Caldwell frequently does in mentioning Mr. Hamme. (J.K.G.)

myself—Mrs Utterback was to see us this afternoon—she says her boy is as big again as Lucy Lee—she has an experienced nurse—and has only to nurse her boy about three times during the day—her nurse dresses and undresses him—and feeds him with his bottle—gets him to sleep without her nursing him—I told her she did admirably to get her.

Mr. Dutart has gone home—he lives 18 miles from Chn—very kindly offered to take any package I may wish to send. I thanked him, but told I had nothing ready at present.

I understand we had a fight at Romney[2] and whipped the Yankees out of the town—Alas, Alas! for poor Lincoln—I fear he will soon have to bow at our feet as he has already done at the feet of the British Throne. How mortifying such conduct was—even we feel it being the same nation—better far to have held them tho' for their sakes I am happy of their release[3]—

I bought with my money Davy's clothes—gave $9 for his pants and shoes—he asked me to give him as much money as would buy him a Coat—he had a coat—so I gave him $4.50—he was well satisfied—I forgot to give him socks—but will write to the old lady about them. I bought Sallie a Linsey dress—had to give $1.00 per yd. is it not enormous—I wished I had bought one from the price you sent—but all has been sold.

Frank begged me to write you a letter—he says

Dear Papa
Willie read your letter to me, I felt glad when I saw my letter and I do love Mama and Lucy Lee—she lays by me in the morning and plays—I want you to send

[2] A reference to Stonewall Jackson's Romney, West Virginia campaign. (J.E.D.)

[3] In late 1861, envoys James Mason of Virginia and John Slidell of Louisiana were named to respective posts in London and Paris. Their departure to Havana from Charleston by blockade runner was scarcely a secret, but the U.S. Navy failed to intercept their ship. Captain Charles Wilkes, commanding the thirteen-gun sloop U.S.S. Jacinto, arrested Mason and Slidell as the "embodiment of despatches" (diplomatic dispatches could be seized as contraband of war) on board the British steamer Trent, and let the ship go.

The northern public greeted Wilkes' act with applause. The House of Representatives passed a resolution lauding Wilkes. But after the first flush of jubilation, second thoughts began to arise. Few expected Britain to take this lying down. The risk of war sent the American stock market into a dive. Government bonds found no buyers. News from Britain confirmed fears of an ugly confrontation. The British expressed outrage of Wilkes' "impressment" of Mason and Slidell. The jingo press clamored for war. Prime Minister Palmerston told his cabinet: "You may stand for this but damned if I will." The cabinet voted to send Washington an ultimatum demanding an apology and release of the Confederate diplomats. Britain ordered troops to Canada and strengthened the western Atlantic fleet. War seemed imminent.

In 1861, British India was the Union's source of saltpeter, the principal ingredient of gunpowder. The [British] government clamped an embargo on all shipments to the United States until the crisis was resolved. No settlement, no saltpeter.

In a crucial Christmas day meeting, Lincoln and his cabinet concluded that they had no choice but to let Mason and Slidell go. Mason and Slidell resumed their interrupted trip to Europe, where they never again came so close to winning foreign intervention as they had done by being captured in November, 1861. Their release punctured the war bubble. The saltpeter left port and was soon turned into gunpowder for the Union army.

The afterglow of this settlement left Anglo-American relations in better shape than before the crisis. "The first effect of the release of Messrs. Mason and Slidell has been extraordinary," wrote young Henry Adams from the American legation in London, where he served as secretary to his father. "The current which ran against us with such extreme violence six weeks ago now seems to be going with equal fury in our favor." James M. McPherson, *Battle Cry of Freedom* (New York: Oxford University Press, 1988), pp. 389-391. (J.M.W.)

me the money you promised me and I will kiss you when you come to Warrenton.

Frank—

Willie has finished his letter—he wrote it himself and feels proud over it—it is very well done—I don't know what Frank means about the money[.] I suppose he bargained with you.

I must close—Lute is waiting for pen and ink—

Good Bye—God bless you my dear husband and preserve you from all sickness and danger—

All join me in love—little ones send kisses—The children were delighted with their letters.

Your affec daughter
S.E.C.

Warrenton Via
Friday Jan. 17th 1862

Dearest Papa

Your letter of the 13th came to hand and I felt it was a blessing—I had been much troubled in mind concerning you—a week had passed by and you had not written to me—or Mr Finks altho goods had been sent to him—you cannot imagine the deep anxiety my heart undergoes during your absence should any letters fail to reach me—I would not be so disturbed in mind if you were in the enjoyment of good health—but knowing how subject you are to cold and that brings about disease. But I felt truly grateful to my Heavenly Parent that all had been well with you, and business alone prevented your writing. If you were to supply yourself with paper and ink you could always write me a nice loving letter on Sundays—I know you are anxious to have me with you in R—but we must bear with our separation patiently, hoping the time is not far distant when we shall be domiciled together in our own home with our little ones around us. The weather is very changeable—we have had some very severe weather—have had snow on the ground since Monday—Willie has a sled and enjoys the fun much.

The children were charmed with their letters—but Willie said you did not mention his Birth day which was on the 10th. I mentioned his Birth day in my letter to you. I gave him a *silver* quarter to put in his portmoneau. He says a lesson nearly every day—he is very anxious to go to school but neither Mrs Diggs[4] [sic] or Mr Latham[5] will take boys—Lute has commenced school. She has lost much in her

[4] Fanny P. Digges, 34 at the time of the 1860 census, was listed as "principal of female school," with personal property amounting to $6,050. (J.M.W.)

[5] R.P. Latham was a professor at Columbian College (now George Washington University) in Washington, D.C. from 1852 to 1854. At this time he was a teacher at the Fauquier Seminary with the former president of Columbian College, Dr. J. S. Bacon. (J.K.G.)

studies and will have to study hard—she was not put in the highest class as she had hoped to be—She is much grown is as tall as I am and quite pretty.

You remember the package of clothing I sent Preston Wescoat—well he *never received them*, nor any of my letters. I sent a letter to him by Mr McCoy and he answered it. I am sorry he did not receive them. He must have concluded I was very indifferent to his request—by not receiving either letter or package from me. I will write him soon again.

Jessie is getting better—but continues fretful and delicate in her appetite. She promises to do all you ask of her. Frank has been complaining for two days past, he eat [sic] *slaw* (cabbage). I think it disagreed with him—he says tell Papa—he will say a lesson every day—as soon as his letter was read, he ran for his book and said a lesson to Dr. Hamme—Willie was charmed with the story of the boy. Grand Ma has taken cold and is not able to attend to housekeeping—seems right feeble.

Lucy Lee improves daily. She is now troubled with a cold in her head—she is very sweet to me—

Jessie has commenced writing you a letter. I can't tell if she will finish it.

I bought Sallie a Linsey dress—gave $1.00 per yd—Mrs Finks at the farm wants to know if she had better have Davy's summer clothes woven up there[,] if so I must send the bunches of cotton[.]

When will the blockade[6] be raised do you imagine?

All join me in love to Papa—

Your devoted
and affec daughter
S.E.C.

Warrenton Fauquier
Wednesday Jan. 22nd 1862

Dearest Papa

Your letter written at your office was received and cordially welcomed as all of them are.

I am pleased to learn you continue well—but am grieved to hear you say—your

---

[6]This is an ironic, if innocent, question. One of Gen. Winfield Scott's supreme contributions to the Federal war strategy was the concept of what was called an "anaconda"—a naval blockade designed to strangle the South into returning to the union.

From the Chesapeake Bay to the Florida Keys, along the shores of the Gulf of Mexico, he favored establishing a deep-water naval blockade to wall the Confederacy off from Europe and whatever aid might come from that direction. Down the length of the Mississippi, from Cairo past New Orleans, he would send an army of "Rough Vigor Fellows" backed by gunboats, thus cutting the Southerners off from the cattle and cereals of Texas, as well as foreign help through the neutral Mexico.

Lincoln welcomed the plan, studied it, and acted on those parts of it he saw fit to at the war's outset. On April 19, 1861—a week after Ft. Sumter, he proclaimed a blockade of the Southern coast. Its effects would be felt increasingly until the end of the war. Shelby Foote, *The Civil War: A Narrative; Fort Sumter To Perryville* (1958), pp. 111-113. (J.M.W.)

appetite is not good—now if you were just to remark to Mrs S. that you do not fancy so much fresh meat—she would now and then gratify your appetite with oysters or ham and eggs—you are not generally fussy and she would understand you—and I feel assured she would readily oblige you—please don't allow yourself to suffer when you are paying for what you can easily obtain by making known your wishes—make the effort—

The box with the oysters came to hand on Monday—Mr F. sent Saturday on receiving the letter—but was told no box had come—and on Monday he was told it had been there since Friday. Have you eaten all your *sugar cakes* that were in the *oyster can*? I have intended to write to you about my putting them in (as I did not mention it to you on packing your trunk) fearing you were not aware of it and they be spoiled—but I hope you have enjoyed them all before this time.

Did you look for the worsted for Lute? Sister wants double zephyer worsted—either *dark blue, dark rose colored, or salfereno*—we cannot get any here—and either one of those colors would make a *hood*—ask Mrs Thayer to look for you—she could get a shade suitable for a girl of fair complexion and blue eyes—takes *3* ounces I think—but I will ask Sister again—you can get it ready to send in the next *box* you send Mr Finks—and save expense.

The oysters were very acceptable. Sister was glad of them as we are now living on Turkey—

Jessie seems to improve each day—her appetite is now good—she says Papa write, dear Jessie Papa love you and send you nice oysters. She enjoys them very much and so does Frank. Sister intends to have a nice dish of fried oysters for dinner—how I wish in my heart you could dine with us and enjoy them—

I have sad news to write—you know the proprietor of Warrenton House, Mr Daschiel's[7] [sic] [...] well poor man—he died yesterday—only sick about two days of pneumonia—Mr. Finks did not know he was much sick, heard him complaining what a distressed family—and how unprepared for death was he—oh! we should live nearer to God and Heaven—for we cannot tell who will be the next one called. Sophronia Yeatmen[8] died of Scarlet fever Monday night—was buried this A.M. Her father is almost beside himself with grief[,] how distressed he must be—wife and daughters all, all gone from him now—*desolated home*. Ned Saunders—lost one of his children, a boy of 10 years old of Typhoid fever—it is truly distressing. And why should we be exempt—we are not worthy to be favored of God—But oh! may the Good Being spare *us* and our *loved ones*. Would that I could feel that I was a true child of God—that I was accepted of Him through Christ and that you my precious Husband could claim Jesus as an Elder Brother and God your portion. You have no time to lose—life is short at best and it does appear to me as if the Almighty is calling his people home—oh! then prepare for Eternity—Let us try and

---

[7] James Deshields, a native of Maryland, was aged 53 years in 1860. He left surviving him a wife, Eliza R. and five children. (J.K.G.)

[8] Sophronia Yeatmen, listed in the 1860 Fauquier County Census as age 17, was the daughter of George E. and Chloe A. Yeatmen, a farming family of considerable wealth. According to this census, Mr. Yeatmen possessed real estate valued at $10,000 and personal property valued at $10,325. (J.M.W.)

live nearer to Jesus—pray for each other—tho separated we can be united—

Grand Ma is much complaining—her old attack of pain in ear—neuralgia—she gets down in Sister's room. Sister suffers with her throat—she calls it dyspepsia. Willie has a cold from getting his feet wet—Frank has been quite sick and I gave Vermifuge which brought 12 worms, he is now well again. Lucy Lee grows finely—she has a cold in her head. I have had an attack of headache but am better to day.

The weather has been very unpleasant. Do take care of yourself. I wish you had bought a more suitable color of clothes for winter—Must I give Mr F. the $16.50 as you charged him with it in bill—I must close with love from all to you. Frank says write to Papa for me and say Dear Papa I love you and want you to send me a *tooth brush*, so I can clean my teeth like Willie.

Jessie[,] with Sallie's help[,] has sent you a letter.

Good Bye. God bless you—

Your ever affec daughter
S.E.C.

You would be amused to see Willie with his books. He rushes for his geography and spelling book as soon as Lute gets her books and studies as hard as she does. I hope it will last and he will learn to love his books.

Undated, 1862

Dearest Papa

Yours of 25th reached me yesterday. I am glad you keep well—Hope your appetite has improved. Mr Finks will write you this evening and I take the opportunity to enclose a note as I tell him to save postage—he laughs at my economy—

I gave him the $16.50—of Mr Saunders—as you had charged him with it in his bill—there is a mistake about the soap bills—he has paid you the $12, he says—so he does not owe it.

Sister begs you not to put yourself to trouble in purchasing articles for Wm Pattie[9]—he remarked the salt cost too much—did not want to take it he paid Mr F. Sister says never buy for him unless he sends money to you—he may make you lose it. If you send a box to Mr F. buy *me* some two or three boxes of *Tapers* to burn at night. None to be had in town, put them in his box, 2 boxes will be sufficient.

Grandma has been quite sick. Sent for Dr Horner[10] he says she has Erysipelis—

---

[9] William A. Pattie, age 39 at the time of the 1860 census, listed his occupation as carpenter, with real estate valued at $1,300 and personal property valued at $1,700. His relation to "Grand Ma," a Pattie by birth, is not known. (J.M.W.)

[10] Frederick Horner, M.D. (1806-1881), son of Dr. Gustavus B. and Frances Harrison (Scott) Horner of Warrenton. He graduated M.D. at the University of Pennsylvania in 1828 and after practicing in Philadelphia and Philipsburg, Pa., returned to Warrenton for a brief period. He engaged in cotton planting in Mississippi from 1835 to 1840 when he returned to Warrenton and for nearly 40 years ministered faithfully to the sick. He was an uncle of Captain John Quincy Marr (C.S.A.). (J.K.G.)

you know what I mean—swelling on the fall from cold—not dangerous. Lucy Lee is improving, but now has a severe cold. Willie, Frank and Jessie are tolerably well—the weather is miserable bad—would that the storms night wreck every fleet of Lincoln's order—I think the times are distressing—no battle—and sickness among the soldiers—we will lose more by disease.

I hope Mrs T succeeded in getting worsted.

Warrenton Via
Friday Feby 14th 1862

Dearest Papa

I have but little time to spare this morning to devote to letter writing—yet I feel as if it will be a source of pleasure to me to write you a short note.

I received a letter from Manly[11] last night. His company is now stationed at *Columbus*—He joined the Tennessee Volunteers last May I think—he belongs to Co. H. 4th Regt. Tenn. Vols. I feel very sad to day—his letter was sad—he remarked at the time of his writing he was in Memphis—having obtained a furlough on account of his wife's illness—She is now very sick, an almost hopeless case of Consumption. He begs me to write to her as often as I can[,] his absence of course depresses her spirits.

Mr. Franklin called yesterday to inquire of me if I wished anything taken to you. I thanked him kindly—but told him I had nothing at present. I wished you had thought to send my package by him. I begged him to see you if he had time—he promised he would. Please if you see him and have the time, send the india rubber *nipples* I wrote for. The one you sent has all split to pieces—too small and very indifferent it was—Please send the *shoe* strings also—Mr. Saunders has none—and all of us want a pair—Inquire of the stores if any *Lamp* oil is to be had—I cannot do without a taper light and there is no oil in town. I have been using *Lard*—that is expensive 20 cts per pound—dont buy any oil until you tell me of the price—so as to calculate which will be the cheapest to burn—Have you bought any tapers. Dr. Stevens sells his at 25 cts. per box—rather expensive business, but I can't do without it.

Judge Tyler[12] died last night of Erysipelas[,] has not been sick over one week—

---

[11] This is her brother, James Manley Jeffords, who is listed as James M. Jeffords, a private in the 4th Cavalry Battalion, which was organized in Knoxville and in other parts of Tennessee, and formally mustered on August 29, 1861. See reference to him by his full name in Susan Caldwell's August 29, 1862 letter. And see note to December 21, 1861 letter. (B.G.C.)

[12] John Webb Tyler, of Prince William County, became the Judge of the District Court following the death of Judge John Scott. At the time of his death Judge Tyler was living with his family in Warrenton. Mr. Joseph A. Jeffries, in his Sketches of the Warrenton Bar, published in 1909, described Judge Tyler as "a dignified man, free from trifling and not easy to approach. He appeared to the young to possess that dignity that doth hedge a king. Whatever may have been the impression he made, he came to this office to administer justice and the effect of his decisions satisfy as to how well he performed his duty." He was age 62 at the time of the 1860 census. (J.K.G.)

We have had very many sudden deaths among adults. I expect it is owing in part to the Hospitals[,] the atmosphere is diseased—not pure as it was wont to be—I feel much sympathy for the family—I believe he was a kind good man. He will be missed in the community—

My heart grew sick when I heard of the defeat of our army on Roanoke Island.[13] I am astonished at the General allowing a man to go at large after uttering words which were calculated to make us know he was against us—and betrayed us into the enemies hands[14]—he should have been put in *irons* and we might have conquered— Poor Wise,[15] he has fallen in a good cause—peace to his ashes—and oh! that his soul rests in the bosom of his God—the sacrifice of souls! How startling to think on— and poor Manly how much danger his is in too.

I judge there will be much ado made over Davis on 22nd[16] would that you could spend that holiday with us. It seems a long time to me [since] you were here—I want you to write to me in all candor and promise me not to volunteer in any company as you are *honorably* exempt being an office holder—you cannot stand a camp life. I would not have you shrink from danger or shirk your duty—but you know as well as I do—you are not necessitated to go.

Mr. Finks says he intends getting a *substitute*[17] if he draws for to go—he knows he can't stand life in the camp—Dr. Hamme says he does not wish to try camp life a second time he has had enough of it—says it is a laborious life to lead. I was sorry to hear Mr Samson[18] & Dr. Smoot[19] had turned against us.

The children are all doing well—Lucy Lee grows nicely—Willie is reading very prettily—Please send him *McGuffey's First Reader*—and *Frank*—*McGuffey's*

---

[13] A few days earlier, on Feb. 7, Gen. A. E. Burnside (U.S.A.) had seized Roanoke Island, N.C., captured more than 2500 men, scattered the remaining men under former Virginia Governor Henry A. Wise, and now held a position from which he might take Norfolk in reverse. Douglas Southall Freeman, *Lee's Lieutenants*, Vol. I (New York: Charles Scribners Sons, 1946), p. 134. (J.M.W.)

[14] One of the keys to Burnside's successful attack was his being briefed of the island's defenses by a 20-year-old contraband who had run away from Roanoke Island the week before and who was thoroughly familiar with the dispositions for defense. Foote, *Sumter To Perryville*, p. 230. (J.M.W.)

[15] O. Jennings Wise, son of former Governor Henry A. Wise, was mortally wounded at Roanoke Island. (J.K.G.)

[16] A few days more than a year earlier, Jefferson Davis had made his inaugural address in Montgomery, Alabama; Susan's reference here is probably to the annual celebration of that event. (J.M.W.)

[17] Mr. Finks was anticipating an official act of a few months later. On April 16, 1862, with so many one year enlistments expiring and so few re-enlistments, the Confederate Congress passed the Conscription Act, enabling the government to draft all white males between 18 and 35 who were not legally exempt. Finks was worried unduly, however, as he was at the time, 44. On April 21, the Congress passed a supplementary law specifying several exempt categories, including Confederate and state civil officials, of which Lycurgus was one. Despite its success in getting more men into the army, conscription was the most unpopular act of the Confederate government. McPherson, *Battle Cry*, pp. 430-32. By 1864 the age limits were 17 and 50. The hiring of substitutes was allowed, and widely used, provided the substitute was not legally eligible himself. Newspapers carried columns of advertisements for substitutes. (J.M.W.)

[18] Rev. George W. Samson, D.D., was ordained in the First Baptist Church of Washington, D.C. in 1843. He was pastor of the Third Baptist Church, later called E Street Baptist Church, from 1843 to 1859, when he became President of Columbian College, now George Washington University. From 1860 to 1863, while still in that capacity, he was pastor of the First Baptist Church. (J.K.G.)

[19] Samuel Clement Smoot, M.D., of Washington, D.C., married Emma Smallwood. Dr. Smoot, an assistant surgeon, U.S. Navy in 1861, was a greatly beloved physician of Washington. (J.K.G.)

Primer—Send Lucy Lee's *rattle* too, she wants one—If you have $10 to spare send it to me, I have been making some purchases[.] I bought a dress for myself and one for the *nurse*. I wish you would buy me a pair of *Corsets*. *Rail Road Corsets* I want. they use to sell for $1.50—to $2.00—get me a *colored* pair No. *21*. Don't give an exorbitant price for them tho'. What about the worsted.

Grand Ma is almost well. Mr Finks is at home with sick headache—

S.E.C.

Warrenton Via
Monday Feb. 24th 1862

Dearest Papa

Hoping to get a letter from you by this evening's mail I will pen a few lines to you this morning. I write this morning more particularly to ask you how are the times serving you? You have not written to us now for more than ten days—and I am getting anxious to hear from you—I also want to ask you if you have any idea of paying us a visit soon? If so, why not come at once and let us enjoy each other's society in comfort for a short time—for we cannot tell when we shall have the blessed privilege of being with each other again—The times look very dark and threatening to me—I have heard that our vast army at Manassas will fall back to Gordonsville—leaving Fauquier and other counties to the mercy of the enemy—who will soon walk in—now in such an event one can hardly decide the best course to pursue—with all my little ones where could I go to be comfortable—every article of food so exorbitant—I know full well that you and Mr Finks cannot remain with us in Warrenton if our Army should go to Gordonsville—you could only be with us as long as we remain behind our army—it is for all this I would be so glad to have you with me now before all come to pass—true such an event may not occur—we may have the assurance henceforth as now that we are secure—but we know not what a day or week will bring forth—Should Fauquier Co. be in possession of the enemy our paper money will do us no good—for this reason it would be advisable to purchase articles of wearing apparel to last for months to come—if we put off goods will increase in prices—I had hoped the Blockade would have been raised through the interference of England—but you see by the Queen's proclamation[20]—she does not

---

[20] Earlier in February, Britain's Foreign Minister Russell announced Britain's position on the blockade: "The fact that various ships may have escaped through it ... will not of itself prevent the blockade from being an effective one by international law" so long as it was enforced by a number of ships "sufficient really to prevent access to [a port] *or to create an evident danger of entering or leaving it.*" By February the northern blockade certainly met this criterion. Another influence working against British acceptance of Southern arguments about paper blockades was a desire not to create a precedent that would boomerang against British security in a future war. As the crown's solicitor general put it: Britain must resist "new fangled notions and interpretations of international law which might make it impossible for us effectively at some future day to institute any blockade, and so destroy our naval authority." Ibid. (J.M.W.)

intend to do one thing—Our people have been waiting on England quite too long—we had much better have been at work ourselves and done as much towards subduing the North—as they have been busied with their fleets of destruction all over the coast I see no place of safety any where—yet I feel no alarm—if I could feel assured of your safety I could stand the time. You cannot stand a camp life—even if you entered the army should the yankees get possession of Warrenton I never could hear from you and you might like thousands gone sicken and die—without my hearing of your whereabouts. I could never live through that thought—I can stand the yankees, bear separation, remain in Warrenton, if I could know of your whereabouts and safety—and could receive and send letters to you. Do write and tell me all you have been thinking of.

I was very much pleased with my dress—it is quite pretty you sent *2* handkerchiefs—did you intend one for Sister? Many thanks to Mrs Lotties for her selection—her taste is excellent—Now I would like if you had the money to spare to get me *2 winter calicoes*—Mrs Lotties will be able to select—in Warrenton we have to pay 37 cts for the same 12 ½ ct. calico—and in Richmond I understand you can get beautiful *chintz calico* for winter for 37 cts *yard wide*. You might speak to Mrs Thayer and Mrs Lotties about them—I judge they know how such goods sell—then I would like a *Mousseline or Merino*—which ever one would be the cheapest, I would like a dark ground Mousseline with a small figure, *rose bud* or something pretty, I don't like large patterns—they are too conspicuous—it will take 12 yds of Mousseline—I merely mention about the dresses if you believe there is danger of the times growing worse and our money be useless then—if all will be right and our paper money good and you do not deem it advisable to spend it at present for winter goods why I am willing and ready to acquiesce. You bought such a *pretty fine* mousseline for Jessie at 50 cts, I thought may be you might get me a nice one about the same. I want an *all wool mousseline*, they last much longer. I would like a *piece* of Bleached cotton suitable for shirts—such as Arkwright or New York Mills—if you can get it at a reasonable price, it is selling here at 37 cts per yd, I would like a piece of Brown cotton—to make up sheeting and for the servant girl's under clothes—

I mention all these articles—but unless you can get them at a reasonable price, I dont wish you to spend out more money than you know to be prudent.

Frank has been quite sick—I had to call in Dr. Horner—he is now almost well again—has been down in the dining room at play to day—the Dr. thinks he is troubled with worms—he says Papa must make haste & come to Warrenton and bring his knife and his toothbrush—

Jessie is little complaining to day bowels disordered—she eat [sic] cake yesterday—and it has not agreed with her.

Willie and Lucy Lee are doing well—as I am better some of my headache—but feel rather nervous—

If you can come home—that is if you intend to come soon—if your business permits you, write and tell me when to expect you—I long to see you to talk with you some—

Mr. F. is very anxious to hear from you—write always to him on business matters quickly as he gets anxious to hear—

Now dont [buy] me a Mousseline dress unless you can afford it, I want it for next winter should I live—I want an all wool suitable for winter and a pretty one—Goodbye, children & all send love to Papa—Don't think I am uneasy because I ask you to come. If you feel that you had better not leave your business to pay us a visit at present, write and tell me all about your own feelings at this time—

Frank seems quite bright and himself again—goodbye—
May God bless you.

Your affec daughter
S.E.C.

Mr. Finks says he has written you three letters since sending on his money to deposit and has not heard from you yet.

Monday Night—I have just received your letter of 23rd, with Davis' message—Mr. F. was greatly relieved to hear you had received his money—please always attend to his letters if possible, he becomes so uneasy—

Mr. Saunders has just sent $21.70—I owe Mr Utterback $11.[,] my washing $3.00—and about $1.00 in other little things so you see it will soon be gone. I bought but few articles from Mr U. such as stockings, sewing silk, ½ dozen spool cotton, and so on—the prices are so exorbitant that $10 will only go a little way—sewing silk is *10* cts a skein—ask the price of it in R—

Please buy me a dozen of colored spool, *black* & dark drab—No. 50 & 60. Get *glace* cotton running 200 yds (There is much cheatery in colored cotton; the indifferent kind only running 100 yds) it is selling at $2.00 per dozen here if you can get it cheaper get us *2* dozen of colored cotton No. 50 & 60—we will want them in making up the children's clothes—

Please price this domestic cotton with you—if you can get it for 25—or 30 cts—you better get a piece—Get the Ladies to make your purchases—they can make better bargains than you—Write me an answer to all I have asked you about all the goods I want you to buy. I want my corsets—What do you mean when you say I must keep $50—or $100. on hand—I have none to keep—and Mr Finks does not owe me any money at present—if you send it I will keep it for you—

Please see about my shoes—half shoes and also a pair of slippers—but don't give too high a price.

Willie says come home soon to see him—

Frank says bring him a spelling book to keep till he grows big to read in it—

You seem to be very courageous—Mr. F. says it is all put on—he knows you are scared up—but won't own it—

Your affec daughter,
S.E.C.

Be sure to get this cotton as thick as you can and good quality—Some are asking 40 cts per yd here for it—extravagant price.

Dearest Papa

I will only write you a few lines to night to give you some idea of the state of the times with us—On Monday an order came up from Manassas to Dr. Fisher, to have all the *sick* removed to Charlottesville—no reason given—All were trying to find out the why's and wherefore's but to no purpose—Mr. Tavenner told Mr Finks that Mrs Gen.l Johnson[21] [sic] received a letter from General Johnson to be ready to leave for Richmond by Saturday. Rumour says that our Army at Centreville intends falling back to Gordonsville—How true I can't say—This evening Tom Franklin informed Dr. Hamme that all the provisions were to be removed from Manassas—he then had 400 barrels of flour on board—Dr. Hamme failed to ask where he intend taking it to—The Butchering at Thourafare[22] [sic] has ceased—and the *bacon* has been ordered to be packed ready to be sent off—Now what does all this mean—and what is best to be done under the circumstances—we can't tell—

Some say Richmond is the safest place—others think Charlottesville—that being behind the army at Gordonsville. Our little town is all in commotion—gentlemen are trying to find out the best and safest place to remove their families—Mr. Finks is very unhappy about his property—he does not like to remove us unless there is real danger—and again he says if he has to leave—we might starve out in the midst of a Yankee army—and if we leave and the house be vacated, should the yankees come—the house and all its contents would of course be destroyed by them—the store also would go in such a case—as Dr. Hamme has to follow the sick—for Mr Finks could do no business here.

Now what say you to us—what would you advise[?] Mr F. says he as yet cannot find out what to do—You must either *write* or come on—we are not any more alarmed than our neighbors—we feel anxious to do the best and save as much as we can of the little we have—We will grieve should we be necessitated to leave our comfortable home at this season—but we must endure what is sent upon us—

---

[21] Mrs. Lydia (McLane) Johnston, wife of General Joseph E. Johnston (C.S.A.), was the daughter of Louis McLane, president of the B&O Railroad. She had joined her husband a few days after First Manassas. Unfortunately, it is not known where she boarded in Warrenton. (J.K.G.)

[22] Against the better judgment of Gen. Johnston, the Confederate Army's Subsistence Department located its slaughter and meat curing facilities at Chapman's Mill in Thoroughfare Gap. "At the beginning of March, 1862, more than two million pounds of meat were being cured or in storage at Thoroughfare, in addition to large herds of hogs and cattle. The meat was stored in the mill. When the order came in March, 1862 for the Confederate Army to evacuate this part of Northern Virginia, the large stores of meat and herds of cattle and hogs were dealt with hastily; whatever could not be carried away by the evacuating army was given to civilians or destroyed. Departing Confederate troops, en route through the Gap, set fire to the mill, burning the remaining meat inside the mill, to prevent its use, or the use of the mill, by the Union Army." Frances L. Jones, "Beverly (Chapman's) Mill, Thoroughfare Gap, Virginia: A History and Preservation Plan" (Master's thesis, George Washington University, 1981), pp. 48-49. (J.K.G.)

Write as soon as you receive this and give us your opinion as to the best way of acting in this emergency—

Should your business be too pressing and you can't leave why write every particular—

How must I write to Ma about it? I know she will feel uneasy about us—

Now about the goods I asked you to purchase—unless you think it advisable, don't make any purchases—I would like some Brown cotton—Mr. F. bought a piece of very good quality for 23 cts—I will need some[,] his is yard wide—don't buy corsets if over $2.00 per pair and the colored spool cotton—if you get any—be very particular to get *Glace* cotton—this *waxed* cotton I mean, *black* and *drab*, Nos. *50* and *60*—running *200* yds spool cotton is selling $2.00 per dozen with us—Don't trouble about my dresses—I know you are too much troubled and perplexed at this time— I spent all of Mr Saunder's money—and am *broke*—I bought dry goods for the *children in time to come*—knowing that soon but little for childrens wear will be in stores. The price of every thing is so exorbitant that $5 is soon gone. Should you price *domestic* cotton and it costs over 25 cts or 30 cts per yd, do not purchase any—as that price will be too high—I should think you might get a piece for *30* cts but I feel so little inclination to go shopping at this time that I dont feel like you are in the mind for it either. You can act your own pleasure about spending your *money* at this distressing time for goods. I will be satisfied either way.

Thursday—Had no one to take my letter to Office last night so I did not finish it—the panic has subsided some to day. Yet all are devising plans for removal—Mrs Genl. Johnson left this morning for Richmond—all the sick have left—

Now I want to ask you this, should our army fall back to Gordonsville—and we remain here exposed, when could you get to us—or we to you—I can bear separation (which I have done now for near 12 months) but I could not remain satisfied to know you were where I could not get to you in case of sickness—or you get to us if any of us were sick—This is what I wish you to settle in your mind. We would like you to come and see us if your business would permit you—if you cannot come, please *write* as soon as you receive this—we will await an answer—

Frank is himself again—altho very weak, his appetite is good and I think he will now improve—

I am sorry to tell you we now have our little darling Jessie quite sick to day— she was taken the same as Frank about 5 O'clock this morning—We sent for Dr. Horner—he has given her calomel—she has high fever[,] he says her digestive organs are out of tune—and he thinks she will be relieved when the calomel acts—There is no symptom of danger—so he told me—he says he has had several cases with children—the liver dont act and food disagrees with them. She is now just as Frank was—and he was much better after taking Calomel. You need not be uneasy—should she grow worse I will write you—dont be anxious, if no letter comes, then you will know she has grown better—which I hope will be by to morrow—Mr. Finks speaks of going to Richmond during the coming week—All the rest of us are well.

I will look for a letter soon—

Your affec daughter
S.E.C.

Warrenton, Via
Saturday Night March 5th 1862

Dearest Papa

Nothing that I can think of at present (excepting your own presence) could have afforded me the delight and pleasure that I enjoyed this evening than hearing from the like of Mr Richard Smith that he had seen you since your arrival in Richmond and that you appeared well to him. *I am truly relieved.* It was but to know you had arrived in safety & that you were in your usual enjoyment of health I was desirous of and over anxious to learn. Now I feel grateful to the Good Being that the way has been opened to me and to night my heart is once again happy in the knowledge that you are safely housed in Richmond. May I ever hereafter put my entire trust in Almighty God Who is ever ready to listen and hear the prayers which are offered up at a Throne of Grace. May you my own loved husband—commit yourself & all your loved ones into the keeping of your Heavenly Parent. Trust Him under all circumstances. Oh! may your health be preserved and you do not allow your mind to be overburthened with anxious cares on our account. We are all well—children are improving every day. They have enjoyed the sunshine, and have lived out doors for the few days past. We are as cheerful in spirits as we can be, no yankees have visited us yet—and it appears that they are not desirous of so doing, for they have left the plains and gone down to the Warrenton Junction. I understood from a reliable source that the yankees had left Centreville and Alexandria and had gone down the Potomac. A skirmish took place at Buckland to day—between Col Mumford's[23] [sic] Cavalry and the yankees—we killed *one* yankee and took two splendid horses—the yankees run [sic] our Cavalry into New Baltimore. They arrived in Warrenton to night—and intend leaving for Waterloo—Our scouts have taken a great many prisoners at different times since they have been around us—The Cavalry are with us[,] that is a portion of them[,] almost every day. I feel very safe as long as we have our own soldiers with us and around the neighborhood. I sometimes fear they may surprise our little force here with overwhelming numbers—but the impression among the yankees seem to be that Jackson is at or near Warrenton with a considerable force. I hope such may continue until our army has time to organize—

I have written you almost daily, by private hand, pickets and scouts all promising me to mail them to Richmond. I hope you have received some of them. I wished so much that Mr Smith had been thoughtful enough to have told you he was coming to W—the pleasure of your sending a letter and our perusal of it would have been unbounded.

But I have much to be grateful for, in hearing of you from one who has so recently seen you—I will continue to write by every opportunity to you. Now promise me not to allow yourself to be over anxious about us—We are as quiet and content as if we never expected a visit from the enemy.

---

[23] Col. Thomas Taylor Munford (C.S.A.), later General, of the 2nd Virginia Cavalry, served under General T. J. "Stonewall" Jackson in the Shenandoah Valley and was in nearly every major engagement of the war. (J.K.G.)

On many farms they have stolen cattle & horses and on others they have behaved better and given their *notes* for what they would take away—Someone from Buckland amused us no little by telling us of Mr Royston[24]—they came and took his rails to make fire to cook by—he became enraged and went out and kicked over the Coffee pots and made a general muss of things not knowing he was seen—but the Yankees soon got possession of him and were about to roast him alive—but they let him go— and I can't say if he has stopped running yet—his rails give him some trouble. He will give them next time.

It is now 11 O'clock—a sweet Good Night—all are well with us. Grand Ma as usual—Mr. F. has a cold. Children & Mama send a bushel of love and kisses—Now please be as happy as you can. It is trying to be so separated—but our lot is a happy one compared to the situation of many others. Bright days are yet in store for us—

Do you ever meet with Mr Brooke and his company?

Good Bye—God bless & preserve you is my very earnest & constant prayer for you—

Your affec and devoted
daughter
S.E.C.

Please mail Lute's letter.

John William Finks to Lycurgus Washington Caldwell

Warrenton March 8th 1862

Dear Sir

I write to let you know what is going on. What I write I know to be so—there is [sic] two Armies beyond Winchester[,] one on Romney Road and one at Charlestown—and two armies on this side of the river between Leesburg and Harpers Ferry[,] one at Lovettsville 13 miles from Leesburg 4000—and ten thousand seven miles above—I suppose they are at Leesburg now as all of our men have fallen back to the Plains in this county. The whole army at Centreville have left and retreating up this way—so you see my prediction has come true—The breaking up of the army—we expect the main body of the Army through here to morrow evening—I do not know what else to do than let them all stay and wait and see how they get along and then get out

I sent you a check some time ago for 45—since the other one for same amt. but you did not acknowledge the receipt.

Yours
JW Finks

---

[24] Marshall Rollins Royston (1816-1887) of Caroline County, Va. He married Martha Cash, February 10, 1838. Mr. Royston was a "fashionable tailor" of Jeffersonton, Warrenton and Buckland, Va. (J.K.G.)

Susan Emeline Jeffords Caldwell to Mary Jeffords[25]

Warrenton Fauquier
Sunday Night March 9th/62

My Dear Sister

I received a letter from Manly some two weeks ago—and would have replied earlier—but could not on account of sickness among my little family. I have had two children very sick—but who now are getting well—

I am sorry to learn that Manly felt himself compelled to join the Army and had to leave you in sickness—I feel very unhappy about him being so far from me and placed in positions of danger—May God preserve his life and return him home well once again to you—These are the times to try men's souls—we are certainly passing through a fiery trial, but if we are able to endure unto the end we shall come off Conqueror—it seems very hard for us to have to give up our loved ones—and be deprived of the comforts and many the necessaries of life—but many have done it. I feel very much concerned in regard to Memphis—and hope she will be unmolested—

I was sorry to learn of your severe indisposition—I hope the remedies used will prove beneficial and your health be restored. The medicine I wrote you has made wonderful cures—perhaps you did not continue it long.

We in this part of Virginia are now undergoing a severe trial—We have been hearing rumours of our Army falling back from Manassas—but did not believe a word of it. Mr C. is in Richmond in Office under government and has several times written to me to come on if I felt the least danger—being so comfortably situated here I felt as if it would be best to remain under all circumstances—and did settle down quietly—Since Yesterday we have been much troubled and perplexed—our Army has fallen back—leaving Fauquier Co. exposed to the Yankees if they see fit to follow on as fast as our Army retreats—some tell us that our pickets[26] will go out below Warrenton, if so we will be a little better off for protection—Under these circumstances I feel at times much depressed and fear my courage will give up—for all communication from this day by Rail Road has been cut off from Richmond— I feel that Mr C. will be unhappy about us if he is deprived of hearing of our welfare— I know not as yet what I shall do—but will do the best I can for the comfort of my little ones—

Should you be able to write[,] direct your letters to L. W. Caldwell, Richmond Via—and I will get them.

Do you hear from Manly often?—I hope soon he may be with you—keep up a good heart and all will be well.

---

[25] Context suggests this letter is to the wife of Susan's brother, Manly, probably the "little Mary Jeffords" referred to in her next letter. She evidently did not survive her illness. See Lycurgus Caldwell's letter of Sept. 16, 1864. (B.G.C.)

[26] A detached body of soldiers, evidently guarding a larger army in or near Warrenton. (J.M.W.)

I am suffering to night with a severe sick headache and only have made the effort at writing as I had opportunity.

Much love to Manly. He must write.

Your affec Sister
S. E. Caldwell

Susan Emeline Jeffords Caldwell to John H. and Mary H. Jeffords

Warrenton Fauquier Co.
Sunday Night March 9th 1862

My Dear Parents

Having this opportunity of getting a letter mailed in Richmond I must write you altho I am suffering with severe headache—I wrote to little Mary Jeffords last night and directed it to you hoping it will arrive safely—

I have bad news to communicate—Since yesterday morning our entire army have left Manassas[27]—altho we had heard rumours to that effect we could not believe that such would ever take place—Now it has really occurred—and our Army falling back not 20 miles from Warrenton leaves no room for the Federalists other than Fauquier and other Counties exposed to the mercy of the Yankees for they it is supposed will follow on after our army—at any rate their pickets will be sent out and may extend to Warrenton we cannot tell—rumour says our pickets will go beyond Warrenton thereby protecting our town—but we cannot tell—

Mr. C. has been much perplexed not knowing what to do—to have us come to Richmond on an uncertainty or remain where we are—we have written about over and again and not hearing positively that our army really would fall back I wrote him I had concluded to remain—for the children would be more comfortable here—Richmond is crowded, board is exorbitant and I have not without buying a sufficiency to keep house on—so I concluded to remain where I could with the children comfortable—I know not how I shall stand it when put to the test. The cars will not run anymore to Richmond—to day was the last and but few persons were aware of this fact. If such be true all communication will be cut off and it will be but seldom I shall hear from Mr Caldwell—How he will bear the separation under such circumstances I cannot tell—as long as Mr Finks can remain, all will be well—but should he be compelled for his own safety to leave us—I cannot say how brave we shall be when night sets in upon us—If about two months ago we could have foreseen all this trouble ahead why of course Mr C. could have made every arrangement for our being with him in Richmond—So far I cannot tell how we shall be situated—it will

---

[27] Confederates withdrew from Manassas toward Richmond when McClellan moved down the Potomac River in transports to start the Peninsular Campaign. (J.E.D.)

take our army some 8 days to leave Manassas—and we may by that time see things in a different light—all is passing strange to each one, that the cars should have stopped so suddenly thereby cutting off all communication in Warrenton from the South—We shall have to find out opportunities and by sending *your letters* to Richmond directed to Mr Caldwell he may find some opportunity to get them to me—I would like to hear from Anna[28] very much—Love to all, keep up a good heart about us until you hear again—Children are getting better.

Your affec child
S.E.C.

John William Finks to Lycurgus Washington Caldwell

Warrenton March 13/62

Dear Sir

Enclosed you will find a check for 341 12/100 which I wish you to pay Brooke who will be in Richmond and take his receipt for in note due—I send you his statement so he will have no difficulty in writing receipt—I also send his a/c or a portion of it which was a cash transaction, which he can call for on the other if her [sic] chooses—If not he can have it open until I see him. I have a store a/c and a bal. on house trade which is to be settled in house rent & trade—

Make Brooke take check. The Yankees were at Gainesville last night eleven miles off. They will be here I suppose by Saturday—

I think I will be in Richmond in ten days, Susan will write by same mail—we do not know what to be at but all are willing to stand any thing that can be put on us for the cause.

Yours
Jno. W Finks

Susan Emeline Jeffords Caldwell to Lycurgus Washington Caldwell

Warrenton Thursday
March 14th 1862

Dearest Papa

Hearing this morning Mr Utterback leaves with Mr Brooke's company I must

---

[28] Anna: Annie, the first wife of William G. Jeffords, Susan Caldwell's older brother; in 1853, William would marry Annie's sister Elizabeth. (B.G.C.)

pen you a few lines and ask him the favor of mailing it at the most available point—

Our troops have nearly all passed on—we have had Major Peyton,[29] one of Beauregard's aids to stay with us since Tuesday—He was in Loudoun—had been ill for three months of Typhoid fever—and came within ten minutes of being *arrested* by the Federalists—he had notice given him by a neighbors son living some ten miles off—said his father had been arrested—he had no time left him to give his *babe a parting kiss*—bade his *young* wife farewell—would have brought her with him but was persuaded from so doing by her Mother—He seems very unhappy about her—as he has heard that her Father has been arrested. He hopes to get a letter by a Servant boy—whom he places most unbounded confidence, he sent him to run the blockade and bring him tidings from his wife and child—after he receives a letter he says he will be happier in mind. He will leave to day to join Beauregard in Tennessee.

I met with Mr James yesterday who was about to leave for Charlottesville—he promised to write you on reaching there—

We are all well—and our spirits as good as can be expected under our difficulties—

So long as you keep your position and keep well and I can occasionally hear from you I shall promise you to keep up a brave heart—

Please promise me not to *join any company* even tho' Richmond be besieged—but get out of the way as quickly as possible for you will be arrested being in Government employ. By no means whatever have any thing to do with Mr Pattie's[30] company—tell him at once and positively you will not *join*—Neither be persuaded by Mr Brooke—when I receive a letter from you with the promise you will remain under government come what will I shall be easy in mind.

I think I shall send this by Mrs Cooper who leaves this morning for Culpepper, she will mail it for me there—

I am anxious for Mr Finks to leave at once. We will do the best we can and if we find we cannot get along—then we will contrive to get out—Mr. F. has sent home 5 barrels of flour—and we have meal & sugar and plenty of other necessary articles—our greatest necessity will be wood, but we have a good supply at present—We will hope to get on—

Excuse this scrawl—but I have no time. Children send bushel of Love and kisses to their dearest Papa—Hoping God will bless him and preserve him and that ere many months we shall see each other—during our separation let us keep up brave hearts, knowing all things work together for good to those who do good—Give ourselves soul and body into the hands of our blessed Redeemer—and He will provide us our strength for our trials—

---

[29] Maj. Henry E. Peyton (C.S.A), a farmer from Waterford, Loudoun County, Va., served on General P. T. Beauregard's staff as Assistant Adjutant General, May 10, 1861; Vol. Aide de Camp, April 6, 1862 and Ass't. Inspector General, June 8, 1862. He served on General R. E. Lee's staff as A.A.G. from July 31, 1863 to Nov. 4, 1864. He was Lt. Col., Inspector General from July 31 to Nov. 4, 1864. (J.K.G.)

[30] James S. Pattie, son of William A. Pattie, a resident of Warrenton in 1860, at which time James S. was 17 years of age. He was a member of Co. K, 17th Va. Regt. (Warrenton Rifles) and later transferred to Co. M, 6th Va. Cav. (Sept., 1862). He was reported to be in a hospital in Charlottesville from June 14 to Sept., 1862. On Jan. 25, 1864 he voluntarily surrendered to the Federals near New Baltimore and took the oath of allegiance in Washington, D.C. on March 12 at the Old Capitol Prison where he was being held. (J.K.G.)

Don't be too anxious about us—you must try and keep your health—and your salary will be of vast benefit to us now—Mr. F. having to give up his business—for if possible I shall prevail on him to leave and go to some town and do business—

God bless you my dearest husband—and I am grateful and appreciate your kindness of heart in trying to get off to see us—But it has all happened for the best, you could not have gotten back to R—without much trouble and inconvenience and that would have made me unhappy—you are not able to walk 10 or 15 miles like many—you would break down and have a spell of sickness, pray never attempt it— Good Bye[.] I will write soon again.

Your affec daughter
S.E.C.

Several officers of Virginia Reg. told us yesterday it was far better for us to remain—we must be polite to any should they come to the house—and he did not think we would be inconvenienced—if we left why every thing would be destroyed as a matter of course.

Much better to remain and so we will and try our fortune—if matters grow too terrible for us why then we will get off—But some how I feel as if we shall get on— my heart has been very brave and I have not been cast down yet. I hope to do well— I know we cannot be as comfortable any where with the children as here—

I have seen and heard enough of the sufferings of those who have left their homes—no resting place and very little to eat or wear—

We will remain for a season at any rate.

God Bless you my dear one.

Your affec Sue

Susan Emeline Jeffords Caldwell to John H. and Mary H. Jeffords

Warrenton Fauquier Co.
Saturday March 15th 1862

My Dearest Parents

Having an opportunity to write to Mr C. I will enclose a letter to you—altho I have no news to write. Our Army have fallen back as far as the Rappahannock River—Some of the Cavalry are with us—I expect they will remain a few days longer scouting around. The Federalists are at *Gainesville* about *12* miles from *Warrenton*. I have not been able to hear from Mr Caldwell—I heard through a friend that he made an effort last Sunday to come home, and got as far as down at Gordonsville and having no connection by cars, he was unable to walk the distance[,] he had to return to Richmond—He regretted it very much—I am anxious to hear from him—I feel as if we will get on tolerably well in Yankeedom. I will keep quiet and treat any who may come around the house with the true politeness and dignity of a lady and I will be treated accordingly by them I judge—

Don't be uneasy about me—I will write you as often as I can—You must write and direct your letters to Mr C—Richmond and he will send them when he sends his—

The children are well—I hope you are well—I would like to hear from Anna; her delicate health causes me to feel anxious about her—My love to them all—

I hope little Mary received my letter. I will write to her soon again—I wrote to Manly's wife last week—Give my love to all friends—

I was very sorry Preston's company did not pass through Warrenton—I would have liked so much to have seen him and several acquaintances I made—

Good Bye—God bless you all. Leave me in the hands of an all wise providence and all will be well.

Your affec daughter
S.E.C.

Susan Emeline Jeffords Caldwell to Lycurgus Washington Caldwell

Warrenton Via
Thursday March 20th 1862

Dearest Papa

How can I express my thanks to you for the letter I received from you yesterday dated Monday, March 17th. It was to me, as an *Oasis* in the desert to a weary traveller. I had to read it over and again—so glad was I to see the familiar hand writing—Again to day have I been charmed with the perusal of the one you sent by Gov. Smith—I am very sorry to learn you have taken cold—please take care of your self—*you are my all*, and now that we are separated—and I cannot well get to you I pray you be particular and not allow yourself to get wet. You must get some good *spirit whiskey* will be best, and put *Cherry bark* in it—and take a wine glass full three times a day— it will do your cold good—and if you will take paregoric on loaf sugar—will be beneficial—

The rumour of a skirmish at Warrenton Junction was a false alarm—not a word of truth—Genl' Stuart is at Warrenton Junction with some 3,000 Cavalry—We have heard to day that the Federalists have fallen back some say as far as Alexandria— at any rate they have all disappeared from Manassas—rumour says that they burned their tents before leaving—their pickets have been called in—Many of the Officers and privates say they do not think the Yankees will visit Warrenton soon—they are rather afraid of being drawn into the interior of the Country knowing we can whip them on land—I wrote you they had been as far as Auburn—that was not so—we hear as many false rumours with us—as you do in Richmond—We are very anxious to hear the news from Missouri—I much prefer it being a drawn battle, than for us to surrender as at Fort Donelson.[31] We suffer for news having no papers—please send us some when ever opportunity offers—

You remarked about your getting a passport—and coming to see us—Now let me advise you not to attempt it—you are unable to walk any distance—and a *horse* cannot be had at any price in our town—I would be delighted to see you for time appears long these days—but I would not have you run the risk—be content to remain and I will promise you to send letters whenever I can get the opportunity— I like you am hoping the day will not be far distant when we shall be gathered around our own fireside there to enjoy the society of each other—Let us keep up a cheerful heart—and do good to all who may chance to cross our path—

I am very glad I was not frightened out of my senses at the bare idea of the yankees coming here as many have been—and have hurried away among strangers leaving houses and furniture unprotected—Mr. Brooke from Culpepper wrote to Mrs Brooke that he felt relieved in mind about leaving his family in Warrenton— having seen the suffering and privations families have been subjected to since leaving their homes—he says that many had neither shelter or food—many had sick children—he wrote he was satisfied his family were in a much better condition at their comfortable home—even tho they should be subjected to inconveniences after the arrival of the Federalists—He told her if she had any influence to tell families with children to remain at home—and be quiet—We are perfectly contented to remain in Warrenton—and await the times—I feel that we are much better off at home—children are comfortable and get healthy food—The children were as glad to see and hear your letter read as I was—and now while I am writing, Willie, Frank and Jessie are all writing to you—Willie is writing very nicely—Frank is actually perspiring with the effort—he makes some letters and some we helped him out by holding his hand. Sallie is writing for Jessie—you shall have them all—

If you should think of it and get the opportunity to send, get a pair of *shoes* No. 2 for Lucy Lee—not one pair can be had here. She will need them very soon.

It is late—I must close—all are doing well. God bless you my dear husband— May you be preserved from sickness—and let us await with patience for brighter days—

Write as often as you can—I will be charmed whenever I may chance to see your familiar hand writing.

The weather is rainy and streets muddy—We have two Lieutenants with us— often times have *four* sometimes to breakfast—The Cavalry[32] are stationed in town— and we are glad of it—They do not know when they shall get marching orders—as long as Stuart remains at Warrenton Junction—

I feel no fear of the yankees—my only trouble is on Mr Finks' account—he says tho he intends to remain with us until the last minute—then if he finds the Yankees

---

[31] On the Tennessee/Kentucky border, Gen. Albert Sidney Johnston's (C.S.A.) defensive strategy for the west had hinged on two forts, hastily built in late 1861 and early 1862. Fort Henry, on the right bank of the Tennessee River, fell to Gen. U.S. Grant (U.S.A.) on Feb. 5, 1862. Fort Donelson, on the left bank of the Cumberland River fell to Grant on Feb. 16th. (J.M.W.)

[32] The cavalry was most likely the 2nd Virginia with Lt. Col. Munford in command. This unit was retreating from Leesburg. (J.E.D.)

are about to arrest persons—he will slip out towards the mountains—Don't be uneasy about us—we will take good care of ourselves—and will write you every opportunity—

Please take Lute's letter to Mr Spiller, and give to Kate—

Your devoted & affec daughter,
S.E.C.

Frank Huntington Caldwell to Lycurgus Washington Caldwell

Undated, 1862

Dear Pa

I love you so much. The Yankees have not come yet. I am not afraid of them. I play out doors this good weather. Lucy Lee and Jessie went to see Grandma White[33] yesterday. We are all well.

Good Night. Dear Papa.

Frank

John William Finks to Lycurgus Washington Caldwell

Warrenton March 21/62

Dear Sir

Col. Scruggs is making an effort to get out the malitia, but will not be able to succeed, there is none left but a few married men, who take the ground they will not leave their families, as this country has been left to the mercy of the enemy[,] nearly all the negroes in this section have left[,] some few are returning[.]

I see that one being grist to a store, is released from the last law—so I will not be compelled to go unless I choose.

The Yankees have returned to Alex. None between here and Fairfax C.H. I do not think they will be here unless they come from Winchester where they are in strong force May have been at Piedmont & Upperville.

Let the money remain in Bank but get a certificate—I sent through you to Brooke in check for some money which if he does not choose to take you can tear up

---

[33] Harriet C. White, aged 71, mother of Miss Octavia White, was noted for her untiring efforts in nursing the wounded brought to Warrenton. The Whites were close neighbors of the Finks and Caldwell families. (J.K.G.)

89

They have not arrested any person in Loudoun. Jimmy was released in a few minutes and was not required to take the oath.

See the Ast. P.M.G. and see if he will not give us a home mail between this and R Road connection, until the Yankees take possession, there is no reason we should be cut off until it is necessary.

Yours
JWF

Warrenton March 25th/62

Dear Sir

On day before yesterday Banks[34] stayed all night at Aldie in Loudoun Co. with twelve thousand Yankee Troops. (This much I know) where he halted to hear from Genl. Shields,[35] who went to attack Genl. Jackson, up the Valley. I have just read a letter from Genl. Asa Rogers[36] from Middleburg who says "A courier has just arrived from Winchester, who reports that Jackson and Shields have been fighting for two days and Jackson whiped him on both days, and Banks has been sent for with his whole command to return—Scruggs who is from Middleburg to day states that he has seen another gentleman who is reliable, just from Winchester who saw Genl. Shield's body brought in being killed in a hand in hand contest with Turner Ashby[37].["]

All the above news comes from such a reliable source Genl. Rogers, I am inclined to believe it. You will therefore inform Mr. Smith of what I have written as I have no doubt but Jackson has whiped them.

Frank, Jessie, other baby & Lute, have been quite sick for several days, in fact Jessie has been sick for a month, but they are all except [sic] to be playing about the room, and getting on Will.

We have had about 300 troops here yet who are destroying everything. The Yankees can't do much worse than they are doing.

The great stand will be made at Hanover Junction. It seems a pity that this fine country should be given up to the Yankees, but I suppose it is for the best.

---

[34] Major General Nathaniel P. Banks' (U.S.A.) troops were to be transferred from the Shenandoah Valley to McClellan for the Peninsular campaign; Stonewall Jackson's mission in the Valley was to prevent this. (J.M.W.)

[35] Brig. General James Shields (U.S.A.) had a division of Gen. Irvin McDowell's forces from Fredericksburg. He was no doubt on his way to the Shenandoah Valley to attempt to trap Gen. 'Stonewall' Jackson. Gen. Stonewall Jackson defeated Gen. John Fremont at Cross Keys on June 8 and then defeated Gen. Shields at Port Republic on the 9th. (J.E.D.)

[36] Gen. Rogers' information was wrong. This is the Battle of Kernstown (3 miles south of Winchester) fought March 22-23, 1862. Gen. James Shields had been slightly wounded on the evening of March 22, and Col. Nathan Kimball was in command of the Union forces (Shield's Division). Kimball defeated "Stonewall" Jackson and caused him to retreat up the Valley. This is known as Jackson's only defeat. (J.E.D.)

[37] Gen. Shields *was not* killed in a hand-to-hand fight with Ashby. He survived the war to be elected, among other offices, a senator from Missouri. (J.E.D.)

We are suffering here for wood as the Army have taken all the wagons and there is nothing to haul in—as soon as they leave I will have to send over and get Davy to bring the wagon down and haul mine if I can do no better.—

Warrenton looks like a deserted place, nearly half or more of the citizens having left.

Hume[38] informed me that he called and left his address for you but did not see you—I also wrote by Sunday week and Capt. Robinson on Saturday who will return in a few days—I hope you will see him. We hardly ever see a paper but know more about what is going on in the Army than the people of Richmond and you will see what I tell you about the fight about Hanover Junction will turn out to be as true as the fall back from Manassas.

Try and find an opportunity to write the letters by Smith & Williamson now. All are well & in good spirits.

Yours
Jno. W Finks

Susan Emeline Jeffords Caldwell to Lycurgus Washington Caldwell

Warrenton Via
Sunday March 30th 1862

Dearest Papa

Mrs Brooke has just sent me word to get a letter ready and send it to her, she would enclose it in one to Mr B. and Mr Lucas would mail it at Culpepper C.H. I have not waited to dress myself so eager I am to get it off in due time—Willie Brooke returned *late* yesterday evening. I soon heard from him as to your whereabouts—he said you looked very much fatigued from your walk from Jefferson to Culpepper—I was very much disturbed in mind on hearing it for I feared you might be suffering from the effects of it. I am glad you rested at Jefferson—I hope Mr C. helped you on your journey from J. to Culpepper as 15 miles was rather too much for you in your debilitated condition—But I will hope for the best. You I hope have recovered.

Don't be uneasy about us—A soldier informed me yesterday that the Yankees were not coming to Warrenton—we need not fear them—they were going towards the springs—

---

[38] William McKay Hume (1823-1872) became the first elected Sheriff of Fauquier County in 1852, a position he held until replaced in 1868 by a carpetbag appointee. He served the county faithfully until the beginning of the war, at which time he was torn between his oath to carry on his duties and his desire to join the army, where, with his experience and background, he could expect a commission. Dutifully he went to see Governor Wise in Richmond. The Governor advised him, in fact ordered him, as the county's last law enforcement officer, to remain on duty. He served during the war, managing somehow to preserve a measure of order in a land ravished by opposing armies. Mr. Hume became Clerk of the Court and at the time of his rather sudden death, was a candidate for the Virginia Senate. (J.K.G.)

Children are all better—

Take good care of yourself—and do not allow your mind to be over anxious about us—We are quiet and contented—

Remember the enemy is not near us yet.

God protect and bless and comfort you my own dear husband under all the trials and separation you must endure.

Children send kisses—

In haste, Dick Brooke[39] is waiting.

Your devoted & affec daughter
S.E.C.

Warrenton Saturday
April 5th 1862

Dearest Papa

I have written you almost daily since you left—but as I have had no tidings from you I know not if you have as yet received one—We expect some half dozen soldiers to breakfast with us this morning[,] scouts belonging to Col. Mumford's regiment. I shall inquire of them the whereabouts of the yankees and write you—I intend to ask them to mail this letter for me. I understood yesterday that the yankees at the Plains had gone to the Warrenton Junction—*giving Warrenton the Good Bye*. Very few persons believe that the *yankees will visit us*—at any rate *not for some time*—they are pressing on to the Rappahannock—*Our soldiers are with us every day*.

I have but few moments to write in so I must hasten. Would that I could hear from you—if I but knew that you had fully recovered from your fatigue I would be satisfied. I am very anxious to hear if you are well and your mind easy about us.

Our Soldiers are in town every day. We have pickets out all the time—our men have captured several yankees and brought them through town. One scout captured 5 at one time—it appeared that one of their Officers had accidentally shot himself and these 5 were sent after a coffin—when our scout captured them. I am sorry I have forgotten the name of the place where they were taken. But sad to relate the poor fellow who captured them—thinking others would be sent after the coffin went again and the yankees being on the alert, *captured him*. I could have cried over him—

I sometimes feel anxious about our soldiers if they remain all day with us, fearing some of the yankees may creep in slyly upon them.

The children are all doing well. Frank and Jessie talk a great deal about you. Frank says *he loves Papa all all*—Jessie says me love Papa all too—and Papa loves Jessie too and will kiss Jessie when he come back again.

Willie says he will have a letter ready next time Mama writes. He says a

---

[39] Richard Norris Brooke, son of James Vass Brooke and age 12 at the time of the 1860 census, would later become a nationally known artist and painter of black domestic scenes; he would also become vice principal of The Corcoran School of Art in Washington, D.C. from 1902 to 1918. (J.M.W.)

lesson now.

The weather is rainy to day—children are compelled to stay in doors. I intended to dress them and send them to the store to see their Uncle—for soon I will not send them fearing the arrival of the yankees—but as long as *our* soldiers are with us, we feel safe to go out—We are very particular with Willie—we do not permit him to run at large now—he does not like it so well—but we make him stay in the *lot*.

Please take good care of yourself if you keep well and are in good spirits I shall be happy all the while. May God bless you and protect you from *danger & sickness*.

The Col. will not allow the men to come down. Sister is preparing their breakfast to send them so I cannot get any further information to write you—but you can rest easy in regard to us—we are quiet and contented, and are satisfied that we will not be troubled soon with the yankees—

We are all well—Grandma is a little complaining—Mr. Finks has a cold.

Please write to Ma, and ease her mind in regard to my situation—

Be content and rest easy—we are safer here than we could be with you in Richmond—if you are well that is all we want to know—

Good bye God bless you

Your affec & devoted daughter
S.E.C.

All join me in love to you. Children send bushel of love & kisses. Don't be the least anxious about us, we are as cheerful as we can. *We want you to be happy*.

The yankees were at the plains yesterday and mistook Col. Radford's[40] Cavalry for *Jackson's* and fled in haste to Thourafare leaving Overcoats, horses and even *watches, which our men soon got* possession of. The men are now in our town and these are facts. The yankees believe Jackson is in Warrenton.

Warrenton Fauquier Co.
Thursday April 10th 1862

Dearest Papa

I wrote you by Mr Richard Smith who left Warrenton Sunday morning about 12 O'clock. I felt so much happier in mind in regard to you since the arrival of Mr. S. that I started for church on Sunday—Mr Finks having just parted with Mr. S on his return to Richmond with letters to you and others informing you and others of our security, our soldiers being still on picket duty around the neighborhood.

As I was telling you we went to the Baptist Church and our friend Dr. Bacon had gone through with the usual singing and prayer—and had opened the Bible to take his text, which was taken from Hebrews 4th Chap. 15 Verse. "For we have not

---

[40] Col. Richard Carlton Walker Radford (C.S.A.), born in Bedford County, July 8, 1822. He attended VMI and graduated from USMA, West Point, in 1845. He served as Lt. and Capt. in the U.S. Cavalry from 1845 to 1856. Commissioned Colonel in the 2nd Va. Cav., May 8, 1861, and dropped at the April 1862 re-organization. Later served as Colonel in the 1st Va. State Line. Died Nov. 2, 1886 in Bedford County. (J.K.G.)

a High Priest which cannot be touched with the feelings of our infirmities, but was in all points tempted like as we are, yet without sin." He commenced by remarking that this sabbath had been the first sabbath since the retreat of our army that we had met for public worship—that it was right & proper that we should meet in public to implore divine aid to strengthen and guide us through our days of trial and even privations that appeared fast approaching upon us—he seemed to be much affected and was very sincere in his remarks and was about discussing his subject at large when a colored man entered the pulpit in a very excited manner and remarked the Dr. had better dismiss the congregation, the *Federal Army* was approaching the town. You can better imagine than I describe the panic produced. Mr Finks called the servant and inquired if they were in town—"Yes Sir" at every point you will meet them—I felt unnerved at the moment for I feared Mr F. would be *arrested* immediately. But he assured me they would not commence that day—so we all started for home—and what a sight to behold, many of the Cavalry had passed on before we were out of church but on looking down the Road towards Bronaugh's[41] you could see them coming as far as the eye could take in—every lady was at her door, no one seemed daunted in the least, the women seemed anxious to see what the *yankee* soldiers were made of. Col. Geary's brigade arrived in the morning, and about 3 O'clock I think the *Dutch*[42] arrived—

During the afternoon Mrs Brooke was waited on by several officers demanding a Secession flag which she had [been] waving to our soldiers on their retreat. She told them she did not have it in the house, and one of them seemed fully satisfied with her statement and requested the others to leave, whereupon she remarked to him that she had had a very small flag about the house that she would give him if he would promise that he did not take it as a *Trophy* or that he had demanded of her—he promised he would not, he was to call in the evening for it which he did and received it[,] she said the reason she offered it to him, he seemed desirous of having one and he had behaved throughout as a gentleman. Of course some one had told them she had it, in fact they said a negro man gave them the information. At the same time others had waited on Mary Smith (the Gov's daughter)[43] and demanded her flag. She was spunky and very unwilling to give it up (I wondered she did not burn it up before them) but had to—the officer remarked to Mr Finks that he admired her much[,] she

---

[41] John T. Bronaugh (1807-1880) and his wife, Mary Gray (Evans) Bronaugh (1827-1905) lived on Main Street, on the southeast corner, diagonally across from the Northern Methodist Church (later the Town Hall and firehouse). Mr. Bronaugh was listed as a farmer in the 1860 census. He had extensive land holdings in the vicinity of Baldwin's Ridge, where the family was probably living during the War. (J.K.G.)

[42] Col. John W. Geary had a brigade consisting of the 28th Penna. Inf., Knap's Battery and a squadron of the 1st Mich. Cav. They had invaded from Harper's Ferry and crossed Loudoun County into Fauquier. Every local account of Gen. Geary's presence refers to his command as "the Dutch," no doubt, from their being from Pennsylvania. (J.E.D.)

[43] Mary Amelia Smith (1825-1911), daughter of Governor (Extra Billy) Smith and his wife, Elizabeth Bell. Governor Smith moved to Warrenton about 1845 where he built his home, 'Monta Rosa,' and where Miss Amelia lived until 1895 when 'Monta Rosa' was sold, and moved to the California House in Warrenton where she spent the rest of her life. She remained an 'unreconstructed rebel' all her life. In 1895 the Black Horse Chapter, UDC, was organized with Miss Mary Amelia Smith as President. It is claimed by some that her constant care of the Confederate graves, every year from the burial of Capt. John Q. Marr on June 1, 1861, with floral tributes, was the beginning of Memorial Day observances—called in the South: Decoration Day. (J.K.G.)

was a whole Secessionist and a very intelligent lady, so much was he pleased with her manner that he called on her. It was very amusing to see the officers riding in town with the citizens who were on their way to their homes and the soldiers hallowing here comes a Secesh'—Mr. Bragg[44] and Dr. Chilton were among the number—they soon released them saying it was only a form—They were marching and counter marching most of the day—planted their flag on the spot our flag was and rode around and having music—they did not leave their flag for which I was glad—

After the arrival of the Dutch they commenced quartering themselves upon private citizens—several houses were filled and at last some one went to the Officers and inquired if such conduct was permitted and they said it should not be that they had no permission from Head Quarters and they must be turned out—which of course was soon done. They took possession of the Northern Methodist Church[45] and also the Presbyterian. The Court House of course they had. Many of them went out to the Grave Yard and cursed the graves & went and *tolled* the Court House Bell in honor of the *dead*. They were all well clothed and seemed well fed.

The most remarkable coincident of the affair was this, it seems as if Mrs Tongue called upon two officers who were standing near, to rid her house of the dutch soldiers who had come in and demanded lodging for the night. They did so and her supper being ready, finding them gentlemen she asked them to supper and she engaged in conversation with one on the times, remarking on Baltimore and her daughter being there and he remarked of many friends he had South, spoke of some in Charleston— whereupon she remarked there was a lady from Charleston residing here—he inquired the name and as soon as she told him—he said I know her—and must see her—it was then about 9 O'clock. Mrs T. told him she thought it was rather late to make a call but he insisted, he did not know how long his regiment might be here— and asked Willie Tongue to show them the way—We were seated in Sister's room when a rap was at the door—I ran up in my room, for I did not want to see a *yankee*. Mr Finks went to the door and he saw two gentlemen all wrapped up—one inquired for me—he told him I had retired—he said he would be pleased to see me[,] he was acquainted with me in Charleston—Mr F. invited them in, thinking they were Southern men, and wondered what he should do with them, the yankees being in town—I soon hurried into the parlor—and who should I find but Mr Mackey[46] of

---

[44] William Bragg, son of Charles Bragg, Mayor and carriage maker of Warrenton. (J.K.G.)

[45] Following the schism of the 1840's, which separated the Methodist Church into two bodies, "North" (Baltimore Conference) and "South" (Virginia Conference) in the borderland between the Potomac and Rappahannock Rivers, many churches in this region were divided in their loyalties. The Baltimore conference faction (Northern Methodist Church) built in 1850 their church on the corner of Main and Fifth Streets (formerly the firehouse and Warrenton Town Hall). The Virginia Conference ("Southern Methodists") erected an imposing church on the corner of Lee and Culpeper Streets (now the site of the Fauquier Court House). Both churches were built by the noted local contractor, John Grigsby Beckham, whose home was the present Fauquier Club on Culpeper Street. John W. Finks was a member and trustee of the Warrenton Methodist Epis. Church, South. (J.K.G.)

[46] 1st Lt. William J. Mackey, Co. P, 28th Regt., Pennsylvania Volunteers. Enlisted at Philadelphia. Transferred to Co. E, 147th Regt., P.V., October 28, 1862. Commanded by General John Geary. Susan's mother had a boarding house, according to the 1850 census, where Lycurgus stayed at about the same time. (J.K.G.) (B.G.C.)

Philadelphia who had boarded with Mother for near two years—he and his wife were boarding at Mother's when I paid my visit to Charleston with Willie—You can judge of my surprise—I felt shocked almost and could only say why Mr Mackey how do I see you—do I meet with you among the enemies of the South—my heart was deeply pained and I saw too he felt it also—he said don't let us talk on that subject—I am so glad to meet with you and it was so remarkable that I should have found you out—he was very much attached to our family. His friend was 2nd Lieu—his name was Tourrisin[47] [sic]—Mr. Mackey was first Lieut—His company is an Independent Company from Phil—attached to Col. Geary's Brigade—They stayed about an hour—and we had a pleasant time. He said he loved the South and if she was conquered—he did not wish to see her humiliated—but wanted it to be written down that she was only subdued if subdued she should be by an overwhelming force as 5 to 1. He abhorred abolition. He and his company had been purely democratic—and it was not until the blow was given to Sumter that they became a united people—but an abolitionist he was not, nor his friend. They were for the Union and was [sic] fighting for that. Mr Finks was very much pleased with their gentlemanly bearing and invited them to break fast if they remained in town. They drank a glass of wine and seemed to enjoy themselves. We spoke our sentiments plainly—they remarked they expected to find 900 of our Cavalry here—I felt proud to tell them our men were beyond their reach—(altho fearing at the same time they were in danger some 50 having left town about 7 O'clock) Lieut Mackey asked me to write a note to his wife and he would call in the morning for it. We told them it was passing strange that we should be seated quietly conversing with those who were our foes—Lieut. M. remarked I had found a friend amidst the foe—and before I should be harmed he would suffer himself—and that we would find it the case among the gentlemen of the Federal Army—we had nothing to fear, we acted wisely in remaining at home. I wrote the letter and he with his friend called Monday morning just before our breakfast hour. Mr F. invited them to break fast—they said they had break fasted early as they were about to leave—he told them they better take a cup of Rye—they consented and went down and had another agreeable chat—Just before breakfast some of the Dutch came and demanded Mr Gaines' horses which he had to give up—we remarked upon it at Break fast table and they promised to intercede, which they did Mr Finks says and Col. Geary has promised to have them returned but as Col. G. is rather ungentlemanly in his bearing towards the rebels, I do not think Mr G. will get them. Before they left Col. Geary's son & others they went into Mr F's store and took just what they chose—leaving a part of every thing and gave him an order on the Washington Government—War Department. They were very polite to him—did not disturb any thing more than they wished—took about $95 worth in all—Part of the soldiers left Monday, several ladies among them—Octavia White, (we did not go out of the house) went up to Mrs Johnson's to see them go by—some one of them inquired of her which way the road led to—she told him she hoped it would

[47] Capt. Ashton S. Tourison, Co. P, 28th Regt., Pennsylvania Volunteers. Trans. to Co. E., 147th Regt., P.V., October 28, 1862. Commanded by General John Geary. (J.K.G.)

lead them all to the Devil—when another remarked she was a _____ "Secesh" don't you see she has the Cannons of the Washington Artillery[48] on her hat—

While the gentlemen were taking from Mr Finks' store, one of the low dutch came to the house and asked for money—Sister told him she had none—he said she did and that he would get more to come and search the house. We sent for an Officer and we told him we had—he soon found his way out—the officer came and said no conduct such as that was allowed and he would be punished if he could be found—During Monday night Dr. Steven's store was pillaged by some of the party—breaking in & taking almost every thing, and turning up every thing he had in the floor. They went down to the Depot and took Sugar Molasses & Flour—Mr. John Spillman[49] Merchant had to open his store and they took about $200 worth of things without pay. Mr Rogers had moved his _shoes_ from the depot at Mr Spillmans and they helped themselves bountifully—they went to the room of Mr Ham White's and cut up his goods he had stored away—stole his blankets and Counterpanes—It is the low Dutch that is cutting up these shines. Col. G.'s brigade would have remained in Warrenton, but he said he would not allow his men to stay with such a low bred act. Most of the Dutch left Tuesday—some 20 have remained on the sick list—but they are not sick—they are here to put mischief in the Darkies head—Mr. Gaines Strother left on Sunday with an innumerable company of darkies—and those who are here the _men_ in particular will not work. Mr Helm went to get his boy—a child about 12 years old who had strayed off with them and they pointed their bayonets at him. They are all at Salem—They say McClellan has an army of 400,000 men on their way to Richmond, they intend to _shell_ the City—How true I cannot tell. May God preserve you my dearest husband—don't act rashly under any circumstance, always bear in mind you have a wife and four little ones dependent on you. We will take care of ourselves with the Good Lord's protection, none of us are alarmed. All send love & kisses. God Bless you and keep you at all times.

Tuesday night. Mr Finks has informed me that Dr. Herndon[50] will not return—He is going to Yorktown to see if he can be of any service there when the battle comes off—Of course, you need not trouble yourself about making the purchase of the articles I wrote for—_When Mrs Lotties goes out shopping she can buy me the yard and eighth of goods like my dress for my cape and you can keep it for me—you may have an opportunity of sending it to me._—If the goods comes in dress patterns of 12 yds why then

---

[48] The Washington Artillery of New Orleans saw action at First Manassas. Freeman, _Lieutenants_, Vol. I, p. 647. (J.M.W.)

[49] John Armistead Spilman (1819-1889) was a native of Jeffersonton, Culpeper County. He was a well-known merchant of Warrenton and lived at 'Conway Grove' on Winchester Street. He married in 1842, Susan Rogers, the daughter of Hugh and Mary (Coombs) Rogers of Loudoun County. Mr. Spilman, a brother of Judge Edward M. Spilman, operated the largest store in Warrenton, near the Depot, and was a member and deacon of the Baptist church. A daughter, Mary Armistead Spilman, married Rev. Francis Ryland Boston, a beloved pastor of the Warrenton Baptist Church, 1884 until his death in 1911. (J.K.G.)

[50] Brodie Strachan Herndon, M.D., born in Culpeper Co., 1834; he was graduated in 1855 from the N.Y. Medical College and settled in Warrenton, where he remained until the outbreak of the war, when he became a full surgeon (C.S.A.). After the war he returned to Warrenton, then removed to Savannah, Ga. and finally to Fredericksburg where he died in 1890. (J.K.G.)

the merchant will not cut a small quantity. Mrs L. will know all about it. I am very sorry Dr. H. will not return directly I felt buoyed up with the hope of having the pleasure of reading a letter from you—You must go to the Hotel and overlook the registers and you may chance to see a name you know and by some means get me a letter—

Jessie has just come in, she went out to present a boquet [sic] to one of the pickets—the first thing she said you solder you killed all de Yankees—hurrah for Jeff Davis—and kept it up until they left—and was among the loudest to say Good Bye—It was quite amusing—Frank ran with a boquet for one—and Willie was on horse back with another all the time they were in town. I have sent you a number of letters—go to the Post Office. It is now too dark to write more.

Mr. Finks is anxious to get to Richmond to hear some news—he misses the papers—

Now be happy and cheerful—we are all well[.] Grandma is complaining some—

The weather is pleasant—children enjoy it much. Please write to Mother—she is anxious for me.

I am so disappointed in hearing Dr. Herndon will not return to Warrenton—

We heard firing at the Junction this afternoon but can't tell what cause, may be cleaning out guns.

Good Night. Be cheerful—

Your devoted daughter,
S.E.C.

Confederate money is good with us—
Children send a bushel of love & kisses. Jessie's eye is well—but a little redness left.

Nine O'clock Tuesday night—Our pickets are very hopeful of a victory at Yorktown[51] and say our army will return in about two weeks—but that is too good to be true. Children all asleep—Good night and a loving kiss for Papa.

Warrenton Fauquier Co
Tuesday April 15th 1862

Dearest Papa

Hearing at dinner to day that Dr. Herndon had some idea of leaving to morrow for Richmond I hasten to write you a few lines.

We were all exultant with joy on Saturday and Sunday over the victory gained by Genl. Beauregard at Corinth, Miss.[52] We are now sad and miserable—Mr Hume brought us on yesterday the intelligence that like at Donelson we were *overpowered* and *have been whipped*—Alas! Alas! for my Country I shall shed bitter tears. I feel that

---

[51] McClellan's peninsular campaign was being met at Yorktown, Va. by Gen. Joseph E. Johnston (C.S.A.). (J.M.W.)

[52] A reference to Beauregard's defeat at Shiloh, by U. S. Grant. (J.M.W.)

my cup is filled to the brim if we are subjugated—never, no never will the South yield to a Northern rule while there are *strong* men to fight her battles. We are very anxious to know the truth and nothing but the truth of all that has transpired in Tennessee under Beauregard. But we must await I suppose Dr. Herndon's return from R. Suspense is terrible when there is so much depending.

I suppose a battle will come off at an early period at Yorktown. Oh! may our men be inspired from on high—and strength be given to each man to aim the deadly blow at each yankee until there [sic] ranks be thinned and we gain a glorious victory as Washington did—when Lord Cornwallis and entire army *surrendered*—then oh then would it not be glorious news to spread throughout our land—and if it would please the Good Lord to send *peace*, once more in our midst—Sometimes I feel as if this state of things cannot last much longer then again I fear it may continue for a much longer period than we can now be willing to bring our minds to,

I send you in this letter a *sample of the goods you bought for me—I have made my dress—but I am very anxious to have a Cape. Please* ask Mrs. Lotties if convenient to her to try and see if she can *purchase me one yard and an eighth* of a yard (1 yd. and ⅛ of yard for a cape to my dress—) also a pair of *shoes*—or *slippers*—for *Lucy Lee No 2.*—you can make the *package small* and Dr. Herndon will put it in his pocket and bring it to me. Be certain to send me a *letter* and a *long one* if you have time to write one—in your letter I want you to put an *india rubber nipple* if you can find one. I want it for a friend of mine—

If Dr. Herndon's stay will not permit you time to make the purchases—why never mind only send me a letter. All I want is 1 yd and an ⅛ of a yard[,] like sample shoes for Lucy Lee, and an india rubber nipple—(if you have time)—

Mr. James Claggett living at New Baltimore arrived in town to day and told us a party of men from Geary's brigade came down to his house and took every thing in the way of eating from him, his sugar, meat and corn—leaving him only *two middlings*.[53] They went to Mr Hunton's[54] (Mrs White's son in law) near Broad Run and stole all his *horses, hay and corn—turkeys*[,] *chickens, meat* and in fact all the man had to live on—I am truly sorry for him—well now for him he has no little ones dependent upon him—Now you see the country people suffer much more than those in town, for parties go out as foraging parties and plunder and steal all they can lay their hands to—and the persons around can have no redress as no officers are at hand to complain to—We have two yankees in town, one very ill—the other as a nurse— We have not been troubled with the sight of the wretches. Our town was all in commotion Sunday night, the negro men were running in every way they said it was reported the Black Horse company were coming in to take all the servants across the lines and those who would resist would be shot—Numbers of them were missing on Monday—but returned to their Masters this morning as they understood it was a false alarm in regard to our men coming in after them.

The gentlemen of the town patrole at night now, to keep the servants in order—

---

[53] A wheat milling product used in animal feeds. (J.M.W.)

[54] Edwin Hunton married Mary A. White, December 23, 1837, Fauquier County, Va. (J.K.G.)

They believe themselves to be free—and are beyond control. The Yankee Capt. set them all at work at their homes before leaving town and ordered them to attend to their business as they had been accustomed to.

While I am writing a number of our pickets have come in, they belong to the Powhatan Cavalry[55] and they say *we have gained a victory out west, have whipped both Columns which were brought against us*—God grant this may be the truth and revive our drooping hearts—

We are all very well. Children are well and happy. Some one asked Jessie if the Yankees had you—she said "No. Good Lord got Pa and take care of him["]—how very encouraging to me were those words. I feel and know that you are in the keeping of Almighty God and we will meet again under more prosperous times when we shall enjoy the society of each other and the company of our little ones. Be happy tho you are separated and always bear in mind your little family ever importune a Throne of Grace for your protection. Don't be over anxious about us—you must be anxious in regard to yourself. Take care of your precious self and regard your health. *Live for us. Keep well* if possible. One of the yankees showed Willie *Ellsworth* Likeness—Willie says—why this is the *man Jackson[56] killed*. The little fellow gloried in telling them he was a Secessionist—Jessie often speaks of the yankees, she says—Daddy [Mr. F.] do you love the Yankees—he will then ask her—she will spunk up and reply No I don't love yankees and you must not either[.]

Should Mr F. have news to tell I will write more.

Good Bye. God bless you and keep you and may you not allow your mind to be disturbed about us—

We are cheerful and not troubled. We don't care for the yankees, they are not going to disturb us.

Please send a letter if you would go to the *Hotels* and *overlook names* you might chance get a letter to me. Bushel of love & kisses from all hands.

Your devoted and affec
daughter
S.E.C.

Apr. 17/62

Dearest Papa

I have at last found a way of sending your trunk. I hope it will reach you in safety and you will find all things in good order. I have endeavored to pack them as well as I know how. I send your few pieces of summer clothes I had at home, because it

---

[55] Powhatan Cavalry: Co. E, 4th Regt. Va. Cav., org. in 1860 by Philip St. George Cooke. The 4th Regt. Va. Cav. was organized on Sept. 19, 1861. Co. H of the 4th Va. was the famed Black Horse Cavalry. General Wm. H. Payne commanded the 4th Regt. from 1863 to 1864. (J.K.G.)

[56] James T. Jackson, proprietor of the Marshall House, Alexandria, Va., shot and killed Col. E. E. Ellsworth (U.S.A.) May 24, 1861, after the latter had removed a Confederate flag from the roof of the hotel. At nearly the same time, Mr. Jackson was killed by Pvt. Francis E. Brownell. The North used the incident widely to create war sentiment. (J.K.G.)

is so very difficult these times to get things to you at the proper season. Your suit of Jeans have been ready since the last of November, but could not find an opportunity. I hope they will fit nicely.

You must enjoy your apples for the childrens sake. The candles I only send for your convenience to have ready at all times in your room. They are very nice tallow candles.

We are all well to night. Children are all asleep—Send bushel of love and kisses. To day has been very cold. Mr F. has not yet arrived. We are looking for him.

Your's affec
S.E. Caldwell

List of Articles in trunk

Sack Coat and pants of Millers factory[57] cloth
2 pair of pants and 2 coats of Summer clothes
1 bed comfort—a few pounds of tallow candles
A carpet bag with apples 3 pair of cotton socks

This trunk is the property of L. W. Caldwell who resides in Richmond and is in service under the Southern Confederacy—I send the said articles to him for his own *individual comfort.*

I have written the above upon learning that all trunks arriving at Culpepper C H were searched and feeling anxious that the trunk should arrive in R—as I have packed it—I thought it best to set down the items hoping the Provost Marshal will be satisfied with the statement and not disturb the trunk.

Susan E. Caldwell

Harriet C. Suares to Susan Emeline Jeffords Caldwell

Charleston April 25th/62

Dearest Susan
Ignorant as I am of the circumstances which surround you I scarcely know how

---

[57] Miller's Woolen Factory, also known as Glen Mills, was located on the Culpeper County side of the Rappahannock River at Waterloo. The mill, on the site of an earlier grist and saw mill, was converted into a woolen factory by Greene, Middleton and Brent Miller. Another woolen mill was erected on the Fauquier County side of the river by Isham Keith. The chimney of the latter is all that remains of this once flourishing enterprise. Edward Armstrong in his reminiscences, published in *Fauquier County, 1759-1959* (Warrenton, Virginia: 1959) p. 117, states, "Both of these factories were making cloth for the Confederate Army. I watched the factories burn from the hill behind the Jett house. Tom Tharpe was cutting grass, and I was in the field with him. Gen. Shields had been defeated in the Valley by Jackson, and he was on his way to Washington after his defeat, when he burned the factories." (J.K.G.) (J.E.D.)

to address you. You cannot imagine our anxiety when the news of the evacuation reached us for I believe the enemy has inspired us with more terror than he has your section (the Lord grant that you have not had cause to judge them more harshly) but your dear welcome letter of the 25th relieved my mind greatly, I hoped and almost believed that should they occupy W. that you would not suffer at their hands[,] but now what do I read your beautiful town taken possession of and the vandals stealing silver, provisions, and whatever comes in their way, And I know not what my dear S. may have suffered, oh how heavily will the time drag on until we can hear something from you but I trust our heavenly Father has not permitted any evil to befall you, all that I can do is to commit you to his holy keeping, oh what sad times have we fallen upon[,] the Lord in his mercy grant that "these days may be shortened." It must have been a severe trial indeed for you to decide between going with your husband and remaining in W. I feel proud of your good judgment in not suffering your feelings to influence you. I hope the chances of hearing from each other may be more frequent than you think for which will compensate in a measure for the loss of each others society. Your dear little ones are I trust all well again and oh that you may all enjoy health during this painful separation. Elvira[58] poor child is very sad at being separated from her husband at this early period of their union[.] I try to cheer her up and I think she would be less sad were it not for the prospect of his being taken prisoner in the event of Charleston being taken, oh when I read of their treatment of prisoners and know not how soon both of the dear boys may be subjected to the same, it makes my heart sick, I feel anxious about them[,] they are on James Island and it will not be long before they will be liable to country fever—Saturday, Thus far had I written when the beloved form of my boy entered looking haggard & sick, upon inquiring I found that he had been suffering from Dysentery for several days, my heart sunk within me (having lost my darling Benjamin[59] with the same complaint) but the Lord blest the remedies I used and he is much better to day, I will try and keep him with me until he is perfectly well, the Battallion [sic] to which he is attached are removed to a more healthy location. I fear it will not be long ere we shall be called to experience some of the horrors of this unholy war, Pulaski was so easily reduced, it is not to be supposed that Sumter will prove impregnable, indeed forts appear to be useless in these days of Ironclad steamers[,] better dismantle them all, oh does not your heart sicken to read of such brave men after such resistance as was offered at fort D. having to succumb at last, the seacoast I am afraid will all go, but that will not be subjugating this south, ours is a just cause and will ultimately receive the blessing of a just God[,] what suffering may be in store for us ere we gain our independence, may the Lord prepare us for, my greatest anxiety is on account of my girls[,][60] it is not convenient for us all to go into the interior, as yet I have not made

---

[58] Elvira Oxlade, Harriet's eldest child, married to Thomas Oxlade of Charleston; see Susan Caldwell's letter of June 25, 1862 to Lycurgus Caldwell. (B.G.C.)

[59] Benjamin Suares: Listed in the 1850 census as 8 years old, he evidently had died by the time the 1860 census was taken. (B.G.C.)

[60] My girls: In the 1860 census, they were: Julia, Ellen, Anna, and Carry. By the end of the year, all but Julia would have died. See note to Susan Caldwell's letter of Dec. 18, 1862. (B.G.C.)

up my mind as to sending them away if the fiends would be satisfied with stealing all I possess in the world it would be nothing could I feel assured that the girls would be protected from dishonor. Well all that we can do is to pray for each other, in these days of anguish. The Lord only knows what we may be called to endure ere we hear from each other again.

All join me in love to you.

Write soon and oh, may there be some way of receiving it. The Lord bless and keep you all is the earnest prayer of your affectionate sister,

H.C.S.

Susan Emeline Jeffords Caldwell to Lycurgus Washington Caldwell

Warrenton Fauquier Co.
April 27th 1862

Dearest Papa

I expected to go to Church this morning but Mr Finks has sent word to us that there will be no service in either the Baptist or Methodist churches. I regret it as Sunday is a long wearisome day unless you can spend a portion of it listening to a sermon from some good man—

I understood yesterday that a gentleman would start on Monday for Richmond and as I always endeavor to embrace every opportunity I hear of in sending you a letter—I have seated myself alone in my room to talk with you some—My heart feels lighter whenever I can get a letter off to you for I know should it reach you it will comfort you in your loneliness—and I feel repaid in the thought that I know you are always happier and easier in mind after the perusal of a letter from home and loved ones at this time. I long—yes I crave a letter from you—could I but be assured that you were in the enjoyment of your usual health and that you were comfortable in mind on our account I would ask no more—all my mind dwells on now is—if you are well—could I get but those words.

I am as cheerful under the circumstances as I can be. I do not repine. I am happily situated—and feel that I have much to be thankful for—for when I look upon the situation of many I know I am truly blessed to be in the midst of such kind friends and such a comfortable home with my dear little ones. My lot is a happy one when compared with yours. You are alone—separated from all your loved ones—and, if *you can gain nerve* sufficient to keep up a *brave heart* and not allow your mind to be too anxious in order to depress your spirits and cause your *bodily health to fail* during the time we shall have to suffer this non-communication—if you can promise me in your mind you will enjoy yourself and keep well, I shall be happy too. I am not unhappy— at times I grow much worried and feel anxious fearing you may have one of your sick turns, we have had such changeable weather, so much rain you were liable to get your

103

feet wet and by that means take cold. But I try to relieve my mind and pray the Good Lord to take care of you and keep you in health and then I grow comfortable, knowing you will be preserved and the time of our separation may not be so long as we now anticipate. Thousands of loved ones are separated—and their lives exposed to death. You have a comfortable home and a good situation to enable you to support your family. We should both be thankful.

The children are all doing well. Lucy Lee has some cold. They talk much about you. Whenever Jessie talks of you she says my Papa cant come home now the old yankees will catch him—she says Daddy can go to Rich to see Papa and come back again—but Papa must stay in Rich. She is very loveable in her little ways—she tries to sing I love the South or God save the South and Dixie—She prays the Good Lord to take care of you and not let the yankees catch her dear Papa.

Willie and Frank often dream about you and it is quite amusing to hear them tell their dreams—Willie says a lesson every day. Frank has commenced to learn— To day is bright and beautiful. The children are all out doors and enjoying themselves—they have been kept in the house so long by the constant rains that they can appreciate pleasant weather. Willie is anxious to go to school but we are undecided about his going. Miss Louisa Sinclair has opened a school for small children—

Jessie's eye is getting the better of the redness. I think soon it will leave and it will be as it once was—

Grand Ma has been much complaining for a week past, has not been down to her meals. She took a severe cold during the few days of warm weather we had. She seems much better to day[,] is now sitting in Sister's room & has a better appetite. She hates the yankees.

I understand that some few of the Warrenton Riflemen[61] intend returning home this week—the year of enlistment being out—only those will return who are 45. Mr Finks thinks Mr Graham[62] will be the only one and he is anxious to return to his family, he has so many children to support. If you could see him, as he will pass through Richmond and send a letter by him to me, would be a pleasant surprise. Mr F. says if you will send letters to Culpepper Co. House to Dr. Gorrell[63] I could get them. I feel assured you have made the effort to get me a letter—but I have not as yet received any—you must keep on trying to find ways to send them and per chance I may get one. Miss Maria English is now in Warrenton—says Mr E. was released after being imprisoned three weeks in Wash—she has not been much inconvenienced by the yankees[,] the house was searched for arms—the yankees being told by their own servant woman that her master had arms concealed. Provisions and dry goods

[61] Warrenton Riflemen returning home: Co. K, 17th Va. Inf. had enlisted for one year from April 26, 1861; with few exceptions, most would reenlist. (J.K.G.)

[62] First Sgt. David E. Graham, Co. K, 17th Va. Inf. (Warrenton Rifles). He was a tailor in Warrenton before the War (see pg. 159 n. 140). Sgt. Graham and Cpl. Hamme were assigned to detached duty as hospital stewards in Warrenton after First Manassas and after Second Manassas, there is no further record of Sgt. Graham. (J.K.G.)

[63] Dr. Joseph B. Gorrell, a druggist at Culpeper Court House who often greeted passing Confederate troops with tubs of ice-cold lemonade. (J.K.G.)

were at their usual prices—We had cheese, salt, coffee, and shoes brought up by those who call themselves suttlers. Salt was selling at $3. a bushel. Mr F. gave $10 a bushel about two weeks ago, but they will only take Silver and gold. They will find they will have to take Virginia money or not find purchasers—as there is but little gold in our midst. Children send a bushel of love & kisses to dear Papa—

We have just heard of the death of Mr R. P. Latham—he died at Culpepper Co. H. of Typhoid pneumonia. It is very distressing indeed. He took his family to Lynchburg after our Warrenton Fauquier Co Army had fallen back—We have not heard any of the particulars of his death. I feel much for Miss Ida—Dr. Bacon dismissed his school to day after hearing the news of his Death.

The yankees are coming in town today. Quite a number up the Street.

Undated, 1862

Dearest Papa

On Thursday last our pickets came dashing in and carried off the *arms* of all the Yankee soldiers—they would have taken all the yankees left to wait on the sick, but some of our citizens begged them not to do so—as Col Geary had sworn vengeance against the town if they were molested, so our pickets consented and none were disturbed—one dutchman begged to go with them saying me be *tamned* Mr. Solder please let me go wid [sic] you me have wife in New Orleans[,] so off he tuddled after our men—During the afternoon Mr Gaines[64] wrote a note to Col Geary—informing him of what had been done—remarking that his men were unharmed and would remain unmolested under protest of the Citizens. Every one in town was down on Mr Gaines for such conduct[,] he said he did it to save our town—(but we know he wanted his horses sent back—but he did not get his horses either). Col. Geary wrote a note of Thanks for his information and said he had sent out 400 of his hell hounds after our pickets—he remarked we were between two fires should his men be disturbed—(Col *Mumford* of our Cavalry says he never acts[,] only threats). But the Cowardly set left our town before next morning and we are undisturbed—and we dont care one cent for a live yankee.

We are all well, go to Post Office for drop letters—send this by one of our pickets.

God Bless you.

Your affectionate daughter
S.E.C.

Saturday—

All well at home. Having a little time left I will add more—We were all

---

[64] William H. Gaines (1807-1885) had come to Warrenton as a young man to clerk in a store. He became the owner of the store and was a very successful merchant. By 1860 he had become a "retired merchant," with large landholdings in Fauquier County, and was later Presiding Justice of the County Court. At the age of 53 in 1860 he was Warrenton's wealthiest resident. (J.K.G.)

mortified to death at the proceedings of Thursday and wished our pickets had taken every last yankee *sick* and *well*—We never will let such doings be allowed in our town again—for the next time we will understand.

Frank Caldwell is in Booneville.

Warrenton Fauquier Co.
Sunday Night May 4th 1862

Dearest Papa

I feel to night as if it would be a comfort to me to sit quietly down and talk with you with pen and paper. I have been looking forward from one week to another with the *hope* that the way may be opened in which a letter from you might come to hand. But alas! the time rolls on and the way is yet blockaded. Many would go to Richmond if they could be assured they would return in safety to their homes. But we cannot tell what a day may bring forth—we are daily expecting to hear of a battle at Yorktown—then again rumour is busy and tells us that McClellan will not fight us at Yorktown—that like a[t] Manassas we are too well fortified—that he has withdrawn all his forces—and Genl. Johnston has done the same, and that a battle may be expected in the open fields without fortifications between Gordonsville and Richmond—Another rumour afloat is that Richmond is to be evacuated and the seat of Government removed to Danville—Now and then we hear some reliable news—Sometimes we get Northern papers with much of the Southern news copied from the Richmond papers—which is true of course.

We have been much distressed on hearing of the evacuation of New Orleans—It is too bad to have to give it up when we had 30,000 men—besides gun boats. New Orleans was to us what New York is to the North—our keystone—Just look at the advantages the North has now over us since they have gained New Orleans[65]—they can now traverse almost every where and will endeavor to surround Beauregard. I am anxious for Savannah, Geo. and Charleston. I have very great fears for Richmond. It was wise in us to remain in Warrenton for we are as safe here as there.

We have not been troubled with the yankees since last week—then they only came in and returned again to the Junction.[66] They find nothing now to steal.

Several persons who were refugees from Alexandria are returning there. I know not if they can get their homes back again—We are told every thing in the way of groceries and dry goods are selling at a reasonable price. Sugar at 8 cts—Coffee at 18 cts. Calico and cotton at 12 ½[,] hearing this has induced several to go back there to live.

---

[65] New Orleans had fallen the last day of April, 1862, when Maj. Gen. Benjamin Butler (U.S.A.) and 18,000 men marched into the city, following a decisive naval battle won from below by Capt. David G. Farragut (U.S.N.). (J.M.W.)

[66] Geary's Brigade was still operating in Fauquier County. (J.E.D.)

Mr. Cross[67] of our town has returned from a visit of two weeks—spending one week in Baltimore and one in Alexandria—We know not what took him from home[,] some say he had business with his sister in Alexandria and then he has a brother in Baltimore whom he went to see. He brings word that business is brisk in Baltimore. He called to see Willa Tongue—she told him Mr Neal was doing a splendid business and everything is cheap[,] writes for her family to come on to Baltimore if Provision is different.

We have hucksters from Washington and Alexandria[,] our own men, they bring Coffee, sugar, tea, cheese, and fruit—they sell at reasonable rates but want *silver* and there is but little of that in town. We are very well off at present—for we have sugar—coffee, flour and bacon on hand. Our garden is very backward, owing to the wet weather, the rats eat all the plants out from the *hot bed*. The peas and potatoes rotted in the ground[,] the strawberries are looking well—but we will have to do without *sugaring* them, be too good these war times.

This has been a charming May day. Children have enjoyed themselves very much out of doors—even Lucy Lee went to paying visits. This morning as soon as Jessie awoke she went to work as usual kissing her Daddy—Sister called to her and asked her if she loved her Daddy more than Anty she said Yes—because he is my Daddy—she heard me wishing for a horse to go to Richmond, and child like she offered me Frank's pony in the middle room—could ride that to Richmond and see Papa—she would go too—She loves to talk about you—is always writing you letters.

I have now to record the death of one of our most prominent Citizens—Mr. Robert Scott.[68] His end was sad indeed. It was on this wise—Since the yankees have had free access to our town the country people have suffered much from many of the stragglers by the way. In this instance there had been two yankee deserters occupying the house of Mr Frank Smith's on the way to Salem. They had plundered and stolen and committed outrageous depredations all around. The neighbors had complained to the officers and they told them to arrest them or shoot them if they resisted— whereupon Mr Robert Scott, with several others started yesterday morning—they were told they were in Frank Smiths house. The gentlemen in party begged Mr Scott not to venture in the house—but he said there was no danger, only two yankees in and they would not resist—but Alas! as soon as he entered he was shot at by one of the wretches, the ball passing through him, in one shoulder through to his back— all he said was I am shot—reeled and fell—dying instantly. Mr Winter Payne[69] then rushed into the house and fired—very probably he would have killed the yankee, but

---

[67] Cyrus Cross, a native of Alexandria, married in Fauquier County, April 29, 1845, Columbia Kemper, daughter of John Peter Kemper. For some years prior to the Civil War he was Jailor of the County and also a cabinet maker. In September 1855, he was appointed by the Warrenton Town Council "to mind, regulate and keep in order the Courthouse clock," for the sum of $12.50 per year. (J.K.G.)

[68] Robert Eden Scott. For a detailed account of this tragedy, see: Ramey & Gott, *The Years of Anguish, Fauquier County, Virginia, 1861-1865* (Warrenton, Virginia: 1965), pp. 152-157. (J.K.G.)

[69] William Richards Hooe Winter Payne (1807-1874) was a native of Fauquier County; he moved to Alabama in 1825 where he married Minerva West Winston. He served in the Alabama legislature and from 1841 to 1847 was a member of the U.S. House of Representatives from Alabama. He retired in 1847 on account of ill health and returned to Fauquier County, and established himself at 'Bellvue' as a farmer. His daughter, Mary, became the wife of General William H. Payne. (J.K.G.)

his pistol snapped whereupon a Mr Matthew[,] a poor man[,] entered the house but was shot dead before he had time to take aim at the yankee. This man leaves a wife and 6 children. Poor man.

I am light hearted on your account. The letters have eased my troubled mind. I can now rest satisfied—and again commit you both soul and body into the keeping of the Good Lord. Who can preserve you if it be in accordance to his will. Give your heart to God and all will be well with you—

Good bye. A bushel of love from one & all.

Your devoted & affec
daughter,
S.E.C.

Warrenton Via
Wednesday May 7th 1862

Dearest Papa

I wrote you yesterday intending to send it by Mr Triplett—but hearing perhaps he would not go for some days—I gave my letters to Mr Hume as he intended starting Saturday for Richmond. I wrote a note in the afternoon and sent it up to Mr Finks to give to Mr Hume, but through some mistake it was handed to Mr Triplett asking you to buy me the piece of goods like my dress if you had sufficient time to do so after the arrival of Mr Hume[,] if he were going to remain the time you would take in asking Mrs Lotties to make the purchase, the package would be small and he could put it in his pocket. As Mr Hume will return to Warrenton he will bring me a package I know if you have it ready in time for him. I feel rather doubtful about getting the goods like my dress. I have made my dress. I only want a piece to make a cape if it can be had without putting you to inconvenience. I would like very much to have a pair of shoes, or slippers for Jessie and Lucy Lee—Jessie wears No 5.[,] Lucy Lee Small size No 2. or largest No 1. I cannot get them with us at present. But dont fail to send me a letter even tho you cannot send the articles. I wrote to you by Dr. Herndon for some little things and I wished so much you had sent them by Mr Triplett for he could have put them in his pocket without being inconvenienced.

Persons from Alexandria are bringing up goods but they will only sell for gold and Silver—or 40 cts discount on Virginia money—making goods cost us a great sum.

Should Mr Triplett reach Richmond before Mr Hume you will be disappointed in receiving so short a note, but when Mr H. arrives you will find the note was to have come by him. I felt that I would have ample time to have written to day by Mr Triplett, hearing he would not leave town as soon as he anticipated. He very kindly called to see me yesterday and told me all about you—that you were in excellent spirits and was very well indeed. That was all I wanted to hear. While I cannot be with you if I can be assured of your good health I shall be content. May the Good Lord preserve you from sickness. Your letters sent by Mr Triplett have given satisfaction to all who have read the contents. Mr Finks has read them to gentlemen up town. They were anxious for the news—

We heard yesterday of the evacuation of Yorktown—we are feeling very anxious about Richmond—fearing it might be given up like New Orleans—I trust we have forces sufficient to keep the wretches from our seat of government—Mrs. Watson begs you to inquire if Mr John English is in Fredericksburg yet or if he and Henry are in Richmond.

I wrote you of the death of Mr R. Scott—but his death is but one among many. Yesterday we heard of the death of Mr Hutchinson[70] of Upperville. It appears he had had some difficulty with Henry Dixon—the said Dixon belonged to the Federal Army and induced some of Geary's blood hounds to go to Upperville and arrest Hutchinson. Mr H. was in his yard when several yankees rode up to the house. He was about to enter his house when they called to him to halt. He did not heed them whereupon they fired killing him instantly at his own door. He was upwards of 70 years old. Now these outrages committed by Geary would shame or far exceed those of Jim Lane in Kansas.[71] The officers are worse than the privates, for I believe they countenance and uphold their men in vileness. We heard of their doings at Mr Stones[,] officers were among them[,] who lives near Mr Bronaugh—he was up Sunday and says out of 27 servants only 3 remain and they small children. They went into his house and stole every thing they could—what they could not take away they broke to pieces—all their furniture. Demanded all their meat and groceries and succeeded in getting the most of it. Mr Stone hid some of his meat. They treated him

---

[70] Lemuel Hutchinson, Postmaster at Upperville, Va. The feud with Henry T. Dixon, the only man in Fauquier County to vote for Abraham Lincoln, was one of long standing. The feud began over a brawl in an Upperville barroom between Hutchinson and Dixon's son Collins. Later Henry T. Dixon and Mr. Hutchinson had an altercation on the road between Upperville and Delaplane resulting in Mr. Hutchinson soundly thrashing Mr. Dixon with a cane and the latter emptying his "pepperbox" at Mr. Hutchinson—missing every shot! Dixon became a Major in the Union Army, serving as Paymaster in Washington and after the war was killed in a street duel in Alexandria by another Fauquier man with whom he carried a spite, Dr. Henry Clay Maddux. (J.K.G.)

[71] Jim Lane, the Grim Chieftain of Kansas as he was called, can, even in kindness, be described only as eminently unscrupulous. A citizen of Indiana where he had been lieutenant governor and congressman, Lane had been a leading pro-slavery Democrat... He had arrived in Kansas in 1855, very likely with the hope of founding and rising with the Democratic party there. Viewing the Kansas situation with cynical objectivity, he had become a Republican, a Free Soil party military and political leader, and a screaming abolitionist. In the summer of 1861...he proceeded, independently of the state government, to recruit "Lane's Brigade"... During Price's raid on Lexington in September, 1861, Lane had developed a unique type of warfare. Rather than strike at Price, the Grim Chieftain had determined to follow in his rear and punish all Missourians who had welcomed the State Guard as it marched north to the river. Informing his troops, largely composed of the most desperate raiders and fighters of the earlier border troubles, that "everything disloyal, from a Shanghai rooster to a Durham cow, must be cleaned out," Lane left Fort Lincoln near Fort Scott and leisurely followed Price's army. As soon as the Kansans entered Missouri, they determined that not a person loyal to the Union lay in their line of march; all should be punished...the column turned into nothing but a looting expedition. Anything that could be carried comfortably was taken: horses, cows, furniture, fowl, clothing, jewelry, and slaves. No family was spared, the homes of men serving with Union forces being robbed with all others. On September 22, 1861, Lane's thieves reached Osceola...a little town of two thousand people... Teams and wagons were first stolen... Nine citizens were courtmartialed and shot, and then all but three buildings were set on fire, including the courthouse which burned to the ground with all the county records. The Kansans left Osceola with 300 of their force drunk in wagons, 350 horses and mules, and 200 Negroes. A million dollars' worth of property had been stolen or destroyed, and Osceola, one of the largest towns in Western Missouri, had ceased to exist. Richard S. Brownlee, *Grey Ghosts of Confederacy, Guerilla Warfare in the West 1861-1865* (Louisiana State University Press, 1958), pp. 37-39. (J.M.W.)

so because he refused to take the oath. After behaving so to him they went into the chamber where his wife and daughters were and demanded their rings and breast pins. Some days after they went to the Methodist church and ripped up the pulpit and threw it out doors, then wrote on the walls all the vileness one can imagine—when done, they went after ... Mr. Stone and brought to the church and with their guns pointed at him made him read what they had written. All alone with them in the church they swore he should take the oath of Allegiance—he refused and they told him they would shoot him instantly if he did not—so on the peril of his life with his family stripped of all their support, now entirely dependent on him—he had to take the oath—He was excusable in so doing—I am truly sorry for him. The vile wretches still remain in the neighborhood and go just when they please to the house and demand their meals cooked. Now yet another. Mr Samuel Bailey whipped one of his Servant women, whereupon she went to the yankee camp and brought home with her quite a number of yankees. They entered the house. Mrs Bailey was alone, (Mr B. was away) and went into her trunks taking out every article of dress that was nice and made this *servant woman dress* in them and took her in the parlor[,] seated her down and bade Mrs Bailey wait on them. They searched every part of the house taking silver jewelry and every thing they fancied. Then they placed a guard over Mrs B. and went to the Barn taking out 20 barrels of Flour and sending it off. They counted what they left in the barn and went to Mrs B. and told her if any was missing on their return, they would burn the house over her head. They left and in course of the day Mr Bailey returned. Of course he was apprised of all that had transpired in his absence—He started to Geary's camp to get redress and complain of the conduct towards his wife. He has never been heard from—whether he has been murdered or arrested we cannot find out. Now look at these things. Geary arrested several gentlemen who went to make complaint. I tell you the Country people suffer. We have not been disturbed in town. We are not afraid of their threats.

Please write by Mr Hume if possible.

I write always so hurriedly my letters are badly written.

Thursday. Mr Finks called on two ladies last night who were direct from Richmond. They were on their way to Balto[.] They said Richmond was secure. That Mr Davis was very sanguine in regard to the battles about to come off. But Yorktown had not been evacuated when she left[,] neither had it been talked of—but she said we had sufficient force to keep the yankees from Richmond. God grant it. I saw the Herald yesterday—and oh! how they are rejoicing over the evacuation of Yorktown—that they had feared thousands of lives would have been sacrificed to have gained possession—and now it was theirs and no blood shed. McClellan is the man for them. They also assert of being able to surround Johnson as they have successfully done Beauregard in the west—I dont believe a word they say—yet I feel very anxious about Johnson—I have not felt as bouyant since the fall of New Orleans. The yankees are gaining ground on us too rapidly.

Oh! how I long for peace—When will it shine in upon our Confederacy? Good people should pray earnestly. Lute begs you to go to Mr Spiller's and inquire of Kate Calvert when she last heard from her Mothers family. She thinks they have left Waynesboro as her Papa cannot run the cars at present. Write her what you may hear.

Willie has commenced school—goes to Miss Sly[72] [sic]. Mrs Tyler's[73] niece. She asks $2.50 per month. Rather exorbitant he begged so hard to go, we thought we would gratify him he seems well pleased so far, is ready always to start she takes in about 9—and lets out about 2 O'clock—and then the boys have all the afternoon to play.

Mr F. understood from Ladies from Alexandria that every *Secession store* has been closed in A. Now I tell you the yankees believe they are bound to win the day. They are now at Culpepper Co H. and have made a few arrests. I missed the chance of sending this to you yesterday by some ladies going to R. Mr F. did not know I had it ready.

You must keep one on hand always so you can send it. Children are all well— send love & kisses to Papa. Frank & Jessie have sent you letters. Sallie writes for them. You will have to study them out. Little Nannie Brooke[74] was here and Sallie wrote one for her which she begs you to give her Papa in Richmond.

Grand Ma continues very poorly, but makes out to get down in Sister's room. Children and Mama send a bushel of love & kisses to dear Papa. Keep up your spirits and keep well is all I crave.

God bless and preserve you from danger & sickness till we be permitted to meet again—Good bye dear one.

Your fond & affec daughter
S.E.C

Undated, 1862
Fragment

… he died serving his country. I feel much for his wife[.] Susan Foster has been out making up a subscription for her—she has had $170. given her—in wheat and money. I hope the poor woman and her little ones will be cared for. Mr Scott's death will be felt throughout the community. Mr Gaskins killed one of the yankees—but the other one with one of Frank Smith's negro men made their escape.

Tuesday. Dearest Papa. How can I thank you enough and Mr Triplett also for those *precious letters* I received last night. The first intelligence save that verbally by Mr R. Smith since you left us. My heart flowed with gratitude to the Good Being who permitted the way to be opened for me to hear from you my dearest husband I have felt for a week past almost ready to despair. My mind has been overburthened with anxious care on your behalf and I said I could endure separation—but I feared I could

---

[72] Gwynetta Slye, age 23 at the time of the 1860 Warrenton census, was listed as "Teacher," living in the home of Judge and Mrs. John W. Tyler. (J.M.W.)

[73] Gwynetta Tyler, age 46 at the 1860 census, was wife of Circuit Court Judge John W. Tyler. (J.M.W.)

[74] Probably Annie A. Brooke, daughter of James Vass Brooke, age 2 at the time of the 1860 Warrenton Census. (J.M.W.)

not stand this suspense of mind in regard to your health much longer—I longed to hear—just a few lines and lo! when the last ray of hope seemed almost gone and I could know of nothing but darkness—what a glorious change now all is light, my soul is relieved of its burden and I feel like *Christian* is Pilgrims Progress—when his burden rolled from his back—I can now abide my time—The Good Lord answers prayers—your dear little ones pray for you every night—and Jesus has heard them and preserved their dearest Papa's health—it is your health that concerns me—I am so fearful you may have an attack of diarrhea and be very sick and I cant hear[.] I shall ever feel grateful to Mrs Lotties for all the kindnesses she has shown towards you. Give my kind regards to her—I have written you many letters. I wrote one by *Dr Herndon* in which I begged you to send me a *few articles*. Particularly *shoes for Lucy Lee*—I suppose tho you did not *receive* the *letter*—I am sorry as Mr Triplett could have brought them in his pocket. He sent the letters last night, and called this morning to tell me he saw you and you were well and in good spirits. He said he would leave Warrenton at 1 O'clock on his way to Richmond as he was rather dubious about remaining in Warrenton—fearing the yankees might come in town any day—said I must write at once.

I am always glad for an opportunity, particularly when I know you will get the letter. Letters are great comforts[.] Strange that neither letters or papers from Rixeyville have ever come to hand. If you write to Dr Gorrell of Culpepper and ask him to send my letters, I will get them—they then can come by the way of the Springs—You must make every effort to send me letters to relieve my mind of anxiety.

The children were delighted with their letters. Frank thought his was a short one—but said he 'sposed Pa did not have time to write any more just then. I told him the other day Lucy Lee loved Mama best—oh! no Mama dont you think she loves Papa best. I know I love Papa best of anybody[,] love Papa like I love the Good Lord—he says he wish [sic] he could go to Richmond—but he would rather live in Washington and play with Calla Wilson if Lincoln did not live there. He hates Lincoln and all yankeydom—Jessie says tell Papa I love him ten thousand dollars and when he comes home she will hug him and kiss him[.] Willie is very anxious to go to school we have some notion of starting him—I hope if he begins he will not tire—he grows very fast. He was delighted with his letter[,] he is anxious to know if you ever got his—

Grand Ma says tell you she was delighted to hear from you once again and that you are well as usual and apparently in good spirits—to take care of yourself and write as often as you can to cheer us up. She has been quite sick, but hopes she may be spared to meet with you again—her cough is very troublesome, she is not able to keep house—but goes to her meals—I hope she will be all right again as soon as warm weather opens fairly upon us. We have had much disagreeable weather. Dont be uneasy about us—we are all doing well. The yankees have not interfered with any one in town. The way is now opened to Alexandria and Baltimore and hucksters are every day bringing up dry goods and groceries. Mr F. bought yesterday Coffee and 50 shad, traded his tobacco—he is to get 2 barrels of Coal oil from Alex. The hucksters are our men, but they want their pay in gold and silver, and we can buy but little from them.

I hope they will bring up children's shoes—for Lucy Lee has not a pair to put on—but I can make her go without till I get some—

My heart was filled with joy and gladness after perusing your letters—but soon was it saddened on reading Ma's letter to you—to hear of Anna's death—I have not received the letter she wrote to me and directed to Warrenton. I feel much symphathy for Brother William and his dear little ones. You better write to him soon for me. I sent a letter to Mrs Suares in one of yours[,] have you received it? If so I hope you mailed it.

Many thanks for the Postage stamps. I dont suppose I shall have any opportunity to send you your summer clothes[,] I am sorry—Dont spend your money unwisely—you better change some into gold and silver if the premium is not too high—If we had *gold* we could get *articles* cheap I must write a letter to Mother now. Good bye. God bless you.

Warrenton Fauquier Co.
Sunday May 11th 1862

Dearest Papa
I was sitting in my room after dinner to day with Lucy Lee when Willie came in saying Mama I will give you the latest news if you will let me kiss Lucy Lee (he knew I always opposed his kissing her when I was getting her to sleep) I supposed he had heard some news or had a paper—I told him yes he might kiss this time, whereupon he says a *letter* for *you from Papa*—he knew I would rejoice over such news. He took as many kisses as he pleased and I read my letter with rapturous delight. Oh! how can I thank you sufficiently for making the effort to send me letters. It is such a relief to the anxious mind. About two evenings ago I heard *your voice* as I imagined in the passage. It gave me the heartache—I feared you may be sick. Altho your letter was written on the 30th of April and 1st of May I feel relieved in mind in regard to your health. I hope you are well up to this date. That is the burthen of my heart.

You remarked you received the last letter dated 20th. I have written you later ones. Have you received any letters from the children[?] I have sent several in my letters to you. I am sorry there is no more like my dress. Not knowing you had received my letters I have written for it in several. Don't trouble yourself about any of the articles I sent for, I know you cannot get the way of sending them even tho you had them, as all the travelling is by *horse back* so should my letters come to hand *still asking* for them you *will not trouble over it*. Mr Triplett has one about my dress goods but when you receive this you will know then that I will not expect you to send any thing to me, as I have received yours telling me it cannot be had.

Virginia money will pass among our own people but the hucksters will not take it unless discounted at 40 per cent. They want gold and silver.

You spoke of sending me $100. You need not do it in paper money. Mr F. has plenty of paper money, all Virginia money too—and he can't do any trading with it unless dis counted. We would like some *gold* and *silver* if there was any reliable person to send by that is if it was not selling at an exorbitant premium. You better rid yourself of all *Confederate notes*. They *won't pass with us now*. If I had *Baltimore notes* I could buy from the hucksters. They are as good as *gold*. You need not send any Virginia or Confederate paper money. Send some gold if you have the chance of a *reliable person*, but do not unless you are certain I will get it. *I am not in want of any thing particularly now. Shoes* for Jessie and Lucy Lee are all that I wish for and I have understood some will be brought up here soon—but we will have to pay a dis count or give gold—

Mr. F. has just brought in a yankee paper—they speak of their having possession of Williamsburg and having had a fight on Monday last. That McC. is in hot pursuit—thinks Richmond will be evacuated. Some how I feel as if we shall gain even tho we are driven out of Richmond. I long to hear the news from our side. Mr F. has also a Richmond Dispatch which speaks of the intervention of Foreign powers—why it will never do to leave Virginia out and put her in Yankee land—no she would rather be a *desert* than submit to such treatment. I hope the Southern states would not be willing to desert her in such a time.

The yankees paid our town a visit to day. They have gone in the direction of the Springs—Mr Royston came up to see us yesterday. He says that the yankees remarked that it was all right speaking of the death of Mr Scott—and the yankee who shot him was *praised* and would perhaps be promoted for his bravery. They rejoiced that he was dead. Called him the Capt. of a gueralla [sic] party. Mind you after the officers had sent word to Mr Scott to shoot them—they were deserters.

I am truly thankful to know you are well. May you continue to enjoy your health. I am also glad you received my letters. I do strive to get them to you by every opportunity. Keep one on hand hoping to find a way.

Children are all well. Send bushel of love and kisses. Grand Ma is yet complaining, better some days than others. I have not had the head ache since getting your first letters. I expect not hearing from you must have had something to do with the head ache—God preserve you my dearest one.

Your ever affec daughter
S.E.C.

We have yet a good supply of provisions on hand.

Warrenton
Monday Afternoon
May 12th 1862

Dearest Papa

Mr. Finks has come home to give us the news. He says he saw a dispatch from Richmond which confirms what we heard of the battle of Monday last at Williamsburg[75] and that Johnson had sent on 900 prisoners to Richmond—also that

---

[75] Battle of Williamsburg, May 5, 1862, as Gen. Johnston withdrew from the Yorktown line. Kemper's Battery was from Alexandria, Va. (J.K.G.)

we had severe fighting on Saturday last, that Kemper's Battery was cut to pieces—he is very unhappy about *Fielding*[,][76] he was under Kemper's command—he says he would come on to Richmond himself to see after him but he is afraid to run the risk fearing he may not be able to get back to Warrenton as soon as he would wish—might be cut off. We cannot tell at this particular crisis what a day may bring forth. He wants you to go to every hospital and make inquiry for Fielding. He may be among the unfortunate ones[,] be on the lookout and search for him as soon as you hear of the wounded being brought in to Rich. Mr F. seems very anxious about him. We are all very anxious to hear of the battle—so much depends on the result of this battle for the peace and comfort of our Confederacy.

Mr. F. also saw a dispatch from McClellan to Washington in which he said a terrific battle had taken place Saturday—and the slaughter was awful number of officers—oh! is it not enough to chill the blood and unnerve the strongest mind to hear of so much sacrifice. Lives too dear to homes to be given up to the vile invader—When I think of the wretches, then the southern blood boils over with revenge Sister says should you find Fielding wounded you must endeavor to find out the where abouts of Mr Joshua Finks[77]—he may have left Waynesboro—he of course would like to know all about Fielding—Of course we know you will do all in your power to relieve him and give him comfort. I fear many of our friends will be taken. Oh may they all be cared for and have every wish gratified.

We expect to hear of much bloodshed during the contest for McClellan seems eager after Rich.

Would that we could get the correct news from our side—suspense is terrible indeed. Look up all of your Warrenton friends—also inquire for the So. Ca. boys—of the Palmetto Guard, Wescoat, Dutart, McCoy. Don't let them suffer if they are wounded.

Mr. Hume will reach Richmond about the middle of the week—we will not expect to get tidings before his return—so long to wait.

While the yankees were in town yesterday Mrs Cox and daughter were on the street walking and as they passed one yankee said to his friend look at them gals—Willie was near[,] he said to the yankee—they are *Ladies* sir—his friend said do you permit that boy to reprove you[,] Willie says he made no remark & on meeting some others yankees I mean Willie went up to them and begged not to kill Mr Jones and Mr Snead, Mr Pollard and Mr West if they should take them prisoners in this battle, they promised him they would not be hurt.

Children are all well. Grand Ma about the same. Love & kisses from all.

Your affec daughter
S.E.C.

God bless & preserve you from all danger.

---

[76] Fielding Finks survived the war, and was living in Warren County, Va. in 1880, aged 43. (T.T.R.)

[77] A reference to Joshua Finks of Waynesboro, Lute Finks' father. (J.M.W.)

Dearest Papa

Your most welcome letter (for next to me is a letter from you penned in your dear familiar hand) came to hand by Monday afternoon through Mr Medideth. Mr M. did not come himself but sent the letters to town. I need not tell you with what eagerness I devour each word your letters contain, it is a pleasure that at present can only be surpassed by the presence of the dear ones themselves.

The Federals are rejoicing over their gaining possession of Norfolk and Portsmouth. They say Genl. Huger[78] withdrew the confederate forces without offering battle. It is also stated in the Sun[79]—that the Merrimac was fired and blown up, the confederates despaired of their iron-monster being of any further use to them since the fall of N. and P. and they preferred to destroy rather than let her fall into the hands of the Federals. The wretches[,] I wish we could have blown theirs up as they were proceeding up to Norfolk. We learn also that McClellan was on Saturday last at New Kent Court House 27 miles from Richmond—That the confederates were in sight but were gradually falling back and it is supposed would make a stand at Bottom bridge in Charles City County only 15 miles from Richmond—and that the Federals had advanced within 7 miles of said place. The Sun also contains a statement of two released prisoners from Richmond saying that a meeting was held on Saturday by the citizens to decide what had best be done with the City on the arrival of the Federals—property holders were willing to surrender while those who had no interest was for burning it—

I see also that the Charlestonians are expecting to be attacked soon and considerable excitement prevailed there. Forts Sumter and Moultrie were furnished with heavy guns. I do not write the above as news to you[,] I only want you to know we can hear sometimes through the Yankee paper of what is going on—we don't believe all we read.

Mr John Spillman left Monday night for Richmond. He was on his way to look up his son who had been wounded on Monday week at Williamsburg and was in the enemy's hands—I suppose our army were compelled to leave them on the battle field, but it is an agonizing thought to the relatives to know it. I hope all may yet be given up to their friends—

---

[78] Benjamin Huger (1805-1877) (pronounced: u' gee) was from an old French Huguenot South Carolina family. No doubt, General Huger was well known to Mrs. Caldwell, whose embarassment, expressed in a number of letters, was shared by many when he withdrew from Norfolk to join the army defending Richmond. He was held responsible for the loss of Roanoke Island and upon investigation was relieved of command and transferred to the West. After the war he owned 'Gordonsdale,' near The Plains, where he lived simply as a farmer. Ezra J. Warner, *Generals in Gray; Lives of the Confederate Commanders* (Louisiana State Univ. Pr., c1959), pp. 143-144. (J.K.G.)

[79] Probably *The Baltimore Sun* newspaper. (J.M.W.)

I was very sorry to hear of the death of Mr William Payne and Col. Phillips' son—I truly sympathize with the bereaved. Oh! how many hearts are aching this night.

We heard to day of the very ungentlemanly conduct of Col. Geary. He made the house of Mr Foster[80] his Head quarters and while at dinner one day he remarked that the Confederate army were composed of the meanest, low bred silt of men that has ever come under his notice whereupon, Miss Kate Foster replied that their [sic] were mean men on both sides then she thought—he instantly arose and drew his sword on her—some of his officers then interfered—he remarked he would not permit her to make such remarks in the presence of his men—Sister says—he is worse than the brute creation and far excels Jim Lane of Kansas—we heard also of his conduct towards two ladies in Middleburg accusing them of stealing his pistol when his son had taken it.

At Thourafare they have plundered every house—Mrs Carter has only one servant girl left her—every servant she had followed the yankees—they took all her provisions leaving her only a half barrel of flour and some meal. At the time of their coming in she had a son and sister extremely ill. The son has since died—they then went on to the Chatman's[81] [sic] and you know they were extensive slave holders—they have been completely stripped of servants and all provisions[,] in fact all the Country people have suffered. The towns and villages are not disturbed to any amount.

The children are well. They were delighted with their letters, Willie particularly. Frank has his carefully put away. I was amused and yet distressed with it too—Last night as Frank knelt to say his prayers, he commenced by saying Jesus please send your angels down to bring me to Heaven for I don't want to stay here if this is *yankeeland*—he hates the name of a yankee—I cannot get him to wear a pair of *blue* pants he has—he says the *yankees* wear blue.

Jessie remarked yesterday to Sallie, she had 4 Ma's. Sallie wanted to know who they were, she says well Mama up stairs, Mamy Anty[,] Grand Ma[,] and Mamy in kitchen. We thought she was smart to count four so correctly. Frank asked her who told her—she says nobody—I say it myself—she is very sweet and interesting. Lucy Lee is coming on—you would not know her—she is very large for her age and has a large foot—I have [been] trying to get her a pair of shoes—the hucksters, (our men) ask $1. in silver for shoes for her and Jessie—I purchased a pair for Jessie and expect to get a pair for Lucy Lee. I have a few dollars in silver—

Willie seems to love his school and tries to learn his lessons. He loves you dearly

---

[80] 'Glenville,' the home of James W. Foster (1807-1866), near The Plains, Va. Kate Foster was the daughter of Major Thomas R. Foster, brother of James William Foster. (J.K.G.)

[81] John Chapman, the last of the large, wealthy family to own the mill in Thoroughfare Gap, had spent a small fortune of his own and that of his brother and sisters plus all he could borrow, in renovating the mill from 1853 to 1858. The Chapman home, Meadowland, was located near the mill. The takeover by the Confederate forces and later devastation by the Union forces proved too much for Mr. Chapman. The maltreatment he received by the Union forces and the final destruction of his property led to a mental breakdown. He died in Dec. 1866 in the Western State Hospital at Staunton, Va. (J.K.G.)

and so do all the little ones—Mr Spillman[82] (the Major) will mail this at Madison C.H. If you were to write immediately and enclose my letter to him at Madison he may be there. He will remain there a few days. I will ask him to inquire for one for himself.

Good night I must now close. I have had a very severe head ache to day & cannot see to write well but could not let the opportunity go by.

Grand Ma is better[,] we are glad I can assure you.

Oh may you be preserved by the Almighty and the time soon roll around when we shall be permitted to be near each other & enjoy the pleasure of our little ones around us.

All join me in love.

Your ever affec daughter
S.E.C.

Warrenton Via
Saturday May 17/62

Dearest Papa

Dr. Ward sent me a letter from you this morning—for which I return many thanks to you. They are to me a source of great pleasure and comfort, now that I am assured it is best for you not to venture to Warrenton, and well do I know the anxiety and suspense I have endured when I was unable of hearing from you.

You remark that up to the 10th of May my letters to you stated I had not heard from you—all that is the truth—for I did not receive any from you until Mr Triplett of Mr J.V. Brooke's company arrived in Warrenton—then I received two—one you sent by Broaddus T—and Mr Tripplett's—I then wrote to you on the receipt of them, but had no opportunity of sending until Saturday 10th I hope by this time some have been received. I write regularly on the receipt of each letter—but as you say it takes some ten days for letters to reach either one of us—Be hopeful as I am—and you will get them all in due time. Whenever I feel despondent, hope rises within and assures me better days are in the distance for me[.] I shall be happy yet again with my dearest husband. Oh! may it please Almighty God to spare your life and that the days may not be far in the distance when we shall sit down under our own vine and fig tree. We must not complain—we must be resigned. I feel the separation keenly—but our

---

[82] Alexander Hamilton Spilman (1806-1875), married, first, in 1825, Culpeper County, Adeline Green Allan; and Mary Russell Brown in 1866, and had 17 children. He first became a tailor and as a member of the State Militia drilled the local company in 'Glasswell's' pasture near Warrenton, which earned him the courtesy title of 'Major.' He was ordained a Baptist minister on August 20, 1849 and during the Civil War he served churches at some distance from Warrenton. One day while on his way to keep a ministerial appointment he was captured by a group of Federal soldiers, who mistakenly thought they had captured a Confederate officer. When they learned he was only a Baptist minister they were sorely disappointed and chagrinned. In 1840 he became Postmaster at Warrenton, a position he held for the next 25 years, until 1865. After being ordained he served as pastor of Carter's Run, Mt. Holly, Bethel and Stevensburg Baptist Churches. Malcolm L. Melville, *Spilman Papers* (Forestville, Calif.: 1965). (J.K.G.)

lot has been cast in pleasant places when compared to others all around us—Look at our dear children—so far God has blessed them with health[,] they have every comfort heart can wish for—they are happy in a good home amidst kind dear relatives and friends—then turn from them to myself—here I am, amid all who love me, those who would share the half of all they possess with me—would it not be ungrateful in me to repine—You are by far the worst off—you are away from all—yet the Good Lord has placed you in the midst of kind friends who would cheerfully add to your comfort all in their power—Yes I say altho debarred the blessed privilege of the society of each other we are made happy and reconciled to our lot by hearing from each other and knowing we are pleasantly situated, as these very distressing times can have us be. Let us be grateful to God.

We are very anxious in regard to Richmond—why was the time put off till now to fill up the river with stones?[83] It seems wondrous strange to me that all these precautionary measures had not been advised long time since—Now we with you fear it is too late—Richmond must be evacuated—no *burn* the city if the inhabitants can get away—let her not fall into McClellan's hands it is his inmost desire—On to Richmond was their boast at the battle of Manassas—and truly does it appear as if they are fast gaining their wishes—Yet as Mrs Suares says—even tho' they gain R they cannot subjugate the South—I would very earnestly beg of you to go where ever the Government goes—you are serving your Country far better in that capacity than if you were in the army—for you know as well as I do your health will not permit you—now please dont talk about entering the army again be satisfied to remain under government. *It is best.*

We were much pleased to hear such news of Mr Jones—we felt as if he would act bravely and nobly—I wish you had cut the pieces out of the paper and sent them to us—We had not heard any thing of it.

We are rejoicing over the good news from Jackson and Beauregard—Would that Johnson could have continued the fight and not retreated.

The yankees pay Warrenton a visit every night, some times they come in few numbers—then again 100 Cavalry[84] will ride about town. Their object must be to inquire if any of our soldiers have returned to their homes. I feel very uneasy about Dr. Ward—he tho' will leave after dinner—it is running too great a risk for persons in the Confederate service to come on to Warrenton. As dearly as I want to see you I would not have you venture at this time. Write as often as you can and I shall promise you to be contented.

I have not seen Dr. Ward. If Mr Finks tells me he saw you in Richmond, very probably I shall call at his house and ask him all about you—

To day is charming—it is growing very warm—how I wish you had your Summer clothes—but you must supply yourself—Get a *coat* and *pants* of Black Drabette—you know what I mean—it is thin goods for summer wear—the

---

[83] Responsibility for the obstruction of the Pamunkey River, to prevent passage by Federal troops into Richmond, was a source of conflict between Gen. Robert E. Lee (C.S.A.) and Gen. Joseph Johnston (C.S.A.) in early May of 1862. Freeman, *Lieutenants*, Vol. 1, pp. 205-206. (J.M.W.)

[84] This cavalry could be some of Col. Geary's 1st Mich. Cav. (J.E.D.)

merchants know if you will spell it "Drab Ette." Save washing and is genteel.

The letters sent by Taylor Scott were received—

The children are all well. I think Frank has commenced to grow some but yet has the *hives*. Grand Ma continues very poorly—her cough has reduced her very much—she is very low spirited at times. God bless you my dearest one. Children send love & kisses.

Be sure you cut out all the news from the papers and send in letters to us[,] we would be charmed to get papers sometimes. Good Bye again. Keep up a brave heart— and should R be evacuated let us hear as soon as possible of your whereabouts.

Your ever affec daugh
S.E.C.

My postage *stamps* have been called for all over town. I have reserved some for myself fearing I may not get more. I know not when this will go.

Wednesday May 21/62

Dearest Papa

I was writing to you on Saturday last in order to be ready for the departure of Dr. Ward—when we heard that Genl. Shields' division were in town. But a circumstance occurred about 2 O'clock before we knew of the arrival of the wretches. Willie was playing by the gate when a soldier in *gray* clothes rode up and asked him if there were any *Southern* soldiers in town—Willie says why you are a yankee soldier—he said oh! no I am a true southern soldier and you must tell me if any southern soldiers are here—Sister overheard the conversation and ran out to call Willie fearing he would speak of the arrival of Dr. W—he did not heed her whereupon she called him again and told him he was talking with a yankee—The soldier on seeing her left the child and addressed her thus "Madam are there any Northern men in town she told him "she left that for him to find out"—he put the question again by saying "I demand of you to inform me if there are Northern men in town["]—she told him she knew nothing of there [sic] whereabouts, he had a pistol in his hand and raising it towards her, (which he now denies) he said I am a Southern man and one of Mumford's Cavalry and demand of you the information, she told him no Southern soldier ever demanded information of a lady with a pistol raised—that seemed to bring him to his senses, for at time Mr F. came in and remarked we were talking to yankees—(I came on the porch a few moments before Mr F.)[.] The soldier on hearing Mr F. said yes he belonged to the Federal army— but was compelled to use deception in order to gain information. Sister told him he might have shot her dead[,] she was not deceived and she knew why he thus addressed her—but she was not in the least thrown off her guard. He apologized as gentlemanly as possible—Sister told him she would only receive on the promise he would never address a Southern lady again in the manner he had done her—Some one asked him if he was retreating from Jackson, he said no—they were on their way to join

McClellan at Richmond[.] Mr F. told him McC. was not in R—he asked him for his Authority, Mr F. told him he had intelligence from R—they were not there, just then another soldier rode up and this one went to him and whispered to him, he then remarked to Mr F. You are my prisoner for a short time. Willie *screamed* you shant take my Uncle. They promised him they would not hurt him. They took him a short distance and let him go. We asked Mr F. why they arrested him—he said he did not know[.] They asked him a few questions and released him—

Dr. Ward was informed of the yankees being in town and left in a hurry[,] we were truly thankful he made his escape for the very soldier left our gate and with half dozen more went and surrounded the Dr.'s house and demanded him—his wife told he was not there[,] they said they had reliable authority he was there, she told him she coined an untruth—that Dr. W. was at home last night she would not hesitate to tell him, but that now he was on his journey and catch him if he could. They did not search the house, seemed satisfied to take her word—they told her they were informed by some of the colored people he had arrived in town—(she asked them who gave them their information) she told them they were heartily welcome to the friendship of the colored race—We soon found out that we would have some 15,000 soldiers in town. About half of the number passed through town during the afternoon Genl. Shields and his staff made their head quarters at Mrs James V. Brooke—Genl. Sullivan[85] arrested Major Spillman on his way to Madison[,] he had a package of letters with him, he says Genl. Sullivan treated him rather as a spy—thought he was a Major of the Confederate army—and stripped him even to his socks and searched him. He was then brought into town and kept as prisoner until Sunday morning. They had a Court Martial called and he was tried. The letters were read and nothing treasonable found in them and he was released. Genl. Shields behaved very gentlemanly to him throughout. We breathed freely once again on hearing he was released for it was through the doing of kindness to the people of Warrenton he had been brought into the difficulty. Several parties of the soldiers went out to search for Taylor Scott but he hid and they were unsuccessful—they stole cattle and committed many acts of depredation. Mrs Lee complained to Genl. Shields and he had all restored. Others went out to Dr. Fisher's and killed all his cattle and sheep—Complaint was made and I have understood that Mrs Fisher was paid $800 for damages done on the farm. Genl. Shields and most of the army behaved very well. Mr Sedwick handed my letter over— I was glad enough to get one from you after hearing such doleful accounts of the intended evacuation of Richmond. I should not judge from the tenor of your letter that you were much afraid of the yankees entering Richmond. I am glad you are in such good spirits & hope you will keep on with the government no matter where it should be removed if in a healthy locality—I forgot to mention that the Federal soldiers left our town Sunday afternoon. On Monday some five or six were straggling about the town—during Monday afternoon we were surprised by a visit from *our scouts*. Col. Radford's men—I tell you they were *welcomed* cordially by the *ladies*[,] all run out to see them—about *8* in number, they came to see if they were any yankees left

---

[85] Possibly Brig. Gen. Jeremiah Sullivan (U.S.A.). (J.K.G.)

behind and went in pursuit, they came in asking no questions but went straight ahead and captured five of them, one of the yankees got away—they were 6 in all. Their arms were hid in old Mary Brown's[86] house—but they could not be found, had been taken away—our scouts went after them and Mary was very impudent and the Citizens ordered her to leave town which she has done—

I am now without a *nurse*. The Mother of my girl called for her Sunday to walk out with her—she went and I have not seen her since. I heard they had left with the yankees. I am sorry because the baby is unsocial and will not take to strangers—

Grand Ma is much better we think[.] I hope her strength will gradually come and she will be herself soon again—

The children were pleased with their letters. Jessie was wishing for you to day to be home to give her some good things. You should have received letters by Mr Triplett and Hume. Before that by Mr Spillman[.] Please enclose these smaller sheets in Sister's letter and she can hear the news—

Thursday—Mrs Brooke has sent to tell me probably she can get my letter off—so I will add a little more. It was rumoured yesterday through our town that a man had been arrested by Mumford's Cavalry as a spy—but upon examination they could find nothing unreasonable. They were doubting about him when he remarked to them he was their friend and showed them a proclamation to Jackson[87] from the state of Maryland[,] names of men in high authority signed—saying that Maryland would rise if Jackson with 50,000 men would come over to their help—he was on his way then to Jackson—I better not name the place he had the paper secreted—Will Jackson go?

Your letter of 13th & 19th were received to day—We are glad you are in such good spirits. Oh that God in his mercy will stay the vile invader but I fear McClellan will not come out to give us battle. He thinks he can starve us into submission—but he will find even such efforts fruitless—We must conquer—I hope Charleston will prove impregnable—She should have been fortified long ago—I hope Ma or any of my family will not leave the City—they are more secure there than in the country.

Please see Frank White if possible and ask him to write home—his people are anxious to hear from him—he must do it.

We are all well. Grand Ma is better. Should you go to L. why you must write. Don't quit your situation. We were charmed at hearing of the honor conferred on Mr Jones—Send my warmest sympathies to Mrs Goodloe. I have no time to write.

The Herald thinks the yankees will get Chn in about two weeks. I trust not— I think the harbor should have been fortified long since. I hope Sister will not leave the city—and hope Ma & Pa will remain also—much better remain in the city than go in the country.

Enclose these in Sister's letter.

---

[86] The only Mary Brown listed in the 1860 Warrenton Census was a free black woman, aged 16 years, living in the home of Mrs. Ann Maria Jennings and listed as a "house maid." (J.M.W.)

[87] Gen. Stonewall Jackson is in the process of driving Gen. Banks from the Shenandoah Valley. (J.E.D.)

Willie told a yankee officer he gloried in the name of rebel—and soon as he was old enough he would join White's[88] Cavalry and make them have a Bull Run. Frank despises the yankees.

You should have received letters by Mr *Hume*. Write a note to Mrs Goodloe for me[,] I feel as much for her—Good bye God bless you.

Warrenton Via
June 1st 1862

Dearest Papa

This is the closing of another sabbath day and instead of having our minds quieted with holy thoughts and religious worship to our Heavenly Parent, we are disquieted and burthened with anxious care about those we love far away from us—and we cannot as much as get intelligence of their whereabouts. One day we are ready to rejoice over victories gained hoping soon to meet in mail communication with friends—and the very next day are our hopes blighted and crushed to hear of the sad reverses come upon our little band of brave hearts. Jackson's brilliant victories in the valley, Front Royal and Winchester gave us encouragement that we would conquer our enemies—we had scarcely rejoiced when we find the enemy has been strongly reinforced and has again taken possession of Front Royal—worse than this we hear that the enemy are in possession of Hanover both the Canal and rail road thereby cutting off our direct communication to Lynchburg—thence to Richmond we will be one day longer getting supplies to Lynchburg by another route—and then we lost *1000* men—We have just heard that Beauregard has evacuated Corinth[89]— my heart is sad. I do dislike our army having to fall back—but oh! may it be for the best. I have implicit confidence in Genl. Beauregard—and almost feel assured that a brilliant victory West will yet crown his patriotism for his country's cause. If Halleck would have but come out in equal numbers or even three to one while we were waiting at Corinth we would have whipped them—just so now is Genl. Johnson at a stand still—McClellan will not meet him—but is trying to surround him and soon we fear we shall learn that Richmond is evacuated, compelled to be so by necessity—and by such means do they intend to starve us into subjugation, but with God's help we will whip them yet. Our cause is a just one and we will conquer.

A gentleman from Alexandria told Mr Finks, he saw four citizens from the

---

[88] Col. Elijah V. White (C.S.A.) organized a company in late 1861, formalized in January, 1862, in Loudoun County. Their first duties were that of scouting and foraging. As the tales of daring became widespread, the organization grew and became the 35th Battalion, Virginia Cavalry. The notoriety of the command was wide spread and no doubt intrigued even the very young. (J.K.G.)

[89] In a bloodless, overnight deception, in the face of a siege of Corinth by more than 100,000 Union soldiers under Maj. Gen. H. W. Halleck (U.S.A.), Gen. P. G. T. Beauregard (C.S.A.) and approximately 50,000 Confederates, 18,000 sick, and all but two local families, had evacuated Corinth on the evening of May 29-30, 1862. (J.M.W.)

country around marched through Alex. to Washington last week. They were *hand-cuffed* and chained, arrested by order of *Geary* on his *retreat*. Geary should be shot—he has no principle whatever. Persons from Warrenton have lately been going to Alex. for goods without disturbance until the past week—and all who went have been arrested and searched. Billy Patterson[90] went after goods and he was taken up & kept in jail for two days—had bought his goods and was putting them in his wagon when he was arrested. His goods were taken from him and a receipt for the goods given him to hand to the owner and say that the goods would be given to them when they came after them. You know that is only a trap to arrest them. Mr F. sent by Mr Yates to get some medicine, but they not [sic] sell him any to bring to Warrenton—At present there is nothing doing—no news can we get and even the yankees have ceased their visits.

We are all getting on as usual. Children are well. Grand Ma is about the same—she gains strength very slowly—and is very thin—

We all want to see you very much. I can't write down how much—but yet I would not have you come to Warrenton at this time—for no sooner is one of our town people here on a visit than they are reported at the Yankee Camp at the Junction by the treacherous negroes—We cannot trust any these days—You would be astounded to hear of the numbers of servants left town for Alex and Washington—

I had to give up my nurse Lucy Jackson's[91] daughter—she was on the order of *Anna* with the children.

Tuesday afternoon—Mrs Johnson leaves in the morning for Culpepper and will mail this letter for me. I hope you will receive it. If you would enclose my letters to Dr. Gorrell[,] Culpepper I would get them.

We heard yesterday of the battle of Saturday with the enemy on Chickahominy—that the fight raged all day till 9 O'clock at night and was thought it would be resumed Sunday—the loss was fearful on both sides[,] the 17th Virg and also the 8th Vir. suffered heavily. Oh! may it please the Good Lord to be on our side and let us gain our cause—and by so doing gain *peace*. About 60,000 troops have been sent up

---

[90] Billy Patterson—the source of an old expression, "Who hit Billy Patterson?" which originated in 1852, was a burly butcher, weighing 240 pounds, who lived in Richmond before the Civil War, and whose chief diversion lay in drinking whiskey and beating his wife. In 1852 the medical national convention met in Richmond. Dr. Alban S. Payne of Fauquier was walking home from a party one evening during the convention in company with Dr. Martin P. Scott and Dr. Blair Burwell. As they were passing near where the St. Clair Hotel once stood, Billy Patterson rushed out of a saloon, dashed into the group of doctors, and knocked some of them down. Springing at Billy Patterson, Dr. Payne struck him two blows which felled him. The doctors then continued on their way to their hotels. On reaching the City Hotel, Dr. Payne sent a servant back to discover what had become of Patterson. The servant returned with the information that "he's breathin' and he's hit mighty hard, but I reckon he'll live." In the meanwhile two policemen appeared at the Hotel inquiring, "Who hit Billy Patterson?" The proprietor sent two boys to ask the officers, "Who hit Billy Patterson?" The repetition of this question on all sides so amused the guests that the policemen retired in disgust. The expression became a by-word on the streets, was taken up by the newspapers, and spread abroad. It is related that Patterson reformed, and that years later the two principals became great friends." Brook Payne, *The Paynes of Virginia* (Harrisonburg, Va.: 1977), p. 142. (J.K.G.)

[91] Lucy Jackson, a free Black, was listed in the 1860 census as being 55 years of age. By occupation she was a "washerwoman" with a personal estate valued at $200. There were three children living in her home, Betsey, aged 14, Frances, aged 12 and Lucy, aged 9. (J.M.W.)

as reinforcement for Banks against Jackson—We heard he was fighting at Harper's Ferry on Sunday. Can't tell how much truth there is in the report. If we could but get the papers sometimes.

Have you seen Mr Hume? I hope you may.

Willie expects to have some company to night to partake of some strawberries and cream—How we all wish our dearest Papa were with us to enjoy some. But we must submit to our privations with patience knowing the Good Lord is taking care of you and you have been enjoying your usual share of good health. We all pray for your protection daily—May you feel that you are kept under the Shadow of His Wing.

The children are all enjoying a good share of health. Lucy Lee improves and is very healthy. She has *two teeth*. I think her very pretty. I was fortunate enough to get her *2* pair of *shoes*. Very nice ones only gave 62 ½ cts per pair.

Grand Ma is very much complaining to day. She is looking very thin—

Please get yourself some *summer* clothes. I have no way to get yours to you. Love from one and all—Children send an amount of kisses.

> Your affec & devoted
> daughter
> S.E.C.

(Undated)

Mr. Coppage saw Mr Finks and he says the yankees have not disturbed any one in Front Royal—your farm and all on it are safe. Davy is there yet. We were glad to hear it—for we knew not in what condition it was at present since the wretches had been at Front Royal—rather remarkable indeed—

Be very certain not to send any Confederate money to me—not even Virginia money. Send gold if you have it by some reliable person. I have no more news and am much hurried just now—so good bye once more.

We have just heard that several of our young men have been wounded. Mr John Spellman's son—he is now ready to start to Richmond to see after him.

Now remember, you must not trouble yourself to purchase any articles for me—I received your letter telling me you could not get any more *poplin*.

I am heart sick to hear that so many of our men and officers are killed & wounded.

God grant we may be victorious. Good bye.

> Your daughter
> S.E.C.

We are all well. Grand Ma is complaining—
Look after all friends who may be wounded.

Dearest Papa

Many thanks must I return for your highly prized letter sent by Mr Sedgwick. True, letters are such treats these times. I felt very grateful to Mr. S. for his kindness to me both in taking, and bringing me letters. My mind is now relieved in regard to your health. I was fearing you may have taken cold this unseasonable weather. Keep on your thick, warm clothing until we have good settled weather. I have had to put flannel on the children again—

We have had much rain. Mr. S. was telling me that Genl. Johnson intended renewing the fight Tuesday last if the *rain* had not set in so furiously. I was sorry for I am so very desirous of driving McClellan off at once. But God is wise and doeth all things well. *He sent the rain.*

How sad it makes the heart to read the names of those who have sacrificed their lives in their Country's cause—how many homes are desolated, children fatherless—sad—too sad.

Your letter has been read by almost every one in Warrenton[,] many say it was more satisfactory to them than the *newspapers*[,] it is now in the country with Mr Hunton—to be sent to Mr Love's[92] family to read. I am glad to give pleasure or comfort in any way. Now when you write—be particular to give all the news in regard to persons with whom we are all interested. You can do much good by your letters. George Jackson[93] says your letters are worth reading—and he is always anxious to get a chance to read them for the news—

Mr. Sedgwick called and gave me $51.70 cts. He changed most of the Confederate money for me. I told him I was hoping to get some Silver and gold from Richmond. He said I must not expect it, as gold was 200 per cent premium—That is worse than the discount here on Virginia money. The hucksters who came from Alexandria will not take Virginia money under *40* per cent discount—they want silver—and we have *none*. So paper money will only buy a little more than half now from them. The stores with us have but few if any useful things in them and of course we are compelled to patronize the hucksters—they are *our men*, who go to Alexandria and they have to pay *Silver* or dis count paper money so you see $50—now will only be worth about $30—I need shoes for the children more than any thing else—and of course they sell *high*. I have succeeded in supplying them.

I am now on the lookout for winter goods for Willie & Frank for *pants*. I must commence in time if I expect to have them warmly clad next winter if life lasts. I will try and get some *jeans* from Alex. if I meet with any one who can judge cloth—We have none with us.

---

[92] The Hunton and Love families lived in the New Baltimore-Buckland area, a few miles from Warrenton. (J.K.G.)

[93] G. W. Jackson was a lawyer, age 30, according to the 1860 Fauquier County census, and a cousin of General Thomas J. "Stonewall" Jackson. (J.M.W.)

Provisions are very cheap in Alex. Sugar 8 cts and 10 cts[,] coffee 20 cts—Salt $2.50 per sack—if any one had the money to spare to lay out in groceries for their family now is the time. But few venture down fearing they may be arrested. We cannot trust the *yankees*.

I was much obliged to you for the postage stamps. Several have sent to me for some.

Please purchase suitable clothing for yourself and be particular in your *dress*. Don't be economical but get all that is necessary for your comfort and appearance. I am pleased to learn you are generous towards the suffering but be careful not to be too lavish—(I would not wish you to be stingy) for very many are undeserving and your good deeds not appreciated—yet again many hearts are truly grateful and are won over by kind words and attention. I see by the papers that the Ladies are making themselves a name for their kind attention to the wounded. May they not tire in their good work for man is cheered and comforted by the presence of the ladies and only reminds them of their own loved ones who would willingly be waiting on them could they be near them. Genl. King's[94] division arrived in Warrenton Friday night. They behaved remarkably well—they intended to make some stay with us—and were all assembled (or some of their regiments in the different churches they had occupied for preaching on Sunday and had commenced services when they received a dispatch for Marching orders—and left very hurriedly some say for Richmond others heard for Maryland.)

Mr Finks met with one of the Genl. who asked him if he could tell him where he could get honey, milk and strawberries that he would exchange groceries or pay silver money—So we thought we had all he wished for and would get some *coffee*. Mr F. took 3 gallons of strawberries, 14 pounds of honey and 2 gallons of milk to the Genl. and received 32 pounds of Coffee for them. I think we made a good exchange— We dislike to have any trade with them, but we are now compelled to buy the necessaries of life—They were also anxious to have bread made and give any thing in exchange for silver money—They were supplied very bountifully with groceries of every kind and good articles. I was anxious to get some tea. Tea is selling in Alexandria $1.25 cts per pound.

Aunt Lucy's son George who left his home last March to go with the Yankees was with King's division. He is waiting on one of Genl. King's aids.[95] He came to see Aunt Lucy. He looks much changed[,] does not carry the same open free countenance he used to wear—He said he would not have left his Master (Mr. Joe Tullus[96] [sic]) if he would have remained at home. (Mr. Tullus is a member of Mr J.

---

[94] General Rufus King (U.S.A.) (1814-1876) was a graduate of USMA, 1833. At the time he appeared in Warrenton, General King commanded a division of General Irvin McDowell's III Corps and occupied the line of the Rappahannock until the campaign of Second Manassas. (J.K.G.)

[95] According to Leon F. Litwack, although the Fugitive Slave Act remained operative until mid-1864, federal legislation in 1862 "barred military personnel from participating in the return of fugitive slaves and decreed that the escaped slaves of disloyal masters would be forever free." *Been in the Storm So Long* (New York: Vintage, 1980), p. 52. (B.G.C.)

[96] Joseph D. Tulloss (1824-1909) served as Sgt. in Brooke's Battery (Battery A, 12th Batt'n., Poague's Battalion, Jackson's Corps). He is buried at Grove Presbyterian Church, Goldvein, Va. (J.K.G.)

V. Brooke's company.) He said his master on leaving home told him he could do as he pleased[,] remain at home or leave—he said he thought he might as well go to the yankees and make his own money—Aunt Lucy seemed very sorry to find him with the yankees and told us she begged him to go back home. George told her that Mr Tullus had taken Anna (her daughter) away with him—she came to me this morning and begged to write and ask you to go and see Mr Tullus and ask him where Anna is—and if she is well and to tell her that her *husband* (Silas) is with George, she saw him and he is well and says he is coming soon to see her—You better tell Mr T. to be on his guard about Anna if her husband comes, it is only to take her away with him—We have had the most implicit confidence in Aunt Lucy, she has been behaving remarkably well for some three months—but of course now since she has seen George we are very suspicious, fearing he may have advised her to get her freedom—it makes us all very unhappy—for we could not well do without her and could hire none in her place, for there are but few servants left in town. She told me to tell you she had no idea of going to the yankees—so I thought as she voluntarily remarked it to be written to you—you had better write her some good advice in my letter so she will know you put confidence in her and expect to meet her and her children when you return home—write to her encouragingly. You must be sure to put Mr Tullus on his guard about *Anna*[,] if her husband finds out her whereabouts, he will get her away.

We have but few servants left in town. Every one from Dr. Bispham have left. And you cannot hire for love or money. Mrs Bispham has now to cook—The soldiers have the daring impudence to say that they hope every last servant will leave so the d____ lazy *southern women* will be made to *work*[.] they actually steal the servants— for the little children are leaving by themselves—Mr Gaines has lost every one from his farm in Prince William—and Strother. Jim and Julia with her two children, (boys) have left him in Warrenton. Carter (Julia's husband) belonging to Mrs Ward was taken up last week being suspected of his intention to take off Julia and was given in charge to Wm Bragg to take to Richmond but unfortunately escaped so that same night they all left town and have not been heard from—Dr. Stevens' woman and four children in broad daylight Sunday left in a wagon before his eyes—he could do nothing the town was filled with soldiers—When owners applied to Genl. King— he said he did not send them, neither would he prevent them[,] they were free to do as they pleased—What times to live in. Had our army not fallen back from Manassas, we would not have suffered such losses. Every one from Mrs Berkeley Ward's farm have left taking wagons and horses—and some have gone from town. Last night our town had quite a number of yankee pickets in it—dressed in citizens clothes finding out if any of our men from the army had come home. They do all the mischief, for they are helping off the servants as rapidly as possible. We will not be able to make any crop. I know not where our *flour* is to come from. It is now selling at $10. and we cannot urge Mr F. to make any purchase. I think it advisable for him to buy in Flour, Sugar, tea, coffee, Salt and many such while they can be had at reasonable prices, but he does not seem willing to buy up at such a dis count—my fears are that in the *fall* we will not be able to buy—there will be no *flour*. It takes a great deal to supply our family, children *eat* all the time—we have been blessed with every comfort and even luxuries, we know not want—but we do not know what times are in store for us—and of course we are concerned. Mr F. cannot make any money now like he has been—he does all he can—he is cheerful under it all. I hope the day is not far distant when good times will return to him and repay him for all his kindness to me and mine these troubled times—that is the reason I say—take care of your hard earned money for it will be needed at home—give to the suffering but be careful not to be wasteful—

I am anxious about yourself—I hope you do not stint yourself in regard to clothes. Keep yourself well clad.

I must tell you something worthy of print in Richmond. Mrs Withers had a Secession flag on her house—the girls had put it up. The yankees spied it Saturday and one of them a youth about 16—attempted to get it, and Mrs Withers seeing him go up the flight of steps, waited until he got to the top when she reached up and knocked him off—he fell from the top down to the bottom, some 50 soldiers were around the house and they raised a shout of laughter at him—he halloed for help. They then demanded the flag I believe whereupon Kate Withers[97] the daughter had it taken down and tore it into small pieces and threw it at them saying they should not have it to say—it was surrendered—They sent her a *Union* flag—she intended to drape in mourning and return it to them but that day she heard through your letter her brother had been captured and she was too much troubled to engage in it—I would like to have witnessed the knock down—

The children are all doing well. On Sunday one of the yankees came down to the bottom of the garden while Sister was gathering strawberries and asked her to sell him some strawberries—she told him it was the *Sabbath*, and moreover she did not wish to sell them. Sister said she saw he was anxious for some, said it reminded him of home. She had some in her dish—and Frank being near she told him to hand the gentleman the dish—he was an officer and said oh! no he could not take them—she told him he was welcome[,] he took them and after distributing them among many of the soldiers he returned the dish with 50 cts (Silver). Sister told him please to take the money—he said he put it there for the little boy—and asked her to give it to him—Frank refused to take it, said he did not want *yankee money*—Sister in order not to give offense begged Frank to receive it. He did so but very unwillingly—he brought it up in my room and told me it was yankee money—he did not want it. I could take it if I would give him money like you had in Richmond—he hates the yankees—won't talk to one of them. Willie never wants to give them any thing to eat, tells us no—it will only give them more strength and help to fatten them to stand marching to get where our brave men are and shoot them. Jessie she says I don't love the yankees—we asked her why she disliked them, she says they are so hateful—and cause they are fools—we tried to impress upon her it was wrong to call them such names.

---

[97] Katherine Elizabeth Withers (1846-1933), daughter of Jesse H. and Frances E. (Carter) Withers, sister of Sarah ("Sallie") Withers, ward of Mr. & Mrs. John W. Finks. Katherine ("Kate") Withers married March 25, 1869, Richard H. Bell of Staunton, Va. (J.K.G.)

Mr. Charles Diggs[98] will leave for Richmond on Thursday—and will give you this letter. He is going to bring his son home. You must write a long letter with all the news—as persons will expect to hear some thing worthwhile when they learn I have a letter. Your letters give general satisfaction throughout the town.

Now I want you to inquire of Mr Diggs how long he will stay and where you can find him to get him to bring me a letter and a small package if you are able to make the purchase. Well I want you to look up some remnants of Cloth for Willie & Frank for winter—*don't give exorbitant prices* tho'. Nice *woollen jeans* or *good heavy cloth, gray* or *brown*, be sure you get it heavy, it takes 1 yard and ¼ for pants for Frank and the same for jacket, and 1 yard and ¾ for pants for Willie—the same for jacket—it takes the same for *Jackets* for each boy as for the pants—get *gray*, or *brown dont want black, black dont suit for children*. You can see what bargains you can get, should you not be able to get it in time for Mr Diggs, you will have other chances. Sister went out to day and not one yd. of woollen goods can be had in town—Frank wont need quite as heavy cloth or *Jeans* as Willie—Do the best you can, but don't give too high price—1 yard and ¾ for pants and 1 yd and ¾ for jacket for Willie, 1 yd. and ¼ for Frank's pants & 1 yd. & ¼ for Jacket—Write me about it Wednesday. We have just heard that Jackson has whipped Shields at Ponds Gap in Augusta Co near Crawfords Springs—would that Jackson could be reinforced with about 50,000 men he would work wonders—We are anxious to hear from Johnson.

Grand Ma is the same, dont seem to gain much strength. She looks very thin and feeble. She seems much disturbed, and fears we will not flour the coming fall and will sell very high. She is for buying up barrels of flour if she had the money—she says it will be like Coffee & Sugar has been—Take good care of yourself. Don't take cold. We all want to see you but must abide our time. I feel that you want to see us and your dear little ones. Time be not far in the distance when the chance will come for you to see us all—dont venture home at present—I would not enjoy the visit fearing the yankees would *nab you*. Love to all[.] Kisses from all your dear ones to their dearest Papa—

Your affec daughter
S.E.C.

Thursday—I had finished my letter, but Jessie says I must write and tell Dr. Hamme she calls him Daddy yet—says she has Papa in Rich—Daddy here—and Dr. Hamme is nother Daddy in Rich where Papa is—she wishes he would come home and bring her some Pea nuts and candy marbles—she loves him—

We have just heard of Jackson's victory over Shields and Freemont taking Shields Artillery and Capturing 1300 men—But we are grieved to learn of the death

---

[98] Charles W. Diggs, Jr., was living in St. Louis, Mo. at the outbreak of the war. He returned to Warrenton, enlisted in the Warrenton Rifles (Co. K, 17th Va); after receiving a severe wound at the Battle of Seven Pines, he was unable to serve further in the infantry; transferred to the Black Horse Cavalry, June 1, 1863. Promoted to Captain and served as aide-de-camp to General William H. Payne until the end of the war. Returned to Missouri where he was a successful merchant and died in January 1907 in Moberly, Missouri. *Confederate Veteran Magazine*, V. 15, No. 5 (May, 1907; Reprint: Broadfoot's Bookmark, Wendell, N.C.), p. 240. (J.K.G.)

of Col. Turner Ashby. He was so brave on the field of battle and his men placed such implicit confidence in him. We mourn his loss—

We are in great trouble to day. Last night about two—light Cinda was missing—and we are pained to believe she has gone to the Yankee Camp. To us, she has ever said she disliked the yankees, and did not care to go on the street when they were about. Generally told us of all the servants leaving their homes and would remark on their ingratitude and say how wrong in them to go where they could not be benefitted. We put confidence in her knowing she was free—But on Sunday last while King's division was in town she went on the street and on her return remarked to Lute that an Officer asked her if she would go with him and wait on his wife—showed her a *ring* he would give her—she said she told him she preferred to remain here and like our soldiers best—Whether this was an inducement or she was taught of George (Aunt Lucy's son) we cannot tell. She has gone from us—she took part of her wearing clothes, took Mr Fink's large carpet bag, two articles of Lute's clothing, and the white muslin dress of mine I was married in—She has asked me for it before but I told her I wished to keep it—I am sorry about my dress—not on account of the worth, but I *valued* it.

Since Cinda has left we begin to distrust Aunt Lucy. Altho she speaks well and has behaved well, Sister wants to know if it will not be best to give her her *freedom* and *hire* her—she knows very well that she can be free by leaving and when she leaves, her place cannot be supplied by any *hired one*, and then it is so uncertain if you can even hire a servant these times, so few are left in town. We are much troubled if Aunt Lucy leaves of course she will take her children with her—the loss will be very great to the family. We would like to know what to do for the best.

Mrs Watson asks you to be so kind as to find out if her brothers John and Henry are in Richmond or Fredericksburg if you can—she cannot hear from them since our Army has fallen back—

Willie seems to love his school and teacher. He has improved. She charges $2.50 per month—The little fellow has $3.35 cts in Silver[.] I offered $5 in Richmond note for it—to send to Alexandria for some Winter clothes for him, but he will not part with it. Please if you can make it convenient look about for the Woollen Jeans for the boys clothes, they will need them as soon as the fall sets in. Frank has worn all of his. At the same time I would not wish you to give an exorbitant price.

Tell Dr. Hamme Frank wants to see him, says he loves him. Sister and all at home send respects to him and would welcome him back to Warrenton if he could but come—

Mr. Sedgwick tells me you are looking very well and are in excellent good spirits. May you continue to enjoy your health. Be careful about your clothing. Get all you need. Buy shirts if you need them. Try and look nice at all times. Have you made any purchases—if so, write me all you have nice.

Good bye and God bless and preserve you. All join me in love & kisses.

> Your affec & devoted daughter
> S.E.C.

Dearest Papa

Though feeling rather too tired to sit down to writing to night I feel that duty to you requires me to exert every nerve so as not to permit an opportunity to go by without sending a letter to you giving you information.

Persons in town are receiving letters every week from Richmond. They are directed to the Care of Cumberland George[,] Culpepper[,]⁹⁹ and he sends them on to Warrenton. Mr Finks says you must write *twice* a week, direct your letters to him to the care of Rev. Cumberland George—Culpepper Co H. and I will get them. And moreover he begs of you to cut *slips* with the *news* from the Richmond papers and enclose in your letters. He is very much disappointed on opening my letters to find that you are so forgetful when he has written to you to send them. You have no idea how bad off we are for papers—cant hear what is going on but through the Northern press—now please cut out the news and have it ready always to enclose in each letter you send to me. Mr F. will be gratified.

Well, there is no jesting in the matter—we certainly have a noble, brave, and daring General in *Stonewall Jackson*.¹⁰⁰ Look at his victorious battles—I understood at this last battle near Winchester on last Sunday and Monday he captured and killed *four Generals* so it is reported. Mr Charles Bragg arrived from Alexandria this evening and asserts that every Church in Alex. is now occupied by the *wounded* from the last two battles under Jackson—that he saw upwards of 100 soldiers being brought into Alex. wounded—some having had their arms shot off—some hands, others fingers— he conversed with one of them who told him that upwards of *1200 lay dead on the field* numbers were deserting, saying they would never encounter Jackson again—they were heard to say that 7 trains of Cars passed on the Manassas Road from Front Royal with well and wounded soldiers—

Mr. Bragg understood for the fact that Genl. McClellan is now in Washington endeavouring to be rid of his position near Richmond—giving as his reasons, his inability to meet the enemy and gain the day on the Peninsula—This is important news if it be true—

Several gentlemen and ladies left for Alex on last Saturday. Mrs Combs¹⁰¹ being one of the party—It appears that every thing was going off nicely, they had purchased their goods and the gentlemen had started with their wagons ahead leaving Mrs Combs sitting in the Rockaway waiting for Miss Fannie Beckham—the wagons moved on some distance out from Alex. when they were overtaken by some Federal

---

⁹⁹ The Rev. Cumberland George (1797-1863) Baptist minister of Culpeper and Fauquier Counties. He was the first Pastor of the Warrenton Baptist Church, organized by him in 1849. (J.K.G.)

¹⁰⁰ A reference to Jackson's recent back-to-back victories on June 8 at Cross Keys and June 9 at Port Republic over U.S. Generals Fremont and Shields in the Shenandoah Valley. (J.E.D.)

¹⁰¹ Mrs. Margaret Combs, aged 45, was living in the home of John L. Fant, at 50 Culpeper Street, in 1860. Very little is known of Mrs. Combs except that she is mentioned in all accounts of Warrenton during the war and praised for her endeavors toward nursing and aiding the wounded brought to the town. (J.K.G.)

Officers, who commenced searching the wagons and also the gentlemen for *letters*, asked them if they were not in company with Mrs Combs—they said yes—and was wondering why she was not meeting up with them. The officers replied she had been *arrested* and was now being *searched* at the Provost Marshal's office by females and that a half bushel of letters for persons in the Southern Army had been found on her. (She had bought $100 worth of *medicine* for Mr Finks[.]) They said she also had medicine sufficient for two regiments and it had been all taken from her—(I am in hopes Mr F. will be able to regain it by writing for it) They did not say when she would be released. They searched the wagons and gentlemen but found no letters and they were allowed to go on to their respective homes. We feel troubled about Mrs C. but as she is a strong minded woman she will make the best of it—

I read a letter from Cash Cologne to day—his Mother it seems had been urging him to get a furlough and come home. He wrote and told her Furloughs were out of the question now, and moreover he would not think of leaving at this critical time when it was important for every man to be at his post—and before he would have as one, or some had done and be disgraced—he would remain even tho he know [sic] he would die—die, or live it was his duty to remain. Mr Jordan Saunders[102] read the letter and was so much pleased with this spirit Cash exhibited, that he told his father *not to urge him home*—that should he fall on the battle field he would have his remains brought home and interred at his own expense also a Stone erected with his words engraved on it, he preferred death to being disgraced. Cash wrote that when in Richmond, you gave him $5. He said he was much in need of it at that time and was very grateful to you for your kindness—Since then he had been paid off and has some by him—Mr Cologne seemed to appreciate your kindness—He is the only one now in town who has any spirit—and hearing Grand Ma needed some, he sent her a pint bottle. It is selling $1. per pint. I pray the Good Being to preserve the life of such a noble boy and may he return home to be a comfort to his parents.

We were sorry William Pattie induced his son to remain at home—better far for him to return back again. I understand Mr Cologne has an idea of going to Richmond on some business—if he has room I shall send you some of your summer clothes—you have scarcely needed them as yet.

The children are all suffering with colds. the weather has been so damp and cold. Lucy Lee has a severe cold—but is bright and playful with it. She is fat and is a good child. Willie, Frank and Jessie live in the strawberry bed—they never tire of eating them. Willie considers himself a big boy these days and will do all the climbing up into cherry trees and gathering cherries for the little ones.

We sent for Daniel Warner to cut Jessie's hair and the poor little soul was frightened out of her wits—she thought he would hurt her—but after a while she became more reconciled and now she looks like a *boy, hair cut short*. I have had a very severe attack of head ache, but to day I am much better—they do not last as long but are very painful.

---

[102] Jordan Saunders lived, after the war, between Warrenton and Fauquier Springs, where he died in 1875, testate. (J.K.G.)

Dr. Chilton with some dozen of our citizens went after *three* yankees who were robbing on Robert Scott's farm—the *yankees* were *deserters* and hearing of it went to Jefferson and give themselves up—Dr C. proposed to take them to the *yankee* camp—but they intreated him not, asked to be sent to Richmond. they were sent.

You will no doubt be surprised to learn I have Mollie Anderson with me again. She asked me to take her back promising to remain. They are objects of charity. Since Mrs A's sons have been in the army, she has had no support. They sent her money from Manassas—but seems as if she cannot hear from them since the army left Manassas—

I hope you have made yourself comfortable in the way of clothing. I am anxious about you in that respect. Be particular. Don't give away more than what is right—we have much at home at this time to demand your means in time to come. But at the same time I would not have you suppose I objected to your doing good among the wounded but you can't do for all.

Grand Ma is looking feeble and seems not to gain any strength.

Children and all join in sending a bushel of love & kisses to our dearest Papa.

May God bless you and preserve you from sickness & danger until it pleases Him we shall meet again. I am much troubled about Charleston and home people. I will write if I have the time.

Good bye my dearest husband.

Your affec daughter
S.E.C.

Lycurgus Washington Caldwell to Susan Emeline Jeffords Caldwell

Richmond, June 22nd 1862

Dear Daughter

I have waited till the last moment before writing to you hoping that something of interest might transpire for me to communicate. But beyond occasional skirmishing, concerning which I wrote you through Triplett & Bronaugh, nothing has happened on our lines here which deserves mention.—The papers which I enclosed (under cover of letter envelope) advises you fully of the bold dash of Stewart's[103] [sic] Cavalry along the whole rear of McClellan's lines during which foray they captured some 150 prisoners, squandered a battallion of 300 Cavalrymen & burned wagons, publications, and three transports worth from $300,000 to $1,000,000 to the Enemy.—I have heard it said here, but cannot vouch for it, that a portion of the

---

[103] Stewart's [sic] Cavalry: this was Gen. J. E. B. Stuart's ride around McClellan's army, east of Richmond, June 12-15, 1862. (J.K.G.)

cavalry captured was a part of the famous corps which attacked Capt. Marr's[104] company at Fairfax Ct. House when the war first commenced.—Among the prisoners however was a Washington Clerk who was wont to hail from Mississippi named *Jewell* (a *precious* scoundrel). He was indebted to Jeff Davis for his Clerkship & had an inexhaustible store of love for Southern rights & institutions. He now turns up a Pa. Yankee cavalry captain. The papers sent you also tell you of a spirited fight on James Island in which the Yankees were gallantly back beaten by our troops.— The names of participants you will read & maybe recognize a number of them.—In a skirmish nearby here last Thursday Capt. Cuthbert was wounded. I did not see that any of his company were hurt; but that some 40 or 50 Georgians were.—I have forgotten the number of ours killed.—An old gentleman went down from here Friday to look after his son, and tells this story upon his return which the papers print. In one of our tents lay a Yankee Capt. mortally wounded. Approached by the old man the Yankee said—"Sir, when I came here I expected to see hard service & maybe meet with gallant foe men but I was not prepared to fight such material as I encountered yesterday.—One of my men & a young Georgian grappled in a hand to hand fight.— My man called for help, but before it could reach him was slain.—Three others then went up & demanded that the Georgian surrender, but nothing daunted he refused & actually managed to kill the three.—I then demanded that he lay down his arms. He refused & I shot him down; but before he died he turned & fired on me, inflicting this mortal wound; and to my knowledge I am the fifth man—who fell before that single soldiers fire.["]—The name of the Georgian is not known.—Our troops have been drawn up in battle array several times during the past week, and rumors of general Engagements imminent are talked of by newsmongers every day.—Genl. Price has been here & may be here now—for aught I know to the contrary; but Beauregard never has been & I dont believe will come although the Dispatch says he is en route for Richmond. I do not believe Hallecks army will come here as some anticipate or that it will go to Washington as the Yankee papers state.—It dares not leave the west so long as Beauregard is in that section.—A withdrawal would lose them all cities in Tenn. and Mo.—One gentleman tells me he is most positively assured Stonewall with 50000 men is at Hanover junction threatening McClellan's rear—that he has seen one of Jackson's Captains, etc. Another less credulous gentleman laughs at the story & says if Jackson was there he would have engaged the enemy before now & permitted no stragglers to leave his lines for this City. What is going to be done is all surmise.—This much is certain[,] the Govt. has brought back here all the public papers which it ordered away a month or so ago. I therefore infer as I have previously written you that the Authorities here are quite surprised of being able to hold this City—Miss Withers' conduct was most heroine & deserves a place in history.—Before this she has probably learned that her brother escaped the Yankees and is with his old comrades. All of the Black Horse troop have got back

---

[104] Captain John Quincy Marr, a prominent Warrenton citizen who was a graduate of and instructor at Virginia Military Institute, as well as Sheriff in Warrenton, was Commander of the Warrenton Rifles at the war's beginning. He became the first Confederate officer killed in action on June 1, 1861 in a skirmish with Union troops at Fairfax C.H. He is buried in the Warrenton Cemetery. (J.K.G.)

except Marsh James, Jno. Newhouse, Robert McCormick, F. Childs, Dick Lewis, John Porter, Brown Willis, & Squib Glasscock [sic].[105]—I wrote you to this effect before, but my letter via Madison C.H. may not have reached you.—I also wrote you Dick Towles was not hurt.—Tilman Weaver is still sick—(consumptive)—and should be discharged. Tom Sanders[106] [sic] is at La. Hospital sick. He is able to go about the streets & expects to go to Danville in next batch of convalescents shipped there.—Frank Jenkins[107] walks all about & has gone (Saturday) to Lynchburg to stay with Cud Spilman.—Alex Day[108] reached Greiner's hospital & he is sick. He has been complaining a week or so of camp fever & loss of appetite.—Dr Fisher does not think him seriously sick.—Allan Carter died there of typhoid fever last week.—Tom Hanback[109] who had apparently only a scalp wound died there (Greiner's) the 21st just. He was walking about for two weeks or more, but grew worse instead of better & finally had a fit. The Drs then trepanned his skull & found the inner part broken & pressing on the brain; several pieces of loose bone were removed; but yesterday he had another fit & died. Examination post-mortem then disclosed unquestionably that his death was caused by his wound.—Eli Fisher[110] and Willie Foster[111] will go to Madison C.H. Tuesday.—Both are doing well. They have doubtless written home.—If I can raise a paper I will send it to Mr F. in A.M. I send you some Yankee money ($14). Tell Mr F. soap & letter paper will command almost any price here. $500 or $1000 worth would pay 4 times cost prices. Love to all.

Yours affectionately,
L.W. Caldwell

Your last letters were worth a heap to me & well written.—I write in my room & tis hot & close & no good materials to use.—I have exhibited the flag. It is pronounced pretty & will be prized by the little girl when I fix it for her. I will write you hereafter about it.—No goods here to buy for children. It is dark now.—Good bye for a short time.—I wrote the children.

L.W.C.

---

[105] Members of the Black Horse Cavalry (Co. H, 4th Va. Cav.) mentioned by Caldwell have been identified by H. Lynn Hopewell, historian of the Black Horse Cavalry: Marsh James - Marshall K. James, 2nd Lt., Sept. 1, 1863; Jno. Newhouse - John P. Newhouse, enl. April 25, 1861; Robert McCormick - Robert E. McCormick, enl. April 25, 1861, promoted to Corporal; F. Childs - Francis A. Childs, enl. March 15, 1862, paroled May 5, 1865 at Fairfax Court House; Dick Lewis - enl. Apr. 25, 1861, promoted to Sgt.; John Porter - John M. Porter, enl. Apr. 25, 1861, paroled May 6, 1865 at Winchester; Brown Willis - Charles Brown Willis, enl. Mar. 15, 1862, captured May 28, 1862 at Hanover Court House with several of his comrades, released from Ft. Delaware, June 15, 1865; Squib Glasscock [sic] - nickname of Orlando F. Glascock, of Kingsley Mills, Pr. Wm. County, enl. Mar. 5, 1862, captured at Hanover C.H. May 31, 1862. (J.K.G.)

[106] Tom Saunders - Thomas B. Saunders, Warrenton Rifles, Co. K., 17th Va. Regt. Wounded at Suffolk, April, 1863 and discharged Aug. 22, 1864. (J.K.G.)

[107] Frank Jenkins - Pvt. George F. Jenkins, Warrenton Rifles. A roster of the company shows him absent, wounded. (J.K.G.)

[108] Pvt. Alexander Day, Warrenton Rifles, died in the service, July 6, 1862. (J.K.G.)

[109] There is no available record on Dick Towles, Tilman Weaver, Allan Carter or Tom Hanback. (J.K.G.)

[110] John Eli Fisher, Warrenton Rifles, Co. K, 17th Va. Regt., was wounded at the Battle of Seven Pines. (J.K.G.)

[111] Sgt. William G. Foster, Warrenton Rifles, enl. July 24, 1861 at Manassas. He was wounded at Seven Pines and admitted to General Hospital No. 18 (formerly Greaner's Hospital) on June 2, 1862. (J.K.G.)

Susan Emeline Jeffords Caldwell to Lycurgus Washington Caldwell

Warrenton Via

Wednesday June 25th 1862

Dearest Papa

I wrote you on Monday last and sent it by some unknown friend who was going to Richmond. This morning my inclination leads me to write again per chance Mr Bronaugh will pass through on his way to Richmond. Mr F. made him promise he would stop with him on his return home. He had come for his wife who is now in Washington. I expect that put you in the notion of wishing to send for me, but we must not be in haste—wait until the times are better settled—don't have us leave a comfortable home and be subjected to trouble and inconvenience—were I alone I would not be from you, but the comfort of the little ones has to be taken into consideration—and it has been solely for their good that we have sacrificed the pleasure of the society of each other for the past twelve months. But perhaps the time is not far distant when we shall be once again reunited—it is a satisfaction even to think of. I have longed to see you if it be but for a few hours. I want to overlook and repair your clothing. I fear you have your clothes in a dilapidated condition—no one to look over them. Be particular and have some one mend them for you.

I hope Mr Charles Digges has reached Richmond—he had two letters for you, one with a Secession flag in it for you—We have had much rain—it will injure the wheat and make flour high the coming year. Mr F. should lay in a good supply at once—but we can't persuade him—How is Dr. Hamme? The children talk often about him. The weather is charming to day—more like a November day. We have had no warm weather as yet.

Grand Ma is looking very thin and she seems to suffer from weakness—she dont gain any strength or flesh—

The children are doing well. They all have colds but have not been sick. Lucy Lee has had a severe cold, but she is as sprightly as ever—I intended having her vaccinated, but the Dr. said must wait until she was well of her cold.

We were much alarmed about Frank a few nights ago. He had gone to bed and was aroused by a fly buzzing about his ear—he tried to fight it off—I went to him and found it was in his *ear* and could hear the buzzing but could not see it. We put whiskey in his ear and sent for the Dr. When he came he filled the ear with oil—and Frank grew easy—but we did not see the fly. The Dr. said it must have been killed by the whiskey—

I wrote you I had Mollie Anderson as nurse. She does very well, the baby has not yet learned to know her, but will soon—

Be careful of yourself—try and keep well. Buy all you need and be comfortable. Don't be too liberal with your money.

I think Bazil Suares[112] and Thomas Oxlade (Elvira's husband) are stationed on

---

[112] This was Susan's cousin, son of Harriet Jeffords Suares who was married to Benjamin C. Suares in South Carolina; Basil Suares would die of typhoid on February 4, 1863. (B.G.C.)

James Island. May they have sufficient force to repulse the vile invaders each time they make the attack.[113]

I am much troubled abut Pa and Ma leaving the City for the Country. I wish they would write to me. I dream of them and I often ask myself if I shall ever behold them face to face again on this earth. It has been 7 years since I have seen Pa and 5 since I have looked upon the face of Ma but hope keeps me bouyed up that chance may throw me in their midst when times are more prosperous.

We heard that the Confederacy has been recognized by the French Government— and that French Fleets are now in Chesapeake Bay and some other point. Can it be true?

I read a very amusing letter from a yankee girl to her Lover—some one found it in our streets. She begged him to *run* when he was in danger of being shot. Prayed that he might shoot Jeff Davis and many of the Generals closed up by saying, she wished the Union boys had such a General as *Jackson*. He was a brave General indeed.

The yankees a few in number came in Sunday morning and searched for Dr. Chilton and Mr Cologne[114]—they said they had gone out after some of their men to arrest them[,] luckily both gentlemen were out of town. Cousin Susan was very much alarmed. They searched every room in the house had their pistols loaded and ready to fire if resistance was made.

Mr F. says he understands *tobacco* is selling very high in R. You must not make a purchase unless on reasonable terms. He says you can use your own good judgment. I wish you could get me some United States money from the prisoners (not counterfeit) notes on Baltimore in exchange for some of your Confederate notes. I then could send it to Alexandria for articles I need. We have not the silver and gold— and only Virginia bank notes are taken and then dis counted at 35 per cent.

Have you tried to purchase any woolen goods for the boys winter clothes? I would not have you give extravagant prices—but if reasonable and heavy & good for the children you better get some and send by Charles Digges or Mr Cologne[,] *don't get black*. Gray or drab—any colour suitable for children (*black don't suit children*)[.]

We are all in good spirits since hearing of the where abouts of Jackson—we are now on the lookout for a very brilliant victory—Would that Beauregard could have carried out his plans—he would have gained the day if Halleck would have given him battle. But why is it that Beauregard and Johnson wait to be attacked[,] why don't they rush upon the enemy as Jackson has done?

I feel an anxiety at present in regard to my own dear native home. I was gratified to read in the paper you sent of the bravery displayed by the Soldiers on James Island.

I have no news. I intend arranging your summer clothes and will send them by

---

[113] On June 16, the Federals had mounted an offensive against Charleston, landing 6500 troops on James Island near the city, but were met and repulsed at Secessionville by Shanks Evans, with less than half as many men. Foote, *Sumter to Perryville*, p. 473. (J.M.W.)

[114] Edgar N. Cologne, Town Sergeant of Warrenton, married Oct. 10, 1838, Susan F. Cash. Susan F. Cash was the daughter of John A. Cash and Lucy Y. (Pattie) Cash. Joseph A. Jeffries said of Mr. Cologne, "he was collector and sergeant of Warrenton from my first knowing him, and continued on account of efficiency to hold the position till near the close of his life." (J.K.G.)

first opportunity. I have bought you 5 pair of nice socks, don't get them lost.

Bushel of love from all to our dear Papa.

Your affec & devoted daughter
S.E.C.

I felt mortified to learn Col. Huger has acted thus and not been ready in time to meet the emergency. I want Carolineans to do bravely.

Warrenton Via
Saturday June 29th 1862

Dearest Papa

I have just heard that I can send a letter to Richmond this morning—so I hasten to write you a few lines.

I must tell you of my disappointment on Thursday last. I had gone to the *Funeral* of old Mrs Jennings[115] at the time Mr Bronaugh arrived in town with his wife. Mr Finks sent to me for my letter I had brought up the street with me—but did not send me word Mr B. had arrived. I imagined he had met with some one on the street going to R and knowing I had a letter with me sent for it. Mr B's arrival never entered my head—altho we had been speaking of him. I sent the letter and after the funeral was over I asked Mr F. who took my letter, he said Mr B—I could scarce refrain my tears in the street. I had set my heart on seeing him, for it is a pleasure to me to meet with those who have *seen you*—and then I intended to ask the favor of him to take your *Summer clothes* which I had gotten ready to send. He was in a carriage and would not have inconvenienced him. I shed many tears, the first I have shed over a disappointment for many years—I have been trying to bear up under all disappointments philosophically—but I give up this time. I was so anxious to see him and for him to see the children. I read in the papers that Butler's proclamation[116]

---

[115] M. Lucy Jennings, widow of Thomas O. Jennings, Esq., died June 25, 1862, aged 70 years. Mrs. Jennings, nee Helm, was the second wife of Thomas O. Jennings, whom he married in Fauquier County, August 25, 1820. (J.K.G.)

[116] The women of occupied New Orleans missed no chance to show their contempt for the blue-clad invaders. Passing them on the street, they forced oncoming yankees to step into the mud. One of them, taking careful aim from an upstairs window, emptied a slopjar onto the head of Capt. David G. Farragut himself. Major General Benjamin F. Butler (U.S.A.) subsequently retaliated with a general order, directing "that hereafter when any female shall, by word, gesture or movement, insult or show contempt for any officer or soldier of the United States, she shall be regarded and held liable to be treated as a woman of the town plying her avocation."

In response, Gen. P. G. T. Beauregard (C.S.A.) issued his own general order: "Men of the South! Shall our mothers, our wives, our daughters and our sisters be thus outraged by the ruffianly soldiers of the North, to whom is given the right to treat, at their pleasure, the ladies of the South as common harlots? Arouse, friends, and drive back from our soil those infamous invaders of our homes and disturbers of our family ties!"

Overseas, Lord Palmerston remarked: "Any Englishman must blush to think that such an act has been committed by one belonging to the Anglo-Saxon race." In Richmond, President Davis branded Butler a felon, an outlaw, and, in the event of his capture, that he be "immediately executed by hanging." Ibid., p. 534. (J.M.W.)

was denounced in the English Parliament while Beauregard's was applauded—but I do not think that either England or France will come to our rescue—altho they are in favor of the Southern Confederacy—oh! how I long for this unholy war to be at an end. I know that a terrible battle is pending now near Richmond and the slaughter will be almost more than we can imagine—yet I am anxious for it to be over.—I feel as if we are not much better off now in regard to the ending of this bloody strife than we were at this time last year.—My mind is much troubled in regard to Charleston, if I could hear from home. I think some might have written to me through you before this time.

Have you met with Mr Charles Digges? I sent you a Secession flag by him— and also to ask you to purchase some woollen goods for Willie's and Frank's winter use—if you can get it at reasonable prices with you. Willie takes 3 yds and ½ for a suit of clothes. Frank takes 1 ¼ yds for Pants. Look out for some.—I expect Mr Henry Diggs can tell you of the whereabouts of Mr Charles Diggs.

We hear yesterday Blinker's[117] [sic] Division was at Flint Hill.—I expect we have nothing left at our farm—I was anxious to buy some Salt for the use of the farm—it is selling at $2.50 per sack in silver in Alex. but when brought up here it sells for $10. Goods are very cheap in Alex. but the trouble is to get them brought up. Very few will bring up goods only for their own use and to speculate. We are afraid to let Mr F. go down—

I must close—I wish I could take a trip to Richmond and see you—but I know I cannot with a young baby. Time may roll around when you can come and see us—

The children are all well. I feel truly thankful they have been so blest in health. Grand Ma does not get any better, she is just able to crawl about the house—and is very thin.

The weather is excessively warm to day—We don't get your papers unless you enclose them in your letters.

Direct your letters to Mr Finks the care of Rev. Cumberland George and he will send them to Warrenton.

Don't buy Tobacco but on reasonable terms. God bless and preserve you until we meet again. My pen is miserable. Try and get some *Federal money* & send me. Virginia money is 40 cts dis count.

Good bye we all send a bushel of love & kisses to our own dearest Papa

Your affec and devoted daughter
S.E.C.

---

[117] Brig. Gen. Louis Blenker (U.S.A.) had been with Gen. John C. Fremont in the Valley; was now on his way back to Washington. (J.E.D.)

John William Finks to Lycurgus Washington Caldwell

Warrenton July 1/62

Dear Sir

I send you a paper which contains much news. When you are done with it hand it to Smith[.]

Buy me some two hundred dollars worth of good tobacco as I presume we have so much money in Bank after Brooks check—By the by what did you do with that check and how much did you pay for the [...] sent Jessie.—

Where is Jno. & Henry English, Mrs. Watson wants to know. Say to Walter Franklin,[118] [sic] his Mother is anxious to hear from him and if he will write and send letter to me I will forward it. It is reported here that our Army has McClellan surrounded and he will be compelled to surrender, and Ewell, Early and several others of our Gen. killed came by telegraph from Gordonsville—It is generally believed but I do not believe more than half the Federal soldiers say there has been no fight—They are however now a great many troops down to McClellan about fifty thousand reported.

Write to care of JB Gorrell Druggist[,] Culpeper C.H. when you have no other choice—send papers also—

I wrote to you a few days ago the pur of Blue Moss, Quinine, Morphene, Ipecac, & Calomel & Castor Oil—Let me know—

Our Troops about fifty rode in here Sunday and had not been gone very long before two Yankees came up near town and learned the fact and they made good time back—The next day Monday some twelve rode through the street and about dark some sixty came in and engaged supper and lodging at the Hotel but while they were making arrangements for supper six of them rode up the st. and Meridith, (Mr. R. Payne's[119] Brother in Law who had been arrested a few days before now released) happened to be in town, saw them; and he put whip to his horse, and the Yankees after him they had it for three quarters of a mile but Meridith beat them. When they

---

[118] Capt. Walter E. Frankland, Co. F, 43rd Batt'n, Va. Cav. (Mosby's Rangers). He had served as a pvt. in Co. K, 17th Va. Inf. (Warrenton Rifles) from 1861 to 1862 when he was discharged. He was among the first to join Mosby in 1863. He took his parole in Winchester in late April 1865, after Mosby disbanded his command at Salem (now Marshall). After the war Capt. Frankland served for a time as postmaster at Stephens City, Va. (J.K.G.)

[119] Rice Winfield Hooe Payne (1818-1884): a member of the Warrenton Bar and known locally as Major Payne. He married America Semmes and after her death, he married Virginia Semmes. About two years before the war Mr. Payne began the construction of his home on Culpeper Street, called 'Mecca,' long celebrated for its spacious and brilliant hospitality. It was completed and occupied early in 1861. A son, Raphael S. Payne, wrote in 1896 that 'Mecca' "was the headquarters and camping-ground of some of the great generals of the northern army, having been occupied by Generals McDowell, Sumner and Russell with their staffs. The spacious drawing-room was used for planning campaigns, and members of the family today who were children then remember to have seen the walls and floors covered with charts, maps and topographical surveys. A telegraph wire, which was a great curiosity at that time, was run into the house, connecting it directly with Washington, and an operator kept on duty day and night to feel the pulse at the capital and post the Secretary of War on every movement of the Army of Northern Virginia. This same drawing-room was the scene of sorrow and suffering, as well as of bright assemblages in those anxious times. It was a hospital for the Confederate and Union soldiers alike, after the great battles at Manassas." (J.K.G.)

returned, reported that they had chased a Rebel picket out of town. The horn soon blew and they left in double quick for Manassas, thinking we had a large force near here, once the picket had gone out to report.

Bragg gives a very amusing account of the race—when Meridith hopped his horse, he says he was laying flat on his horse whipping with both hands; kicking with his feet and butting with his head, one hundred yards a head.

Billy Payne reached here on Sunday and will be well in a short time. Tell Mr. Smith Ben is at work but I am fearful he is not doing altogether right as his wagon passed through to here early the other morning home—He may have been moving off some other negroes who had run off. Inform R. Payne of M. race. He is in Richmond.

Yours
Finks

Susan Emeline Jeffords Caldwell to Lycurgus Washington Caldwell

Undated, 1862
(Fragment)

...(are they putting it into effect. For instance) Mrs Fairbanks a lady from Baltimore (milliner) who occupies Mrs Schackleford's[120] [sic] house has been ordered to move out, and give up the house to a Capt, for the accommodation of his family[,] she asked permission to retain two rooms, and it was coldly granted—they have taken possession of every thing belonging to Mrs Schackleford—even to the *cooking* stove— use all the vegetables from the garden them selves—say it is *Rebel* property and it belongs to them since the confiscation bill[121] has passed.—I understand they have taken Rice Payne's house as the Head Quarters of the General—and Dr Bacon's seminary as a Hospital—they have turned their *mules* into Dr Bacon's garden, Mrs Fant's and all the lots are now filled with their horses and mules—our land will be laid waste and we have no hope of a crop the coming season—*Keith's factory* was burned yesterday—and every barrel of Flour taken from John White—and the mill dam opened to allow the water to run in—the destruction of property is awful to think on and have it to realize they destroy as they march on—even stone fences are destroyed. Geary's division or brigade has been through. Lieut. Tourrison called— he told us Mr Mackey was at home in Philadelphia very ill of Typhoid fever—was

---

[120] Benjamin H. and Rebecca Shackleford, were ages 40 and 29 respectively at the time of the 1860 census. Mr. Shackleford listed his occupation as lawyer and farmer, with real estate valued at $10,940 and personal property valued at $25,190. (J.M.W.)

[121] The confiscation act was passed in July, 1862, and punished "traitors" by confiscating their property, including slaves who "shall be deemed captives of war and shall be forever free." The act was important as a symbol of what the war was becoming—a war to overturn the southern social order as a means of reconstructing the union. McPherson, *Battle Cry*, p. 500. (J.M.W.)

taken home in a delirious state not expected to recover. Lieu. T. seemed sick and tired of the war—he heartily wished he was at home—he seemed very sad and much changed.

You would scarcely recognize our town—streets are filled with soldiers—and every little shantee filled with goods brought up by the dutch and all kinds of yankeedom. Most of our stores are closed—The yankees only sell for specia—and we do not patronize them of course—I could not be seen in one of their stores—

The Stars and Stripes are flying from the Court House—hard indeed is it for us to bear with any degree of patience. Very seldom are the ladies seen on the streets, only on very urgent business—Mr F. will not permit us to go out[,] not even the children—in fact we do not desire to go out—we have been compelled to go out now and then, but we have never walked under the *flag*.

The cars are running twice a day from Washington—the very whistling of the cars makes the heart sick[.] The telegraph wires are in operation—and to look out one would suppose we would never have our town again in our possession[,] but we never allow our minds to dwell on the dark side of the picture that is now turned towards us—the cloud will soon disperse and the bright sun shine will be ours again—It may be we will have to endure the burthen for months, but help will come if we trust in Almighty God—We are now in their power and God grant it may be short lived—oh! may we be freed before the winter sets in—wood is scarce—what we will do when winter comes we cannot now tell—we must say with the Good Book—"Sufficient unto the day is the evil thereof"—My heart grows sad when I give up my mind to dwell on our condition—cut off from all communication—I could even bear it better if I could send you letters to comfort you in this day of trial, even tho I received none in return from you. If I knew your mind could be relieved of the anxiety for us, I could try to bear[.] When, oh! when are we to be blessed with the society of each other. God give us grace to bear our trials with submission. I have no patience with Genl's Magruder and Huger—Huger particularly—I have little faith in him—I was astonished he was assigned such a post after his conduct at *Roanoke*— had he brought up his force in time McClellan would have been surrounded—his men own it. How important was it then to have had an Officer in whom confidence had been placed. I am mortified to know Huger is from So. Carolina[.]

Mr. Sedwick has returned—he said you were well and you were to meet him at such a time—but he left a day earlier than he expected and did not meet with you. I was sorry but such circumstances cannot be controled[.] We must be satisfied with hearing from our friends verbally. Mr S. left his son near Jefferson and came on fearing to bring him to Warrenton—but the yankees pushed on to Jefferson and took him prisoner[,] brought him to Warrenton and *paroled* him as he was wounded in his right arm and was unfit for military service—so he now has two of his sons at home. A few days ago several prisoners were brought in, they were captured at Culpepper Co House. George Shumate[122] was one, they were put in the Court House and strictly

---

[122] George Harden Shumate, Cpl., Co. H, 4th Va. Cav. (Black Horse Cavalry) enlisted April 25, 1861, and discharged, according to roster compiled by H. Lynn Hopewell, Oct. 31, 1861 on account of deafness. George H. Shumate was the husband of Mary N. (Ogilvie) Shumate whom he married May 23, 1853. (J.K.G.)

guarded. Most of them, 7 in number, were without coats—the gentlemen and ladies supplied them with clothing and eatables—they were taken to Washington. I could freely shed tears on account of Mr Shumate—he was not allowed even to write to his family & had not time sufficient between his being brought to town and his leaving in the *cars* for Washington for his wife to learn of the news of his capture so as to have come in town. I am sorry for both of them—separation is too painful under easy circumstances, but doubly so under these severe trials. I hope they will soon be exchanged. They have captured about 17 I think in the past few days—5 of Radford's Cavalry were brought in to day—captured at Madison C.H. Willie knew them, went to see them and took them breakfast, Willie was very anxious for them to come home with him, could not at first understand why they were not allowed to go out until explained to him. He grieves at our soldiers being taken[,] prays for Jackson and all his friends in the army every night.

We have no *sabbath* now—wagons and troops are passing on every day alike—we have no preaching—and even now the sabbath school has ceased—We often wish we were out of hearing of the yankee nation—but where shall we go News has come that the Federals have possession of *Gordonsville*, taken without opposition—I had hoped we had force sufficient to hold it—

I am very anxious to hear from Charleston. Would that you had sent Mother's letter by mail[,] then I would have been able to have gotten it before the arrival of Genl. Pope's division.[123]

We have all been blest with a good share of health. The children have been vaccinated and taken well. Lucy Lee did not mind it, made her a little fretful—

Jessie talks about you and asks if the yankees have you the reason you dont come home—Frank says he *loves you* the best of all and wishes you could come—Willie[,] he wants to go to Richmond to see you. I tell them all we must be content, you cannot venture now to Warrenton[,] we will have to wait until the yankees leave. Would that Jackson could be spared and have a sufficient force to go into Maryland—then Pope would tell us Good Bye.

Warrenton Fauquier Co.
Monday August 12th 1862

Dearest Papa

Having heard through a friend to day that possibly a letter might reach you if one was sent by some one of the Federal Officers en route for Culpepper[,] he may find some means of having it conveyed across the lines—I hail the opportunity of writing and may Heaven's choicest blessing rest upon the unknown stranger friend who may forward it to you—should it reach you it will relieve your anxious heart in regard to the welfare of your dear family. Long have been the days, weeks, and now

---

[123] In July, 1862, Maj. Gen. John Pope (U.S.A.) arrived from the west to take command of the newly designated Army of Virginia, formed from the divisions of Banks, Fremont and McDowell that had chased Stonewall Jackson so futilely in the Shenandoah Valley. McPherson, *Battle Cry*, p. 501. (J.M.W.)

months to you since you have been waiting for a letter from home. God speed this one to you is my earnest heart felt prayer. May you be made happy by its perusal.

Your dear little ones have been in the enjoyment of excellent health during the summer. Since this extreme warm weather has set in Jessie & Frank have had a slight attack of fever—from heat only sick a few days. Both are now well again. Willie is well. Lucy Lee enjoys excellent health. She is very interesting, can say a few words— would that you could see her. Perhaps the time is not far in the distance when we shall be once again a united family. The children inquire daily when they shall see dear Papa. They send you love and kisses by the bushel.

Rest assured dearest Papa that we are all well and comfortable in our home. We have not wanted for anything. We have all the comforts of life—all, all, I want now is, that I could hear from you as I have heretofore been doing, to be assured of your good health. I know it would not be well for the children to be in a City at this season of the year, and that you cannot be here with us—so that for these reasons I submit to separation—and would not murmur could I but hear from you sometimes.

To quiet your mind the money sent me came safely to hand.

I cannot say if you will have the pleasure to peruse these few hasty lines (I feel as if I could write you a volume tis so long since I have written to you) but should good fortune favor us—and you get this, rest assured we are more comfortable here than we could be any where else—and if I could but know you were well and your mind freed from over anxious cares on our account[,] all would be well with me. Hope is the anchor of my soul and I do take strong hold on it.

I feel that brighter days are in store for us and some day we shall be a united happy family. God bless and preserve you dearest one.

Your affec daughter
S.E.C.

Monday night. The children had a package of very nice candy given them this afternoon. Some of the candies had the motto—"Hope on, Hope ever" Willie was anxious to have one piece sent to you in this letter. He I supposed thought the sentiment would cheer you—I told him I had to send it open and it would be lost.

Sister says my letter is like the Irishmen's—made up with a great many "if's"[.]

The little ones are all asleep—May God protect and preserve their lives till you are permitted to meet with them again.

All join me in love to you. Good night.

May you be preserved through all danger and enjoy your health.

The weather is excessively warm.

Your affec daughter
S.E.C.

Monday August 18th 1862

Dearest Papa

How much pleasure it has been to me to sit down alone in my room and pen my thoughts to you knowing my letter would soon reach you and the contents afford you comfort while you were absent from loved ones. Now I write when I hear of an opportunity, but I cannot know if you ever receive one—*Oh this cruel war. God grant it may soon end*, and families be once again re-united and spend their remaining days happy.

I sent you a letter by a stranger friend of the Federal Army last week, he promised to mail it or send it should opportunity offer. Would that I could know if you have received it, for you are anxious to hear from us. I am writing this morning hoping by some means this may come to hand and you be made aware of our very comfortable condition. We have not wanted for any of the necessaries of life—in fact we are living about as usual. Since the Federal Soldiers have been in our town Mr F. has taken in a good amount of Northern Money which has enabled him to make purchases in groceries—we have a good supply on hand, particularly coffee—We have much to be grateful for—

During the sojourn of Genl. Pope's army in our town and country I must say we were treated kindly and they were all respectful and gentlemanly. We had occasion to meet with them almost daily—for they would call for vegetables and milk—paid in silver and gold. Sister made about $20 in gold for honey and milk—Whenever we conversed with them in regard to Genl. Pope's order,[124] they seemed mortified and said such means would only swell the Southern army and give new life to the Soldiers. Many of the poor fellows were anxious to get home once again—had no idea the war would have continued so long when they volunteered. A very nice gentleman from New York (a Civilian) we became acquainted with and he became very much interested for Mr F. He said if the Citizens were to keep quiet, he did not think Genl. Pope's order would be carried out—he was a kind generous hearted Union man and truly sympathized with us in our condition and it was *he who sent my letter to you through one of the Federal Officers*—He was particularly kind to the children—and on parting with them the day he left for New York—he placed $5 in the hands of both boys.

The soldiers of the 9th New York were gentlemen—they were two soldiers from Massachusetts that were much interested in. They used to call for milk & vegetables—on having orders to leave for Culpepper one of them called to bid us "Good bye" (he was not 21 years) and asked permission to leave a *gold* dollar with Jessie to remember him by—he left with his eyes filled with tears—he wished he was

---

[124] Among a series of general orders issued during mid and late July, Pope announced that his troops (then in and around Warrenton and Culpeper) were expected to live off the enemy's country: "Vouchers will be given to the owners [of confiscated supplies], stating on their face that they will be payable at the conclusion of the war, as upon sufficient testimony being furnished that such owners have been loyal citizens of the Union states since the date of the vouchers."

Sabotage or guerilla activities were to be dealt with in an exceedingly modern manner: "If a soldier or legitimate follower of the army be fired upon from any house the house shall be razed to the ground, and the inhabitants sent prisoners to the headquarters of this army... Any persons detected in such outrages ... shall be shot, without awaiting civil process." F. E. Vandiver, *Mighty Stonewall* (McGraw-Hill, New York, 1957), p. 327. He also issued orders "authorizing his officers to seize the rebel property without compensation, to shoot captured guerillas who had fired on Union troops, to expel from occupied territory any civilians who refused to take the oath of allegiance, and to treat them as spies if they returned." McPherson, *Battle Cry*, p. 501. (J.M.W.)

going home to his Mother—The other was an elderly man—he eat some dinner[,] one day came to the house hungry and tired—and Sister invited him to eat, we had just finished dinner—he at first refused, but at last consented—after he finished he turned to Sister and said Good Lady how could you find it in your heart to ask me an enemy to sit down at your table to eat your meat and bread—he says it choked me, I could hardly eat[,] my feelings were so tried[,] he was truly grateful and on going insisted to have one of the boys keep a *gold* dollar, saying when you look at this remember an old warrior gave it to you—one who sat down at your table and partook of your Aunt's hospitality—at the same time had left his home with the intention perhaps of killing even your own father if he is in the army unawares—he brushed away his tears and left—We have never seen him since—

We have not been disturbed in the least, our corns and gardens are unmolested—others on the edge of town have been much annoyed—had their corn & potatoes stolen. Mr F. has been sick—I believe his mind was much disturbed in regard to Pope's order—he did not wish to be separated from his family—and of course he did not intend to take the oath—Many of the gentlemen are all prepared to start should it be administered. But we think now as our town has been freed from all of his Army that the order will not be carried out. My mind was much perplexed to know if I must remain or go to you—at last I concluded I would remain on the children's account. Richmond would not suit them during the Summer—had I no little ones I should be at your side—but I must think of the good of our little ones and do all in my power to preserve their health—here they have every comfort and pure air—in R—we would have to board and be subject to every inconvenience—so I concluded you would think I acted wisely to remain—If I could but hear from you to know if you were well and was satisfied in regard to our condition I would feel relieved—God grant I may hear from you soon—I think of you by day and dream of you by night.

Warrenton Fauquier
Saturday August 23rd 1862

Dearest Papa
Our town was thrown in the greatest state of excitement yesterday afternoon by the presence of Genl. Stuarts'[125] Cavalry. About 5000 rode rapidly in town. You

---

[125] Stuart's Catlett's Station Raid, August 22-23, 1862. Gen. Stuart, in retaliation for losing his hat and cloak to General Pope, got permission to raid the railroad behind Pope's lines. He crossed the Rappahannock River on the morning of the 22nd at Waterloo, with two cannons and 1500 men, encompassing the brigades of B.H. Robertson and Fitzhugh Lee. Without opposition they reached Warrenton and Auburn after dark. A storm and darkness hampered the operation until a captured Negro, who was known to Gen. Stuart, offered to lead him to Pope's baggage trains. The 9th Va. Cav. attacked the camp and captured a number of officers belonging to General Pope's staff, a large sum of money, the dispatch book and other papers of General Pope, including his personal baggage. The 1st and 5th Va. Cav. attacked another part of the camp and attempted to burn the railroad bridge over Cedar Run, but the rain-soaked timber refused to burn. The captured papers gave General Lee vital information that aided in a successful Second Manassas. Some of General Pope's uniform was put on public display in Richmond. (J.E.D.)

can better imagine than I describe the joy that soon pervaded the hearts of man, woman & child. The streets were thronged with all who could walk—and Secession flags were every where displayed. Kate Withers (Sister to the one in the Black Horse) was standing at Mrs White's corner waving her flag when a soldier rode up to her and said Genl. Stuart would like to have that flag. She cheerfully handed it to him and was pleased with the attention.

The Cavalry came in the direction of Waterloo—Some of them remained in town all night. Mr F. treated as many as he could to Soda water—until the fountain was exhausted—it was a glorious treat to them—and Coffee seemed to do them good. Genl Stuart tho' had no time to tarry to enjoy luxuries. He had come to accomplish some work and altho' the rain was pouring in torrents he hurried his men on towards Catletts station to get behind Pope's Army, which charge proved very successful. He captured 200 prisoners, the Pay Master with $25,000. and burnt many wagons, I also understood they tore up some part of the rail road track. I know not how many were killed or wounded on either side as no one could tell. One young man of Comp. E. was wounded badly, and we were told he died this morning—his name is Berry.

We supped about 16 last night, and breakfasted about 20 this morning. I tell you every hand in the house was kept busy for a Soldier's time is precious. Genl. Stuart sent for them and they had to go. They left for the Springs to return to morrow. I gave one of them a letter to mail to you which he promised faithfully to do.

We heard Cannonading all yesterday. They were fighting across the Rappahannock—

The Soldiers seem very sanguine of success—say that McClellan is just where they would have him be. I hope it may prove so.

Several yankees were in town[,] some 14[,] when our Cavalry rode in and were captured. Even the Ambrotypist[126] was caught and taken with the soldiers.

Our hearts have rejoiced over the events which have taken place since yesterday. We can scarcely realize that our little town is now in possession of our own men and that not a yankee face is visable [sic] on the streets. The fighting yesterday at Foxville some miles below the Springs on the Rappahannock was very severe—We have not heard of the killed and wounded. We now are anxiously awaiting to know what next Genl. Stuart will be doing—Oh! that this cruel war was at an end. The Black Horse were among the Cavalry and Mrs. Tongue had the pleasure of seeing her Son, and many hearts were made glad at the sight of loved ones, yet their pleasure was mingled with pain for parting came again—and when gone we knew not who would return again in life. Many fervent prayers were offered in their behalf, and God in mercy answered them by returning loved ones again this morning.

I had the children's likenesses taken hoping I would have had an opportunity of sending them to you—but not being successful they are awaiting your arrival to take them with you. The boys are taken very well for a *Country* fix. Jessie was in such an ill humour that her face is spoiled, I could not get her to sit again. I fully intended

---

[126] An ambrotype: A positive picture made of a photographic negative on glass backed by a dark surface. (J.M.W.)

to try her over, but the man has left. The children have all suffered from the extreme heat[,] they are thin and debilated, yet not sick. Lucy Lee keeps well altho teething.

We are longing to see you and hope now the day is not far distant when you can come with impunity.

Lute had the pleasure of seeing one of her Beaus from Waynesboro. He called aloud for her on the Sts.[,] said he knew she was in Warrenton and asked for her at the first house he came to. He gave her much news from home having been there only two weeks ago. She was well nigh crazy all day yesterday. She gave her beautiful flag away to one of the Southern boys.

Oh! dearest Papa may I expect to see you soon—time has been long and dreary but I have managed to keep up my spirits wonderfully well. My dreams of you have generally been pleasant and I have fervently prayed that your life may be spared to be once again united to your family. The Lord has been good to us all.

We heard from the *farm, nothing has been disturbed* and we have had a plenty of every thing to *eat* here[,] we have not been inconvenienced in the least. My trouble was that all communication was cut off and I knew how anxious you would be about us. God bless you till we be permitted to meet again—Children send bushels of love & kisses.

Your affec daughter
S.E.C.

Warrenton Fauquier Co
Thursday August 28th 1862

Dearest Papa

I wrote you hastily last week, hoping my letter would have reached you ere this, (Mr John Spillman hearing of the illness of his son at Charlottesville was endeavoring to get to him and in so doing would have mailed my letter to you but all his efforts were unavailing—before he was able to make his arrangements after hearing the sad news the Federal Army were in town and of course he could not pass out through their pickets without a permit, and at such momentous times as at present no permits are granted) but here it lies—no way of getting it to you now. Of course you have heard of Stewarts [sic] raid at Catlett's Station. He captured very many of Genl. Pope's wagons and destroyed part of the rail road I think. One of our men was killed and one severely wounded. The Cavalry had not left town many hours on Friday last before the Federal Army arrived. Genl. Seigel[127] [sic] it is said captured 2000 of our men on the Rappahannock—he (Seigel) had his *Artillery in Ambush*[,] erected a bridge and made a faint [sic] retreat, *our men of course were not aware that they had* their Artillery in ambush and crossed over on the bridge—no sooner had they landed than Seigel opened his Artillery upon them cutting them to pieces, in the meantime burning the

---

[127] Gen. Franz Sigel (U.S.A.) commanded the First Corps of Pope's Army of Virginia. (J.E.D.)

bridge[,] cutting them off thereby capturing 2000 prisoners—but we have not yet seen that number, some 8 have passed through. We conversed with some of Seigel's men and they seem to think that Jackson has his equal in *Seigel*[,] that he can make as many retreats and strategic moves as Jackson and unless we have a very large force to meet them some one in the Southern Army will be *hurt*. We laugh heartily at them and ask them why [they] have left the Rappahannock and Rapidan—if Seigel was doing such wonders—all have returned to Warrenton again[,] they say it is a strategic move only known to the Generals. Oh! I never have seen such tired nay worn looking beings almost starved to death, come begging to sell them bread and milk—they say they are worn down marching back and forth, for no purpose. Yesterday all day were they pouring in and marching on towards Manassas to meet Jackson.[128] To day our town is clear of all and we are now in hourly expectation of seeing some of our men—for this reason I am writing hoping to get some one to take this and mail it for me.

I am grieved to tell you the Hotel and buildings at Fauquier White Sulpher Springs have been laid in ashes—some of the soldiers say it was accident, a bomb bursting—(the pickets were shelling each other) others report they were burned[129] by order of Genl. Seigel. I am sorry for Mr Hodgkins the proprietor—he has done in all he could to get along with the yankee sick while they remained at the springs—and now they have turned him out of doors a ruined man—Another calamity occurred in the neighborhood about 6 miles from us—some of Seigel's crowd went to Dr. Beal's[130] [sic], Richard Smith's cousin, house to *search* (unauthorized of course) (the house has been searched three different times) when the Dr's brother remonstrated with them, told them it had been searched several times putting the family to much trouble and annoyance unnecessarily, and he would not permit unless an Officer was among them—whereupon, they levelled their guns before any one could get out of the way and fired[,] killing the Dr instantly at his own door—now can we submit to such wretches—we can get no redress when we complain—tis true such deeds are done by the vile portion, and the General will say they are not permitted to do so, and if they could be identified would be punished. But they can never be found out—

---

[128] This would be the beginning of the Battle of Second Manassas. Jackson crossed the upper reaches of the Rappahannock (Hedgeman) at Hinson's Ford with his wing of the army and camped at Salem on the night of August 25-26th. He then followed present Route 55 through Thoroughfare Gap to Gainesville thence to Bristow Station. Gen. Lee, travelling with Longstreet's wing, followed Jackson's line of march to camp at Salem on the night of the 27th. On the night of the 28th Lee stayed at 'Avenel,' home of the Beverley's, at Thoroughfare Gap. Robert E. Lee and his staff were nearly captured in Salem by U.S. cavalry operating from Warrenton. (J.E.D.)

[129] There was controversy as she states. Critics claimed that Sigel burned it, others claim that the fire started from the artillery. (J.K.G.)

[130] John Gillison Beale, M.D., son of John Gordon Beale and Mary Lee (Gillison) Beale. The Beales lived at 'Herd Farm,' near Midland. According to Marvin D. Gore, in the W.P.A. Historical Survey of Fauquier County, 1938, "the Federals came to search 'Herd Farm' for Confederates. Dr. Beale told them that they had just searched the house the day before, and also that morning, and that there were no Rebels there. The Federals told him to get out of the way, and when he did not move fast enough, one of them stuck a pistol to his head and blew his brains out." The Beale genealogist is more specific, he "was shot and killed in his father's house by a Yankee Irish soldier while trying to defend his brother, William, who was paralyzed." Dr. Beale married in 1839, Eliza Digges, daughter of Ludwell Digges. Their two sons, Dr. Ludwell Beale and John Gordon Beale served in the Black Horse Cavalry. (J.K.G.)

They fly as soon as their deed is done. Every garden in the town has been robbed of corn[,] tomatoes and potatoes since this last visit—they tell us they must steal or die of starvation,[131] Mr F. has had all his corn in barrels stolen[,] also most of his hay and all along the country as they came by have they killed sheep and beef, and laid waste the corn fields. They do much worse after our men have been in and leave. They tell us as soon {as} they leave we will see our men—and then after they (our men) leave, they will return again in a larger force—and it will be so. I fear we will have no chance of hearing from Rich for some time to come. I would not have you to think of coming at present. Times are too uncertain. If I could but get a note from you to say you were well and easy in mind about us I could rest satisfied.

We are all very well. The children are all up and about, but the warm weather keeps them thin and fretful—yet we have much to be thankful for that their lives have been preserved. Oh! may the Good Lord preserve the life of my dear husband—and the lives of us all here till we be once more permitted to meet. The children are thinking now that Papa can venture home soon—would that I could believe it—but I feel the times as yet too insecure—All send bushels of kisses and love to dearest Papa. God bless you—

Your affec daughter
S.E.C.

Warrenton Via
Sunday, August 29

Dearest Papa

I hope you have received all my letters—

I had quite a laugh on Mr F. & Sister. They started yesterday for the farm—with Willie and Jessie—and the wagon broke down some 5 miles from town—they had to come back—I was sorry but enjoyed the fun—Mr F. was much disappointed[,] he says it must be fated his trip. But they intend to start again to morrow—Frank was to have gone this time, but Sister could not take charge of so many and it is thought the trip will be very beneficial to Jessie[,] so Frank said he would stay at home with me. Dr. Hamme will sleep at the house.

Mr. F. says you must write and direct your letters to him Care of Mr Nelson[,] Culpepper C. House and I will be certain to get them[,] someone coming from there daily. No tidings from tobacco yet—I feel worried about it—We hear it is at Gordonsville and cant get *transportation*. Mr James V. Brooke has received his—I hope we will be able to get ours—times are so very uncertain and so much to risk. The weather is charming to day. I feel well and can enjoy it—I hope you are well— I have felt very anxious about you fearing your Battallion may be ordered out. I pray

---

[131] Gen. Sigel's First Corps was apparently living off the land as they withdrew from the line of the Rappahannock. (J.E.D.)

not. Write soon by way of Culpepper. Direct Mrs Goodloe's letter for me—Please direct Manly's letter for me. James Manly Jeffords—Convalescent Camp Company B. Care of Sergeant George Locke[,] Atlanta Georgia.

Love & kisses from all. Good bye God bless you my own loved one.

Your own devoted daughter
S.E.C.

Warrenton Fauquier
Wednesday night Sept 3

Dearest Papa

I have been looking for you daily since Monday and have had the heart ache at your non-arrival—This afternoon Dr. Hamme arrived bringing me *two* letters—I tell you he received a warm welcome home after such a long absence—How I wish you had come with him—Please come[,] don't wait so long as you mentioned in your letter—I am impatient to see you. Dr. Hamme says you are overtasking your strenth [sic] by working for others—now pray leave their work for themselves to do & you come home—and get leave of absence for *one month*—now not less than *one* blessed *4* weeks—remember you have not been with your family for 6 months. I will look for you every day *till you come*. Mr Finks says if you could find out the *Couriers* who are passing from Richmond through Warrenton and send a letter by them immediately on the receipt of this and name the day you will be in Culpepper—he will meet you with a conveyance. He has a *horse* he is keeping for some Major—

We have about 1500 soldiers sick and wounded in our town[132]—I have been going all day and feel very tired to night—quite a number of So. Ca. I do all I can—Having no nurse my time is limited—

The children are all complaining[,] have colds—and Willie & Frank have had fever and head ache of an evening[,] they are up and about with all their aches and pains—Jessie is not well seems weak and has no appetite—yet she keeps up all day and plays about. Lucy Lee keeps well—eats hearty and grows nicely—

I have been trying to have some *shirts* ready for you—sorry you have had to give such a price for them—Provision is scarce with us—and so many soldiers in town unprovided for are a task on the people—if we knew where to purchase more when this is gone we would not be troubled and could give more than we do but Sugar and tea cant be had—*Flour* is scarce—

I called to see a Capt Murden of *So. Ca.* to day—he handed me a receipt and asked me if I could get him the package from Richmond, it was left at Spottswood Hotel, *some Shirts*. I thought you might call for them and if you knew of any one

---

[132] 1500 sick soldiers would have been Confederates from the Second Manassas Campaign, August 28-30, 1862. (J.E.D.)

coming to Warrenton to send them on by as the gentleman is in need of them and no goods can be had in town to make shirts of—if no one comes before you do why then you can bring them on for him—left at *Spottswood hotel*.

All are gone to bed and I must go too. I am grateful to know you are well. Now pray come on—don't wait—we will expect you soon. I have had the pleasure of seeing Preston Wescoat at last, he was much worsted in clothing and almost starved—

The soldiers are all hungry and tired.

Good bye—God protect you till we meet again—Chidren send love & kisses to Papa—

Your affec daughter
S.E.C.

Thursday—

All well as usual. Children are better. Come home soon.

John William Finks to Lycurgus Washington Caldwell

Warrenton Sept. 29th 1862

Dear Sir

We reached home about five o'clock the day we left Culp. without any accident—Will very tired.

Dr. Massey reached here this morning from Winchester, and says our Army has all fallen back to that place, and the Yankees are crossing at Harpers Ferry in very large force, and from the best information that he can get our Army will fall back to the Rapid Ann River which I think will be the case—I would as soon take his judgement as any men in the Army except them that know—

In that event I am in trouble again, as I do not wish to remain here with them, and if I leave I will loose all I have, if I stay I may do the same—If I stay and send the negroes off I will have no person to cook[,] if I keep them they may all leave.

I will send over this week after the two calls and see them or send them to Culpeper, so you can get them and sell, if I can get any one to go after them. If they remain they will be taken by the Yankees certain.

There is no Yankees near here than Grouten, where there [sic] pickets extend. We are getting off the wounded very fast.

The children and all are well. Write as soon as you receive this and let me know what about

the ...

Yours
JW Finks

Since writing the above the Yankees[,] about 400[,] have made their appear-

153

ance in Warrenton, and paroled upwards of 800 of our men—They also captured [R.P.], who had about three quarters of an hours notice, but instead of his leaving he mounted his horse and rode up and down the street and at last rode in their midst—The report says, (which I have no doubt of) *he was awfully drunk*. They left about dark taking [P] with them, by which the S.C. have lost nothing—They behaved well and disturbed neither private or public property. If the S.C. have such management every where as here, they had better wind up[,] if they do not it will soon be done for them—the Yankees left about 1500 at Horner's place—show this to Mr. Smith, but tell him to say nothing about [P]'s being drunk, as the family would never forgive me.

...They broke 50 muskets and carried off about as many more.

Susan Emeline Jeffords Caldwell to Lycurgus Washington Caldwell

Warrenton Via
Tuesday Night Sept 30th/62

Dearest Papa

Having an opportunity of mailing a letter to morrow I will pen you a few lines hoping you may receive them.

Our town was visited yesterday by *Yankee Cavalry*.[133] We had quite an excitement throughout the town for a few hours—[M.R.P.] had been informed some hours before their arrival that they were near town and instead of getting the guns and *well* men out of town he went riding about on Academy Hill and elsewhere to be assured for himself and in the Cavalry rode and *nabbed* the Major on his horse, he was much excited and of course had to surrender and all his business unattended to—they behaved very gentlemanly, did not disturb any medicines or provisions, they found some 50 guns and broke them to unfit them for service. We had some 900 men here, and of course were all paroled, now waiting their exchange. I feel vexed to think we had to put up with such work as that—Government should not have allowed this place to have been made a hospital of and then left it *unprotected*. Those only at any rate should have been left whose wounds would not permit them to be moved. They made a grand frolic of it—I am glad you left before their arrival—

To morrow will be the *Anniversary* of our *wedding day. 11 years have we been married* and oh! may it please our Heavenly Parent that we may yet live to see our three score years and ten with each other—and may no cloud intervene to mar our life—

---

[133] This was Lt. Col. Joseph Karge with a small brigade from the 1st N.J., 2nd N.Y. and 1st Pa. Cav. He reported: "Every house in town was filled with sick and wounded, with about 50 deaths daily." Dr. Samuel Fisher was the surgeon in charge with about 40 surgeons in attendance. Col. Karge further reported that he paroled between 1300 and 1400 in a two day expedition. (J.E.D.)

Lucy Lee will be *one* year old to morrow—May her precious life be spared to comfort us in old age should we be spared also—

We spend our time as when you were with us, engaged all day in caring for and nursing the wounded—we have about 800 wounded in town, we sent to Richmond last Thursday and Friday about 1000 I think. Several have died whom we knew[.] Rev Mr Tally's son in Mr Finks' office died to day. Mr McCormick who was moved to Mrs McClearen's[134] [sic] died this evening. He was from South Carolina. Mr Anderson left us last Saturday for Richmond. He hoped to gain his discharge—

The children are about the same as when you left. I think Jessie improves each day in health—Willie & Frank have colds.

I wrote you by Mrs Cooper. I hope you have received it by now.

The weather is uncomfortably warm—I have paid Mr F. for drawers & collars—Should the way be opened I shall buy all I can in clothing for all hands—Please send me *stamps*—

Mrs Watson's daughter Joe[135] is quite sick of Typhoid fever—but not considered dangerous.

We all miss you—it seems like a dream to me that you have been here—how did you find your business on your return? Should Mr Skinner go home, get him to get you a suit of clothes and *boots* if he will. Send love for me to Mrs G. by him—

Be sure to get *clothes* for your winter wear. Write soon[,] direct to Warrenton of course all join in love. Children send kisses & love

Your ever fond & affec daughter
S.E.C.

Warrenton Via
Monday Night Oct 6th/62

Dearest Papa

Your letters of the 5th to Mr Finks and myself sent by Mr Lindsey came safely to hand to day and have been perused with pleasure—Tho but a week elapsed on Thursday last it seemed long to me and I wondered why you delayed writing—we have a regular mail twice a week at present—I have written you twice since you left—

I am pleased to learn you arrived in Richmond safely and your health about as usual—Oh! it is my earnest prayer that your health be preserved and the time soon roll around when we shall be reunited around our own home circle—I will abide my time patiently—for here the little ones have every comfort earth can afford. They would suffer many privations in a City—The health of our little ones have greatly

---

[134] Mary F. McClearan (nee: Pattie), wife of Thos. C. McClearan, was listed in the 1860 Warrenton census as being 31 and a housekeeper. She was married Feb. 9, 1848. (J.K.G.)

[135] Probably Mary J. Watson, daughter of Joseph H. and Mary E. Watson, who was eight years old at the time of the 1860 Warrenton census. (J.M.W.)

improved. Jessie is getting herself again looking much brighter. Willie and Frank are well and happy as birds. Lucy Lee is better in disposition than when you were here—

Rev Mr Talley's son died last Tuesday—Mr Warren of Geo. who waited upon him is now at leisure and calls often here, he has taken a fancy either to Willie or the girls for he seems hard to get off when he comes—He went *fishing* with Willie & pleased the little fellow—he is all the time cutting or making some little play thing for the children.

Quite a number of soldiers have died—I learned last night that a Mr Henry Lockwood of Charleston was dying down at the depot—I was sorry I had not known he was there earlier—he was connected to the Bonnells—I learned several Charlestonians had died there but did not learn their names—

Please call at Spotswood Hotel and inquire about Capt. Murden's shirts—sent by Express to him. You better get my *old letters* out of Post Office, has the Express Bill in it for them—

I feel much troubled in regard to Lincoln's proclamation[136] in regard to the servants—I don't expect we will have one left any where in Via.

You do not appear to be as hopeful of *Peace* being declared by Christmas as when you were here—I put great faith then in what you said and really felt as if it would certainly come to pass.

Mr. Utterback has been extremely ill—yesterday the Dr had but little hope of his recovery—but he had a good night's sleep last night and he is considered much better to day—I am happy to hear of the change in him for the family were much distressed—

Please don't ever mention again about your going into the *Army*—you know our opinion on that subject—*we never would consent*—*your* health is too *delicate* and instead of its making you *robust* you would soon be laid under the silent dust—then who would provide for your little ones in the cold heartless world—No—remain where you are—you have a permanent situation and in a short time we may be so situated we can be with each other—Please don't name the subject again—I see enough of the life of a soldier in the suffering of the wounded—they die uncared for and are left to die alone—Oftentimes the nurses are not aware when their breath has gone and life is extinct—Oh! how different it would be were they at their own dear homes with their loved ones around.

Mrs Watson's little Joe is very ill—I hope soon her disease may change for the better—Mrs W. is much distressed—

We are all as busy as ever in preparing food for the Hospitals—they seem to be as much in need of light diet at present as they did at first—Would that I had the

---

[136] On September 22, five days after the battle of Antietam, Lincoln called his cabinet into session. He had made a covenant with God, said the president, that if the army drove the enemy from Maryland he would issue his Emancipation Proclamation. "I think the time has come." He continued, "I wish it were a better time. I wish that we were in a better condition. The action of the army against the rebels has not been quite what I should have best liked." Nevertheless, Antietam was a victory, and Lincoln intended to warn the rebel states that unless they returned to the Union by January 1 the slaves "shall be then, thenceforward, and forever free." McPherson, *Battle Cry*, p. 557. (J.M.W.)

means to relieve many more. I must close. Keep an easy mind in regard to us—we will all do well. God bless & protect you.

Children send bushels of love & kisses to dear Papa. Write to Mother often—Tell her Dr Chazal of Chn is here[,] one of the head Surgeons—I have not seen him yet—I know him very well—but don't think he would remember me—Did you review my letter of the 30th Sept?

Your affec daughter
S.E.C.

Warrenton Fauquier Co
Friday Oct 10th 1862

Dearest Papa

Having an opportunity of writing to you I lay aside all things and pen you a few lines.

I have no news to write you—of course you read of our defeat at Corinth—I was grieved to hear of it. Oh! that we could have peace to reign once again in our dear land and prosperity abound—The cloud seems to darken again over and around us—and I feel that your prophecy will not be fulfilled—God grant that it may. My heart yearns for *peace*. I long for families to be reunited—when I go about and see the wounded and dying in our midst, I feel as if there never will be happiness here below any more to many families—so many have died lately. So many married men leaving wives and little ones to suffer in this cold heartless world—and then to die alone with out a loved one near—the nurses who wait upon them scarcely ever know when the last spark of life is extinct—is it not sad. I have heard and seen so much that I can think of but little else.

Have you received a letter from me dated 30th Sept.[?] I have written one since then also.

The weather has been very warm—we suffer very much at night with *musquietoes*[sic]—something new with us—the baby some nights cannot sleep—

There is a great deal of sickness in town among children, several cases of Typhoid, and scarlet fever—also diptheria—we have had great cause to be thankful to Almighty God for His protecting care over our dear little ones—God grant to spare their precious lives to us yet longer if it be in accordance to His Holy Will—They are very dear to us.

Willie and Frank are about as usual—Willie has been suffering from head ache—he will eat apples in great quantities, hard apples—and Frank does the same—it is impossible to keep them from it—they get them from Mrs Cooper's tree, and they are not yet fully ripe—they will have to fare as other boys. Jessie has been fretful for a few days past[,] I think she is troubled with worms—there is no Vermifuge to be had—medicine of all kinds are scarce—Jessie tho' has improved very much since you left. Lucy Lee is very well—she eats very hearty—has cut another tooth—She has no idea of standing alone.

Grand Ma has been rather more complaining lately. Mr F. has been threatened with *Jaundice*—he is better now—but has fallen off very much. The cars have commenced running again—We expect to send off quite a number of our wounded to morrow, those who are able to be moved. Mr Young[,] the gentleman in the brick house of Mr Ball's[,] left this morning for South Carolina—Mr Donelly from Court House leaves in the morning—Mr Utterback is mending slowly. Little Joe Watson is considered out of danger—

Mr. Finks has purchased an *Umbrella* for you. Mr F. says tell you to buy him a lot of *very fine* tobacco if you can—

We have had the good luck to buy a suit of Factory clothes for Willie $3 per yard—*nothing extra.* Mr Edward Spillman went out to Miller's factory and purchased 100 yds at $3.00 per yard and let Mr F. have 7 yards of it. Had you taken my advice when you were here and gone out there as I begged you to do you could have had clothes for yourself and children. I am going to try to see if any more can be had—it is thin, but better than nothing these hard times.

I must bid you Good Night, it is after 10 O'clock and Lucy Lee is stirring.

Sister has hired a white girl, so far she seems to do well—

Dr Hamme was not paroled—his name was not given in the list. Mr Anderson had left town the day before the yankees came—

The Yankees are now at Centreville—Our Cavalry are in every day—

Provision is very scarce. Butter & Eggs 50 cts[,] Beef 15 cts per pound—

Good night once again. Take good care of yourself. I hope Mr F. will be able to purchase you some clothes—

All little ones send kisses & love to Papa. God bless and preserve you my own dear one.

> Your affec & devoted daughter
> S.E.C.

Lute wants to know if a bundle can be sent to her from Waynesboro. She wants clothes & shoes, tell her Papa if you see him again in R—

Have you found my old letter with Capt Murden's Express bill in it—he will be in Richmond Monday.

Please don't think of joining Mr B's company. I never will consent.

> Warrenton Fauquier
> Friday Nov 29th 1862

Dearest Papa

I have written you some four letters—would that I could get one line from you. Tis true I have heard of you through many who saw you both at Gordonsville and in Richmond. My greatest anxiety is for your health. Please take good care of yourself during the coming winter. Keep dry feet. I feel that from the sign of the times we will not be able to get to Richmond this winter. Oh! that this cruel war was over and families could once again enjoy the blessed privilege of being once again gathered around their own board and fire side. It is now near two years since we left Washington[137] and each year we have hoped to be with each other—but our patience shall be put to the test yet again for I see no chance this side of Christmas.

Would that the Armies would meet at once and fight this last battle before going in Winter quarters and let us see what the result will be—for if we go into winter quarters without a battle—Spring will find us where we are now and the suffering of families this winter is heart rending—The yankees on this last tour through our County took every thing they could find from farmers and families.

Flour is selling at $14, brought from the upper end of the County. The yankees destroyed Minter's mill[138] on this last trip. One good luck we had tho' before they burnt Millers factory[139] our men had been there and taken all the cloth that was made—

We made the attempt on last Sunday to send to the farm for the wagon—Martin got as far as Chester Gap or some such place and was turned back by *our* men, would not let him go on. We were very sorry to find it so as we are anxious to get the things before hard winter sets in the roads will be in a bad condition for the wagon—but we must trust to luck—some good time will come for us to get them. Fritz Horner has not brought the horse to Warrenton yet. I think if he would remember the expense you were at in having to pay for the time the horse is away from Billy Patterson he would have had it home. Mr F. has been very fortunate in getting Sugar[,] Coffee Salt, Soap and some pork—has also bought several loads of wood—and now has hands employed in cutting wood preparatory to hauling. He has hired a team and horses for so doing. If we had the *flour* and fruit from farm we would be doing first rate.

The piece of heavy factory cloth Mr F. bought so very reasonable from the yankee and we intended to make your Coat of—Mr Graham[140] thought it was not suitable (only used for Overcoats) and so he has managed to cut you a sack coat and pants out of the two pieces we had here that Mr F. had bought for Willie (and made pants out of the heavy piece for school clothes for Willie)[,] now we are anxious to get them made—but that seems to be a difficult matter just now, (would that they were made and could be sent to you by this good chance) and the children need so much attention that neither Sister or myself can take up our sewing during the day. Mr Graham says it will be a beautiful suit when made[,] we are trying to get lining and buttons for them both. We intended and did send to Alexandria for trimmings but the man could not get up on account of our men. Mr F. has bought

---

[137] Evidently, a reference to the Caldwell Family's departure from Washington, D.C. to Warrenton, in the face of the pending war. (J.M.W.)

[138] Minter's Mill was already an old mill in 1862. It is located on Great Run, between Warrenton and Fauquier Springs, on Rt. 802, immediately before the road crosses the bridge. (J.K.G.)

[139] See pg. 101, note 57. (J.M.W.)

[140] David E. Graham, Warrenton tailor, married April 16, 1844, Mary Jane Cologne, daughter of Vincent Cologne and sister of Edgar N. Cologne. (J.K.G.)

you a nice pair of Shoes which we will send you. He also bought a pair of boots—(Willie bought them for you with his Silver) but he thinks they are too large No 10. and will keep them till you come. *Willie* says if they don't *fit you* he can get *$25* for them.

The children are doing first rate. Frank has been down in Sister's room and looks really well and fat. His ears trouble him some—but Dr Horner thinks he wil get over it soon. He eats very hearty.

Jessie is improving slowly. She has not been dressed yet—but sits up in the rocking chair and in anyone's lap most of the day—She has had a severe time, but now we hope she is getting on nicely and will soon be playing all about the room with Frank. You would have been pleased to have witnessed the meeting between Frank and Jessie the first time. (I always felt that they fondly loved each other) They hugged and kissed each other over and again and their eyes were full of love and pleasure to see each other again. Lucy Lee & Willie are doing well. Both have had colds, but don't make them sick. Lucy Lee tries to walk—

What do you think—every one of Mr Leary's[141] servants have gone to the yankees, excepting Aunt Harriet and the *Mother* of all the children. Lucinda I think her name is.

There is scarcely a servant in town. We cannot get any one to help us in the house or even get washing done is a task—we have to work hard ourselves, that is one reason we have no time during the day to *sew*[.]

Have you received your shirt and drawers sent to you by Dr. Christian who was going on to Richmond?

All join in love to dear Papa and send bushel of kisses. Have you heard from Charleston? I am so anxious to hear.

Mr. Finks begs you to send him some *papers*. Send papers and letters to the care of *Marcus Cooper*, Culpepper and we will get them. Please send some soon, we are anxious to hear from you. Good bye we all want to see you. God bless you and preserve you—

Your ever affec & devoted
daughter
S.E.C.

The yankees have been up as far as New Baltimore again.

Send back to Sister the old *flannel shirt* of Mr F. you wore away—She wants to make one for Willie.

O O O O O O
Kisses

---

[141] John Leary, in an article by Joseph A. Jeffries, was "an educated Irishman of fine intelligence, had retired from school teaching [in 1854 when Mr. Jeffries came to Warrenton] at which calling he had gained a competence. Many of Warrenton's substantial men of the past generation sat at his feet." Records indicate that he taught at the Warren Academy and was a tutor of Lycurgus W. Caldwell. When asked about his occupation by the census taker in 1860, Mr. Leary replied, "Supervisor of my own affairs." (J.K.G.)

My Dearest Papa

Mrs Caldwell[142] (late of Richmond) arrived in Warrenton yesterday about 3 O'clock. Sister received her very cordially and made her feel at home at once. She is an excellent lady and we are all quite charmed with her. She is very agreeable—

Your letters gave much pleasure to us all. The children were delighted and were handing them around for perusal. Willie could manage to read his very well. She brought the trunk and left it at Mr Miller's. Having so much baggage of her own the conveyance could not take the trunk also—it is as safe as if it were here. I think she was very kind to take charge of it. The cost of transportation was only $1.00 to Mr Miller's. She gave me $7, the surplus left. *How very reasonable.* As yet Mr F. can see no chance for getting her to Alex. The law is very strict in yankeedom and if one ventures down they are detained and all their effects taken, so no one cares to run the risk of losing horses & wagon. We will try and make her time pass pleasantly while she so joins with us—She seems very anxious to get to W—

Dr Dwight of So Ca called on me this evening and tells me he leaves for Richmond to morrow and will take this note to you—Should he need your services— if you have the time wait on him. He is a nice gentleman and has behaved very kindly towards me—

In the package of letters was $20 and trunk key, also a letter of mine to you—did you send it in mistake? I thought perhaps you may not have received it—

Fritz Horner has sent me $2 North Carolina bill, $1.00 in Silver—you wrote me he had $4. N.C. note—He sent no yarn. I intend to send and ask him for it.

The children are getting on very well. Jessie seems very well to day—Frank is as lively as a cricket.

They are all expecting you *Christmas*. Can you come?

How I wish your suit of clothes were finished—this would be such an admirable opportunity—The Ladies (Mrs Palmer & daughter) have empty trunks with them. Perhaps your coat may be finished, we will try and find out if possible—and may send it, If we do send it you must put it carefully away until your pants come on so as to wear the suit—How I wish they were ready.

I am happy to know you are well. That is my chief anxiety about you. Have you received your package by Dr Christian of flannel shirt & drawers—and shoes by Charles Sedwick—also hat & boots by Mr Bolt. Write and tell us. Bushel of love & kisses.

S.E.C.

---

[142] Mrs. Caldwell's identity cannot be ascertained, nor her relationship to the Warrenton family. (J.K.G.)

Warrenton Fauquier
Sunday Night Dec 14th/62

Dearest Papa

I have been expecting a letter from you daily but each day I am disappointed. Gentlemen are coming from Culpepper constantly and then we have a mail from there also—Please write me as often as *twice* a week if you cannot oftener. I feel to night as if you must be sick or you would have written surely—I write by every opportunity if I can possibly do so—sometimes my time is so occupied with Lucy Lee I cannot avail myself of all but I do the very best I can in order to have your mind at ease. Separation is painful, but with it an anxious heart is almost unbearable—When I hear from you and feel assured you are well I am content with my lot and feel I am so much better situated than many who are compelled to be separated.

You have not acknowledged the receipt of any package sent you. First I sent your flannel shirt and drawers and pocket handkerchief by Dr Christian. Next I sent by Charles Sedwick a pair of yarn socks and a pair of Shoes—On Friday week Mr Bolt had a felt hat and a pair of boots—We are anxious to hear from you—and know how you were pleased with all sent. We had hoped to have sent you by Dr Dwight your Coat—but could not get it in time then Mr F. thought he would send it by Mr Beckham, but found he had no way of taking care of it—but we are on the lookout. The suit is now at home, Coat (Saeque) and pants. They are made very nicely. I wished so much for you to have had them this pleasant weather and you would not need an overcoat. Should we not get an opportunity to send them, you can get them *Christmas* (which is now but *two* weeks off) when you come—We are all expecting you.

Frank and Jessie are well I think we can safely say. Frank is very fat, he has improved rapidly and is as merry as a cricket. He has a *pistol* to show you Christmas given by Dr Hamme—Willie has one also—Jessie is weak, but bright and happy, wants to see you. Lucy Lee & Willie keep up very well. No fever have they taken.

Mrs Caldwell is yet with us. She has been disappointed twice in getting away. Persons are afraid to risk their horses. She has the promise of being taken down on Tuesday next. She is very anxious to get back to W—to see her daughter. We are all very much pleased with her. She is a very pleasant companion—Mr F. has not as yet sent for the *trunk*. Has not found an opportunity. I wanted it home on account of the package due Mrs Pence—but she must abide the time and in course of time it will arrive—

The wagon from the farm arrived with all your purchases—the peaches are very nice—We could not get any more butter. It was selling at $1.00 per pound. Turkeys $4. a piece—Soap $1.00 per pound such prices for the country. The old lady seemed shocked at the prices—

Fritz H. sent me $1.00 in silver and $2. N. Carolina note also the yarn—said you lost some of the yarn out of your pocket—He sent no Stockings for Lute, the old lady wrote she sent her a pair by you.

We have heard many report regarding Fredericksburg being shelled. To night we heard only four houses were burned and Burnside had crossed the Rappahannock just as Lee desired that the fighting commenced Thursday last. Cannon was heard to day and the rumour is that they have been at hard fighting all day. (Sunday is generally selected for the big battle.[143]) Two deserters came in to day. Father and son—gave themselves up and were paroled. They left Fredericksburg Thursday—dont want to fight any more—They are on their way home. Oh! for peace and prosperity once more in our land.

Mrs Caldwell tells me of the fabulous prices for every thing in Richmond, says it would take a small fortune to board myself and children there.

The weather is charming. I went to Episcopal Church to day with Mrs Caldwell—

Don't be troubled about my money matters. I have nothing save *washing* to spend money for. I sent my $10 Federal money to Alex—and the man could not buy any thing to bring out, would not be permitted to bring a spool of cotton—he spent both my money and Mr F.'s for board he was detained there 2 weeks—he has sent me $5. I don't expect to get the rest. Mr F. lost $6. by another man this week. Said yankees took it. He declares he will not trust another one. All send you a bushel of love & kisses—do please write and direct to Dr Gorrell & we will get them.

Your ever affec & devoted
daughter
S.E.C.

Good night's rest to you. May God bless and preserve you my own loved one.

Warrenton Via
Thursday Night Dec. 18th/62

Dearest Papa

I have no idea when this letter will reach you, but I feel as if I would like to talk some with you to night. It is now 8 O'clock. I have just put our Lucy Lee in her cradle asleep—all the little ones are in bed fast asleep[,] warm and apparently well & comfortable. My letters and package with the childrens letters were duly received and afforded as much satisfaction & pleasure particularly in your letter where you remarked you "were unusually well." I thank God for your health and you be preserved from the fatal sickness now so peculiar as you have stated—keep camphor about you—I dread the smallpox—It is prevailing to some extent in Alexandria. Mr Albert English lost a servant boy with it. There was one thing in your letter you mentioned I have been much distrubed in mind about, your not having a sufficiency of bed clothes. Now I think the lady from whom you rent your room should make

---

[143] *...the Richmond Examiner...*proclaimed the battle a "stunning defeat to the invader, a splendid victory to the defender of the sacred soil." The equally critical *Charleston Mercury*, though admitting concern lest the enemy deliver another blow, reflected confidently: "General Lee knows his business and that army has yet known no such word as fail." Freeman, *Lee's Lieutenants* Vol. II, pp. 383-4. (J.M.W.)

you comfortable. Has she no more to furnish you with?—pray inquire of her—and if she cannot find you, why buy a *blanket*. Should you come home Christmas I can spare you some comforts or blankets either. You can take them in your trunk. You must have all the necessary comforts of life, for you certainly are denied the luxuries and pleasures of home. Promise me to ask your Landlady for warm bed clothes—Take Mr Skinner's during his absence—

I am sorry your boots and shoes do not fit—if you can change for suitable ones, equally as good leather and make[,] better do so for you will need boots during the winter. How much I regret not buying many more pairs for you. I thought I would buy all I needed from the Sutler who was to bring up shoes and dry goods to Mr F— & you would have been bountifully supplied with every article you were in need of had not Stuart's Cavalry[144] come in so soon. There is no chance now of getting anything from Alexandria. No one is allowed to bring the smallest package out—we have all most [sic] all we need. Willie is well supplied. Frank has two very nice pairs of warm winter pants and boots and shoes to take him through the winter—don't be troubled about us—we have all we need at present. You have never mentioned having received a package by Dr Christian containing your *flannel* shirt—Write if you did—I hope so as you need your shirt—Willie was glad you sent Uncle Will's to him—Did you mail the letters sent by Mr Bolt? I was sorry to hear of Mrs Suares'[145] deep affliction. She has had much trouble to bear. I hope her children were spared to her altho I feel in that disease it is hopeless. Oh! my dear husband how grateful and truly thankful we should feel towards our Heavenly Parent for His kindness in sparing our dear ones to us when so many Parents have been called upon to give up their children. When I look at Frank and Jessie playing about as usual I wonder if it has been so that they have been snatched from the grave. They were very ill children. Jessie now shows the effects. She continues to be troubled some with Erysipelis.

The *Candy* was quite a treat. I saved some for Christmas—Just to think Christmas only one week off—this time last year we have never felt the power of the yankees—never dreamed our soil would have been down trodden and polluted by them—and our homes and farms plundered. We have been rejoicing over the good news from Fredericksburg heard we have whipped them finely—and also that Bragg has gained a victory visit—I hope such is reliable. Many deserters are daily coming in from Fredericksburg—

Mrs Caldwell left this morning—she will stop at Alex and from the house of a Mr Gardner there get transportation to Georgetown. She had a charming day for travelling. I hope she may soon arrive at her home—she seemed so anxious. Say to her son that she will endeavor to communicate to him and he can write and send

---

[144] There is no evidence of Stuart personally being in the area, but Wade Hampton's brigade was on a scouting expedition from December 18 to 22nd; she may be referring to the results of Stuart's Catlett raid earlier—that supplies from Federal troops were no longer available. (J.E.D.) (J.M.W.)

[145] In 1862 typhoid swept the family of Harriet and Benjamin Suares of South Carolina: The Charleston Death Records reflect the deaths of Ellen Suares, 16 (11/6/62); Anna Suares, 15 (12/3/62); and Carrie Suares, 11 (12/4/62). (B.G.C.)

letters to Mr F. and he will look out for chances to send them to her—She will not suffer for any thing, she knows how to get on in this world and I expect her *sons* are of the same way.

We are having only two meals a day, like we used to in Washington. I like it—saves much labour—I went to day to see Mrs Spillmans (Mayor's wife) about a nurse—She does not give her a very exulted character, I am undecided about taking her—times are so hard to get servants clothing—

Lucy Lee cannot walk alone yet. I think her very backward. Jinne Utterback's boy can walk all about and talks very well[.]

I wish you had your coat and pants, but see no chance at present—we are hoping you will come for them. I hope you asked Mr. Skinner to get you *pants* in North Ca. if you had a pair extra you could wear your old coat—

I am sorry you are without your trunk & carpet bag—how do you manage with your clothes, pray dont lose them.

Mr F. says your hat will stretch to your head after wearing it. We have had charming weather. We have taken Frank & Jessie on the front porch to enjoy some fresh air. They go down regularly now to their meals in dining room—How wonderful that Willie has escaped so far—he has so much taken with Lucy Lee's letter you wrote. Dr Horner has sent in his bill[,] $48.00 cts[,] and asks to be paid as he is necessitated to do so at this time. Mr F. promised me to settle with him at once—By the bye that was unfortunate in the Lieu. losing his money but of course you will not lose it by his doing so—will you? The gentleman who borrowed should be responsible till you received it in your hand—and would not lose it—times are too hard—and I do try to be economical and I say I cant afford to lose it. Mr F. wants you to purchase 100 pounds more of tobacco, this you sent is first rate he is much pleased with it.

It seems a long time since you were here. How I wish you could come Christmas—come if you can—you must get to see Mr Bolt if he remains in Richmond. He is a nice gentleman. Give our respects to him—

Mr F. hauled 22 loads of wood I think, or will have done so by Saturday next. Thinks he will have a ... for Winter—What a blessing these hard times. We have all we need in abundance—live happy and comfortable. Now in your next tell me about your *bed clothes*. Children send kisses. All send love.

Your affec & devoted daughter
S.E.C.

Warrenton
Sunday Dec 28th

Dearest Papa
Your kind letter sent by Mr Wm Pattie has been received. Until its perusal I had hoped you would have been with us during the Christmas. I felt the disappoint-

ment but I too knew that you felt it even more keenly than I, for it would have been a source of much pleasure for you to have enjoyed the companionship of your family and children—They laugh at me when I say I hope yet to see you before New Year's day. Sometimes I think you may come for a few days.

On Christmas morning the children ran into the parlor hoping to find a "Tree laden with presents and niceties." They were much disappointed at the appearance of the room and we told them "Old Chriss" was a yankee and our pickets would not permit him to pass through our lines. They were satisfied and were happy all day. They found their little stockings well filled with Candy, cake and apples. We could not find a book or toy all over Warrenton. Mr F. found some nice apples at $4 a bushel and bought them. If we could have just had *you* with us, we would have been all right.

The weather has been charming and the children have enjoyed themselves finely. It has been a great help to Frank and Jessie[,] enabled them to regain their strength much faster by being in the open air. They are improving rapidly. Frank seems better in health than he has ever been.

I have been so anxious for you to have your trunk and suit of clothes, but I see no chance at present. I often dream that your pants are out at the knees, or you are *ragged*. I hope dreams go by contraries and you are in a good condition. Lucy Lee is very backward in walking. I cannot persuade her to walk alone. She is quite pretty and sweet. I ask her who loves Lucy Lee—and she very softly answers "Papa"—ask her whose baby is she and she will say Papa's—now I did not teach her—it is purely *natur* [sic] taught her—*dont laugh*.

Jessie is devoted to Dr Hamme calls herself his little boy and has named herself Jimmy.

Willie has been a good boy to me since the cold weather[,] brings up all my wood and chips. He says if you need the *boots* you had better exchange them for a pair to fit you. He would much rather you have your feet kept warm and dry than have any amount of money for them.

Did you send for pants for yourself by Mr Skinner? I hope you did. You might have sent for childrens shoes—I am not in need of any at present tho' I am happy to say the children are all supplied with enough to last them through the Winter but I am always ready to buy if I can get at a *reasonable* price. I bought a very nice pair of yarn stockings for Frank for $1.00 and Aunt Martha Royston has knit him 3 pair out of the yarn so the little fellow's feet are kept nice and comfortable[.] Aunt Martha is now knitting some for Jessie—

Write me if you will need yarn stockings this winter, or will what you have last till you put on cotton socks. I thought of getting Aunt Martha to knit you some and pay her for them.

We contemplated giving the soldiers an elegant and handsomely gotton up dinner Christmas day, but the day before Christmas wagons came in with the news that all the soldiers who could be moved must be sent on to Richmond—Now I thought that was too bad to take all away just the day before the frolic—why we were only going to set tables for those who were able to be seated at them but the mandate had to be obeyed—prepare to go was the word and could you have seen the ladies running home to get all the goodies that was prepared, some turkeys, some pies, cakes and many niceties, for good Christmas dinner they should have on leaving—and they had it and enjoyed it even tho' no tables were set—and "onward to Richmond" they went I hope to eat a good New Years dinner. On Christmas day the ladies assembled and set tables in the Baptist Church for the soldiers who remained (they could not come around the tables but could enjoy the variety[,] it was a change) and I tell you could the yankees have seen those tables they would never again have the impudence to say the oldest citizen of Warrenton "would scarcely recognize coffee were he to see it"—We had every thing in abundance. Turkeys[,] hams, meats of all kinds, cakes—custards, pies[,] jellies and every nicety. To have seen the quantity of cake and custard, one would have supposed the yankees had returned all the *hens* they stole and we could get eggs plentifully—but eggs were scarce & were selling at 75 cts per dozen—butter at $1.00 and turkeys from $2. to 4. The yankees may try to starve us out—but they cannot. We have all we want.

This morning an ambulance arrived in town with a lady escorted by four yankees under a flag of truce. The lady was Mrs Roberson, the hotel keepers daughter of Culpepper. It appears that she had gone to Baltimore for groceries—and is now on her way home again. Our pickets had been called in and therefore the ambulance came into Warrenton unmolested and the yankees were going until stopped by some of the Black Horse who were in town. They said they were instructed to go by flag of truce all the way to Culpepper—Now I think it looks very suspicious of the lady—being enabled to go to Baltimore and purchase goods, being allowed to bring them out and escorted by yankees home. Our men sent the yankees back and told them they could go no farther into our lines[,] the lady would not be molested, would get home.

News came in that the bridge across the Rappahannock was being rebuilt—that Stuart and Lee were about to cross and winter about Culpepper—then again we heard that the yankees were advancing and a fight was expected near Fauquier. We have been expecting the yankees daily but we cannot tell what a day will bring forth.

I do not suppose there will be any hiring on New Years day—for there are but few servants in town, and even now they are talking about this new law after 1st of Jan meaning Emancipation bill—The darkies know every thing.

I must close[,] I want to write to Ma—take good care of yourself. I hope you have more bed clothes. Come on as soon as you are through your hurried work. All wish you a Happy New Year! Send bushels of love and kisses.

Your devoted & affec daughter
SEC

The lady who came up under Flag of Truce, had letters from some of the Influential Generals of the Yankees to gain a permit. The yankees had made a hospital of her Mother's house at one time and she had been kind to the sick and gained the good will of many of the officers, so this letter was written for her to go down to Alex and buy groceries. She is yet in town[,] will leave as soon as can get a conveyance.

Good night my dearest one. God bless you and preserve you is my constant prayer in your behalf.

S.E.C.

Lycurgus Washington Caldwell to Jessie Caldwell

Undated, 1862

Dear Jessie,

I wrote you by Mrs Smith to get a pin cushion & keep an account for me.—How many pins are in it now—You must soon learn to darn my socks.—You would laugh to see me darning & patching.—I want a house & a little girl to keep it clean for me & Mama—Can you do it.—

Papa

Susan Emeline Jeffords Caldwell to Lycurgus Washington Caldwell

Fragment

Monday—Miss Roberta Phillips has just handed me a letter from you dated Dec. 25. I am always grateful to those who so kindly bring letters from you to me. She tells me you are looking so well—I am truly thankful to kind Providence for preserving your health. Continue to take good care of yourself—and may we spend many, very many happy years together in peace and prosperity.

We are anxiously awaiting the signs of the times to know the intention of Lee in rebuilding the bridges. Many suppose we will have a battle soon near Fauquier. We understood that Burnside's Army is at Union Mill near Bull Run. Hampton's Legion was at Dumfries yesterday. We are expecting the Yankees daily. Mr F. says he does not expect them this winter, but I think it very reasonable to suppose they will make the attempt.

We have been visiting today, went to see Mrs Branaugh—it was a delightful walk—charming day. I must close all well with us—

Miss Roberta tells us Calico is $2.00 per yard, bonnets $7 and a silk dress is worth $200. Great goodness I better come on with my *trunk*. I would make a small fortune—

I received the money by Mr Pattie—also the $3.00 enclosed in letter by Miss R—

Good night in haste.
God bless you

1863

Susan Emeline Jeffords Caldwell to Lycurgus Washington Caldwell

Warrenton Fauquier
Monday Jan 5th 1863

Dearest Papa

Hearing Mr Sedwick would leave for Richmond in the morning I hasten to write you a few lines. I had hoped to send your trunk also, but Mr Smarr asks $5. to take it to Culpepper. Perhaps another opportunity may offer soon on more reasonable terms. I am so anxious for you to get your clothes.

I received your letter by Miss Phillips and have not heard since then. Why dont you write by the way of Culpepper—mail comes in frequently.

I cannot write much. I am suffering with one of my violent sick head aches—have just taken a dose of Blue Mass—hoping it will relieve me.

What glorious news—Braggs victory out West.[1] Oh! that the yankees would lay down their arms and let us enjoy our Independence—

I have to day received a letter from Charleston from Bazil Suares.[2] He writes his Mother has lost by Typhoid fever three daughters—what an affliction.

The children are all doing well I am happy to say. Please take *extra* good care of yourself. I hear there is much sickness in Richmond. Small pox & fever.

We had quite an exciting time here one day and night of last week—the yankee Cavalry[3] dashed in and charged all around town. We thought of course the Infantry were near at hand and they were about to make our town their winter quarters, but happily for us they left by early morn—They did more damage and destroyed more in one night among the citizens in town than any *army* has ever done. They encamped on Main Street, built fires on the pavements—broke open meat houses—took every piece of meat from Mr Saunders near us—and robbed many of chickens and so on—we were not disturbed. Mr Finks sat up all night. Uncle John had just returned from the farm with the black colt and we were fearful they would take him—but none entered the lot, much to Willie's joy—

I must close hoping you continue well—Write to Mother if you have time—all send love and kisses by the bushel—

Your affec & devoted
daughter
S.E.C.

The $20 you sent by Wm Pattie & the $20 you sent by Mrs Caldwell I paid Dr Horner—

---

[1] This is a reference to the Battle of Murfreesboro, Tenn. Dec. 31-Jan. 1, between Gen. Braxton Bragg (C.S.A.) and Gen. Rosecrans (U.S.A.). Bragg had the initial advantage but abandoned the field under Union attack on Jan. 5th. (J.E.D.)

[2] Basil Suares was about to follow his three little sisters. He was to die within the month, on Feb. 2, 1863, at the age of 22. (B.G.C.)

[3] Federal Cavalry not identified; could be from the Washington defenses. (J.E.D.)

Dearest Papa

Mr. Sedwick leaves to day for Richmond and I embrace the opportunity of writing you a few lines. I received your last letter through Mr. Branaugh—you mentioned your intention of sending it by Mrs Smith[.] I am sorry you were compelled to purchase such a common pair of pants for such an exorbitant price but I am glad you did so—had I been aware you would have been kept out of your clothing and trunk such a length of time I would have sent piece at the time. But never mind—I am grieved to know your clothes were in such a delapidated condition for such a long time in the City. I only regretted you did not purchase them sooner and been made comfortable[.] I hope your trunk and contents arrived in safety.

Mr F. says you need not purchase any more tobacco to send to Warrenton as there is but slow sale for it and it only commands 70 cts per pound in Loudoun— I was sorry to learn it was selling at such a reduced price for my idea was to get you to send some to me to exchange for goods in Loudoun—but after hearing of the prices there for Tobacco, of course it would be a losing business.

Mr Finks purchased a velvet bonnet and cloth cloak for Sister—but she says she does not wish to keep them and as Mr S. has kindly offered to take them to R for her she will send them. Roberta Phillips told her that a bonnet like this one, she priced and it sold for $100 and the cloak sold for same amount—the straw bonnets with very indifferent trimming sold for $25. These are the prices the Miliners ask of course with profit. We cannot expect to get such prices because if they should purchase, they would wish to make the same profit as they have heretofore been doing—I would suggest that you better take the band ... to Mrs. Lotties or any lady at your boarding house who could tell you the most fashionable milliner to take it to—or they would go with you—the cloak should bring $80 I think. Mr F. says if you cannot get good ...

Friday Night. Hearing the mail would leave for Culpepper to morrow Mr F. thought best to send this[.] Mr. Sedwick declined going to Richmond this week—but will leave for R next week. You can in the mean time make inquiries regarding the sale of bonnets and cloak—The bonnet is a black silk velvet with the finest french flowers—the cloak is black cloth they are the latest fashions from Baltimore. Try and get the highest prices for all—the cloak to pay for all risk and trouble[,] ought to bring $80 and by Roberta Phillips' account one would suppose it would bring $100 as easy as if only a few dollars in by gone days—

I have kept a straw bonnet for myself for the spring thinking I might need it then. Mr F. only charges me what he gave. I choose the best and finest one. Sister persuaded me to get one so I have now a very fashionable bonnet from Balto and by looking at the ones sent[,] you can judge what a figure I will cut in mine.

Please write by Culpepper and tell me if you received your trunk.

We are all well—Children send love[.] Mr. Williamson[,] Methodist preacher[,] shot himself Wednesday night—cause unknown, very sad. The Conscript law has gotten Mr. Watson. Mrs. W. is in hopes he will get off[.] I hope so for we all know he is too delicate. Dr Chilton & Fisher said he was able to go—They are mistaken.

Have you seen Dr Hamme?

Good night. We all long to see you—Mr F. thinks of making another trip next week. I hope he will do as well as the first.

God bless you
Your affec daughter

Warrenton, Via
Friday Night Jany 16th/63

Dearest Papa

I write to night on an uncertainty. I have partly had the promise of Mr John Grant[4] to take your trunk to Richmond as he will leave for said place to morrow. He will call and see the size of trunk and will then know if he has sufficient room in his wagon for it. I hope he will be able to accommodate me as I am very desirous of your getting it. If he cannot take trunk I shall prevail on him to take your suit of clothes as I know you must need them. Mr Sedwick told me you were looking quite well. I am made happy and contented to hear such good news from you. Oh May the Good Lord continue the richest of blessings to you[,] health is one of God's best of blessings.

I am sorry to tell you that Fritz Horner died on Thursday night—poor boy he came home to die. Quite an affliction to his parents—this is their first affliction by death and a grown son.

Mr Graham lost his eldest daughter on last Wednesday[,] only sick a few days. What a warning to every one of us. Death is knocking at doors all around us. Let us live for the future—Oh that I could say I was prepared but I feel that I too frequently neglect my religious duties, and give as a cause my wont of time—such excuses will not be taken at the Judgment day. Great God assist me by Thy grace to live this year as becometh a disciple of Jesus—and may my dearest husband be enabled to lead a life worthy of the name of a Christian, and hereafter we may never m ...

Mr F. has not yet returned, but we are expecting him. Some of the Black Horse captured 10 prisoners near Centreville to day.[5]

I have understood that Halleck and McClellan quarrelled and fought a fist fight in Washington. Would they would all get fighting and kill the ring leaders of this unholy war—I can see no bright prospect ahead—all seems dark & dreary. I hope Genl. Lee will not go into winter quarters until he gives them another whipping—

Sister says you will find a few sugar cakes in your trunk as for Lunch. Frank was given some of the cakes—and when he asked for more his Anty told him she made

---

[4] John Grant, age 37 at the time of the 1860 Warrenton Census, was listed as a "machinest" with real estate valued at $800 and personal property worth $1,310. He was married, on Dec. 23, 1844, to Lucy A. Latham. (J.M.W.)

[5] This must have been an unreported raid by Co. H. (Black Horse) alone, for the rest of the 4th Va. Cav. was on picket duty in the vicinity of Kelly's Ford. (J.E.D.)

them to send to you & would he eat them himself or prefer you to enjoy them. He cheerfully said he would wish you to have them and has not asked for another. He loves Papa dearly and so does Willie and Jessie—they are getting very anxious to see you. Talk of you every day.

Frank is very anxious to learn. He knows his large letters and is now learning his small ones—

If the Candle Wick is 50 cts per pound get some 6 pounds and send by Mr Corant, but wrap it up or put in a small box so he will not see what it is or he will be for buying all up. Sister paid $2. per pound for the last she purchased—

The wind is whistling mournfully through the trees to night and it is quite cold.

I would like to see you when you open your trunk[.] I hope the apples will be in good condition. I have had them some three weeks packed. I picked out the best and largest and kept the small ones for children. They have been very fortunate so far in getting apples this winter. Lucy Lee generally eats 2 before breakfast. She is a fat pig. Children are all doing well—love and a bushel of kisses from your ....

Warrenton Via
Thursday Feby 5 1863

Dearest Papa

It seems a long while since I heard from you. I am always on the lookout for a letter from you when I hear of an arrival from Culpepper, but I am generally disappointed. You seldom direct letters there.

We are having very severe weather bitter, biting cold. Snow commenced falling last Wednesday night I think and continued all Thursday—had quite a deep snow. On Saturday it snowed some little again and since then we have had two slight snows. To day it has been snowing since morning—the weather is truly very severe on our poor soldiers—I pity them from my soul.

The children are all doing well. Frank now much complaining yesterday—but is bright and well again. Jessie seems very well—she has grown fat and improves. Willie is well. During all this hard weather we could not prevail upon the little fellow to remain at home—to school he would go—said he was *head* in his definitions and could not think of going down foot. He studies very hard. Has commenced your plan of studying before break fast.

Lucy Lee growing finely—she walks all about and tries very hard to talk. She is very fond of Mr Finks. Sister has been some complaining lately—but is up and about. Grand Ma has been only tolerable lately. After all the information of others I must now say that I wish I could sell my *head* and buy another, as I am tired of the head aches. I have them regularly every week. I suffer violent agony for a day & night and then it passes off—

Have you seen Mr Black? And if so of course you received the bonnet—*Mrs.* Shackleford bought the cloak for herself. It was a beautiful one.

Mr. F. has been expecting to go over again, but the weather has been too unfavorable. I am sorry as I was anxious for him to get some more shoes & other things. He very kindly offered to get me all I needed. I know I will be able some time to return him the money. Bank notes of $5. are all the kind in use and Mr F. said I must not discount my confederate money—that he would supply me with what I should need—He is very good and kind to us.

I understand we are falling in Richmond. How comes on Dr Hamme. I supposed he would have been here before this time—I often wish for you to be here, but really I sometimes fear it is unsafe on account of the yankee raids—and they seem to me as if nothing upon the face of the earth is too villainously bad for them to commit—Just read of the cold blooded murder of Rev. Dr Boyd[6] in the very presence of his wife and children—

We were all thrown in a great state of excitement on last Monday night. I was very thankful Mr Finks was at home—Uncle John is very faithful and as soon as any Yankees are about, he runs for the Black colt and will hide him as he says so no *ankees* [sic] can get him.

I will now tell you of the Yankees thieving expedition. On Monday night last about half past twelve O'clock our town was disturbed by the sound of the tramping of horses and yells of the yankee Cavalry commanded by Col. Windham[7] [sic] (acting as General). They had been in town but a short time when they commenced their rascality. Mr & Mrs Watson heard them as they passed on Main Street and immediately got up—very soon some of them were on foot and commenced knocking at her front door with their guns and kicking with their heels. Mr W. went into his parlor on second floor—raised the window and inquired what they wished at that hour—they asked him if he had seen any yankees—Mr W. said *yes*. I see some now—this seemed to enrage them and they ordered him to tell them where they could procure whiskey and tobacco—Mr W. not giving them any satisfaction[,] they told him if he did not take his head in they would blow his brains out. Mrs W. then came up and talked with them and succeeded in getting them off—From there they went over to the Warrenton House and succeeded in finding about 20 gallons of Whiskey which of course they stole[,] and being made drunk then their work of villany commenced in earnest. They went over the house and stole spoons, knives and all such things that were compatible. After leaving there they went to Mr Finks (Hamme & Finks drug store)[,] broke open the door and smashed the large plate glass of both windows, shivered to atoms all the glass in show cases, one of them they threw

[6] Probably refers to the Rev. Andrew H. H. Boyd, D.D. (1814-1865), pastor of the Loudoun Street Presbyterian Church, Winchester, Va. He was an ardent, outspoken Southerner and several times was seized by the Federal military authorities as a hostage, and his death, while not occurring as stated by Mrs. Caldwell, was eventually due to his illegal, prolonged imprisonments under less than humane conditions. (J.K.G.)

[7] Col. Sir Percy Wyndham, an Englishman, was in charge of the outposts around Fairfax Court House early in 1863. He found the tactics of the newly organized command of John S. Mosby very annoying and proceeded to eliminate, if possible, the presence of the annoyance. He made raids into Loudoun County and the surrounding countryside to accomplish the task. Becoming agitated himself, Mosby, in early March proceeded to Fairfax Court House, through the Union lines in the darkness of night, to capture this English upstart. They found that Col. Wyndham had gone to Washington that afternoon and the raid became nationally known from the capture of the officer in command, Brig. Gen. Edwin H. Stoughton. (J.K.G.) (See pg. 182 n. 14.)

into the street and broke it up, mixed and destroyed the medicines, broke up the bottles, upset the drawers, stole about $100 worth of Tobacco, went into the money drawer and stole about $50 in money, most bank notes, and in fact, they stole every article in the store of any value—cannot mention every article, it would be too long a letter—from this store. They returned to Mr Watson's Jewelry store, broke the door open, smashed the show cases and stole about thirty watches, the most of which belonged to customers. Whilst one party were robbing the store, another still broke into the dwelling. Mrs W. hearing them, met them as they entered the passage and asked them what they wished—they said a candle—she gave them one and asked them why they were disturbing persons at that hour, inquired for an officer—when lo! it was an officer who asked for the candle—he replied his men were doing attending to their business—she at last succeeded in getting them out, they then joined the party in the store and stole all they wished. They broke into Mr Cologne's, Mr Galway's, Mr Rinsburg and many others, they did much damage at Galway's in fact, everywhere. The General finding they were doing so much mischief blew the Bugle and ordered them to leave town. Before leaving, they broke open the Warren Green Hotel stable and meat house and stole seven horses and meat. Stole these horses from Wm Pattie. Stole about 15 horses from Citizens and members of the Black Horse. A party searched Mrs Martin Brookes' house under pretence [sic] of searching for Charles Digg's sons, who are members of the Black Horse—During the time they were pretending to search for them, they were making many excuses—saying it was very disagreeable business to be engaged in—(The ladies had not time to dress themselves before the wretches entered their rooms) but with all their excuses they managed to steal Mrs Brooks' gold watch from mantle piece. The sum of the matter was this. This Col Windham actually brought them to Warrenton to plunder and steal all they could find for he was anxious to hire wagons[.] I suppose he wanted to get as much meat as he could carry off—

It is reported to day that about 10,000 are at Kelly's Ford[8] about 15 miles from here. I hope they do not intend to come this side again for we shall be starved out. They do more damage each time they come. Virginia has suffered terribly[,] particularly in the counties of Fauquier, Prince William, Fairfax and others. I oftentimes wish we could have a force here sufficient to keep the yankees at their distance if not that, that no confederate soldier be in the town for any time, so the yankees could have no excuse to come on any expedition.

I am so tired out with this war. We have had good news from Charleston. Beauregard[9] is my admiration, I know he will ever do well.

Mr. F. says you better read my letter to Mr Tyler and let him make an edatorial [sic] of it. Please before you do it (should you do so) correct and revise it to the best advantage.

---

[8] Kelly's Ford, a much used crossing on the Rappahannock River some 4-5 miles below Remington, in Fauquier. In a battle here on March 17, 1863, the Confederacy would lose one of its most promising artillery officers, Major John Pelham. (J.M.W.)

[9] The "Hero of Sumter," as he had been known since 1861, Beauregard was now charged with the defense of Charleston. (J.M.W.)

I would like to see you, but would prefer you to remain until the times were more settled with the yankees in and around Warrenton.

All send love & kisses to our dearest Papa.

Your devoted & affec
daughter
S.E.C.

P.S. When Mrs Watson asked the officer what he wished and where were his men— he said he wished a light and his men were attending to their business—meaning of course they had broken in Mr Watson's store and were stealing as fast as possible.

Warrenton Via
Sunday Feby 22nd 1863

Dearest Papa

I have not written since Dr Hamme's arrival—first because I had no way of sending a letter by a friend, and then the mail could not go out even to Culpepper on account of the bridge being washed away—I hope tho' you have in the meantime received two letters that were on the way when Dr H. left Richmond. He said you had not received the letter I wrote giving you the particulars of the Yankee raid in town some time since in which the store was almost ruined. I saw the particulars of the raid in one of the papers Dr H. brought with him.

I received the money sent me by Dr Hamme. Mr F. thinks it would not be well to buy *flour* to *speculate* on—in the first place there is but little flour for sale—and he thinks it will be running a risk to get many barrels to keep in the house on account of the *yankees*, for each raid they make they enter some house and *steal* all they can take away or destroy it in some way and if I were to buy *wheat*, there is no place to put it away in the house. He says he cannot see any thing to speculate on here in *Confederate* money.

The Dr says you are very comfortably situated. Your board is excellent with the exception of *Rye* coffee. I wish oftentimes since you had a cup of our good strong *coffee*, real good *Rio* Coffee. We certainly have not as yet felt the effects of *war*. We have been supplied with all necessary comforts which many would call *luxuries*. How grateful should we feel to Mr F. in being willing to keep our children so comfortably supplied during these trying times. But I feel assured he will not lose, some day it will all be returned to him—perhaps in a day when it will come to hand in the time it may prove the most useful and beneficial. He seems to have a sufficiency of money to answer his purposes. He expects to go over to Berlin[10] if the weather permits, he has been disappointed twice on account of the snow. And then we heard the yankees were there endeavoring to prevent the trade. Many persons were captured and all their goods confiscated.

---

[10] Berlin - the former name of Brunswick, Maryland, across the Potomac River from Loudoun County, Va. (J.K.G.)

Mrs Brooke (James V. B's wife) started for Baltimore on Tuesday last. She expects to get groceries for her family. I believe she has *money* in Baltimore and she thought it best to go on herself and make purchases than to trust to another party. Her family are well cared for. Has a relative staying with them. Mrs Combs returned from Baltimore last week. She says business is brisk—cotton goods are selling high. She does not think the citizens of Baltimore and Philadelphia approve of Lincoln's last act, of his intention in raising a negro regiment to supply the places of the soldiers whose time will be out in April.[11] I cannot think old *Abe* will be successful in his undertaking. May God prevent it—for of all acts of Lincoln, this is the vilest.

We are having a heavy fall of snow to day and it drifts furiously. We have had many snows this month. I hope this will prove to be the last.

Mr. F. has purchased a wagon in partnership with Mr Jackson. Gave $100 in Confederate money. Broadus Triplett sent down by Penny Triplett $300 for the Black colt, but Mr F. would not sell him, said he ought to bring more. I felt inclined to sell him fearing the yankees may come in on us unexpectedly and capture him— but Uncle John is very careful and seems to know when the yankees will be about and *hides* the colt—so that Mr F. thinks he can with safety keep him until spring and sell him for $500. Splendid price I think.

Have you sold the bonnet? I hope you have gotten the price you named—for Mr F. did not make but $10 on the cloak—and if he gets $70 for the bonnet why then it will be a good sale—I think. Mrs S. did not pay him well for the cloak—it was a beautiful one—she paid him $60 in Confederate money and I believe it would have brought over $100. in Richmond. I understand goods are cheaper in R at present.

I have been fortunate enough to get you a *cloth* vest. I bought the pattern and had the vest made[,] it costs me $10. but Dr Hamme says you cannot buy a vest in R—for less than $20.

The children were delighted to see Dr Hamme Jessie particularly, she calls herself *Jimmy Hamme* and loves the Dr dearly.

Willie has improved very much in writing[.] I have been trying to persuade him to write you a letter but he cannot remain still long enough. Frank is anxious to learn, spells in three letters but cannot pronounce them himself.

Jessie talks about you and wants you to come home. She thinks you have been in R. long enough. She tries to make peace between the boys—but Lucy Lee has taken her place in that respect—as little as she is[,] of her own accord[,] as soon as she sees the boys or Jessie in trouble, she will go up to them and kiss them very sweetly. She is very interesting[,] walks nicely and commences to talk. I am anxious for you to see her. She has had a severe cold the past week—but is now doing well.

---

[11] Here was a revolution in earnest. Armed blacks were truly the *bete noire* of southern nightmares. The idea of black soldiers did not, of course, spring full-blown from Lincoln's head at the time of the Emancipation Proclamation. The notion had been around since the beginning of the war, when northern blacks in several cities had volunteered for the Union army. But on the principle that it was "a white man's war," the War Department had refused to accept them... By March, 1863, the president was writing to Andrew Johnson, military governor of Tennessee: "The bare sight of fifty thousand armed, and drilled black soldiers on the banks of the Mississippi, would end the rebellion at once. And who doubts that we can present that sight, if we but take hold in earnest?" McPherson, *Battle Cry,* pp. 563, 565. (J.M.W.)

When are you coming home[?] We are very anxious to see you—we will *hide* you if the yankees should come. Mr F. says the yankees wont trouble you should you be here—I must close, do write soon and tell us when you will be *coming*.

Good bye. God bless you my loved one. May you be protected All join me in love to you.

Your affec daughter
S.E.C.

Monday—All well[,] Dr Hamme begs of you to be so kind as to inquire of the *prices* of the articles on the paper—don't forget it & write them down in next letter.

Deep snow[,] Mr F. cannot get to Loudoun this week—we are sorry. Good bye. God bless you dear one.

S.E.C

John W. Finks to Lycurgus Washington Caldwell

Warrenton Feby 25/63

Dear Sir

I wish you to see Mr. R.M. Smith, hand him five Dollars, to pay for six months sub. to the Sentinel, (Daily)[.] Tell him the five handed him for the Enquire was that much lost, as I never received a single copy of the paper since—I think Tyler ought to send it—

Also ask him if he will sell some old trees standing in his woods—if so I will have them cut[,] corded and pay him a good price per cord—There is no chance of getting over to Loudoun on account of the roads—We never get any papers here as Coon's has no horse and walks with the mail—when it comes some times in ten days, we get nothing—ask Orford to have some person put in who will carry or stop it altogether.

Yours
JWF

Susan Emeline Jeffords Caldwell to Lycurgus Washington Caldwell

Warrenton Via
Saturday Feby 28th 1863

Dearest Papa

I have written you a week ago but there has been no travel, waters so high could not cross the river. I heard to day Miss Henrietta at Mr Rinsburg would leave in the morning if she could get across, for Richmond, so I will send you a hasty note.

I received a package of letters from you, one from Manly and Cousin Ellen[12]— I was relieved to see once again the familiar hand writing of my dearest Manly, poor fellow he too has to endure the hardships and privations of the soldier—May his life be preserved—Poor Sister[,] is she not deeply afflicted. Her pride, her fondest hopes crushed—how dearly she loved her only boy—to think of *four grown* children in *two* months taken from *one fireside*—who can bear up under such trials and yet tis said she bears up with wonderful fortitude[,] what a Christian she must be. May she ever feel that God doeth all things well. I was sorry to learn my letter did not reach the dear boy, for he wrote a beautiful and affectionate letter to me and I fully intended to write him a good long letter as soon as I had leisure time. We cannot tell what a day may bring forth. Little did I think to hear of his death. Oh! that I could write a comforting letter to his broken hearted Mother but I feel incompetent to the task. When I look upon our dear little ones and know what they have passed through, I feel as if I am ungrateful to the Good Being for their preservation through their illness[,] dear children they have been spared to comfort us I hope.

About 1500 (fifteen hundred) yankee cavalry rode into town yesterday. They did not disturb anyone, did not get off their horses. It was said they were going to destroy the bridge and again it was said they were on their way to Falmouth to join their Army. The Black Horse captured 6 of them who remained in town. We are on the lookout for their return this way again. Col Windham was in company—you remember he was the one who brought up those yankees on their thieving tour. One of the officers pointed out Mrs Watson's house as one of the houses they had broken into during that night and laughed heartily over it.

The children are all very well. They are getting very anxious to see you. Frank is trying to learn to make better on the slate so as to write you a letter. He is now by me begging me to write one for him. I have not the time. Jessie calls herself Jimmy Hamme—wishes she was a boy. Lucy Lee is getting on first rate, walks and talks well.

I have hired a very nice nurse—she is about 13 years old and suits me exactly. Give [sic] $25 for her—she has but few clothes, which is bad on me as I cannot get goods except from Yankee land. I have tho already made her look very genteel. Lucy Lee likes her very well.

Mrs James V. Brooke started to Yankee land, and was unfortunately betrayed by a man by the name of Slack, he was from Culpepper and was acting as a detective for U.S. She was arrested as a spy and was a prisoner 5 days, escaped by walking 2 miles at night in the snow up to her knees—She looks very badly and feels miserably now whenever she relates her trials. She got home Thursday. I must close. All well. Good Night.

Your affec daughter

You better call on Miss Henrietta[,] if you find out where she lives she can tell you all about Warrenton.

When do you think of coming?

---

[12] According to the Charleston Death Records, Ellen Suares died on Nov. 16, 1862. (B.G.C.)

Warrenton Via
March 1863

Dearest Papa

    Mr. Sedwick leaves Tuesday and I will send you a vest. I hope you will be pleased with it and it will fit you. It cost me $10. I think it very pretty and quite a bargain—

    I think I shall send you an Embroidered suit of clothes. Perhaps Mrs Lotties can sell them for me, to enable me to get other clothing in the place of them[.] They are not soiled and at this time I do not think they are suitable for Frank—I think they should bring about $30. But she can do the best for me and I shall be indebted to her for her kindness—Of course if they cannot be sold at a good price why dont part with them for they fit Frank and can be worn—but my object is to get a good price and buy more suitable clothing for the Country during these war times—

    We have had good news in the capture of the Queen of the West.[13] We will soon have a navy if we meet with such success every time—I am glad the yankees have given up the idea of taking Charleston—I do wish that they would give up Virginia and carry their war into some other state (if they wont give us peace) and permit us to try and raise grain and provisions for our support the coming year. I feel as if we will suffer the next year. Mr F. speaks of going over to the farm and I will give him Money to buy *Wheat* and get the old lady to take care of it and buy *hogs* to raise for meat. None are about Warrenton.

    I wish you would send me by Mr Sedwick some three or four pounds of *Candle wick*. It is selling at 50 cts a lb so I see by the papers—and there is not a pound of wick in town, and now that we cannot get Coal oil—we use many candles and I thought I would like a few pounds—

    What think you of trying to get Mr Skinner to purchase 2 pieces of cotton— *bleached* and *unbleached*, heavy and stout for *shirts* and *sheeting* while it is selling so cheap in North Carolina—

    I do not know when Mr F. will go to Loudoun for since Mrs Brooke met with so much trouble I feel afraid of encouraging him to make the trip—

    We are all well. Children send love and kisses—please write me if you ever received a letter from me to be mailed to Mollie Hungerford?—please mail the enclosed letters—examine Manly's envelope if I have directed correctly.

    Make haste and pay us a visit. Mr F. says the yankees wont disturb you—they wont look at you.

    Good bye. God bless you.

Your affec daughter
S.E.C.

Monday—All well. I send your vest. You must wear it and keep it nice to last you.

---

[13] On Valentine's Day, the Federal steamboat "Queen of the West" ran aground on a mud flat on the Red River in Mississippi and was taken suddenly under fire by enemy gunners, and sunk. A few days later, the Confederates had patched her hull and resurrected her. Shelby Foote, *The Civil War: A Narrative; Fredericksburg to Meridian* (1958), pp. 195-7. (J.M.W.)

If you cannot sell the suit of boy's clothes for a good price, keep them and return them home when you come, or opportunity offers—

Lycurgus Washington Caldwell to Susan Emeline Jeffords Caldwell

Richmond 8 P.M.
Tuesday March 17, 1863

Dear Daughter

I was cheered this afternoon by the receipt of a letter from you by mail without date—telling me of the state of your health, the capture of Genl. Stoughton & c.[14] I hope ere this you have my letters by Stewart & Sedwick—I sent none by Mr Carter. I wrote once to go by him, but it rained too hard that night & the next morning for

---

[14] Susan's letter of Capt. J. S. Mosby's (C.S.A.) capture of Brig. Gen. E. H. Stoughton (U.S.A.) in bed is missing from this collection; however, the following account of Stoughton's escort into Warrenton, dated March 17, 1863, in the Richmond *Sentinel*, sheds some light on the public's sentiments: "Scenes in Warrenton, Virginia. Chance threw me on the 9th Inst., upon the main street of the formerly busy and beautiful, but now almost deserted town, which is the county seat of down-trodden, but irrepressible Fauquier. On the slope of the hill which descends from the front of the court-house, there were grouped old men and boys with eyes towards the Alexandria turnpike. Approaching this group, an expression of quiet satisfaction was perceived on each countenance. A number of Yankee prisoners, including a Brigadier General and his staff, were expected. Trays and baskets of cold bread and meats, and of crackers and cheese, were placed upon the stone steps of the now closed temple of justice, and a few ladies, children and noble attendants, were standing near. I passed and took position amongst them. In a few moments a long cavalcade made its appearance, and the pale blue livery of despotism left no room for doubt, the Yankees were near. Slowly and in good order, Brigadier General Stoughton and a portion of his staff, some thirty privates, all mounted, some bareheaded and riding barebacked, escorted by a portion of Captain Mosby's cavalry, ascended the hill, and, upon reaching its summit, were met by persons bearing the trays and baskets, before referred to. A prominent and wealthy citizen advanced and offered the Brigadier this cold collation, which he declined, but his attendants and followers partook, and with seeming gusto. Enquiry was made for the road to Culpeper, and the party moved on until it came to the residence of J. G. Beckham [now known as the Fauquier Club, on Culpeper St.], where a halt was ordered. General Stoughton was a graduate of West Point and an acquaintance of Major F. M. Beckham of General G. W. Smith's staff, and called at his father's residence, where he refreshed himself and tarried until Captain Mosby suggested further delay was inexpedient.

The story of Gen. Stoughton's capture, as told by Capt. M., is briefly this: Sunday night was cloudy and rainy. A raid upon Fairfax Court-house, and the capture of Gen. Wyndham was projected. Captain M. and twenty-nine men set out upon this daring and hazardous enterprise. General Wyndham escaped by being in Washington City. General Stoughton, acting Major-General, was taken instead. He was confident of being recaptured. The party on their retreat passed so near the breastworks at Centreville as to be hailed by the sentinels. No rescue came. The gallant Captain took the General in an unexpected direction, and if any pursuit were made, it was in vain.

Captain Mosby, though well pleased with the result of his adventure, would have been better satisfied to take Wyndham, as this pseudo nobleman had sent him repeated messages, announcing a purpose to hang the Captain, when caught. The Captain bore his honors meekly. General Stoughton's sword hung at his saddle bow, and with one attendant, he formed the rear guard of the cavalcade. After replenishing his inner man and his haversack, he went where the Yankees will hear from him again.

In November last, as I was informed, Gen. Stoughton passed through Warrenton with Gen. Burnside's hosts, which came 'like the grasshoppers for multitude,' and devoured this people's substance. Traces of their desolating march are still visible on every hand. The former haughty invader now enters an humbled prisoner, and those, it may be, who were robbed under his very eyes kindly offer meat and drink. The man who bore the offering had lost his thousands by the Yankees. 'If thine enemy hunger, feed him.' The spectacle was touching." Viator. (J.M.W.)

me to go out, and I did not venture too because Mr Sedwick was here & would take you one.—I tell you what[,] I have been working hard all day since I saw you, to bring up work and make my desk so far in advance I could go again. That is the reason I have not written you more or oftener.—Tell Mr F. to lay out his confederate money in property.—Tell him Mr Smith refers him to his brother Blackwell about buying wood.—Blackwell is authorized to sell.—Mr F. had better buy an acre or two of wood land.—He must raise a good garden, and if possible, get every one else to do so and also plant a patch of corn somewhere.—Bread & meat will be hard to get in times near at hand.—Tell him to persuade poor people to buy and plant.—Impressment will come and money will not buy after a while. That is why I wrote you to buy even if you were robbed. Buy for Mrs Brook and Pugh,—or tell them to buy.—We have beaten off the Yankee fleet at Port Hudson.[15]—No battle can be anticipated near Fredericksburg, as Genl. Lee has been here several day.—I do not know that he is here now.—The No. Carolinians are delighted that Genl D H Hill[16] has been sent there.— I do not know when I shall start for Warrenton.—In a weeks time though I think.— I want to see you all mighty.—I have been busy & it keeps me from thinking and promotes my health I think.—I keep very well.—

I can see little use in sending Mr F. papers by mail as Coons does not take them Mr Sedwick says.—He is no account.—The Dept. cant do better or wont.—How is it Coons is not Conscripted.—I am much pleased that Willie & Frank are trying to learn.—I expect there will be active campaigning in a week or two and fear I shall be hampered or molested during my next trip.—If I do not start in ten days I will defer it for one month. At that time I could stay longer.—But the boys are jealous already and I better shave close.—Cuss the Yankees.—They are a heap of bother. Kiss the boys and little girls for papa.—And remember me to Hamme. Love to Mother, Lucy & Mr F. It is 9 P.M. and I fear Mr Diggs is asleep.—I'll bring the Candle wick.—

Yours most lovingly
L W Caldwell

Susan Emeline Jeffords Caldwell to Lycurgus Washington Caldwell

Warrenton Fauquier Co.
Friday April 17th 1863

Dearest Papa
I will endeavor to write you an account of the entrance of the Yankee Cavalry

---

[15] On the Mississippi River; beginning of the Vicksburg Campaign. (J.E.D.)

[16] Gen. Daniel Harvey Hill, native North Carolinian, formerly had a division in the Army of Northern Virginia. He was a brother-in-law of Stonewall Jackson. (J.E.D.)

into our town of Tuesday—Early Tuesday morning it was reported the yankees were in sight. Johnsey Tongue had been in town about midnight bearing a dispatch to Genl. Lee—he was in haste to deliver it. About 12 O'clock quite a number of the Black Horse rode out towards Mrs Branaugh's to see if the yankees were in sight and in a short time there was a great excitement up town[,] our men were in full gallop through town and the yankees in hot pursuit after them. (Col. Payne[17] had just arrived in town and dismounted was in the act of kissing his little son when the excitement commenced, so without going into the house he was soon mounted and with the Black Horse.) The yankees were so near our men that you could scarcely distinguish them from each other. Such yells and cursing were never before heard in our town. Several shots were exchanged (which greatly alarmed the ladies fearing a regular skirmish)[,] one of their shots took effect in mortally wounding Mr Dulan a member of Hampton's Legion. He would have escaped with the others, but his horse became unmanageable and turned into the midst of the yankees. He was shot by a Captain—after he fell[—]the Capt sent for Dr Owens the hospital Surgeon to dress his wounds—The Black Horse fled towards the Mountains and a party of Illinois Cavalry[18] were pursuing them[,] overtaking them at Winter Payne's farm when our men[,] 18 in number[,] turned and had a skirmish. We lost one man[,] a Mr Cushing. The yankees suffered no loss; our force was too small to meet so many more against us. We have since understood that they have been captured by Genl Lee. They crossed the river after leaving Payne's farm and the heavy rains swelled the river so they were unable to return. But this is rumour, cannot vouch for the truth. Lieut Payne[19] rode in town Thursday with a Yankee Lieut, having captured him the other side of the river. On coming to the River they found the river too high to cross, so they would have to swim. Lieut. Payne made the first attempt, and would have been drowned had not the yankee Lieut jumped in and saved him (How generous! Noble hearted yankee he was indeed, one with a soul has been left in our midst). It appeared that the water was higher at that point than lower down but the Lieut was not aware of it when he attempted to swim. There were 5 of our soldiers in company with Lieut Payne who could have saved him as well as the yankee—but the yankee took no thought, but was ready to save the life of his enemy—Lieut Payne wrote an account of it to Genl. Lee. I hope he will be released soon.

Mr. Brooke left Tuesday morning. He had a hard time getting across the river, the water was very high and he was thrown twice from his horse, once he lost his crutches, but he arrived safely in Culpepper after all difficulties. Mrs B. received a letter.

---

[17] Lt. Col. W. H. F. Payne, an original member of the Black Horse. (J.E.D.)

[18] Of all the Federal units which operated in Mosby's Confederacy, especially those which sought out and engaged with the troops of the Partisan leader, none were more relentless, nor respected more by Mosby's Men than the 8th Illinois Cavalry Regiment. Operating almost independently from around Fairfax Court House, the 8th Illinois, led by Brig. Gen. William Gamble (see pg. 260 n. 11) and Brig. Gen. David R. Clendennin, came closer to matching the guerrilla tactics of Col. John S. Mosby than any other Union cavalry. The major historians of Mosby's famed 43rd Batt'n. Va. Cav., James J. Williamson, John H. Alexander and even Col. Mosby in his memoirs, attest to the bravery and ability of this regiment. (J.K.G.)

[19] Alexander Dixon Payne (1837-1893) enlisted in the Black Horse Cavalry (Co. H, 4th Va. Cav.) April 25, 1861; 2nd Lt., Sept. 19, 1861; 1st Lt., April 25, 1862 and promoted to Capt. Sept. 1, 1863. (J.K.G.)

During Tuesday night about 150 of our men rode through town and stopped at Mr Helmn's for a *guide,* making it a profound secret as to their where abouts—they returned back the same night. We would see some of our men during part of the days and then again they would scamper and the yankees would ride in. The yankees rode in Wednesday with Johnsey Tongue's horse. His mother was much troubled fearing he had been killed but after the Yankees left that day, quite a number of the Black horse came in and Johnsey with them. He said his horse gave out after riding so fast on Tuesday night and he was sitting down to rest when he heard them so he left his horse and hid himself in the pines until they rode by[,] he said he could hear their conversation, but they overlooked him—Ned Cologne and Mr Willis remained all Tuesday night in the woods in the drenching rains. The yankees were near all night, but they escaped and came to town. Now it is getting rather dangerous for our soldiers to be around or in town for it is rumoured that a large force of Cavalry men are near town.

Quite an excitement up town[,] the Black Horse are in full speed and the yankees are up the street. We have just heard of the death of Richard Lee[20] a member of the Black Horse. An officer was at John M. Fants'[21] and was in conversation with the Ladies when Lee heard of it, and although Lee was persuaded not to go he persisted saying he would make him surrender—he rushed in the house—some say he fired first, others say the officer fired first and shot him dead on the spot. Poor fellow we all knew him. It is Capt Farnsworth who shot him. Better for him to have remained away unless he had had more with him—some say that others were there and two were captured.

I forgot to tell you of Peter's (the slave of Mr Gaines) adventure home on Tuesday evening from Culpepper. He was halted by a party of yankees and searched. He had Peter Bell Smith's[22] trunk in the wagon[,] they broke it open and distributed the clothing around[.] Peter then saw an Officer and went to him and entreated him to have the clothing returned which he did, made each give up what he had. Peter was very faithful.

Mr F. sent some wheat and corn to the mill and very fortunately for him has gotten it home all right altho the yankees have been dodging in and out every day.

Sunday night, 19th April—Lute and myself went to the Grave yard this afternoon and took down the names of the Soldiers. Have you Dr Britton's name down[?] He was from Sumter District/So. Ca. We had not been home half an hour before 200 yankee Cavalry were in town. We have just heard of the Capture of Lieut Payne (he

---

[20] There is no record of Richard Lee having been a member of the Black Horse Cavalry. Not infrequently men in the area, home on furlough or passing through, "rode with" the Black Horse Cavalry leaving no official record. The same is found with Mosby's battalion—traditions of men having been members of the outfit, without having been officially listed on any roster. (J.K.G.)

[21] John L. Fant (1789-1874), son of George Fant and veteran of the War of 1812, was listed in the 1860 Census as a farmer with a considerable estate. His wife, Lucy E. D. M. Fant (maiden name unknown) was 69 years of age in 1860. (J.K.G.)

[22] Peter Bell Smith was a son of Governor William ("Extra Billy") Smith. (J.K.G.)

who captured the yankee Lieut) and 6 of the Black Horse. Mr Helman's son would not surrender and they shot at him, taking effect in his hand, he lost one of his fingers[.]

Monday April 20th—Mr Gaines returned home to day[,] on his way he heard of the yankees being in town and left all his packages at Mr Charles Kemper's—but it was false the Yankees had not been in Monday—about 6 O'clock we sent Uncle John for the package and when he reached Mr Kemper's he found the fields covered with yankee Cavalry and Miss Kemper told him not to risk taking the package[,] the yankees would take it from him, for they had been searching the house and seemed to be suspicious of every one, so we have not been able to get it. Since Monday we have had encamped on Payne's farm and around the country upwards of 10,000 Cavalry men.—There are Three Generals—Averill[23] [sic] is one—Very many horses have been stolen and cattle killed. Mr Kemper has suffered severely and all the farmers around have lost nearly every thing.

The strictest surveillance has been observed throughout town ever since the yankees been here[,] pickets stand at every cross street and every corner—On the hill near us not even a child is permitted to pass to go to school, on last *Saturday 26th* Sister and myself started to pay Mrs Grant for milk (we forgot about the pickets) and just as we reached the hill we were halted and would have been turned back but the Capt. rode up and made inquiries and permitted us to go, but watched us all the while—

One order was that no person should be on the street after 7 O'clock and no light seen in houses after 9. In fact the officers went to the hotel and several private houses and ordered the lights to be put out—

On Wednesday night we were all in a state of excitement[.] Mr Bragg had been waited on by a party of Cavalry and was ordered to notify every man to appear at Head quarters, if he failed to appear the houses would be searched. We all thought the *oath* was to be administered—we were much troubled. Mr Finks of course had to go—after all the men had left their homes a rumour was afloat the houses would be searched & all eatables stolen—so every one was busy hiding. About ½ past 9 O'clock much to our relief Mr F. came home having been released. He said they were anxious to find out if we had any *rebels* in town and questioned each man of his age and the number of sons and their ages. Mr F. having no sons in his family was released. 14 of the citizens were detained all night, why no one could tell. Next morning they released 7 and kept 7—They detained boys such as Stacy Bispham[24] 15 years old and John Saunders[25]—said they were able to enter the Confederate army—and they would not permit them—It seemed as if they were aiming to get the Conscripts.

---

[23] Maj. Gen. William W. Averell (U.S.A.), commanded the 2nd Cav. Div. and noted for his victory over the Confederate cavalry at Kelly's Ford in March, 1863, signifying the turning point of the effectiveness of the Union cavalry, which to this point had not been a match for the Confederate counterpart. (J.E.D.)

[24] Stacy Budd Bispham (1847-1909) son of Dr. William N. Bispham. He served with Mosby during the War. He became a travelling salesman and later a merchant at Charlotte, N.C. where he died. He married Ellen Lewis Hill, July 2, 1874, at Culpeper, a niece of Lt. Gen. Ambrose P. Hill, C.S.A. (J.K.G.)

[25] John A. Saunders, 18-year old son of Alfred and Ann Saunders of Warrenton. He served in Co. D, 43rd Batt'n, Va. Cav. (Mosby's Rangers) with Stacy B. Bispham. (J.K.G.)

Dr Hamme was one of the 7 detained—we were very uneasy fearing they would make them enter the Federal Army[.] Dr Bispham got Stacy away on account of his age and Willie Beckham[26] was also released, the rest were detained until Friday when all were released excepting *Towson*. He told them he was from Baltimore and left because he could not live in peace there, came here found it was the same and had concluded to enter the Southern service. They told him they would give him better employment— and he is yet a prisoner. Dr Hamme says they treated the prisoners with kindness— the guard were ever ready to wait upon them in any way. While he was there they brought in several prisoners—Dr. Fisher's son was captured and his fine horse— Walter Franklin & another soldier, name unknown to me—Walter Franklin was questioned where Mosby[27] was, he told them it was none of their business—and the General then ordered him to walk the *ring* 4 hours for impertinent answers as punishment. I was sorry he was subjected to the insult, but when we are in their power it is useless to permit ourselves to be abusive. Dr H. said the General punished his men severely when any one complained of the depredations, he said it was not permitted, but he knew many did so and went unpunished because they were not found out. The order in town was that nothing should be disturbed, but *corn* and *hay* was stolen from every stable. Mr F. had all his hay taken from the stable one morning before any one was up—but no fences were burned and no gardens disturbed. They were very respectful, in fact the pickets did not seem disposed to be held in conversation and would not exchange Sugar or coffee; it was against their orders.

Sunday 27th—I went to church this morning and heard Rev. Mr Bartain[28] [sic]. I found seated quite a number of yankees—among them Genl. Averell and many officers—Mr B's text was lead me to the Rock which is higher than I. He was very bold in his remarks—spoke of the trials and difficulties by which we were now surrounded—that we had had comparative quiet for a few months past—but now we were again in the midst of our enemies—but we must not be discouraged—God would lead us on as He had ever done in times gone by—that he would not pray for us to be delivered, but that the furnace be heated seven times as hot, if God would

---

[26] William Beckham, son of John G. and Mary C. Beckham. (J.K.G.)

[27] After serving as a cavalry scout for Jeb Stuart, [John Singleton] Mosby raised a guerilla company under the Partisan Ranger Act of April, 1862... Never totalling more than 800 men, Mosby's partisans operated in squads of twenty to eighty and attacked Union outposts, wagon trains, and stragglers with such fury and efficiency that whole counties [including Fauquier] became known as Mosby's Confederacy. No Union supplies could move in this area except under heavy guard. McPherson, *Battle Cry*, pp. 737-8. (J.M.W.)

[28] The Rev. Otto S. Barten succeeded Dr. George H. Norton as Rector of Hamilton Parish on January 23, 1859. "Dr. Barten passed the most of his term of service in this community under insurmountable difficulties. He spent less than seven years in the parish, five of which stretched through the long dark days of war. I doubt that any man could have been found in all the land who would have risen more perfectly to the stern duties of this trying time than Dr. Barten. Sympathetic, indomitable in energy, inexhaustible in resource, he went in and out among a people stricken with poverty, torn by alarms and broken-hearted with bereavements to help, to strengthen and console. He closed his pastorate here [St. James] on Sunday, December 3, 1865." Rev. John S. Lindsay, *Hamilton Parish, 1730-1876* (Baltimore: 1876), p. 11. Dr. Barten's photograph is today displayed in St. James Episcopal Church on Culpeper Street. (J.K.G.)

but *strengthen* us to bear up under all—That even through the darkest cloud there was yet a ray of light—I was pleased with his sentiments as they were so clothed that no offence [sic] could be instly taken. He remarked that the service for the coloured people would be omitted on account of the order to pickets not allowing persons on the street after 7 O'clock—

Wednesday 29th—Well let us be joyful the yankees have taken French leave, no one knows when they left, must have gone last night—I heard Monday that they had captured a Mr Lewis[,] member of the Black Horse They had a skirmish last week with Mosby—it was at that time Walter Franklin was taken—I heard Mosby captured quite a number of them and they are so much afraid of Mosby that on Sunday night they rather expected him and made a fortification in front of Mr Bragg's[29] shop by placing wagon bodies and every kind of timber in front of a mud hole so that if Mosby should leap over he would be stuck in a mud hole below—it was a curiosity and nearly every person in town went to see the breastworks—Mr Bragg placed a log of wood on it for a mounted cannon so it was called Fort Warrenton and Bragg's Battery. On Monday night about 150 servants left town on the cars (the cars have been running up to the water tank daily)[.] It looks as if the yankee soldiers were here for the very purpose of getting all off that would go—telling them Jeff Davis intended arresting all free and slave and making them either go into the army or work on the cotton fields—The negroes were as bold as they could be—those who were house keeping had auctions and sold out all their goods—A Major Pope was seen conversing with very many servants urging them to leave. Mr Rice Payne had every one to leave him. Inman Payne the same, 9 left Mr Jolly—8 from Warren Green Hotel—two from Dr Chilton. Bell, Cinda's sister and quite a number from the country—John Lucas took his family—and Ditcher the white washer—

Many more were to leave last night and regularly sold out. Lucy Jackson and her family were going but this morning it was found out that the cars did not come for them as was expected. Kitty and her child (Ham White's or rather Bettie Kuch's servants) left last night—I dont think there will be many servants left. Aunty Lucy seems faithful—but I dont feel like trusting any servant. One servant came to Mr Gaines with $100 saying he could have it[,] that her son from Washington had come for her—she belonged to Thompson's estate—he cursed and bid her begone with her money. It was amusing last week when a portion of the Cavalry came in to see the *mules* packed with *cracker* boxes on their backs—that portion came from Waterlo[30]—

Numbers of persons are sending out to the camp this morning and are getting hay, oats and corn left by the yankees last night—Uncle John went and said he heard yankees were there, but it was not so for many wagons have passed laden with hay and corn—drove him back purposely.

---

[29] Bragg's carriage and wagon shops were located on Winchester Street in Warrenton, just east of 'Paradise,' the 18th century residence still standing. (J.K.G.)

[30] Believed to be the pack train of Col. B. F. 'Grimes,' Davis, union brigade commander who had been at Waterloo guarding along the upper Rappahannock River. (J.E.D.)

Warrenton Via

Sunday May 31st 1863

Dearest Papa

Mr F. arrived safely yesterday from his trip over in Loudoun. He was not successful in getting the cloth you wrote to him. The yankees were in the place and he could not get to the Factory. He purchased a barrel of very nice Molasses costing $53 in Virginia money, 40 pounds of Sugar at 62 cts, 10 pounds of coffee at $1.25[,] also several pounds of sole leather at $3 per pound. No person is permitted to cross over the river to buy goods unless they take the oath of Allegiance—He will make another trip if the yankees are not about. I think he has given up his trip to Richmond.

The yankees were in Friday night[31] about ½ past 10 O'clock. Charles Tyler[32] and another soldier had come to town for bread for some of the scouts who were hid in the pines and instead of keeping on out of town they stopped to have some chit-chat with the Miss Lucas' and the yankees chased them and shot several times—they *hid* themselves, but lost all their bread, so much for the girls keeping them in town. We were alarmed as we generally are when we hear the pistol shots—but they soon left after the rebels disappeared—

About 150 came in yesterday afternoon and arrested every citizen on the street[,] took them out of town and questioned them to know if they had ever been in the rebel army[,] after a short time they were all released—

About 700 went through town this morning towards Waterloo but returned again before evening—did not disturb anyone.

Saturday June 12th I had intended finishing this to send by Mr Sam Chilton[33] but he went unexpectedly after all—he however had a letter from me to you.

We are very anxious to get the papers to hear the truth as regards the battles out West. We heard that Johnson had gotten in the rear of Grant's army and routed them[,] that Grant was killed—then again he was wounded. Then at Port Hudson we heard Banks was killed, some say he has only lost a leg[34]—

I was sorry to learn Genl. Stuart permitted himself to be surprised by the

---

[31] This would have been a unit from the Army of the Potomac whose cavalry were now along the north bank of the Rappahannock. (J.E.D.)

[32] Charles E. Tyler was a member of the Black Horse Cavalry (Co. H, 4th Va. Cav.). (J.K.G.)

[33] The Hon. Samuel Chilton "was a distinguished figure in Warrenton for some sixty years. Tall, straight, well filled out, he was attractive of person and comely of feature. He was possessed of superior legal ability with clearness of enunciation that added force to his addresses. He served in the U.S. Congress from the district including Fauquier County. About 1851 he changed his residence to Washington, D.C. to gain a larger field, but continued to practice in Warrenton until the Civil War. The defense of Daniel E. Sickles, who killed Philip Barton Key, and John Brown and his co-conspirators, were two prominent cases in which he was leading attorney. He was the grandson of Capt. John Chilton who fell at the battle of Brandywine during the American Revolution. He returned, with his family, to Warrenton at the outbreak of the Civil War and passed away in 1867, in his sixty-second year." Joseph A. Jeffries, *Sketch of the Warrenton Bar* (1909). (J.K.G.)

[34] She is referring to the Vicksburg and Port Hudson campaigns on the Mississippi River. None of these deaths or injuries occurred; by July 4, Vicksburg would fall to Grant, and by July 9, Port Hudson to Banks. (J.M.W.)

yankees and suffered such a heavy loss[35]—tis true his loss was small compared to the yankees, but then he would not have suffered so heavily had his men been ready for action—but tis said had it not been for the bravery of his men—his loss would have been greater. Capt. Farley of So. Ca.—was killed—he was a brave soldier. I deeply deplore his untimely end. Several of our soldiers passed through town Thursday evening on a scouting party—some said they intended going into Maryland. Mr F. says that is not so—

Mr. F. intended making another trip over into Loudoun but the yankees are in force and he is afraid to go.

Do you know any thing about William Norris[36]—I heard he was sentenced to be shot, has deserted twice—I hope it is not so—His mother has gone to Culpepper to see about him—Poor boy[,] they say he is a coward—

I have been sick for three days past with violent headache—the most severe one I have had for some months past. I feel very weak to day and am scarcely able to write but Dr Owens leaves in the morning and I must write you by him[.]

The children are all well with the exception of slight colds caused by the high winds—We are very much in want of rain, every garden is suffering. Our cherries are ripe, how I wish you were here to enjoy them with us, as yet I have not eaten any having had such headaches—my eyes are so painful I can scarcely write properly— if we had the means or way of getting a package to you we would send you some ginger cakes—and a loaf of nice bread—but we have no one who would take any thing at all.

I have succeeded nicely in making gaiters for Jessie and Lucy Lee. I believe I could get $10 or 15 for them in Richmond—you never at any time mentioned the luck you had in disposing of your *cravats*—

Please write to Charleston and insist upon them writing to me—they must know I am very anxious to hear from them and also from Manley—

So Mr J. V. Brooke has been elected to the Legislature—I wonder who will be Captain now. Lieut. Pugh[37] is very unpopular so it is said—

Please write me how you are getting on in the boarding line—butter and eggs are now selling at 50 cts with us—but I cannot get them to you so it is useless for me to buy—I thought I would buy tallow and mould up candles—

I must close. Good bye. God bless and preserve you until we meet again—I know not when the yankees will let you come here again—they are here every day—

---

[35] This is a reference to the Battle of Brandy Station on June 9th, the largest cavalry battle of the war. Richmond newspapers and many Confederates were critical of Gen. Stuart. He had been so engrossed in his grand review of "Pomp and Ceremony" (according to an account in Volume III of Freeman's *Lee's Lieutenants,* Stuart "now had five cavalry Brigades of 9536 officers and men—more than ever he had commanded. Lee must see them, Lee and all the young ladies of the Piedmont region of Virginia." Stuart, in the days before the battle, had been preoccupied with two reviews; in the evenings, there were balls to attend.), that he was surprised and barely hung on to drive the enemy back. Capt. W. D. Farley, of South Carolina, a scout on Stuart's staff, was killed. (J.E.D.) (J.M.W.)

[36] William Norris is possibly the William C. Norriss, listed in the 1860 census as a distiller of Warrenton. (J.K.G.)

[37] John W. Pugh, Lt., Brooke's Artillery (Battery A, 12th Batt'n, Poague's Battalion of Artillery, Jackson's Corps). (J.K.G.)

they are up the street now while I am writing—Good bye once more. Love & kisses from all of your dear ones—

Your affec daughter
S.E.C.

Tuesday June 16th You will see that I was very much disappointed in not getting my letter off—The yankees came in large force Saturday night and remained until about 1 O'clock last night—they were about 5000 Cavalry men[,][38] their leave taking was unexpected to them—they had rather expected to have been with us some days—the cars were to have brought up supplies yesterday and many Citizens had the promise of coffee and sugar in exchange for bread—but were rather disappointed—but as many say we rather be without sugar than be with the yankees. I must say tho they behaved very well—some little stealing of meat went on with some of our people. Mrs Fant and Mrs John Smith[39] suffered at their hands—could the parties have been detected they would have been punished. The Col. told some of the Citizens that our army was nearing on to Bull Run again and they must hasten on to flank them. Most of this Cavalry were from the Western states—Two very nice young men were sitting on the pump last night[,] were attracted by the singing of Tave White—Mr F. went out by the rail and they asked him to request the lady to sing "Bonny Blue Flag"—she told them she did not know the words but any how she was not singing for *their benefit*[,] rather tart I thought for her to reply from such a polite request. One of them asked Willie if any rebels were about—he said "Sir that's for you to find out—and if I was 16 years old I would be one of them"—The yankee said by that time all the rebels will be *starved out*. Willie told him no indeed never. I have bought a *Calf skin*—Mr Tongue has promised to tan it. Send me your *measure* for shoes and if any yankees come in with shoes I will try and get you a pair—Good Bye—All quiet with us this morning—but the report since break fast is that more yankees are on their way to Warrenton.[40]

Wednesday Night

Dearest Papa

Mr John Spillman leaves in the morning for Richmond hoping to get there by some means—The rivers are so high Mr F. cannot venture to Culpepper—

I received your note sent by Mr Sedgwick this evening. He was detained from

---

[38] This would be Gen. John Buford's Cavalry Division just prior to the cavalry battles at Aldie, Middleburg and Upperville. (J.E.D.)

[39] Mrs. John Smith, nee Ann Adams, daughter of Thomas Adams of Fauquier County. The Adams, Smith and Kerfoot families were old northern Fauquier County families. (J.K.G.)

[40] There follows a strange silence, or break in the letters, as much was happening at this time. Stuart's Cavalry crossed Fauquier County. Brig. Gen. Wade Hampton's Cavalry Brigade was in Warrenton on June 17-18th, and there's no mention of the great battle at Gettysburg. One exception: the fall of Vicksburg in her letter of July 13th. (J.E.D.)

home by sickness of one of his sons your note is dated June 4th and tells me you were well—I have also received one dated June 14th in which you speak of the Organizing of clerks and citizens into companies for Home defense—pardon me for saying that I think you have acted very unwisely—and I cannot agree with you in saying that it is "discreditable in some of the clerks refusing to sign—" No, they feel as I do that there are now a sufficient number in the field with their lives in their hands—no hour to call their own—and perhaps they have a wife with helpless children dependent upon them—no, no, I say they acted with true wisdom and are as brave at heart. Moreover you say the department will not receive these companies for less than 3 years. My heart is troubled. I feel as if this step is but the beginning of troubles to come. God grant it may prove otherwise—had I received your letter sooner I would have *implored* you not to have committed yourself for you knew too well the inmost desires of my heart in regard to your being engaged in military duty. I do grieve over the step you have taken[.] Would that you had reflected over it—Now that you are enrolled and have gone out once you will be compelled to be ready to go when and where, sick or well will be alike to you. I do not censure you but I feel grieved to think you have done what was not compulsory—for you to be exposed to sickness and death I feel it is hard for me to be submissive. Please write me all about it—I shall be unhappy until I hear from you again—

Mr. F. says if he does not succeed in selling his goods here he may come to Richmond soon[.]

Willie wishes he had his letter to send—feels sorry he was so lazy but says he has a great deal of business on hand—in your letter of 14 was the children's letters and a tract. If I can get you a pair of shoes I will do so—you forgot to put your measure in—Mr F. says he sent money by Mr James to pay for Sugar[.]

All the little ones are asleep and are all in very good health to night. I am happy to know you have been enjoying such good health. God grant such a blessing you may ever enjoy. Love and bushel of it from all hands.

Your affec & devoted
daugh
S.E.C.

Warrenton Via
Tuesday July 13th 1863

Dearest Papa

I have received two letters from you dated 7th and 9th—you marked them 13 and 15. I have received none in between. I have not received one third of your letters lately[,] I always welcome your letters—but not as with the last two[,] instead of gaining comfort and pleasure from them my mind has been filled with apprehension for your welfare—I have strived hard for the past two years to be cheerful under all the trying circumstances that has passed over our country and even tho being compelled by necessity on the childrens account to be separated from you I have carried the greater portion of the time a cheerful countenance, *hoping* that as each month and year rolled by we were so much nearer being again united in our own home. I say I have borne the separation patiently feeling that you were highly blessed by the Good Being in being permitted to be in a position of good standing, doing your Country's service and maintaining your little ones without being exposed to the deadly missiles of the invading foe—but now what has come upon me—all the quietude of mind gone. I have ever sympathized with those who have had their loved ones torn from them and exposed to death at any moment but not till now did I know what anguish of soul they have endured for so many long weary months of this cruel war. Your being arrayed in *Uniform* and ready at a moments call to withstand an enemy[41] outnumbering you has come upon me like a thunderbolt and I feel as if I cannot rally my spirits again while you are in such an exposed situation.

I had buoyed myself up with firm belief that you would never be *compelled* to leave your *desk* and don a uniform—Now tell me *candidly, are you compelled?* Are there no *clerks* left in the office when the militia are called out? Please tell me if you could not have avoided this trial to me? I would not have you act cowardly but I feel as if you were not necessitated to this act—if all are compelled to go in duty for Home defense then I must bow in submission to my fate (tho trying it may be) but it has come upon me very unexpectedly—and Oh! my dearest husband may God overshadow you and protect your defenseless head in time of danger—my head grows giddy while I pen such sentiment in regard to you. I long to get a satisfactory letter from you telling me all about it—but I do hope Richmond may be guarded by a force sufficient not to need the Home guard called again to aid in repulsing the enemy—if I am wrong, do not censure me—it is the feelings of my inmost soul, it seems to me if I could but be relieved of this dread apprehension which haunts me fearing you may be placed in some trying position—for how you know not what duties may be placed upon you to bear—'tis such thoughts passing through my mind in regard to what you have undertaken which causes me to be despondent—Would that it had not been so—oh! how I have been deceived in believing that you would *ever be exempt from military* duty—Now I want you to write me exactly what duties are expected of you, and if it is so that clerks are kept in the office to do government work, why *you preferred* to do *military* duty—tell me if you are to be placed in perilous positions—you say you would not like to be *absent* if the *yankees* should come—

The surrender of Vicksburg[42] has been a down fall to us tis true but that should

---

[41] In times of emergency the clerks in the various departments of the Confederate government as well as laborers in the defense mills of Richmond, were organized and called out to aid the regular forces. Lycurgus W. Caldwell was in Co. F, 3 Va. Inf., Local Defense. This company was also known as Departmental, Henley's and McAnerney's Batt'n Va. Inf., Local Defense. Capt. Bolling Baker's Co., Henley's Batt'n, Local Defense Vols. was mustered in on June 20, 1863, with L.W. Caldwell as Cpl. He was Sgt. dating from Aug. 31, 1863. (J.K.G.)

[42] July 3, 1863 was a bitter and disappointing day for the Confederacy on a number of fronts. Lee was massing for his all-or-nothing assault on Cemetery Ridge at Gettysburg; Gen. Joseph E. Johnston was preparing to cross the Big Black River near Vicksburg; Lt. Gen. Richard Taylor was threatening to re-take New Orleans; Lt. Gen. T. H. Holmes was moving into position for his assault on Helena, Arkansas. All four failed; and not one of the generals—Lee, Johnston, Taylor or Holmes—was aware that on July 3 and 4, 1863 Vicksburg, Mississippi was being surrendered by Lt. Gen. John C. Pemberton (C.S.A.), after 46 days and 45 nights of siege, to Gen. Ulysses S. Grant (U.S.A.). Foote, *Fredericksburg to Meridian,* pp. 606-612. (J.M.W.)

not cause you to want to sacrifice your life and leave in this cold and heartless world during such times (...) as are to be little helpless children—I do not intend to censure you for your patriotism—no—I prefer to hear you speak your mind in such noble language—but I feel the precious blood and of that too much already has been spilt and yet this inhumane war is still raging in all its fury—and your *one arm* cannot help much—so do not let the love for your Country gain the ascendency of your better judgment and you rush into duties which may cost you your life—the bible says take care of your own household and while you are in the employ of the government you are certainly doing your country's service. But enough of this, you will tire of reading it but—upon this alone I feel to day as if I must write—because I have ever objected to your being out on duty as a soldier—

Sister and Grand Ma are both much troubled about you. Mr F. expects to send you a box of goods—he will start for Culpepper as soon as he can cross the river—the box sent by Mr James was saturated in water and several articles damaged so that they had to be sent home.

Jessie has had a severe attack with her ear again[,] we have had to poultice it—she has been unable to rest at night for a week—she is a little better of it to day—Willie, Frank and Lucy Lee are doing well—All want to see you—think it is time for you to be coming, and that you much better be away from Richmond when the yankees are about than be with them. I heard the attack has been renewed at Charleston—I am heartily tired of the war.

We have heard from the Sugar—it has been sent to Jefferson. Mr F. will bring it home with him on his return from Cul. If sugar *should fall* I think it would be well to buy another barrel. It would *sell* rapidly in Warrenton. I wish I could pay you a visit. I would if I could leave Lucy Lee at home—but it would be imposing too much care on Sister.

I will make an effort to get you a pair of shoes. Take good care of your *winter clothes* for everything seems scarce and very high—

Jessie is very anxious to see you. She prays every night without being told and begs the Good Lord to take care of Papa.

Willie commenced a letter to you but has not finished it. He keeps himself busy with the pigs and horse. How are goods selling now in Richmond? I have been told things have fallen since the Army left—is it so?

Mr James has the money for the barrel of Sugar—

The yankees were in Upperville Monday[43] I think—I expect they will pay us another visit soon again.

I feel very uneasy in regard to Richmond fearing the yankees will take advantage of Lee's absence, but I hope the Lord is on our side—We must trust Him.

The weather has been inclement for some two weeks. The children have been indulging too freely in Gooseberries and Frank was unwell last night, but is up and frisky this morning—

Dr Hamme says he is afraid to pay Richmond a visit at this time—he may be put in the Army—

---

[43] This could have been the van of the Union Army on its return from Gettysburg. (J.E.D.)

194

Good bye. God bless and keep you—write me a letter to comfort me under this trial—

Your devoted & affec
daugh
S.E.C.

Warrenton Via
Sunday July 19th 1863

Dearest Papa

I have received letters by Mr James and Mr Saunders. But in all your letters you speak of *drilling* and being in readiness to go again on the same expedition as some weeks ago—and that you are able to stand the march and so on—Would that you had never signed your name for I am *unhappy* about you. I am fearing the future—perhaps your services may be needed and the Governor will not scruple to send the company any where—please if you can *quit with credit do it at once* or write and ease my mind about it[,] I feel *miserable* on account of it, indeed I am—I am thankful your health has been good—God grant you may continue to enjoy health and every blessing which may conduce to your happiness in this world. Mr Saunders has $100 you sent me—he will hand it to Mr F. to morrow—There is neither Bacon or butter brought to Warrenton for sale these days—no one has any meat to sell—and country people use their butter in place of meat. Yankees—taken all their meat. There is no Cider Vinegar to be had—so you see I cannot buy the articles you mentioned for *love* or *money* here. Mr F. says Tobacco will sell first rate—you can buy it, it commands $2. and $2.25 per pound with us[,] *buy some for me.* I can get *Virginia* money for it.

Sugar would sell at good price—but it sells at too high a price in Richmond at this time to speculate on. If it should fall in price and you had the means you better buy a barrel for me to speculate in. Be sure to buy the *tobacco.* I can sell that for *money* which will be current with us here—We can buy but little with confederate money and I will not *dis count* it at such a *sacrifice.* I have bought some things from Mr Finks and I will pay him in Virginia money when I get it—so if you send tobacco I can pay him pretty soon for it sells high and fast[.]

I have a pair of *shoes* for you if I can get some one to take them to you for me—Should you see Mr Brooke or Spillman talk with them about this company you have joined so they can tell me all about it. Mr Finks will make an effort this week to go for his Sugar—may start to morrow—it is reported the yankees are near us again—We may look for them now any day—Mr F. says if Lee falls back towards Richmond, we will have the *yankees* very soon and he thinks your chance for coming will be *slim.* But I hope the wretches will keep away so you can come soon if possible.

Jessie was charmed with her present. They are exquisite. I shall make her take good care of them. I asked what would she send Mr Phillips for them, she said $4, and much obliged to him—We were all pleased with them.

You have never written me about the cravats you carried with you—did you part with them—you promised to buy tobacco with the funds for me to speculate on.

We are all well. God bless you my dear husband—I cannot but feel uneasy about Charleston. May God preserve the City and my loved ones in it. I love my dear old home. Please write to Mother and encourage her to keep up a good heart—I would write but fear of headache[,] cannot write at night and Mr Brooke leaves early in the morning—

Mr Finks may send you a box of goods by Express soon. He intends taking them to Culpepper to sell, but if he cannot get good prices will express the box to you and in the box you will find a list with the prices he gave in yankee money and, of course should bring a big price in Confederate—do the very best you can for big prices should he send it on—He will send it to Post Office department as you room there—you might even inquire at Express Office if any box has arrived towards the close of this week—

Should Sugar fall—buy a barrel say to $1.30—or 40[,] I see by papers *Leather* is more reasonable in Richmond than in Warrenton. Sole leather is $3.00 and upper $5 with us. I expect a calf skin in October—

Please try to keep your situation in Office and not be persuaded to go again with your company any where. I am truly miserable about you—I dream about you and always in trouble about you—

All send love to you—Children were pleased with their letters—Willie will write soon—

I delivered the note to Mrs F. I did not let on I knew what it was—

Good night once more God bless you—my pen is miserable and the best I have.[44]

Warrenton Fauquier
Friday Sept. 11/63

Dearest Papa

Through the kindness of a stranger friend this note may reach you—We are all well[,] dont be uneasy about us—I know not when we shall have a mail regular again—This is now seven weeks since communication has been cut off—and by the signs it may be as long again—but I trust not—

Could I get a line from you to assure me you were well, I would be too happy—Try every possible means to get a line to me. We have been blessed with health and

---

[44] There are two serious gaps in her letters. The first occurs between July 19 and Sept. 22. In that time the Union Army moving south from Gettysburg entered Fauquier on July 20-21. By the 24th, Meade had concentrated his army around Warrenton. Lee's A.N.V. was to the south near the Rapidan. Thus Confederate correspondence was interrupted. Gen. John Sedgwick's VI Corps occupied the Warrenton area for nearly seven weeks. By Sept. 22nd, they were gone. Also, from October 3rd to November 27th is another break. This period would have covered the Bristoe Campaign in October when both armies moved across Fauquier. Lee, in attempting to get behind Meade and force a battle, brought two corps, Ewell and A.P. Hill, to Warrenton, New Baltimore and Auburn while Stuart fought the Union cavalry along the Warrenton turnpike to Buckland. (J.E.D.)

are all doing very well—dont be uneasy about us—Keep up good heart—all will be right some day—

May God bless and preserve you is my earnest prayer—

I am anxious about Charleston. I see the Northern papers daily and they are ever ... their success—

Good bye no ... more at present.

Be cheerful.

Your affec

S.E.C.

Warrenton Fauquier Co.

Sunday Sept. 12th 1863

Dearest Papa

The Good Being has granted my petition and has opened unto me a way to communicate with you. I said if I could but send you a line it would lighten your burthened heart for I knew how anxious you were about us. I have made many efforts even by flag of truce, but all have been failures until now—I have written once by Flag of Truce—and have been promised assuredly that it would reach Richmond—then I have sent another in a different direction—Mr F. wrote you on yesterday and I have heard of another opportunity to day. I do not expect to receive answers from you—but you must make inquiries and use every available effort as I do and chance may throw an opportunity by the way as it has been in my case.

I write to assure you we are doing remarkably well—we have never been without *butter*—when nearly every family have been without—we have had the privilege of sending our *wheat* to the mill—and we have had sufficiency of flour—Corn meal is scarce but we have been enabled to get it several times—Bacon is scarce, but we now have the promise of 100 weight which will be quite a consideration these times—we have supplied ourselves with coffee, sugar, candles, soap and are daily trying to get more—The *Commissary* department supplies us at first at government prices—coffee at 40 cts, sugar at 13. We have been treated very kindly this time by the *enemy*—We have bought upwards of three bushels of salt at $1.00 bushel—Good whiskey at $1.00—whiskey is sold to be used for medicinal purposes—and it has helped the children—I was glad enough to know Mr F. could get some—We have bought good Molasses at 60 cts gallon—we bought some flour at Commissary at 4 cts per pound first rate flour—The Commissary had *dried fruit*, we bought some of that. Sutlers have been up and brought up every variety of goods, shoes and groceries—if *Federal* money was plentiful with *me* I could buy lots—but I cannot even buy it, the *Confed money goes begging*[45]—I have made several purchases through

---

[45] In all areas of the Confederacy, inflation ran uncontrolled. In this section, Confederate money became worthless earlier than in others for it could not compete with U.S. Currency. (J.E.D.)

Mr F. I am trying now to get shoes for them children. I think Mr F. has been blessed in getting the right kind of money to enable him to buy groceries and a nice suit of clothes—he bought beautiful Cassimere at $2 per yard—

I have made the acquaintance of Capt. Barry—he has been South for many years travelling in the different states—he knows Brother William having had business with Adger—if I had money he would bring up any articles I would name but I know Mr F. has *groceries* to buy and it would be wrong in us to spend money for *clothing* at this time—

Dont be uneasy about us—we have been truly highly favored during these trying times—

I fear the army will remain here for *time indefinite* and it will be peculiarly trying to *you* to be *separated* from us so long—but dont get low spirited—all will be well soon I hope—I feel confident there is a bright day in the distance for us—so be cheerful and happy if you possibly can—I will write you by every possible chance and live in hope of hearing from you—I pray the Good Lord to preserve your precious life till we can meet again[,] I feel as if He will hear my unworthy petitions in your behalf. Be careful of yourself under all circumstances. Nearly every servant has left town—Aunt Lucy has heard from her son (George)[,] he is in Washington and we cannot tell what she intends doing—but she says she is never going to the Yankees—I hope she will not be so foolish—

The children are all well, are *well fed* and *clothed*, in fact they have never felt the effects of *war* and *blockade*. They enjoy every thing in abundance—

Now be happy we are all well and doing well—if you keep well tis all I crave—as I know I cannot see you for some time to come—then again the town may be evacuated at the shortest possible notice—but the signs are now they may be here for weeks longer—

I think you better buy yourself a nice *coat* and *pants* if you can buy them reasonable at this season in Richmond buy the *cloth* and we can get them made up—or buy them already made if they *fit well*. I have a very nice *vest* for you—also 2 *Merino under shirts* for winter, and I am trying to get you a pair of drawers to match your winter one.

I think of having Lucy Lee's daguerrotype if she will be still. Sister says she will keep some nice cheese for you to *toast* at your leisure on your next visit—

I cannot get the correct news from Charleston—the papers say the Enemy have possession of Morris Island—can it be so?

Good Bye. Love and kisses from little ones and all—God bless and protect your health is the constant earnest prayer of your affec

S.E.C.

Warrenton Sept. 22 1863

Dearest Papa
Our town is freed once again of the enemy. Would that the country was freed

even as far as the road to Richmond—if such were the case I would be in daily expectation of seeing you once again—but the enemy's movements have been towards Culpepper and we cannot tell what day we may have them return again—for I am assured they will be repulsed by us—I am *heart sick* of this *cruel war* instead of realizing the comforts of family and home as each year draws to' a close—the separation grows wider and of longer duration and the stay of the enemy increases each time, so that it is painful to bear separation when all communication is cut off—I have embraced every available opportunity to write to you during the blockade—how successful I have been you are to judge, for I have not received a line from you since the middle of July—What times we are living in—

I have seen several of our soldiers and they are all sanguine of success. Some speak very hopeful of Charleston that is to say Beauregard will never surrender the City.[46] I hope he never will. I dont want to hear of the 2nd New Orleans disaster—I am deeply anxious about my dear home[,] we cannot get any reliable information—the scouts dont know any news. I was troubled when I learned the enemy had gained such a strong foot hold on Morris Island[47]—Battery Wagner from the yankees accounts was in a wretched condition on their arrival—oh how my heart sickened at the perusal.

Your dear little ones have enjoyed the blessing of health this summer[.] Willie was complaining for a short time, but is well again—Jessie has suffered at periods with the risings behind her ear—she is a great sufferer at such times. I do pity her from my heart, but she bears her pain like a heroine—The children talk about Papa. Jessie said she prayed the Good Lord to take care of you—she said she knew the Good Lord cared for Papa now the yankees were here[,] it was really touching at times to hear the children give expression to their feelings in regard to you. Amidst all of our trials and troubles we have much to be grateful for—Mr F. has been enabled to get a few groceries and some wearing apparel and was about to lay in quite a large supply, but they left very suddenly. The sutler was not able to return—it takes time to get Federal money together to buy. Mr F. was caught in Culpepper when the army came[48] in and had to leave Wagon and horse at Mr Cooper's—he is so much in need of his wagon that he has determined to run the risk and will send Uncle John for it to day hoping the old man will be enabled to bring it safely home without interruption.

I am anxious in regard to this conscription bill[49]—please promise me to *remain* in your position, dont give up your situation. Mr F. says he knows you have not quite

---

[46] The siege of Charleston is on; enemy capture of several forts and batteries would lead to the final fall of this great port of the Confederacy. (J.E.D.)

[47] Morris Island, one of two natural guardians of the Port of Charleston, fell on Sept. 7, 1863. (J.M.W.)

[48] The Union Army has moved on through to the line of the Rappahannock, apparently without depredations. (J.E.D.)

[49] The South was scraping the bottom of the manpower barrel. The Confederate Congress abolished the privilege of substitution (making those who had previously bought substitutes liable to conscription) and required soldiers whose three-year enlistments were about to expire to remain in the army. Congress also stretched the upper and lower age limits to fifty and seventeen. Despite these efforts to maintain the army's strength, Southern forces numbered fewer than half the enemy's as spring sunshine began to dry the red clay roads of Virginia and Georgia. McPherson, *Battle Cry,* pp. 718-9. (J.M.W.)

lost your mind, that you of course will not *dream* of joining the army and support your family on $11 per month. God bless you, protect you and keep you from all sickness is the constant prayer of your affec daughter,

S.E.C.

Don't be uneasy about us, all are doing well. Loving kisses from all to Papa.

Warrenton Via
Saturday Sept 26th 1863

Dearest Papa

Miss Octavia White leaves to morrow for Mossy Creek in Augusta Co. and promises to take a letter and mail it for me—now if you are fortunate enough to receive this—sit down at once and answer it directing to Miss O. White, Care of Thomas White, Mossy Creek Augusta Co. and I may per chance receive it through her. I am so anxious to hear from you. I have embraced every opportunity in writing to you, with what success you alone can know. I hope sincerely some has reached you. The enemy after sojourning with us for 8 weeks took their departure I hoped for ever—but alas how mistaken I was, for we had a visit to day from a scouting party. How I wished they were removed from this side of the country—

We cannot hear any reliable news, because we are afraid to send for the mail at Culpepper—the enemy are all around us. We did hear all fighting had ceased at Charleston, but the enemy had gained possession of Morris Island—I am very anxious to hear from home. Mr Finks begs me to write and say to you that he has about 400 Ladies gaiters and about 100 Misses leather shoes and gaiters and about 75 pairs of childrens gaiters—he wishes to know what prices they will bring in Confederate money or Virginia money—wishes to know the dis count on our money in Virginia money—we dont know any thing these times, we are *know nothings*[.] Mr F. has some handsome gentlemen cravats—socks—ladies stockings, wants to know if such things would command good prices in Richmond[.]

Mr F. gets $4.50 in Federal money here very readily for ladies shoes—

I have just heard to night that the Enemy were at Waterloo guarding a bridge— also that 2 corps[50] have gone from Virginia to reinforce Rozencranz, [sic] that Bragg repulsed R in Tennessee. God grant we may be enabled to give them a severe whipping out West. I know there is yet a good day coming to us. The Confederacy must prosper. I understand Gov. Letcher has called out all from 16 to 60—now you are not included in that number—you need never leave your situation so Mr F. tells me—that clerks are as necessary to the government as Soldiers in the Army so pray be contented and do not for a moment have your mind disturbed about *soldiering*.

Last night one of our soldiers was shot by a 2nd South Carolinean—they met

---

[50] The XI and XII Corps were sent from Virginia to the aid of Rosecrans at Chattanooga. She heard the news quickly as they started loading at Warrenton Junction and Brandy Station on Sept. 25th. (J.E.D.)

in the street and the S.C. hallowed the other soldier, who was a Virginian, inquired who he was whereupon the Virginian jumped from his horse and run—saying he was one of the *New York boys*—South Carolina not wishing to associate with a New Yorker poped [sic] away and shot the poor fellow in his head—Sad mistake he made, the poor boy was a Virginian and a boy only 16 years old from Balto. He took the Carolinian for a yankee and felt he was safe by saying he was from New York—The poor boy's name is Smith and to night he is not expected to live. The So. Ca. was justifiable of course.

Oh! how we all long to see you—but I know it would be running too much of a risk to venture at present—but be on the lookout and come the very first opportunity—I dream of you and you are always well and happy[.] Oh! how I long to be with you once again if I could but get one line from you, I hope soon to hear from you—

Children are all doing well—they all long to see you—may the day soon come when we shall all be happy with each one again. God bless you my own dear one. Good night. We are all comfortable[,] dont be uneasy about us—

Your devoted daughter
S.E.C.

Warrenton Via
Saturday Oct 3rd/63

Dearest Papa

Your letter of the 14th September has just reached me through Mr W. Franklin—How very and truly thankful am I once again to peruse a letter from you my own dearest husband—and to hear you have been and are well. Oh! you cannot imagine how happy I am at this moment to hold this dear letter of yours in my hand—Tis next to seeing you, Oh! how I do long to see you—time has been very long and I have been heart sick for the past month—I long to see you—but I would not have you run the risk of meeting with the yankees for they are in town almost daily on scouting parties.

I am sorry to hear you have been on another campaign—please dont go unless compelled. Mr F. says you are not *compelled* to leave your office, for some one must attend to government business—Please dont go any more—I will be so unhappy about you—for the cold winter is now coming on. Please take good care of your precious self—for you are my *all*. God bless you dearest one. I know you will come as soon as the way is opened for you are now longing to see us all—particularly the little ones—So far all have been well excepting dear little Jessie—her eye and ear has given her much trouble—rising almost every four weeks—and when the water discharges, it scalds her little face and makes it sore—she was grieving yesterday about her face, said it would not be well by the time Papa would come home—she bears her sufferings like a little martyr. The children will be delighted with their toys—Willie will start to school Monday—and I intend to open school for Frank myself—The times have been so exciting that I have not put him regularly to his books—He will soon learn to read. We have gotten on remarkably well during the sojourn of the yankees, we got a supply of coffee[,] sugar and several gallons of Molasses and many other articles very useful to us—The children are supplied with shoes and good many articles of clothing[,] I bought you two nice under shirts & drawers, also a black felt hat.

If Virginia money does not sell too high, you better purchase me some little— but dont do it if you will have to make *much sacrifice.* Please send me some stamps if you have opportunity. None in town—

I am pleased to hear such good news in regard to Charleston and our army— oh! how I long for this cruel war to be over[.]

Now please promise me not to go out again—or think of joining the army— you are not able, and some one will be compelled to be at the Office—I pray you not to go—for you will not stand the winter—I am in earnest.

Don't be uneasy about us—we are doing well—I hope you soon will be able to come and see us. All send love to you—I have a splendid calf skin to make you a pair of boots when you come home to get your measure—

All join me in love & kisses, my time is limited and I write hurriedly. Good bye. I have written you many letters—but as I have never received any from you—it has been the same with you.

Your affec
S.E.C.

Warrenton Via
Friday Nov 27th 1863

Dearest Papa

I wrote you a few days ago and enclosed a letter to Ma in it. I hope good fortune has favored you in the receiving of it for I know you are anxious to hear from us. Would that I could be near you so you could hear from my lips the sad recital which I had to write on paper—Fearing that—that letter may not reach you I will write you its contents, knowing that this will come safely to hand[.]

We have passed through a heavy affliction. Our dear Mother[51] has fallen asleep in Jesus her Saviour. Our loss is her eternal gain, but oh! how we *miss her—loneliness* pervades the house—she was ever with us and near us—now she is far from us but I feel that she is near us in *spirit* watching over her loved ones left behind. Grand Ma seemed to be enjoying her usual degree of health[,] up to the 10th of this month she had indulged in eating fresh fish which gave her cramp colic, but she was relieved by remedies we used for her, altho she never regained her strength she was enabled to be up in her room the best portion of each day. We sent for Dr C. and he said she

---

[51] Frances (Pattie) Caldwell, widow of James Caldwell and mother of Lycurgus W. Caldwell. (J.M.W.)

was no worse than she was ten years ago—she was not aware herself of her situation for she never spoke seriously to us about it. She would say she feared she would not get up again but we did not think her ill—but she was for her spirit passed away on the Sabbath morn quietly and peacefully as an infant falls asleep—on the 15th— Sister mourns her loss, she feels as if life has no bright spot for her now and she would willingly die to go and be with her once again. I feel deeply for her for she has ever been a devoted and an affectionate child[.] I try to comfort her in her sad trial.

Mr F. had every thing done that was necessary. He has been very kind and acted the same in every particular as a Son—I felt very grateful to him and I knew that you would ever feel gratitude in your heart towards him for his acts of kindness and love. Sister intends changing her dress—she wishes me to do the same if it meets your approval. I know that you are not in favor of mourning as a dress—but you may wish me to show that respect due your Mother, and she was *mine too.* I have been so closely identified with the family that I have ever felt as *one.* I will await your answer before I make any change—Mr F. thinks I best not make any change but I think Sister desires it if it meets your approval—

We long to see you dearest Papa, but I know you cannot run the risk at present for the *enemy* is *between* us—We have heard heavy firing for the past two days, but have not heard the result.

The children are in very good health. I was anxious to have Lee's likeness taken and sent you, but she will not be quiet[.] I shall make the effort when I am able to go out. She will make a lovely picture. This letter will be handed you by Mrs Dixon[52]—she has kindly offered to take the letter and deliver it herself—I feel under many obligations for such a disinterested act of kindness. She will return to W—in about 10 days after her arrival and she will bring me a letter from you. She expects to stop at the Exchange Hotel and you can call on her. I assured her you would appreciate her kindness. She says she will cheerfully bring a small package to me if you have any—you might send the childrens' toys you made[,] I hope you will be able to see her before she leaves Richmond—if not at the Exchange—make inquiries of Mr Memmize. Please send about $5 worth of *postage stamps* as I have none. Please write by every opportunity. I have been so anxious about you—and feel my heart often sink within me fearing you may be sick and need me near you—oh! I long for this cruel war to be over so I shall once again have a home and you be near me. All send much love to you and a bushel of kisses. A heart full of love from your affec & loving daughter

S.E.C.

---

[52] Rosina (Ashton) Dixon, widow of Lucius Dixon, of 'North Wales' and 'Ashley.' Alexander Hunter, in his *Women of the Debatable Land* (Washington, D.C.: Cobden Publishing Co., 1912), mentions the daughter of Mrs. Dixon: "I know of but one instance, and one only, where the love of sex triumphed over the *amor patrae,* and that was Miss Nannie Dixon, a beautiful maiden, who fell madly in love with a Federal captain of cavalry [Anna Ashton married Aug. 16, 1866, at 'North Wales,' Col. L. W. Russell (U.S.A.) of Salem, N.Y.] and gave up, for a time at least, her friends, her country and kinsmen for the belted and spurred dragoon." According to a descendant of the Russells, Miss Dixon was riding from 'North Wales' to Warrenton and found the gate carefully guarded by Union forces. She, determined not to let that stop her, urged on her horse and made a beautiful jump over the nearby fence. Witnessing this display of superb horsemanship, Col. Russell turned to a fellow officer and remarked, "Any lovely woman who can ride like that is destined to be my wife." And, so she became. (J.K.G.)

Warrenton Fauquier
Monday Night Dec. 7th 1863

Dearest Papa

I have written you many, many letters since the yankee army has left us, but have not as yet had an answer to one. I received one from you dated 27th Oct. I hope some of my letters have reached you. Not knowing if you have my letters each time I have been compelled to pen the painful tidings of the sad affliction which has taken place in our little family circle—we have had *our dear Mother* taken from us. Her death was very unexpected to us—she had been complaining only a few days but she must have been much worse than we thought her to me or even she could have thought, she did not mention the subject as being so near at hand. She died on Sunday morning Nov 15 as quietly as an infant falling to sleep. But Papa we miss her so much. We cannot realize that we shall never have her with us any more. We miss her all the day long and oh! I do feel so lonesome at night when I go up to my room and know that the next room has no occupant. But we should not murmur[,] our loss is her gain, she is freed from all pain and is now happy in Heaven.

We have been blessed thus far in our children. They have had very good health. Jessie's ear rises sometimes but has never been as painful since we had it lanced during the summer—her general health is excellent. She is very fat and as happy as a bird. You will be astonished to see how Lee has grown and how well she can talk. She says prayers every night for her Papa. Willie grows fast and learns well—he studies Geography, Philosophy, definitions, Spelling, Arithmetic, and writes. Frank does not love his book as well as he loves play[,] he is so tiny I dislike to call him in from the yard. The children long to see you, but I tell them I am afraid to have you come till the yankees go into Winter quarters. I hope you will be enabled to get here before the close of the year—but I would not have you run any risk because they [sic] are so many ill disposed persons in W. who are ever ready to inform upon persons to the yankees. I understand the yankee army is at Brandy Station,[53] but we are *"know nothings"* in Warrenton, we never get a paper and we see very few from across the lines. What do you think of 100 weight of Pork costing $200 of *Confederate money.* Confed money is worth nothing with us. Cant buy clothing of any kind or eatables. We have no cause to complain—we have had plenty of Coffee, sugar, molasses, flour and meat, never have been without. Our children have not been deprived of any thing during this war. I have a sufficiency of clothing for them all. I bought very nice shoes for Frank and Jessie—I make the baby's shoes—I have a nice little stock on hand for you—a hat[,] a pair of drawers, under shirts, pocket handkerchiefs and a pair of shoes—also a fine calf skin to make you a pair of boots—so hurry home and take a peep at them all—

Mr. F. and I have grieved over our loss of *tobacco* at Culpepper C H—we were not aware you had sent any there on account of the yankees—and only heard it

---

[53] The Union cavalry occupied the line along the Rappahannock River and around Brandy Station. (J.E.D.)

through Mr Withers[54] who told him he was an eye witness to the yankees taking it out of Mr Cooper's store. How much money did you spend in tobacco? If we could have had it in Warrenton during this last visit of the yankees, we would have gained a small *fortune* in yankee money—but we were very unfortunate to lose it—your means are so limited—but do not be worried about it yourself—I have $100 in Confed money and you can *borrow* that amount and buy *tobacco for me* should you have a chance of coming home and bring it with you—but dont run any risk by leaving it any where—the times are too uncertain. You could pack chewing tobacco in a carpet bag, borrow one if you have none.

If you will write and direct your letters to Mr Dudley Pattie, Charlottesville, I may be enabled to get them. Try every means for I am very anxious to hear from you. My heart aches often not knowing if you are in the enjoyment of good health. Separation is painful at all times, but is aggravated when all communication ceases and we cannot hear from our loved ones—When will this cruel war be over and our little family circle be once again reunited. I long for a home, and a home with you— I have no home, because you alone can constitute my home. But I have been blest far above most persons during this cruel war—I have been pleasantly situated with every comfort heart could wish for—in a home where I am loved and our dear children are loved and well cared for[.] May God bless my dear Sister and Mr F. for their unbounded kindness to us—we can never repay them.

The weather is charming—how much the children would enjoy a visit from you—Come as soon as the coast is clear of the yankees—but I cannot tell you when that will be, for their movements are very uncertain. God bless and preserve you is my constant prayer. Oh may you soon be with us.

Good bye love and kisses from all—

Your affec daughter
S.E.C.

Mrs. Withers begs the favor of you to do your best in regard to finding out the whereabouts of her son who was captured at Hanover with the Black Horse. She understood he had escaped—but has not heard from him—how would it to do to find out through an advertisement in the Enquirer. She is so anxious to hear from him.

---

[54] Thornton Withers (1807-1878), from an old Fauquier County family, was born in Kentucky. He moved to Fauquier County where he was married on February 7, 1831 to Katherine Nelson. After her death, he married in 1841 Agnes A. Nelson. He bought the Farmers' Hotel in Warrenton, which he later deeded to his wife and children. Mrs. Withers married very shortly after her husband's death, George G. Booth. (J.K.G.)

1864

Susan Emeline Jeffords Caldwell to Lycurgus Washington Caldwell

Warrenton Fauquier Co
Wednesday February 17th 1864

Dearest Papa

Hearing of an opportunity to send you a letter I hasten to write you a few lines, altho one nearly freezes to be away from the Chimney corner—it is so cold to night, yea it is severely cold—never has been so cold for many winters past—the water freezes in my room if left for fifteen minutes so you must excuse the brevity of this note—

I am very anxious to hear from you since this recent attack upon Richmond by Butler[1]—it was Butler's intention to make a raid into Richmond, destroy as much of public property as possible, *free the prisoners*, then retire but the desertion of one of their men to our army prevented their plan being put into execution. Oh! I feel so grateful their plans were frustrated, for I supposed the Home Guard would have been brought into active duties on such an occasion. God overruled all. I trust I am grateful so far as I know of your safety. Oh! dearest Papa I am so tired of the war and separation from you—life is so short at best—I long for *reunion* but I try to be happy under all circumstances—our little ones are comfortable here, more so I think than they would be in Richmond. We have every comfort—We have a store opened in Warrenton, kept by Mr Howard Skinker[2]—he takes orders and charges 50 per cent on the original price—calicoes sells at 45 cts—shirting 60 cents—and soon if I had United States (or yankee green backs) money I would like to make many purchases. Mr F. is very kind and offers to get me all I need—but he has but little yankee money, and I prefer him to lay it out in provisions—we cannot buy a cent's worth of any thing with confederate money—We understood Mr Cooper sold some of the tobacco for yankee money—Mr F. wrote Mr Cooper to that effect by Mr Skinker when he went to Culpepper—but Mr Cooper was absent from home and we could not hear anything about the sale—I was sorry on account of wishing for it just now—but we will have the store as long as the army remains and I will have the opportunity to make purchases—

The children are all well—and doing well—We all long to see you but cannot think of it at present—I wait with patience for the coming Spring—May our lives be spared and we all be permitted to meet again and be happy again in the midst of our family—God grant you health. Please write us now if you have sold the *bonnet*.

I must now close—Please write to Ma for me—My time is much occupied for all hands are compelled to do some part in housework—I have the same girl this year that you saw when you were here last year—and she with my *help* does my *washing*

---

[1] Gen. Benjamin Butler landed troops on the peninsula east of Richmond on February 9th. Advancing from Yorktown, he attempted to release prisoners from Richmond. After skirmishes at Bottoms Bridge and Baltimore Store, he withdrew. (J.E.D.)

[2] Howard Skinker, much to the disgrace of his family, was a Union sympathizer and spy; he was also always ready to aid anyone in need and frequently gave Confederate soldiers refuge under his roof. (J.K.G.)

and ironing, and it is quite an undertaking during the winter—I cannot get an article washed unless yankee money is paid—so I do the best I can and it is astonishing how well I can get on—I don't have as much time to devote to sewing as I would like—

Good night dearest Papa—may the time pass quickly when you can come home without risk—Bushel of love and kisses from all you love dearly—Sister's spirits are the same—she does not get the better of her affliction.

Your own dear daughter,
S.E.C.

Lycurgus Washington Caldwell to Susan Emeline Jeffords Caldwell

Richmond, Va. March 9th 1864

Dear Daughter,

I have your letters of Jany 27 and Feby 17th and on receipt of each wrote to your parents—They were well at last accounts and would remain with Mag Fitzgerald at Blackville, living off the money for which they sold Jim.—I have it from several acquaintances that provisions are plentiful in So. Ca. and sell at about ¼ what they bring here.—I told the old folks to write me every fortnight so I might give you the latest news when opportunity offers for me to visit Warrenton.—Wm. is Steward of a hospital in Chn.—Manly is attached to an engineer company and he says will hereafter be less exposed to bullets. He has been in several hard fought battles under Genl. Cheatam[3] [sic] and has never been hurt.—The health of all your Carolina friends is good.—

Tell Lute her Mother sent me a nice box of substantials, and occasionally writes to me to hear from her. She must neglect no opportunity to write to her Mother and be ready to go to Waynesboro when I next visit Warrenton.—

I sold the velvet bonnet early last Fall for $90 in Confeds.—borrowed $500 from Josh. B. Finks and added $300 of my own, and with the whole $890 bought tobacco[,] two cases smoking and one box chewing tobacco. That was the lot I left with Cooper when I tried to get home—and which you said Thornton Withers reported to have been stolen by the Yankees.—If as you hear later he sold some for Yankee funds, it may be one of the cases of smoking tobacco.—I wrote him to sell that and I would buy more chewing tobacco, as I got letters from you after my return from Culpepper which induced me to so instruct him.—If the tobacco is a total loss, I could not help it; and Cooper would not take it in store at all unless I assumed the

---

[3] Maj. Gen. Benjamin Franklin Cheatham (C.S.A.), a native Tennessean who distinguished himself as a brigade, division and corps commander in every engagement of the Army of Tennessee, from Shiloh to Atlanta. (J.E.D.)

risk against the Yankees. Lee's army was then on the South Side of the Rappahannock, having lately driven Meade to Centreville, and I did not think would winter South of the Rapid Ann. Besides I had no idea Meade would allow the robbery of private stores in town. I did what I thought was for the best for Mr F. & you and have no censure for myself. I do not believe I would retaliate for my personal wrongs, for the other night when our battallion[sic] repulsed the raiders on Richmond and took several wounded prisoners I only felt compassion for their suffering and not revengeful—

Now about that fight. It was a small affair, but as I was in it *you* will want to have particulars.—It was very like, on a quadruple scale, the fight of the Warrenton Rifles at Fairfax C.H. at the commencement of the War.—You doubtless heard of the escape of 109 Federal Officers from Libby prison[4] some six weeks ago—57 of whom were recaptured and the remaining 52 got off.[5] The latest dates from the North state that the notorious Col. Streight [sic] stated he remained in a score of miles of Richmond (most likely in the City) a week after his exit from Libby—was cared for by Union men & his squad rationed & armed and piloted beyond our lines after the excitement had died out—that in passing our batteries he found them unmanned; that we had only about 3000 regular troops around the City and most of these were engaged in guarding the Military prisons & Belle Isle and that the Home Guard numbering some 2000 could not be depended on. Much other important information he pretended to have or indeed had, but the writer for the Northern papers said it would be communicated to the Federal Govt. & it would be improper to publish.— Now Streights story as printed was indeed too true; and hence the late raid under Kilpatrick, Custur [sic] & Dahlgreen on Richmond;[6] Custur made a diversion on Charlottesville—the others struck with picked men for this place. They were at Frederick Hall on the Central road before we knew it, and were only one hour too late for the Capture of Genl Robt. E. Lee who left Rd that day.—Crossing the country into Goochland they followed a negro guide to the James with the view [of] fording it and coming down the South Side of the James, secure the little bridge to Belle Isle & free the 8000 Yankee soldiers, put arms in their hands & with turpentine and sakum balls, cross Mayo's bridge & fire the City in a thousand places, hang Davis & Cabinet &c &c.—But the River had risen by late rains & they could not ford it, and believing their negro guide had deceived them, they hung him. Cavorting around

---

[4] Libby Prison was located, along with the Belle Island Prison, on the James River in the center of Richmond. (J.M.W.)

[5] Col. A. D. Straight and 109 Federal officers escaped from Libby Prison on February 9th. (J.M.W.)

[6] The Kilpatrick-Dahlgren Raid to Richmond, Feb 28 - March 4, 1864. The noted, abortive raid planned by Union Gen. Hugh Judson Kilpatrick and Col. Ulric Dahlgren was to storm into Richmond, release the Union prisoners held there and capture or kill President Jefferson Davis and his Cabinet. The two leaders separated at Spotsylvania, with plans to meet and surprise the Confederates on the outskirts of Richmond. The plan failed due to information concerning their approach reaching the Confederate War Department. Encountering forces too strong to assault, Gen. Kilpatrick retreated east to New Kent Court House. Col. Dahlgren continued his march to the James River which was too swollen to ford and again facing heavy opposition, he withdrew. Pursued by Confederate forces, Dahlgren retreated to King and Queen Court House, where he rode into a trap, was killed, and most of his men captured. For a definitive study of the raid, see: V. C. Jones, *Eight Hours Before Richmond* (New York: Holt Publishing, 1957), p. 27. (J.K.G.)

the City, and making feints on batteries to the North of the town during the day (from 800 to 2000) they got a guide (an Irish man once a prisoner) sent to them by one Jno. C. Babcock and made a demonstration on the River Road West of the City.—About an hour by sun they came up with the Armory battallion, and catching them by surprise with unloaded guns captured 60 or 70, killed three and wholly dispersed the rest.—A few stragglers from the Armory battallion informed ours (the Departmental Battallion) that the Yankees were a little way ahead in force & that their battallion was *falling* back. So we loaded our rifles about a mile beyond the outer fortifications, marched on 1/4 of a mile and deploying to the right of the road, drew up in battle line in an open field.—The Quarter Masters battallion filed off to the left of the road & formed a line of battle on that side of the road.—Our battallion threw out 3 skirmishes from each company 15 paces in our front and advanced about 30 yards when we heard the Yanks coming up. Our Major then ordered us to lie down & wait for the word before firing, telling us to let the enemy get well up. By this time it was dark as midnight & raining hard.—Our boys kept their guns dry, and soon the opposing skirmishers met, & the head of the Yankee column got within 20 yards of the companies on our right. The Skirmishes then fired & ours fell down or back and our boys poured in a beautiful volley from right to left which caused the enemy to rein up & fall back and as they retired[,] a desultory second fire was directed at them.—Lt. Dement (a Confederate prisoner with the Yanks) said we killed 11 & wounded 20 Yanks[,] principally the first fire. They left 5 dead & 4 wounded in our lines almost and more of the mortally wounded at a farm house & cabins in their rear. After our 2nd fire there was the greatest hubbub in our ranks, & little discipline for 10 minutes, friend calling for friend & excited fools firing their guns in the air. Between the 1st & 2nd fires (our Major being on the right) a part of the right by order & half of the rest by fear, were some 30 yards in the rear of the line of battle & just then three Yanks lapping our lines or breaking them charged between the original & confused lines and not reining up or asking quarter were fired at by fifteen or 25 rifles or more & killed.—That fire revealed to me in the front that the flag was 30 yards to the rear & all of us in the original line fell back and dressed on the colors.— In going from the original line to the colors (my place was six files from the flag) I stumbled on the body of Capt. Ellery, and mistaking it for old Skinner by his white hair, I kneeled down beside it & begged him to tell me how much he was hurt.— He groaned but once and could not speak.—I called to two passers by and they told me it was Ellery—feeling his person (I could not see in the pitchy darkness) I concluded it was E & not S. & so left him—Knowing he was dead & I could do him no good. The reason I took more pains than others as to this was when we were ordered to lie down (being a sergeant) I passed to the left where old Skinner was & told him I would see after him that night, but that I must go to my post near the flag.—I kept my word and was mighty glad to hear the old fellow's voice when I halloed for him along the 2nd line.—The confusion was produced by intense darkness & the blazing firing at the 3 Yanks in our rear.—Indeed we in the front were in most danger from our own men and at that time.—But the whole battallion redeemed itself by falling in a second time and advancing to the original ground or nearly so & waiting there till ordered to the rear by our commanding officer—the 8th & 56 Va. Regts. Huntons

Brigade[7] in the meantime coming up to the batteries a mile in our rear.—Those Regts. then advanced & we fell back to a pine thicket a couple of hundred yards from the batteries and encamped for the night, around brush & plank fires.—Hamme's over-coat kept me dry & warm, altho it rained, sleeted & snowed.—Next day was clear & we manned the batteries at daylight, got wood, crowed, cooked &c.—The next night I was Sergeant of the guard & during forty eight hours only slept 15 minutes. During the 2nd night one sentinel reported a noise, like cavalry riding down fences in front, and the Lieut. ordered me with two men to make a tour of observations & report.—I did so and believe the Sentinal's alarm was caused by cows instead of horsemen & so the camp kept still & others slept while I was awake.—The next day we were ordered to the City to bury Capt. Ellery & back again to batteries.— The 3rd night I slept on the ground & the next night in my bed.—I know I did my whole duty as a soldier.—

Richmond Tuesday 15 March 1864

Dear Daughter,

Last P.M. I rec'd a letter from your Mother and also one from Manley. I have several letters for you. Your Mother & father were still well, but somewhat troubled about living or rather at the prospect of losing 33 ⅓ per cent on their funds. If however the new currency will buy one-third more than the old, their troubles are only imaginary.—They & Mag send love to you.—McMillan has gone to Florida with his company—Mag wrote you a long letter some months ago and I sent it to you.—You must write to her if you can find time. Miss Sam'l J. says she sent back to Chn my letter to your Mother containing money ($40.) But it has never been heard from. I called at Dead Letter Office today & nothing was entered there concerning it.—Manly says he wants a detail—anything rather than a private, but after passage of last Military laws, there is no chance for him so long as he remains well as he is at present. He lately heard from his wife in Memphis, and it greatly rejoiced him.— Gilmore appears to have given up the siege of Chn,[8] but shells are still thrown at the City from Morris Islan.—Another gun-boat, the Ashley, has been just launched at Chn and Confederate blockade ships occasionally run into that port with goods.— There is nothing additional from our armies.—Mosby and McNeil in Va[9] occasionally forward a squad of prisoners to the Libby and Bell Isle—About 400 or 500 Yanks are sent for here every day or two for Ga.[10] in order to feed them the more readily.— If exchange is resumed, they will be shipped from Savh. There is still about 6 or 7,000 privates on Belle Isle & several hundred officers in the Libby. Four simon-pure nigger

---

[7] Hunton's Brigade: Eppa Hunton had been raised in the New Baltimore-Buckland area of Fauquier County. He was now in command of Gen. Garnett's old brigade which had Cos. B & K of the 8th Va. Inf. from Fauquier County. (J.E.D.)

[8] Brig. Gen. Quincey A. Gilmore had directed an attack as part of the siege against Charleston, S.C. (J.E.D.)

[9] John S. Mosby and John H. McNeil, Partisan Rangers. (J.E.D.)

[10] Probably to Andersonville Prison, where food was, ironically, hardly any more readily available. (J.M.W.)

soldiers, caught at Suffolk are housed at Libby with Dahlgreen's [sic] raiding officers—Yanks white dont like the proximity of black Yanks.[11]—The niggers will never be any account as soldiers.[12] News from Europe—especially France—excites pleasing emotions—not matters of hope.—The signs at home and abroad are cheering for the Confederate cause—About 1000 returned Confederate prisoners are now coming up Main street—making 1800—exchanged without the Agency of Beast Butler—I must go out & see them. They are escorted by Music—There was a great crowd at Rockets to greet them several hours ago but delay has driven the major part home.—

Wednesday March 16, 1864—Near about 1 year since I last started home—no prospect just now.—The Yankees are a great bother.—What is to be the Confederate programe [sic] is not known here. The Yankee threat to try Rd. again with 250,000 men cannot be done.—Their draft has failed & been postponed. The Nigger element is a cause of weakness.—They will surely lose Va or Kty & Tenn soon. The disposition of our troops it would not be proper to state—I am clearly of opinion we will have more veteran troops than the Yanks when active operations. All our old armies have re-enlisted and there never was a time when a better feeling prevailed among our troops. There is indeed reason to base cheering hopes upon the coming campaigns.—Again much love to all home.—Be a good girl till I see you.

Yrs affectionately
L W Caldwell

10 P.M.

I understand W E F will convey this to you.—I also send Mr F. some clippings—by same hand—I expect some one will be down from Warrenton soon looking after bonds—See to it—$100. & all over $5. loss 33 ⅓ percent after Apr 1st.—$100. bills 10 each month there after till funded.—Only some 500 privates & some 50 officers arrived today from Point Look Out. Broadus not among them—Gov Smith treated all to coffee & cakes—I did intend to write W & F letters—but too late now.—Love a heart brim full of it to you, Willie, Frank, Jessie, Lucy Lee, Lucy, Lute & Mr F. & Kindest regards to Dr. H. Tell Hamme to put me aside a quart of best old Rye & sweetening—Dont see Sugar these times—Butter retails $10. pound—Now good night—God bless you, my love—

Yrs affectionately
L.W. Caldwell

---

[11] The recruitment of black soldiers did not produce an instantaneous change in northern racial attitudes. Indeed, to some degree it intensified the Democratic backlash against Emancipation and exacerbated racial tensions in the army. The black regiments reflected the Jim Crow mores of the society that reluctantly accepted them: they were segregated, given less pay than white soldiers, commanded by white officers, some of whom regarded their men as "niggers," and intended for use mainly as garrison and labor battalions. One of the first battles these black troops had to fight was for a chance to prove themselves in combat. James M. McPherson, *Battle Cry of Freedom* (New York: Oxford University Press, 1988), p. 565. (J.M.W.)

[12] Six months after the Emancipation Proclamation, more than thirty black regiments had been organized; by December, 1863, over 50,000 blacks were enrolled in the Union Army; before the end of the war, more than 186,000 would be enrolled. Leon F. Litwack, *Been in the Storm So Long* (New York: Vintage, 1980), pp. 70-71. (B.G.C.)

Susan Emeline Jeffords Caldwell to Lycurgus Washington Caldwell

Warrenton Fauquier
March 18th 1864

Dearest Papa

It did not occur to me 'till now that I could write you by "Flag of Truce" and I have taken this opportunity to do so hoping these few lines may reach you, and I presume that through the same medium I may *hear from you*. It has been a *long long* time since I have heard from you and have grown very anxious concerning the condition of your health fearing it has become delicate since my last intelligence from you.

Judging from my own experience that you are as equally concerned about the children and myself as I have been about you I am happy to inform you that we have been very comfortable all winter and the little ones have enjoyed their usual health. We have had all we desired and as yet never wanted for any thing so do not be unhappy in mind on our account, we are doing well. If I could have communication with you my anxiety of mind would be greatly relieved and I hope that here after through this medium we may enjoy this source of pleasure.

We have had severely cold weather this winter. The ice houses in town have all been filled and I hope we shall have this luxury through the long summer months.

I long to hear from Charleston and my loved ones there. May their health be preserved and I may once again have the pleasure of meeting them. When I think of my dear brother Manly far away from all of us oh! how my heart aches—May the Almighty shield his defenseless head when exposed to danger. It has been some months since I have had any intelligence from him.

Willie has commenced school again but I do not think he improves very much, that is to say not as much so as I would desire. He is studying grammar and is fond of it. Frank can spell and can read short sentences. He dreams of you very often and expresses anxious desire to be with you.

Jessie and Lucy are both well and would love to see you once again at home. We all wish very much to see you, but I try to keep up a brave heart and bear this *long*, long separation as well as I can. This month last year you were with us. 'Tis well for us we cannot see into the future, or we would but seldom wear a smiling face.

Sister has not enjoyed good health this winter. Time alone will heal the wound. She grieves deeply over the loss of our dear Mother. Mr F. has had a severe cold and cough this winter.

Hoping these few lines may reach you I shall await anxiously a reply from you.

May God bless you and preserve your health 'till we are permitted to meet again.

Your affectionate and devoted
daughter,
S.E.C.

Warrenton Fauquier Co

Sunday April 19th 1863[13]

Dearest Papa

How truly grateful am I to my Heavenly Parent that you were permitted to leave home in peace and comfort. You went at the right time[,] I feel assured of that[,] you could not have enjoyed another day of pleasure for we have lived in an excited state up to the present. The yankees have been in and out during the week—one part of the day we would see the yankees, then our men would come in and remain until run off by a large force. But a most lamentable occurrence took place Wednesday afternoon. Mr Scruggs and Tom Pattie[14] were in Mr Jackson's[15] room engaged in a game of cards—they had both been drinking and fell out in some way about the game[,] had high words to pass between them and got up and came down into the streets, (there were others in the room but did not think any thing about their leaving) after getting into the streets they talked loud and struck at each other[,] Mr Scruggs falling and Tom Pattie fell on him. Mr S. struggled to get Tom from him— Tom did not seem to be doing any thing to Scruggs. Mrs Tongue was eye witness to it and when they fell she begged some one to part them. Mr Ross came out of the Hotel and raised Tom up but he fell life less on the pavement. Mr Scruggs got up and seeing the condition of Tom as he lay as if dead the blood streaming from his throat— screamed he had murdered Tom—he did not intend it and ran home all covered with blood to his wife telling her he had killed Tom and begged for a gun for some one to shoot him—The Dr was sent for and Tom taken into Mr Jackson's office—they tried to find the artery that was severed and did not succeed until about 11 O'clock at night when reaction took place and he roused. About 5 O'clock next morning he conversed rationally and inquired about his wife and children—at 10 O'clock the Court House bell rang—he asked the reason and was told they did not know—he supposing it was a meeting for Scruggs—said tell them to let him alone, he did not mean to kill me. His wife came to town about 11 O'clock and he knew her—asked after all the children—she was much distressed and could not control her feeling which seemed to excite him, he soon fell off into a heavy sleep and was not conscious again—he died at 5 O'clock, just 24 hours after he was struck with the pen knife by Mr Scruggs—He died very hard having convulsions. Mr Scruggs hearing he was living Wednesday seemed to hope his life might be saved—but when on Thursday he heard he was dead he raved like a maniac—Mr John Spillman went his bail. Tom's family are much distressed—his wife has a young baby and three other children, the eldest about 10 years old. His mother says it will kill her—William Pattie says he will spend the last dollar to have the law enforced—Oh! the distress brought on those two families by drink and deep rooted passion—I dont believe Mr S. intended

---

[13] Probably misdated, as Kilpatrick's raid on Richmond referred to late in the letter, did not occur until 1864. (J.E.D.)

[14] Tom Pattie, who was killed by Mr. Scruggs, has not been identified. Mr. Ross was a carriage maker of Warrenton and a native of Cassel-Hesse, Germany. (J.K.G.)

[15] Possibly G. W. Jackson (see pg.126 n. 93). (J.M.W.)

murder—no his passion led him to the deed. He left this morning for Culpepper where his trial will take place—the yankees caught him once and brought him to town but he has succeeded in getting off to day—

Tuesday —

Mr Yates got home yesterday (brought in by the yankees but released) and brings the news that Mr Scruggs was making his way to Texas but was caught by Dudley Pattie and taken to Culpepper again—poor unhappy man.

Now for some home talk—Lucy Lee missed you Monday and would call for you—Tuesday morning on awaking she looked over the bed and called you. Frank has been troubled with a cold, but is better—we are all doing very well—I hope soon to get my letter left at Mr Kempers.

Monday Night. I received a package to day from you and also some papers for Mr Finks—My letter was dated 9th March. You spoke of having been called out to drive the yankees from Richmond. I have been very miserable concerning you since the raid My heart was sad all the time[.] I read the account you gave of your first call to arms— Oh! how can I be thankful enough to Almighty God for his preservation of your life during the severe trial you have passed through. We cannot see into the future for I knew not of Kilpatrick's raid until it was over. May your precious life never be so exposed to danger again—Pray never enter the army—you are serving the country in your position. I want you to promise me you will not expose yourself if you can possibly avoid it. You have a very dependent family. Think of it and keep your health that some day we may enjoy the society of each other as in by gone days.

I have read several of the many extracts, the one giving the account of the stolen *watch* was very interesting, pray was it yourself or did you only place your name to create some fun because you must have lost all the flesh you gained, and I did not believe your *uniform* had grown thread bare so soon as Mrs D. told me all the *clerks* wore uniform, at present. Please write me if you are in such a dilapidated condition. You must purchase some good clothes. I have Cassimere to make you Coat and pants[.] I was pleased to learn of the compliment paid to Robert Martin[,][16] he is a very deserving young man and a splendid soldier. Write me what you need the most in the clothing line—I have a very nice hat for you—I wish your suit was made to send you but it is difficult to get persons to take packages—

Many thanks to Mrs Joshua Finks for her kindness to you. I have some 20 pounds of *real* coffee if I could manage to get it to you. I wish you had the sugar you sent to Culpepper. So you sold the velvet bonnet—got a big price for it too—I am very sorry we lost the tobacco, but such acts of robbery go on daily. Love to you from all—

---

[16] 1st Sgt. Robert E. Martin, Co. K, 17th Va. Inf. Regt. (Warrenton Rifles). Mrs. Caldwell might have been the first to cite Sgt. Martin's bravery; he was later known as the "Bravest Man in Lee's Army." For a full account of Sgt. Martin, see: Lynn Hopewell, "Robert E. Martin; the 'Bravest Man in Lee's Army,'" in: *Fauquier Magazine,* Vol. I, No. 8 (June, 1988), pp. 16-22. (J.K.G.)

Dearest Papa

We have once again beheld the "Greycoats" and have heard from "Rebeldom."
I read letters from Mr. Utterback which has encouraged me to hope for better days
to come. May my turn come next to get letters from you. Even one *line* would suffice
just to know you were in the enjoyment of health. Mr. F saw Charles Bragg today—
he told he had seen you lately and you were well. Said you were on the raid but was
not hurt. My mind feels much relieved. I hope he is correct. Mr. F saw a gentleman
today lately from Richmond but could not give him any news in regard to you—had
not seen you. Mrs. Brooke received two letters from M. B—why are there no letters
for me? Must surely be some on the road. I wrote you yesterday—hope the soldier
will be faithful to mail it for me—but I do not put much faith in the soldier. He will
oftentimes forget and letters are not mailed, only in their *pockets*. We are all so eager
for letters and papers when the Greycoats come in. Quite a number were in today—
but their pleasure was of short duration for the cry was soon abroad the "yankees" are
coming and it was too true—the yankees did come in a scouting party,[17] raced all over
town to find some rebels, remained about an hour and left. I sometimes think I would
prefer the army here—for these scouting parties to dash in unawares upon us at all
times of the day and night. We are never free of the yankees—we cannot tell when
will return to make any stay, but they will be scouting around us all the while—I
hope soon tho for the time to roll around when Warrenton shall be freed and you be
enabled to come home—or we come to you—tis hard to live thus separated from each
other for so many months at a time. I do know you long to see us—and may be
gratified. Some think we shall have another raid into Pennsylvania. What say you to
that. Can it be so—if so I hope Lee will be more successful than he was at Gettysburg.
We have had a glorious victory in the West.[18] The yankees feel assured that Grant
will be successful in the capture of Richmond. He has a very large army but many
are heartily sick of the war and say they do not intend to reenlist. Their time will be
out in August and they are going home to stay—I hope they will be true to their
word.

Mr. Brooke writes he has heard various rumours in regard to the ladies of
Warrenton. Tell him not to believe one word. We are all loyal—we are very
peculiarly situated and no people would do even as well as we do in the midst of an
enemy. We at some times are completely in their power and cannot help ourselves.
We must exist and are dependent on the wretches for many things but {would not}
yet have sold ourselves for sugar and coffee. We keep *true* to the South amid all our
sore trials—and at times are to be pitied. To have the enemy around you and come
in and take your horses, your meat, corn & wheat at their pleasure and compelled to
submit quietly. It is now 11 o'clock P.M. and my little Lee has not gone to sleep—

---

[17] These scouting parties apparently were in search of Col. Mosby. (J.E.D.)

[18] This must have been the capture of Ft. Pillow, Tenn. Apr. 12th. (J.E.D.)

my foot is on the cradle and I cannot write steadily so please excuse the scrawl. On receiving this if you will write and direct your letters to the Care of Lieut. Col. John I. S. Mosby, Glen Welby, near Salem,[19] I will get them. Mosby has his headquarters at Major Richard Carter's and his farm is called Glen Welby and I was told to have my letters so directed as Mosby has a regular mail at or near Salem. I shall look for one from you very soon.

I have some clothing for you—how would you like some colored flannel overshirts like the soldiers in place of white cotton ones—would they be useful to you? I have two—gave $4 a piece in yankee money. Have you any idea when you can come home? We are all well at present. Sister's spirits are yet much depressed. Has not been out yet.

All send bushels of love and kisses to you. We do long to see your face once home again. Good night—most 12 O'clock. Good night. God bless and preserve you. Should you come bring some smoking tobacco if you can without sustaining losses on the roadside. Good night.

May your precious life be preserved.

Your ever devoted
S.E.C.

Undated, 1864

Dearest Papa

Mr. Grant arrived home Saturday but having failed to see you had no letter from you. I was much disappointed for it is now some time since I heard from you. I was glad to learn you received the trunk and am anxious to know if the clothes were a good fit and if you were pleased.

There is no news. Mr. Sedwick does not know when he will go to Richmond. I am anxious for him to go in order the ... can get there before the winter is over.

We are all doing well—send love & kisses. Lucy Lee has commenced to walk alone.

Good Bye. Love to you from all. There is no telling when Mr. Sedwick will leave for R.

Your affec daughter
S.E.C.

I would like to write you a long letter but my envelope is filled. Mr. Bronaugh

---

[19] 'Glen Welby,' the home of Major Richard H. Carter, is located between Marshall (Salem) and Rectortown. The family was noted for its hospitality to Col. John S. Mosby and his men. That he assumed one more responsibility of civil government, that of postal functions, is not surprising. He was the only government employee in "Mosby's Confederacy" and was recognized for his civil, as well as military, activities in the area. This arrangement for mail, however, has not been mentioned by the several writers on Mosby's Rangers. (J.K.G.)

gave Mr. F the letters. I was glad enough to hear from you. You must enjoy your apples yourself. Don't be too generous in handing them around for I sent them for *your special* benefit during the evenings. I was sorry your *coat* was so *short tailored*, but it was *that or no coat*. Never mind—I am trying hard to get you another suit if it is possible. I was delighted to hear from Mollie Hungerford. I was sorry to hear of little Fannie's death. I loved her as a baby. I shall write to her very soon.

The children are learning their letters. Willie seems to love his school. He studies and is generally perfect in his lessons. He will *not* remain at home schooldays, never mind if it rains, or snows. He has just returned from school and it is snowing furiously but he said he could not stay away, he did not want to be afoot in his definitions. I am glad to see him anxious to attend regularly to school.

Frank is learning Ba Be Bo. We are all very well.

Quite a number of Yankee deserters are coming in daily. They sell their overcoats for all they can to pay their way.

Warrenton Fauquier
Monday April 25th 1864

Dearest Papa

Could you but know how much my troubled and anxious heart has been relieved since the perusal of your much welcomed letter of the 17th[.] I know you would consider yourself well repaid for your early rising to be in the right time at depot. I know my heart feels grateful to Almighty God for his innumerable kindnesses to you in the many months I have not been permitted to hear from you or even of your welfare. I have striven hard to keep up my usual cheerful disposition— and have done so until this raid of Kilpatrick's. I knew all the clerks had been ordered out and read extracts from the Richmond papers that many had suffered severely from the exposure and forced marches—I would dream of you but my dreams made me miserable during the day—Oh! how my heart has yearned but for *one line*[,] I en- treated the yankees to send a letter for me[,] they did so[,] I wrote by "Flag of Truce" but judge you never received it. I have written to you by every possible opportunity and did hope you would hear from me 'tho I was denied letters from you. How thankful we should be to our Heavenly Parent for his preservation of us all during such months of severe trial we have had to pass through this winter; and now we are in constant suspense fearing we know not what, Grant's proclamation did not amount to any thing with us. The Cavalry were ordered off very suddenly from our town. Should they have remained a longer period with us after Grant's arrival he might have been apt to have carried such threats into execution. So far we have ever been treated kindly by the Army. The country people have suffered severely. We have been permitted to buy of the Commissaries groceries at very reasonable prices. Sugar at 15 cts, coffee at 40. Then we had a dry goods store established selling tho at rather high prices calicoes at 40 cts cotton at 70. If I had, had plenty of Green backs I could have bought you boots and every article you would have needed at reasonable prices for these exorbitant times. Boots were selling at $8 and 12—excellent ones. All the ladies had to work hard to make money to buy groceries and dry goods. The yankees you know are very fond of *pies* and *cakes* and they buy or exchange for coffee as many as would be sent to camp. I made about $25 and bought shoes and other articles for children[,] paid for your *Cassimere* I purchased in the fall. I had borrowed the money. I have several articles for you—a very nice black hat. If I knew you could not get here soon I would make an effort to send them to you—you must write me word what articles you need the worst. I have 4 white cotton shirts made to send you if I can get them to you by Dick Brooke—but these times every body's carpet bag is filled with articles they wish for themselves and but with little *extra* room for a *neighbour*. I will abide my time hoping you may be able soon to get home and take all your clothing with you. What are we to expect this year? Are we to be thus separated again? How about our coming to Richmond? Are the times too uncertain for us to be with you in Richmond? Write and tell me what you think will be best for us the coming summer. I am willing to abide your decision—Tell me if you can keep your spirits up when separated so long from those you love. Do you ever become d[e]sparate? Mrs Brooke tells me Mr B. is crazy to see her—but is afraid to venture home. He writes *love letters* to her half dozen at a time—Oh! how I long for this cruel war to be over— I feel *ten years* older.

We have made some pleasant acquaintances among the army—We are in the midst of them and are in their power—we only treat those kindly where kindness has been extended to us by them. I understand various rumours are afloat across the lines in regard to the Ladies of Warrenton—We are as *loyal* now as ever—and if the very persons were similarly situated as we are who circulate these false reports I doubt if they would [have behaved] as consistently as we have done. Our situation is a very trying one. Col. Taylor and Col Gardner proved themselves very gentlemanly during their stay with us. Several officers had their wives with them. Very many persons from Washington came up during the winter. I heard from Mrs Smoot several times. Dr Samson teaches the college boys in his house, the college having been taken for a hospital. There are a number of secessionists in Washington but they are compelled to keep quiet.

The yankees made a raid in town on Friday last and captured William Bragg— he is one of Mosby's men—He had just come in to see his wife and they were about to start out for the country when the cry was the yankees are coming[,] he then jumped on his brother's horse hoping to escape, but his *horse* was rather too fat to run fast and poor fellow he was caught—now to lie in prison for time indefinite, very little pleasure for friends to visit in Warrenton during the time the yankees are about.

Please write me every particular about yourself and what you think will be best for us the coming months—Write and direct your letter to the Care of Lieut Col J. S. Mosby. Mosby's head quarters are at Major Richard Carters and Glen Welby[,] Fauquier Co. Va. His farm bears the name of Glen Welby and I will be sure to get them if so directed[.]

I did not understand what you meant by saying I must "keep the children well at home the coming 6 weeks" and also what did you mean by having a "branch Gov in the Trans Mississippi" explain in your next—.

Please dont mention any thing again about your desire to join the Army—you are now oftentimes called into danger and such should satisfy you I think. I shall never consent to your joining the army—I am miserable enough at best and should you take such a step life would be worth nothing to me but to make preparation for eternity—and I am so moved in mind at times that I fear I do not think of the future as I should. We should be more mindful of our home in heaven[.]

The day is lovely, very warm—I must hasten to my sewing as the little ones will need their spring fixings—

Mr. F. has suffered very much with colds during the winter he is getting the better of it at present—he is anxious to get to Richmond for a short time to see how things are working but he fears to leave home at such critical times.

I must close. Dick Brooke will leave in the morning for Richmond and you will meet with him—Give me an idea if you are coming on soon[.]

Frank wants to see you, he dreams oftentimes of you and is trying to learn, but he is rather too fond of playing out doors. He has had a sick turn, but is now well and out doors at play[.]

Good bye. A bushel of kisses from all hands and a heart full of love is sent you in this letter from all. I will write to Mother if I have time—God bless you dear one

Your ever affec daughter
S.E.C.

Warrenton Via
Thursday May 5th 1864

Dearest Papa

I am sorely disappointed in not being able to get some few articles to you that I know you are in need of. But Dick has no room to spare and Mr S. has as much as he can toddle under. May be some good Samaritan may pass by me some day and offer to take you a *shirt collar* or pocket handkerchief or perhaps a cravat. Mr Sedwick thinks of going to Richmond when the way is clear of *yankees*[,] then you will get a package—

I have 3 flannel shirts, 3 white cotton shirts, 6 pair cotton socks, 4 handkerchiefs, 8 collars, 2 pair of cotton drawers—cravat vest and a suit of Cassimere clothes—Sister has a hat for you—Now of all these articles tell me which of the many you will need most, so I can send to you as I can only send a few at a time. I have also 2 under shirts and a pair of flannel drawers—and some 11 pounds of *real good coffee*— Oh! that I could get them all to you in good order at this early period. I am hoping you may get home yourself after the battle is over which of course will come off soon now—

We understand the yankees are in the valley. We are in daily expectation of them. I wish you could pay us a visit but I prefer you to remain where you are until there is more quiet with the raiding yankees. No pleasure now for friends to visit Warrenton.

On last Saturday at Rectortown a party of yankees from Harpers Ferry[20] were led in by one Mr James—and behaved most shamefully, killed one of Mosby's men after he had surrendered—you see there were but three of Mosby's men in the place and they were surrounded—Lieut Nelson escaped—Goff was killed, Glascock severely wounded & captured. These three soldiers were near Salem not Rectortown, they did fight at Rectortown & Middleburg I understand. I much prefer an army around me than these raiding parties. But we have been very kindly treated by the yankees—Mr F. has always been able to get groceries, he has now 2 barrels of Sugar and one of coffee, 8 barrels of flour and supply of bacon—We have never wanted for any thing. I have clothes for myself and children as much as I ever had and hope you do not allow yourself to want for any comfort. Keep yourself supplied if you please in good comfortable clothing and good nourishing food. It is deprivation enough for you to be separated from loved ones—I feel for you and if wishing and praying would or could have us once again united we would soon be—

The children are all well—Jessie suffers a great deal with *tooth* ache. We are going to make an effort to have the tooth extracted.

I just had a talk with Mr Williamson, Willie's school teacher, he speaks in praise of Willie's quickness to learn but says he is very *mischievous* and is compelled to correct him. He is learning Geography and Grammar—

Frank can spell but prefers to play out doors, he is so very delicate I dont urge him at his book. I let him run out doors all day long. I have promised myself to commence soon now to hear him daily—

Jessie and Lucy are sweet little creatures, would love to walk up street with Papa if the yankees would stay away. Aunt Lucy is with us yet—I hardly think she will go[,] I hope not for we would have to break up housekeeping[.] Mr F. has no way at present to send Lute home—if her Father can meet her at any point he must write and tell him and he will get her to him—She has quit school and I think would be better off now at her *Mother's home*. She is rather hard to manage, and Sister feels as if she ought to be with her Mother—*don't mention* the fact tho. Find out what Mr Joshua intends for to be done and let us hear. Lute wants to see them all at home very much—

Why dont you write—only had two letters—17 April & 9th March. My pen is miserable, perfect scratch, excuse scribble in haste have but little time to write in, did not know Dick was going till half hour ago—

Take good care of yourself and if you do not hear from me soon—know the yankees are about. Be easy about us, we get on nicely—

Direct some of your letters to Care of Col. J. S. Mosby—Glen Welby, Fauquier Warrenton and I will get them—I think. Write me how much you weigh & how many *clothes* you have—I have a pair of heavy shoes for you—

---

[20] She may be mistaken in saying "yankees from Harpers Ferry." The existing reports indicate that these Union troops were from Col. Charles R. Lowell's brigade at Vienna. (J.E.D.)

Be ever easy about us—take good care of yourself Write to Manly & my dear parents for me.

Undated, 1864

Dearest Papa—Mr Franklin tells me he met with you last week and you were well and in excellent health. I am truly thankful to the Good Being in His kindness and protecting care of you my loved one—I have felt very great uneasiness concerning you, not had one line from you since the 17th April—please write to me. When may I expect you home oh! how I long to gaze upon your dear face once more if but for an hour. Write me if you have any idea of coming home at an early day—I have quite a number of articles for you but have no way of getting them to you. I do wish you had your suit of clothes I have for you—I have a bag of coffee[.] I intend asking Mr Walter F. to take it to you but I fear he cannot do it. We are well & do hope your health will continue good—write to me what articles you are in most need of—and I will try my utmost to get them to you. Be sure to write to Mother & Manly for me— Good bye Loved One[.] Oh! may we soon meet again, may this cruel war soon end and we be once again united never more to be *parted* till by the cruel monster "death."

Bushels of love from me & all[.]

Your own devoted & affectionate
daughter
S.E.C.

Lycurgus Washington Caldwell to Susan Emeline Jeffords Caldwell

Richmond, Va May 25 1864

My Very Dear Daughter

I have two letters from you, (thro' Dick B. I presume;) one dated April 25th with pencil addenda of April 30, and the other May 5th.—The last reached me first in camp on the Williamsburg road last Friday, the first was advertised and only taken from the Post Office last night when I reached the City.—I wrote to you on the 20th inst., but my letter got no further than Mr Phillips room up to last night.—It took 4 days to go three miles.—So much for letters thro' soldier friends.—I am I trust profoundly grateful to Almighty God to learn that Mr F. has a good stock of commissary stores, and that you and all the needy of my native town have been kept warm during the Winter. That you all now enjoy a goodly share of health, and have raiment is also a source of gratification.—Your privations so far have been less than tens of thousands, and should teach you lessons of thankfulness and resignation.—Rest assured of this,—I am comfortably clad and have plenty of wholesome food.—I have not suffered in body at all.—My chief and nearly whole concern is for you and the children,—for Lucy & Mr F.—Beyond my family circle little transpires to excite disquietude. I do not think I ever breathe a prayer for myself except to ask God to bless me with continued health and safety for your sakes—for I love you all better than I do myself and wish to be able to serve you. I know each of you pray for me, and confiding in the purity of your lives believe I shall be spared in Gods own time to provide for and take care of you all, in answer to your own, if not my own, supplications.—I confidently believe we shall soon meet and on bended knee return Heaven thanksgiving.—Be of good cheer.

I have worn my uniform[21] all winter and saved my citizen clothes.—I shall have plenty for 12 months even if I do not get home.—If I had two or three marino under shirts this fall I could make my cotton shirts hold out for 18 months more or two years.—I wear out a great many shoes on raids, but have had foresight to purchase long ago, and now half sole & patches will keep me going till next Jany.—I wrote the dream for fun, but much of it is now literally true of Clerks here with *families*.—Few of them have meat for their little ones and most of them look seedy.—Indeed some of them actually suffer.—My mess-mates (Skinner, Phillips & Judge Baker) still keep together.—P. gets a good deal from the Quarter Master of Marine Corps and S. from interior N.C.—At present we have 50 pounds bacon & 1 ½ bushels meat &c.—enough to last us a month—till Grant is whipped. Now that transportation is suspended & the R. Roads occasionally threatened, and gardners of the vicinage alarmed, prices rule very, very high—indeed little can be bought at any price.—Just now every thing is higher than ever, but down South prices are tumbling.—Here meal is $100. per bushel—bacon $10. per pound—butter $20. per pound, eggs $10. per dozen—onions $2. for four.—&c. In Chn meal is $2.50[,] bacon $3.50[,] &c. But as soon as Lee fights a decisive battle everything here will tumble. Few persons have left the City, and as Lee falls back this way, every thing goes higher.—In the three great battles recently fought[22] it is estimated that we have lost between 15,000 and 25,000 men killed, wounded & missing and the Yankees confess to 45,000 while some of their papers put it down at 70,000 & for so doing have been suppressed.—The cause of the discrepancy was due to the fact that for the first time our men fought principally in entrenched positions or on ground of their own choosing.—Grant was forced to make the attacks.—It is thought now that another great battle is near at hand if not now progressing along the line of the Central Rail road above Hanover junction… [Here a two-page lapse in the correspondence exists.]

---

[21] See *The Day Richmond Died*, by A. A. and Mary Hoehling (A. S. Barnes & Company, Inc., 1981), pp. 78-9, for a descriptive paragraph on the unit to which Lycurgus was attached: "Not far away, near Chaffin's Bluff and Fort Harrison, was a patched up tatterdemalion brigade under the command of Custis Lee (see pg. 228 n.24). It was composed of some 1,300 local guards from Richmond, chiefly clerks, 'augmented' by an artillery group of six battalions so rusty in active service that they scarcely knew a cannon's breech from a muzzle. Yet they all were jaunty in scarlet caps with trim that set them apart from ragged trenchmates, many of whom wore nothing that could be described as a "uniform." (J.K.G.)

[22] The Wilderness, Spotsylvania and North Anna. (J.E.D.)

... They left their dead (five) in the woods, but bore back the wounded; & those slightly wounded came back without help. All the while there was an interchange of cannonading—some of the enemys shells passing over the heads of our entrenched men quarter of a mile to the rear. When Gracie[23] had gotten out about 300 yards from our lines (breastworks) a call was made for all non-commissioned officers, save one sergeant & 30 men from each company of our battallion. Being a non-commissioned officer I promptly obeyed and the force called for was in line of battle in 10 minutes.—All of us then expected to be led into the woods with Gracie's Brigade; but other counsel prevailed and after keeping us two hours standing up in pelting rain, we were ordered back to the trenches.—In the meantime other forces had arrived and they formed a new line of battle and pressed through the woods only to find the Yankees had ... the bridge and retreated.—I got the credit of being a good soldier &c., but I tell you old 'oman, I was very glad I did not have to bush-whack for Yanks that day for they were 3 to one & had splendid cover from behind big trees, underbrush & deep ravines to fight.—Our papers lament their escape, but I congratulate my countrymen that they left.—Our Cavalry hung on their rear as they came to Richmond & could not venture a general fight. They were pronounced mounted infantry by our wounded men as they passed us, for they said cavalry would never have fought at all.—They thought we had a large force & were scared off as their retreat has been cut off by our cavalry attempting the destruction of bridges & this it was which alarmed them.—Now you may ask why I did not ask to be the sergeant left in the breastworks.—It was the duty of the Capt. to elect one and I feel prouder that he did not name me.—I went to sleep in the P.M. while our devoted soldiers were piling up knapsacks and singing pious hymns preparatory to joining battle as they imagined, for I had not slept over 4 hours in 48.—Our battn. was out 19 days, and during that time it rained once or more hard in every 24 hours; but for the first time, we halted. We had tents to shelter us & so kept dry and comfortable.—One night some dogs stole about $80. or $100. worth of bacon from my mess.—I saw them in our pot nosing after hock and corn dodgers.—But some two legged dogs soon played the same trick on the other messes.—The Govt. gave us 2 oz. bacon & pound corn bread per day—or about sugar & coffee enough to make a cup full per man instead of meat.—It cost me as much in camp as at home, for there are many lazy spongers.— Soon we shall be ordered out again perhaps, but I am sure we shall only fight in emergency.—You would not have me play sick or act cowardly I know, and I believe I shall not be hurt.—I do military service cheerfully from a sense of duty and abominate the skulkers.—I know I have no choice about the matter, but do not pout and grumble like children or darkies.—I did not write you I wished or desired to join the army; but that a rumor was afloat which if true would make it preferable to civil life—viz: going with Govt. to Montgomery.—In that event I wanted to see you & then join Mosby.—There was ground for it—the 2nd Auditor was ordered to pack up papers and the ladies on Treasy notes were sent to Cola. We have a branch of the

---

[23] Archibald Gracie, Jr. commanded a brigade on the Petersburg lines until his death in December, 1864. (J.E.D.)

226

Treasy and P.O. Depts. at Shreveport La.—or soon will have.—They will settle trans-Mississippi affairs.—I may have referred to that as giving me additional work at the time I wrote.—We had books to copy &c. for them.—

Susan Emeline Jeffords Caldwell to Lycurgus Washington Caldwell

Warrenton Via
Monday June 14th 1864

Dearest Papa

I hastily pen you these few lines to beg of you to write to me.—I feel as if I cannot exist these times if I am denied the only comfort left me that of hearing from you.— I write you by every opportunity but I know not how many letters you may receive from me—Write me all you are doing—if you are in service, or at your writing desk—oh! that I could see you just a little while—tis so wearisome—has been so long since you were here—

Mr John Roberts is at our house, he lives in Charlottesville and tells me if you will write and enclose your letters to John Roberts[,] Charlottesville—or Dudley Pattie[,] Charlottesville[.] Mr Roberts comes to Warrenton every two weeks and will deliver my letters to me—now you will have no excuse—write as soon as you receive this and I will get it very soon—I will be on the lookout for a letter from you now in a few days[.]

The little ones are all well—I have not been well for some days but am getting much better.

I hope you have received some of the packages I have sent you—sent one package by Walter Franklin one through Mrs Garratt by the way of Lynchburg— and Mrs Tongue had one for you—Mr Tavenner has some coffee and sugar for you— Jessie sent you a box with some cake—Lee a candy strawberry—The Conscript officer is in town creating quite an excitement, but I believe they will not take heads of families, I feel much worried about Mr Finks but he says he knows he can get off should they take him—but I hope they will pass over old men at 45—

Send some papers if you can—I would like you to hunt all the papers with the battles & lists of killed and wounded—

Please write to Mother. Oh! how I want to see the dear old people—have you written to Manly?—Now be sure and write me, tell me if you have received any thing from me—and what you may stand in need of—

Good bye—God bless and preserve you my own loved one[.] Oh! may we be permitted to meet again—

Love & kisses from all your loved ones—

Your devoted daughter,
S.E.C.

227

Lycurgus Washington Caldwell to Susan Emeline Jeffords Caldwell

Richmond City June 27th, '64

Dear Daughter

I came in from Camp lst night on 24 hours furlough and have had many things to attend to for our company. I have not filled all requests yet and now it is 1 P.M. and I must leave at 3 ½ or walk 8 ½ miles before 8 P.M.—I got your package per Mrs Tongue today. Regret I did not know in time she was here. I asked for 30 days furlough, but could not get it.—I think the Civil Offices will be almost entirely suspended till Grant's campaign is over and that our Battallion will be kept in the field till then.—We have been 26 days out this time and many of us are tired of marching—building breastworks and felling forest trees. I do not believe we will be placed in posts of very imminent peril, because the stake is too great to depend on the untried qualities of the local Confederate troops, composed of Clerks from the Depts. and Mechanics from the workshops.—Our Brigade is under Custis Lee[,][24] son of Robt. E. Lee[,] and number about 1700 men.—On the 21st inst. all of us were kept in line of battle 4 or 5 miles below Chaffins Bluff at a place on the River called Deep Bottom.[25] I have endorsed on one of your letters a few lines which you would like to see.—They were the thoughts that then filled my heart and mind.—I am not afraid and trust the Lord will shield me from all danger, ward off all sickness and soon restore me to you and those whom it is my duty and pleasure to take care of.—There have been many foolish and cruel reports circulated concerning our Battn. Do not let such idle stories disturb your quiet.—Look daily to the moral & religious instruction of our little ones and tell them their loving papa will fly to their embrace as soon as circumstances will permit—Now may be the best time to visit you but let us patiently wait God's pleasure—His (not our) will be done—

Now I have no news—half I see in the papers and most all I hear in Camp are lies.—Tell Sister I would like to eat a good dinner with her and hope soon to do so.— The Yanks are trying to destroy our Rail Roads and think starvation will force us to make disadvantageous battle.—I however hear we have army supplies here for 3 months and am sure Grant will not take a 4th July dinner here. *Pride* may force him to make a desperate effort to do so and then may give our men again opportunity to fire behind breastworks—

Charleston is still annoyed by Foster's[26] shells but in no danger.—Yankee officers are now put in the shelled localities and it may stop the barbarous procedure. They can hope for nothing in the vile practice but criminal annoyance.—They

---

[24] Maj. Gen. George Washington Custis Lee (C.S.A.) (1832-1913), was the eldest son of General Robert E. Lee. He was a graduate of USMA, West Point, 1854, and saw duty in the U.S. Army to 1861. He was commissioned Capt. of the Confederate Engineers and assigned to superintend the fortifications of Richmond. In August, 1861 he was commissioned Col. and A.D.C. to President Jefferson Davis. He trained the local defense brigade at Richmond and commanded it in the Kilpatrick-Dahlgren Raid. Under General Ewell he retreated from Richmond and was captured at Sailor's Creek, on April 6, 1865. (J.K.G.)

[25] Deep Bottom, on the James River. (J.E.D.)

[26] Union Commander John G. Foster attacking Charleston. (J.E.D.)

confess their inability to capture the proud old City.—The temporary success of Yankee[s] in the Va Valley has been checked and they now flee from the wrath of Breckenridge[27] & Early.[28]—Josh. B. F. is all right, so says Agt of Va Central.— Enemy did not go to Waynesboro.—In a week or so the Road will be repaired.— Johnston is getting the better of Sherman in North Ga.—and in trans-Mississippi the Yanks have been most signally whipped.—All looks well for our side just now. I hope we shall soon demolish Grant and that peace will follow victory.—How proud it would make me to be herald of peace to old Fauquier. Tell Mr Finks to stay at home. I have not seen any reserve Militia from border Counties.—Saw Gov. Smith a moment in Market this A.M. & he said he would send to Fauquier in a few days and transmit a letter for me.—I will tell John Garrett to give Gaskins a paper to send Mr F. every opportunity.—Jno. has no package yet. Nothing yet by Mr Franklin— Corse' Brigade is on South side of James River & 4th Cavalry on North side last night.—Have not seen any Warrenton boys—and can give no news of them this time.—Soon as my battn. is ordered to Rd. I will get leave to start home.—Campbell will accompany me.—He, Carlin, Chilton and Beckham are in my camp.—Do not give way.—I look confidently forward to a brighter day a short distance ahead.—Be of good cheer & write me long letters & tell me all about our little responsibilities.— I want some of their talk dotted down.—I looked at you all this A.M. God preserve us.—I must now look for Goodloe's boarding house & carry him a change of clothes.—I was 4 weeks out without change of shirts.—The articles by Mrs. T are too fine for Camp.—Keep all clothes you have for me save colored shirts for soldiering till I see you.—

Sweetly and tenderly kiss all the children for me and tell them softly each day Papa prays they will be very good children. Love to Lucy, Lute and Mr F. Kind regards to Dr H & friends.—Remember me to Aunt Lucy, the faithful among the faithless.— The cruelty of Yankees to negroes are sending numbers home.—Goodbye and, my dear daughter, remember, I think of you and the children always.—If not for my own, God will spare me for your sakes.—I will strive to discharge faithfully the trust—

Ever affectionately I am yours truly
L W Caldwell

Written at Sentinel Office & bad pen.
RM.S will send this & Miss—letters—

Richmond August 6th 1864

My Dear Daughter
    I have such miserable conveniences for writing at my room, that I am tempted

---

[27] Confederate General John C. Breckenridge, who had defeated Sigel at New Market May 15th, with the help of VMI's Cadet Corps. (J.E.D.)

[28] Confederate General Jubal A. Early, who drove Gen. David Hunter from the Valley in June. (J.E.D.)

to pen you a few lines during office hours as I hear of an opportunity to send you a letter by Mr. Norris, who says he leaves tomorrow.—I have no news to tell you except that General Lee wants more men and it is rumored has made a requisition for 10,000 of the reserved forces of Va. He has troops enough for defensive operations, but wants to strike as well as parry. The evacuation of Atlanta is much regretted; but as Hood's Army[29] is still in heart and hope, military critics in bomb proof positions should be more lenient and less despondent.—Gen'l. Jno. H. Morgan,[30] the gallant partisan leader, is no more. It appears that he was surprised at Greenville on the Va and Ten. R.R. and killed—his staff being captured.—He had recently been relieved of his command of the Dept. of South Western Va and Genl Echols[31] put in his stead.— For this reason Kentuckians are very bitter on Gen'l Bragg. It is said that Order No. 65 by Gen'l Cooper is bringing in many deserters in front of Lee's lines.—It appears … German this morning in the Examiner.—Charleston still holds out, and there is no prospect of its capture.—Like Petersburg it is occasionally shelled.—Every thing at Mobile is now at a stand still.—Wheeler[32] is said to be threatening Nashville in Sherman's rear.—But what if he does cut S.'s communication with his base of supplies, the Yankees will forage all the more upon the abundant harvests in the heart of Ga. from whence the Confederates here have been drawing supplies for 12 months; and moreover, they (the Yanks) soon repair damages.—Forest[33] [sic] seems to be checkmating Federal troops in Miss.—From trans-Mississippi we hear little but that little is encouraging.—Kirby Smith[34] is having every thing his own way there.—I wish he could cross over 20,000 men to reinforce Hood; but I do not believe his men would obey such an order even though he could make a safe ferriage over the Miss. River.—It would not surprise me if Early secretly withdrew from Sheridan's[35] front all save his Cavalry and go to Hood's Assistance. Then possibly the Yanks would overrun nearly all Va. again.—Oh! if we had only 30 or 40,000 more men to throw in Shermans rear! It seems to me he has ventured now so far into the heart of Ga. that his capture would be inevitable.—Indeed I am almost willing to see Gen'l Lee evacuate Va. entirely for a time with the view of taking Sherman's army.—The Democratic party in the North are now aroused and talk of peace—recognizing slavery and all rights under the Federal constitution.—The Republicans will let the

---

[29] Gen. John B. Hood (C.S.A.) had just been driven from Atlanta by Lt. Gen. W. T. Sherman, (U.S.A.). (J.E.D.)

[30] This letter is probably incorrectly dated *August* instead of *September*. Brig. Gen. John Hunt Morgan (C.S.A.) (1825-1864), legendary cavalry leader of the Confederacy from Kentucky, was killed on September 3, 1864 in an early morning surprise attack by a detachment of Union cavalry at Greenville, Tenn. (J.K.G.)

[31] Brig. Gen. John D. Echols (C.S.A.), in command of Southwest Va. (J.E.D.)

[32] Lt. Gen. Joseph Wheeler (C.S.A.), cavalryman with the army in Tenn. (J.E.D.)

[33] Lt. Gen. Nathan Bedford Forrest (C.S.A.) (1821-1877), one of the greatest cavalry commanders of the South. (J.E.D.)

[34] Gen. E. Kirby Smith (C.S.A.), "was clinging precariously to what was left of Texas, Louisiana, Arkansas, and the Indian Territory—'Kirby Smithdom,' this last but empty stretch of the continent was called—and resisted all efforts by Richmond and homesick subordinates to persuade him to go over to the offensive, either toward New Orleans or St. Louis." Shelby Foote, *The Civil War: A Narrative; Red River to Appomattox* (1958), pp. 574-5. (J.M.W.)

[35] Gen. Philip Sheridan, Union Commander in the Shenandoah Valley. (J.E.D.)

South go rather than recognize slavery.—An issue is made and a few months will give us all a clearer insight into the future than we have been capable of seeing in the past.—I do not think I can consent to live separated another Presidential term, and expect we had better prepare to live in a log hut.—House rent is outrageously high.—I think we might live if we could cultivate a garden and get pasterrage [sic] for a nannie goat.—Do you think you could feel contented in an humble abode and keep ward and watch if I were now and then called off on a raid? Another four years of war and there will be a general scatteration.—But possibly we shall have peace in a few months and then we can live uninterruptedly and comfortably.—I sometimes think and think till I grow dizzy in thought.—And suddenly waking from a reverie I say it is useless to think.—It troubles me no little to think I am in no situation to help you and the children.—How many thousands now striving for political independence are laying the foundations of pecuniary servitude for all time to them individually? We shall have pledged all we had saved before the war even if it ends now, and if we come out with honor, though penniless we can be frugal & economical and enjoy life yet. I will not despair.—It may be peace is but a little way off.—But I must not dwell on the probabilities of a continuance of war.—In all time I will strive to do the best I can to serve my family and leave the rest to God.—

I wonder if Lucy Lee is tripping on tip-toe today and munching apples? Possibly Jessie is singing a lullaby to Mary McCafferty.—Frank is doubtless counting the goodies in his saving box, and Willie bridling the colt or old Charley, preparatory to riding them to water.—Lucy is looking over her specs at her sewing now—and anon at the litter our little scamps have made in her chamber. You are perhaps running tucks in Willie's pants and wondering if they would be a good fit for Frank if measured by his summer breaches.—I would like to pop in unawares and kiss right and left, and spend a month, yes a lifetime with you all.—There is a misty rain falling and such days there is racket at home I know, but to me now it would be sweet music.—How much I would enjoy a wild romp with the little ones.—How many anxious thoughts they give you! Well daughter, imagine what you would have them be, and live yourself precisely that character perpetually before them; and they will always be good children and worthy members of society.—The little things are continually aping and copying the manners of those they love. Being so much away from home you will have had more influence in fashioning and moulding their characters and conduct than I; but this does not relieve me of my responsibility to them and God. Dear little souls—Heaven's choicest blessings rest upon their heads!—

Lutie Finks was here one day last week, and I took dinner with her at the Calvert's at the Powhatan conducted on the European style.—She has had her teeth fixed and looked quite pretty.—I read her your letter of the 24th alto. being the latest news from Warrenton.—She says all are well at her fathers.—

Tom Saunders was to have inquired of Stofer[36] about the tobacco and reported

---

[36] Alfred J. Stofer, Editor and publisher of the *Culpeper Observer* for many years prior to, and after, the Civil War. (J.K.G.)

to Mr Finks. Did he do so? Evans has written me he sent on the tobacco the day after Mr Cooper passed up with the permit and hopes it is at Stofer's—I trust Mr F. will get it.—

I wish your parents had a little country residence within 10 miles of Richmond and you were located nearer me.—Like the old hog which wandered all around the field & came out of the hole he went in at[,] I have written and written and come back to the old place.—Well I'll quit.—

Love, much love, to you, to Willie, F., J., L. L. & Lucy & Mr F—Respects to Dr H. Remember me to Alice & Aunt Lucy & her darkies[.]

Yours truly & affectionately
L W Caldwell

Confederate States of America
General Post Office Department,
Auditor's Office,
Richmond, Va., Augt 7th 1864

Dear Daughter

I understand Jas. Chilton left for Warrenton the day after my arrival, but I did not know of his going or I would have written by him to assure you of my safe arrival.—Ed Fant called at my room yesterday to see Phillips & said Mr F. & Willie had got safely back. I saw Carlin today and he said his room-mate and homeward companion (Hodgkins) had lost for him all his greenbacks, being captured by Yankee scouts the day I left for the Mountains and robbed.—Carlin says we were tearing up track beyond Culpepper C.H.—If true it looks as though you would have Yanks with you soon again.—The Black horse & all Fitzhugh Lee's[37] Cavalry passed thru Rd today for Early or Culpepper. I did not see Ned C.[38] as I was not on the street in time.—There is said to be a big movement on foot—but today is Sunday—Sensation day.—Beauregard[39] blew up a Yankee mine Saturday P.M. and produced confusion in their Camp. All quiet at Chn and rumor says the opposing Generals there have agreed to exchange the officers which both sides have put under fire tho' prisoners.[40]—

---

[37] Gen. Fitzhugh Lee's cavalry was headed for the Valley to help Gen. Early in his campaign against Sheridan. (J.E.D.)

[38] Edward M. Cologne, son of Edgar N. and Susan T. (Cash) Cologne, aged 22 years. Enlisted October 20, 1862 in the Black Horse Cavalry by Capt. Robert Randolph and was paroled at Winchester, Va. May 1, 1865. (J.K.G.)

[39] Confederate General P. G. T. Beauregard, on the Petersburg lines. (J.E.D)

[40] This had become a bad situation, when Confederates held Union prisoners under fire to prevent the Federals from firing into the city of Charleston. The Union in return held Confederate prisoners under fire on Morris Island and Fort Pulaski. This was the basis for post war organization of The Immortal 600, composed of officers who had refused to break under the shelling. It was quite a badge of honor throughout the South to have been one of these. (J.E.D.)

At Mobile we have lost a Naval fight, but military men say the City is not endangered thereby.—Forest did not capture Yankee Gen'l Stoneman, but Brig. Iverson[41] did.— Two raiding parties have recently been bagged in Ga. and today Gen'l Hood reports that the Enemy made a demonstration yesterday which was handsomely repulsed with loss to them.—Nothing is positively known here at Kirby Smith's crossing the Miss. River bound Eastward. Our Dept. Battn. was on duty only 24 hours during my absence, and the impression prevails that we will not be ordered out again.—The Auditor says he will let me go home again about Christmas perhaps.—I forgot to tell Mr F. the tobacco cost $911 to get it to Gordonsville I paid Cooper $500. & will pay balance on his return in 10 days. Skinner drew my salary & put in $300 for me in a club which has sent to N.C. for provisions. The Secy has sent to us for a list of the number & ages of our family.—Some say a scheme is on foot to furnish us rations— others that Secy Trenholm[42] will import clothes for us—others again that the single men are to be conscripted.—There are 4 lady clerks in our Bureau now and may be others will be appointed.—Provisions have fallen some since I was here.—Butter is $6. now and flour is retailing at one store for $1. per pound. Butter was $10. & flour $2.50 when I left.—The corn crop in this State will be miserably short every where so far as I saw and can hear. I saw Col. K. of Warren Co. Said Mr. F's father was well and would make plenty bread. They had a good season.—Tom Triplett had lost his leg below knee in battle of Kernstown.—Alice and Co T.[43] had been to see Tom.— No news from Fielding—presumed still in prison.—Capt Alick Payne is here.— Philips saw him.—He was kicked on thigh by a horse and was not quite able to keep his saddle. Dr Jones has his box.—Utterback has not yet called for his.—I hope it will not be long before he and W. Foster[44] get their packages.—In my absence Philips got package from L. Spilman sent by Taverner, and commenced on sugar & coffee.—I got package—shirt, shoes, shoe strings & blacking thro' Jno Garrett.—Tom Franklin was not at Gordonsville & I will not get that package for some time. I am sorry you

---

[41] Brig. Gen. Alfred Iverson, Jr. (C.S.A.) (1829-1911), commanded a brigade of Cavalry in Martin's Division of Wheeler's corps. He captured the Union General George Stoneman and 700 of his men at Sunshine Church, Ga. in the Atlanta Campaign. (J.E.D.)

[42] George A. Trenholm, Confederate Secretary of the Treasury. (J.E.D.)

[43] Co. T, Alice and Tom: Col. William Hedgman Triplett (1798-1876) lived in Warren County near the parents of John W. Finks. He was Finks' uncle, 62 years old in 1860. He served briefly in the War of 1812, at the age of 16, substituting for a Mr. Cutley, as a private. He filed a pension application in 1870 and received $8 a month beginning Feb. 1871. "Colonel" may have been a courtesy title, or he may have served in the militia at some time. He married, July 8, 1833, Eliza Ann Bayliss and had the following children:

    Edwin Mundy, b: 1834;

    William Broadus, b: 1835, m: 1867 Emily A. Wood. These letters indicate that he tried to buy John W. Fink's colt, but JWF wouldn't sell;

    Thomas Henry (Tom) b: 1837. One record has him killed in battle but, in fact, he lost a leg at Kernstown and, is believed to have died of wounds. No record exists of him after 1864;

    Mary Porter, b: 1837, m: Davis. One record has her a twin of Tom;

    Frances Alice, b: 1841, m: 1867 James R. Thornton;

    Elizabeth (Bettie) b: 1844, m: McDonald;

    James Pendleton, b: 1847. "Penny;"

    Carrie Belle, b: 1849, m: 1870, Charles Fielding Finks (Fielding). (T.T.R.)

[44] Capt. James William Foster, Co. A., 43rd Bn, had been a P.O.W. since 1863. (J.E.D.)

and Lucy or some one sent more Coffee & sugar in carpet bag by me.—We can get on without such things so well and they would be so useful to you all.—All I care for is bread & meat. And then the cake! It is good; but why make it for me when it hurts my conscience to witness the waste of sugar &c.

Susan Emeline Jeffords Caldwell to Lycurgus Washington Caldwell

Warrenton Fauquier
Sunday August 14th/64

Dearest Papa

I received your most welcome letter through Mr Marshall and answered it by Mr Ross—who left town last Tuesday—

Yesterday I received another from you through Mr Brooke. I was glad enough to hear from you[,] wish very I could hear oftener. I am sorry your good things gave out so soon. I had hoped you would have reserved some for *your special benefit* and not *divided* it all away so rapidly and extravagantly. I hope you will *reserve* the *sugar* and *coffee* in your box for your own use. You say Mr P. goes out to tea almost every evening so I would only use my sugar when he is absent if he will not buy Sugar & coffee[,] then of course you are not bound to give him what is sent to you for your own private use.—Have you used up the sugar & coffee sent by Mr Tavenner?—I feel worried every time I think of your package being opened while you were absent—if they use they should replace it when out at their own expense so that you then will enjoy it a longer period[,] it is my wish you should enjoy Sugar & coffee daily—I know you can afford it. I wish you could make arrangements to have some one come and *cook* your dinners this *hot* weather, cant you? It is too bad for you to have to be worried such weather as this. It is a great trouble to me and whenever I go to the table I feel as if I would give up any thing I possessed to be with you so you could have some palatable food—

Mr Marshall leaves to morrow and if all were as accommodating as *you* I could soon fix up some goodies—but oh! all are too selfish about these parts to render a kind act to friends at a distance. Oh! that I could send you some nice bread. Pray buy some *tomattoes* [sic] and enjoy them. Dont be so economical. I hope Mr Skinner will be successful and get good things at reasonable prices. Be particular about your *winter* clothes and shirts—put tobacco[45] in them. Did you give the *shoes* to Mrs Lotties? Mr F. started for the farm last week but returned fearing he would be cut off from home while the army is on the move. Willie was much disappointed. He thinks of going to Culpepper this week to see about Tobacco—He paid Mr Cooper $450.00—and

---

[45] The placing of raw tobacco in closets, chests and other places of storage for clothing to keep out moths was common before the use of moth balls. (J.K.G.)

authorized Marcus Cooper to pay the balance not hearing from you—he thought you then could lay out your extra money if you had any as you felt inclined. I hope he will be prompt to pay the money as it will then help to defray expenses.

Jessie has been much complaining since you left—her face has broken out with sores as it was last year[,] another piece of bone has come out of her ear. The weather being so very warm and her hair so thick and long caused her much trouble at night so Sister and I concluded to have it cut off which we had done yesterday and the little creature has been much relieved. I was sorry to lose her *curls*, but it was for the good of the child.

I have had one headache since you left. We heard from Lute since her arrival[.] I am very glad you gave the honey to Mrs Davis—her note was prettily worded. The weather is intensely hot with us. I feel so thankful your Battallion is in the City. Hope you may not be ordered out again. 'Tis Sunday and how lonesome I am[.] Wish you were here. Jessie has an apple keeping for you when you come home again—asks you if she must send you a *curl*.

All join me in love & kisses to dear Papa. God bless you & preserve you till we be permitted to meet[.] Direct my letters for me and mail them—

Your affec daughter
S.E.C.

Monday. All well. Sister expects to go to Culpepper to morrow with Mr Finks & Pattie [and] I will be all *alone*.

Warrenton Fauquier
Friday morning August 26th/64

Dearest Papa

I will write you a hurried note by Mr Utterback. I understood he would not leave until Saturday and fully intended to write you and Mrs Goodloe lengthy letters. Mr F. told me last night Mr U. would leave Friday—I was suffering again yesterday (just one week ago I had one) with sick headache and was unable to write last night. It is now about 6 O'clock A.M. and my head is aching badly but I cant think of having Mr U. leave without my penmanship. You will excuse brevity[.] Mr F. and Sister will leave to morrow for the *farm*. I dont know which of the children will go. Dr Hamme will sleep in the house at night. Mr F. wants to get Uncle John to go with him there and work the ground. No *signs* of the *tobacco* yet. Please attend to it if you can fearing the *yankees*. I am grieved to learn the yankees have one portion of the Petersburg Weldon Road—Mr Brooke paid over the money to Mr Bronaugh—says he paid you $28 and now has $10 in his hands—so I understood Mr F. The children are all well but Jessie—her face is very sore, she does not suffer pain but it annoys her. I hope it will soon cure up—would have sent you a *box* of *eatables* but did not like to ask Mr U—altho he kindly asked what I had for him to take to you.

Good bye. God bless you & preserve you. My head is aching and I must go back to bed. Good bye—all join me in love.

Your affec daughter
S.E.C.

Lycurgus Washington Caldwell to Susan Emeline Jeffords Caldwell

Richmond, Sunday Augt. 28, 1864

Dear Daughter

R. M. Smith & Capt. Utterback (thanks to you, who notwithstanding sick head aches wrote to me) delivered me the letter today.—It does me good to hear from home and you. Poor little Jessie, I hope she will not lose her hearing or beauty—You did right to cut off her hair.—Save the curls. Do not send them. Papa will claim one when he next sees Warrenton. Tell Frank I have consulted many Doctors here and also deaf persons and they agree that he must keep his ears well clean.—I fear he will be always bothered with the offensive matter from them.—Doctors give much encouragement.—I wish you would if you could get some tissue or blotting paper and make little rolls of it (like old fashioned tapers for candle lighters) about 3 inches long and tell F to carry half dozen a day in his pocket.—Before he uses them direct him to moisten the end in his mouth and then run it round his ear as a sponge—so as to keep the ears as clean as can be.—Jessie must do same.—Two or three times a day they should wash the ears well with casteel soap.—Use paper instead of your hair pins—but put no hard or printed paper in the ear.—Dear little afflicted ones, I cant help thinking of their misfortune. Tell F. what I request him to do, and to remember there is an old man in my office with both feet turned inwards, worse than Rob Whites, and the old man looks at his lameness and says his parents were careless and should have made him press his feet straight when young. McVeigh deaf from scarlet fever, says he tried all the doctors in N Yk & Boston to cure him before the war & they only made him worse.—F & J may outgrow it.—God grant it.—Lee must be good and not cry or papa will say she is ugly.—Willie must have his fun, but never at the expense of making any one uncomfortable.—He must read the fable of the boys and the frogs.—I hope he will excel all the boys at school and be ambitious of having it said of him that he is incapable of any thing dishonorable.—Willie, Frank, Jessie, & Lee, little pledges of your own and my own good conduct—Let us live worthy the examples for their dear sakes.—I got your old letters and forwarded all to destination. You did not tell me why. Only said of Mrs Davis' not to—I wrote you by Mr. Dick Cooper Friday and sent Mr F. a file of papers to that date.—He said the tobacco reached Culpepper the day after Mr F. left there & he told Silas to send Mr F. a note to that effect.—You misunderstood Mr F. about giving Mr Cooper $450. on the tobacco I ... —He says Mr F. gave him an order on Marcus Cooper which he will collect.—He also promised to see Mr C. about am't due me & get it.—I offered to pay him the $411. balance, but he did not then want to receive it.—I reckon Mr Dick C. attended to the tobacco as he went up Friday and Tom Saunders promises to look for it & ...

Susan Emeline Jeffords Caldwell to Lycurgus Washington Caldwell

Warrenton Via
Monday August 29th/64

Dearest Papa

My heart rejoiced at the sight of your penmanship as Dr Hamme handed me your letter—I was sorry you have allowed yourself to grow home-sick—cheer up dearest one and hope in truth for better days—I shall ever keep this last letter of yours around about me and peruse its contents over and again and will promise you I will earnestly pray to have more patience and preserve if possible an evenness of disposition. It will be a struggle for I am so very impulsive—I am angry in an instant and as soon as my reason returns I can do as kind an act to the very object I was angry with—

Miss you—you cannot miss me more—I yearn after you—I long to be near you—I am constantly stretching my mind to catch at something to give me the perfect happiness I once enjoyed, but am not able to obtain it day or night—but I strive to be cheerful and make home happy to others[.]

Mr. F.[,] Sister, Willie and Jessie started at ½ past 4 this morning for Front Royal—if I had only received your letter yesterday Mr F. would have gone to Culpepper after tobacco—you say you are certain it is there—strange Mr Stofer has not written to Mr F. He promised him he would write as soon as tobacco arrived in Culpepper—well we must take chances—trust we may get it yet safe in Warrenton without loss—I enclose a pair of gloves and an odd one for you to give to Mr Joshua Finks for Lute. Sister sends the gloves to her—her odd one she left at Mrs W and Eva brought it home—please write a note to Lute for me enclosing articles[,] telling her Sister received her letter and did answer her first one—Fix the gloves securely so her Father or who ever you may send them by will not lose them.

I am glad you have all your packages—buy all your appetite craves and enjoy yourself[.]

I am grieved your Battallion had to go out again[,] pray you will not have any more duty to perform. I have been busy all day putting the house in order. Dr Hamme will sleep in the house at night and my neighbors are all very kind[.]

Children and myself are well—In great haste—

Yours devotedly daughter
S.E.C.

237

Lycurgus Washington Caldwell to Susan Emeline Jefford Caldwell

Richmond Sept. 16, 1864

My Dear Daughter

The order for our battallion to assemble at 5 P.M. today for active service was countermanded before we left the City, and I gladly put off my knapsack and laid aside my gun; because I am hurrying up my work so as to get holiday and embrace you.—I know that heavy sighs well up from the very depths of your bereaved heart every hour of the day, and that you crave my presence to beguile and cheer you.— If our loveliest child[46] has been taken from us, remember this, that being the youngest, she was least accountable and most certain of an abundant entrance into Heaven. If the Master's hand has sorely touched our hearts by Lee's death, possibly it was necessary for him to do so in order to attune them for His praise.—I feel that I have been justly chastened, and pray God to spare me similar inflictions in future.

I have written to your father and to Manly—The latter desires a situation here—He has lost his health, & his wife is dead.—He has been assigned to light duty.—I wrote to Dr Moore today in his behalf.—What he can or may do I know not.—

There is more despondency in Richmond now than I have before observed during the war.—I do not think the Citizens fear Lee will be outgeneralled or defeated but they had expected peace from the action of the Chicago Convention, and McClellan's letter of acceptance has destroyed all such hopes.—

I saw Mr Heart today. His head quarters are in Charleston.—He says that the City is still shelled.—That a few nights before he left he had to take in a family whose house two squares below him had been penetrated and cracked above their heads without hurting any one.—The people have got used to the dangerous music and do not seem to mind it.—

General Lee has been in Richmond several days conferring with the President.— Outsiders do not know what is going forward.—What they pretend to know is merely guess work.—Grant is building a railway in rear of his lines,[47] and both Armies are preparing to make themselves comfortable this Winter.—Mr. Skinner was in Tallahassee, Fla. in the 4th inst. and apprehensions are felt among the Clerks that he may not be able to get our supplies through. No one however is willing to sell his share in the investment.—

The tobacco was sent to Culpeper the day after Mr F. left there, and J. B. F. says Stofer never called for it.—

The Reserves from adjacent Counties ordered here in May are still in service around the City.—The two Regts. of City Militia do prison and guard duty.

---

[46] Lucy Lee Caldwell died of scarlet fever on Sept. 10, 1864. (J.M.W.)

[47] This was the military railroad built from Grant's headquarters and supply base at City Point to supply his troops attacking Confederate lines around Petersburg. (J.E.D.)

There seems to be no present prospect for an exchange of prisoners.—

My hopes now for a speedy termination of the war rest only in making it more savage than it has been.—Everything is at a stand still in Ga. as Mobile & around Petersburg.—But preparations are going on and a battle may be joined before a month goes by.—

The dear little trio—Willie, Frank & Jessie—how do they come on?—Hug & Kiss them for me and write me what they have to say.—

Love to Lucy & Mr F.—and kind remembrances to every one.—

Good night. It is eleven oclock.—I will hand this to … Chilton in A.M.—I am well.—I wish I could speak peace to your sorrowing soul—I recommend you to God—the God of peace and love.—May he abide with you and approve your life.—

Yours affectionately
LW Caldwell

Tuesday night Sept. 27, 1864

Well—well—I did not know you ever tried to write poetry.—The effort is a good one.—You deserve a compliment—and if you do not receive one—remember it is better to merit than to obtain commendation. I shall preserve your effusions.—You know daughter I love you too dearly to use flattery to you.—

You ask me if you may not wear black.—You have too many things already to remind you of your bereavement and oppress your spirits—and our pecuniary circumstances, will not permit it.—I too wish to see little change in your personal appearance as time will allow.—Little Lee is now clad in raiment white as snow. Oh, do not you put on black.—In times of peace and prosperity general usage might have induced me to withhold objections to the custom—but war and penury are upon us, and it would be unwise to put away the clothes we might wear and buy others. We must look at the matter rationally—Even if you had the money to buy them, ask yourself if it would not be better laid out in the purchase of necessaries of life for yourself and children or in providing a meal for the poor around you.—In God's sight, which would be more acceptable?

I thank God our little boys have hearts brimful of sympathy for you.—There is great comfort in having their arms encircle your neck when unbidden tears and sighs betray heaviness of soul.—Be thou, my dear daughter, God's instrument to establish their characters. Jessie, must also be an object of special regard.—Do not be blind to their faults.—If God chasteneth whom he loveth—does he not expect parents to be guided by his example.—Study the effect of causes—and help them develop the good and eradicate evil.—I write thus in most every letter not because I think you unmindful of the high trust reposed in you, but because I am full of such thoughts.—

Now I must close—God bless you—bless each one of you—with every needful good.—Tell Lucy & Mrs F. to write me—and you & the children write me.—I feel that your prayer beside the bed at our parting will be granted.—Be not concerned about me.—I am well—have good nutritious food—and every necessary bodily want.—My chief concern is about my family.—I see good even now ahead—Let us be hopeful.

Yours most truly & affectionately
LW Caldwell

Susan Emeline Jeffords Caldwell to Lycurgus Washington Caldwell

Warrenton Via
Sunday Oct 2nd 1864

Dearest Papa

Yours of the 23rd and 26th of Sept were received to day and hearing of an opportunity I hasten to reply—

We received the news of Early's defeats[48] much to our sorrow—We are all gloomy enough in regard to our gaining the day—Oh! how my heart grieves over the loss of our brave and gallant men—Dearest Papa you tell me to [...] give myself no uneasiness on your account—I can't help it—my heart drinks deep of the cup of sorrow and trouble. I long to be with you to be near you—oh! how very heavy my heart is all the time I feel as if at times I am sinning and bringing down upon me heavier afflictions that God will yet humble this rebellious heart. I cannot help it[,] I do yearn after my darling babe[,] to catch yet once again one glimpse of her sweet face I would be willing to stem the storm—oh! it seems so long since I have seen her and felt her near me and heard the sweet sounds of her voice as she would whisper. "I love Mama best"—I can find no comfort any where—God grant peace of mind to me[.] I can only think of Lee as lost to me[,] gone forever from my sight—but love her oh I love her more fondly than ever. Papa you dont [know] how much I miss her but enough, my time is limited.

The tobacco has arrived in Warrenton[,] Mr F. has it at the store. Too large boxes to have at the house.

The report to day is the yankees both Cavalry and infantry are at Warrenton Junction[49]—of course will be here soon it is supposed.

Children are all well. *I did not compose* the *poetry*[,] I copied it—I thought the lines were beautiful and only changed some lines to suit my own darling, I love to read them, so truthlike. Yesterday was our *Wedding* day & my darling Lee's *birth day*.

---

[48] This refers to Gen. J. A. Early's (C.S.A.) defeats in the Valley at the hands of General Sheridan (U.S.A.). (J.E.D.)

[49] This is unidentified, but could possibly be patrols from the Washington defenses attempting to keep Mosby from damaging the railroad. (J.E.D.)

I had anticipated so much pleasure—but what a sad, sorrowful day I spent, no loved baby to nestle in my lap and with loving arms to encircle my neck and whispers words of love. My dress at present corresponds but little with my mournful aching heart but I am willing to do as you wish me. Please write several times a week[,] send them by the way of Culpepper or Charlottesville or any way—so as to relieve my mind. Oh! may you be spared to me is my earnest prayer—a bushel of Love from all. In haste.

Your affec daughter
S.E.C.

I hope you will not have to go out on a raid[.]

Warrenton Via
Sunday Oct 9th 1864

Dearest Papa

Your welcome letter of the 26 & 27th of Sept were received. Since then I have understood that the *clerks* have been ordered out. Oh! how troubled my heart is. My dreams are distressingly painful. I awake and start not knowing where or scarcely who I am—This cruel war[,] the sorrow and anguish of heart it costs the many thousands of beings. Would that I could hear from you *daily*, it would comfort my aching heart. Oh! Papa you dont know how much I suffer—I feel at times that God will punish me yet more severely because I cannot gain power over my own rebellious heart to say *God's Will be done*. Oh! how hard to be submissive.

I am glad to learn you will be soon so well provisioned. I want you to be comfortable—live at your ease and do not give yourself too much anxiety on our account. Oh! Papa I feel some times that could I have gone with you even for a short time and had taken my *darling one* with me she would may be have been spared the taken of that dreadful fever—to think there has been no other case in town—she was taken so suddenly ill and of such a malignant and violent character—where and how did she take it is in my thoughts day and night. Lee had been very sprightly all the week—I was at home alone you remember I wrote you Mr F.[,] Sister, Willie & Jessie had gone to the farm. Every thing had gone on nicely[,] no trouble at all, until Thursday evening when Lee begged me to put her to sleep before supper—she went to sleep and awaked with some fever, but nothing more than she had often complained of many times before. I gave her some calomel and in the morning a dose of vermifuge thinking the fever was produced from worms—her fever continued so high I sent for Dr Chilton (Sister had not gotten home from the farm and did not come until the following Monday night[,] I sent for them) Friday morning at 6 O'clock—he said what I done was all right but she was very ill—he called again in an hour and pronounced the disease Scarlet fever—I was alarmed not because I believed she would not recover but fearing the bad effects she might be left with as Jessie & Frank. She continued to grow very ill during the day and on Saturday had violent spasms. From

241

that time the Dr gave me no hope *but I clung to hope and could not believe otherwise but she would get well.* She was a very great sufferer—she never spoke during her illness, sometimes answered yes and no in a whisper—too ill to notice or talk, she may have known me but did not show it. She never recognized Sister or Mr F. Oh! my Papa how I long to see my baby—I want my baby—I cannot remember her features during her life—she changed from the first day of her sickness and did not look like herself. How I long for her daguerreotype. Strange I did not persevere more to get it. Oh! my *darling babe—Mama's heart aches all day and night for you.* I feel at times as if my heart will *break when I know I cannot get my baby back to me any more.* Lee, Mama loved you more than she can tell. Miss you darling—yes every moment of the day—to morrow will be one month but it seems to your desolate Mama 6 months or more. Oh! that God had permitted you to have stayed with Mama—you were my comfort & sunshine.

Write me as often as you can. Tell me if your battallion has been out. We are all well. Frank wants me to write him a letter. He tries very hard to comfort me in my trouble. I wish much for the time to come when I shall see you.

Your affec daughter
S.E.C.

Love from all—

Mary Humbert Jeffords to Susan Emeline Jeffords Caldwell

Blackville October 17 1864

My Own Dearest Daughter

I received your kind letter and was truly pained to hear that you had been called to resign your dear babe, believe me My Dear Child that you have the warmest sympathy of my heart; how I wish I could be with you in this your dark hour of trial and affliction to cheer and sustain you—A kind Saviour has removed your little lamb from your tender Care to his own bosom, where it is now free from all harm, and happily singing its Dear Saviour['s] praise, the stroke has been a severe and bitter one but a Father's hand has dealt the blow, and he has said he chasteneth the Children of his love for some wise purpose, you must try My Dear Child and feel that God doeth but wisely and that though fond nature bleeds at the thought of joys departed and of the dear little one no more to be with you on earth yet that it is well, with the Child so early removed from earth, temptations sorrows and cares, May God grant you of his rich grace abundantly and his precious promises and be enable[d] to say his will be done oh God.

My Dear Susan I know well of how to feel for you, I have had to go through the same, I hope and pray that your Heavenly Father will grant you strength and fortitude[,] you must look to him for strength, I am thankful that all of your Children are well—Your Father has been quite ill in bed for five weeks with billious [sic] fever—he is now better, he is all about the house, but very weak—I am quite well[,] thank God for my good health—

I heard from Manly—he is quite well he sed[sic] give his love to you, give my love to your Sister and L. C. I dream I see him and help him, I thought he looked the lame, but oh my it was but a dream,

Kiss the dear Children for me, Mag sends love to you, she's looking [to]day to be sick, Julia has twin's both girls you must know what trouble her mother has, I feel sorry for Lucy, Julia[50] still has the fits, your Father sends love to you. Lucy tells you howdy.

I remain ever your Affectionate

Mother

Lycurgus Washington Caldwell to Susan Emeline Jeffords Caldwell

Richmond Va
Wednesday Oct. 26 1864

Dear Daughter

I have just returned from the "*front*" on a special detail and *mailed* you a letter misdated the 27th inst. of the 26th. In it was a beautiful letter from your Mother telling you your father had been sick with bilious fever 5 weeks but was convalescing rapidly—being able to go about now. I think her expressions of sympathy and condolence equal to any letter I ever read.—If her orthography and punctuation had been good it would compare well with printed compositions.—I hope you will get it in due time.—In writing me hereafter concerning the dear little departed one do not write as if addressing her, but me. It makes one apprehend that you may not be equal to the affliction put upon us.—You must partially forget your grief by endeavoring to have the duties of life absorb your thoughts.—And the highest and holiest of those duties are the moral and mental training of our three living children.—How to advance Jessie, Frank and Willie so as to have them good and wise is your first, your chief employment. And as the night closes on your labour, ask yourself for the evidences of your teachings during the past day.—If they have exhibited forbearance, self negative-generosity or readiness and aptitude for book lessons, congratulate yourself & pray that on the morrow you may have other

---

[50] Probably Julia Suares, daughter of Harriet and Benjamin Suares, 17 at the time of the 1860 census. She was one of two surviving children of the six born to the Suares. (B.G.C.)

243

illustrations of their improvement.—You will soon get to love such labour and a hundred examples of enabling deeds will encourage you to persevere in your instruction.—I do believe my children are peculiarly blessed in having an educated Aunt & Mother and pious examples—and the thought is precious and cheering during my separation.—I could embrace them and say good bye for a time because I *know* you & Lucy & Mr F. strive to give tone and stamina to their good *impulses*.— A Child, Daughter, has no principle.—Example & culture form principle from *impulse*.—When you wish to restrain them persuade them. You grieve over their misconduct. When you wish to encourage them convince them of what would give you pleasure.—Your countenance should speak as well as your tongue. If possible never let them see you angry or hear you utter a word in a tone you would not have them mimic.—

Tell Willie I hope he will advance at a gallop in his studies and keep head in his classes at school.—If he would be as generous to Frank as he is to me it would make me shed tears of real joy—Brothers, I know are not always good to each other as they are to their sweethearts, but I would like my boys to be that good to each other.— Willie will do as I say or try and that is the first step towards doing it, because he loves to please me.—Frank must meet Will half way and both I hope will be happy in each other's company.—Jessie must always be pacificator—for girls who wish to pass for Ladies are very amiable & peace loving.—*Gentlemen* will not bandy taunts and in- sults in presence of ladies and there is no room for quarrels therefore in Aunty's house.—I ask the good Lord to spare my life that I may contribute towards rearing my children properly.—If they are bad God may think I am of little use to them— Certainly they would not have the Almighty think that.—By every means awaken in them good thoughts and nurse them as tenderly as you would an infant till you fix in them proper ideas. Old Mr Stephen Fletcher was my Sunday school teacher and I have not yet forgot passages of scripture I memorized to repeat to him.—I res- pect him highly—a man never forgets the lessons he learned in childhood.—Tell my children to bow very respectfully to that good old man whenever they meet him.—

I judge from your letter of the 16th (rec'd in camp thro' R.M.S.) that you are acquainted now with the position of the opposing forces at Chafins farm.[51]—For want of troops we lost 1 ½ miles of breastworks there before my Regt (no longer a battn) was ordered out.—But the enemy only occupy about one acre of the line—and that is at Fort Harrison.[52]—From that point to the River is perhaps 2 ¼ miles.—At that time Genl Lee was sadly in want of men—Col Chas Marshall[53] told his brother-in- law ... that 5000 men would be of great service—10,000 make his position secure and 20,000 enable him to take the offensive.—Since then over 11,000 have been registered at Camp Lee alone. I understood from Col Sullivan of our Regt. that

---

[51] Formerly part of the Confederate defenses before Richmond; now in Union hands. (J.E.D.)

[52] Formerly part of the Confederate defenses before Richmond; now in Union hands. (J.E.D.)

[53] Charles Marshall was Gen. Lee's military secretary. (J.E.D.)

Pickets[54] [sic] division had been filled up—each Company sending 64 men and that Genl. Hoke's[55] division was being rapidly[.]

The boat on which I came up the River last night carried down a load of Enfield rifles (for the new recruits I guess) directed to Genl Hoke.—I guess there were 500 rifles on the boat.—The opinion prevails that Lincoln will be elected and the war vigorously pressed.—Our soldiers are tired & want peace—but they will not clamor for it from Lincoln.—They will fight him to the bitter end.—The way public sentiment is running it would not surprise me if the Confederates employed negro soldiers next year.—The resolutions of the Convention of Southern Governors look that way.—The question I am told will be brought to the attention of our next Congress.[56]—Genl. Early confesses his defeat and reads his soldiers a severe lecture.— I hope his troops may be withdrawn & others substituted there.—The Yanks gave our lines the benefit of a shotted salute in honor of Sheridan's success in the Valley— but luckily hurt no one.—Perfect quiet pervades our whole line. Both parties are busy strengthening their line & making bomb-proof for protection & winter quarters. We have a fast 500 yards from Harrison & some persons surmise that Grant is winning it. I hardly think so for we picket soldiers as to enable us to watch his operations—Many funny things are said by opposing pickets, for at present there is a truce between sharp shooters.—One of them had even the courtesy to hallow just previous to the shotted salute the other day "Lay low Johnny Rebs, we are going to fire."—Desertions are frequent from one of the Local battallions from the Tredegar[57] Works and as yet not one of them have been shot tho' fired at all most every night.— Last summer a single picket gun caused the whole Camp to go to the ditches—Now we hardly turn over on our straw if a dozen shots are fired in our front. To prevent desertion from that battn. videttes are withdrawn & any man who goes 3 paces beyond the picket line ordered to be shot without being hailed.—The deserters are foreigners & Yanks—Mechanics who have hitherto been exempt.—They should be withdrawn as they are useful to us as citizens.—No one has deserted from our Regt.—and it has the best name in the local brigade.—Our Gen'l (Custis Lee) has been promoted—is now a Major General.—I hope our command will soon be ordered to Richmond as the business in the Depts is now behind and the appointment of ladies does not work well.—

I must conclude. Good night.—God bless you all—I write at Sentinel Offices with bad materials.

Yours affectionately
LW Caldwell

---

[54] Gen. George Pickett's Division had been filled after being nearly destroyed at Gettysburg in July, 1863. (J.E.D.)

[55] Gen. Robert F. Hoke of North Carolina had his division guarding Darbytown Road north of the James River. (J.E.D.)

[56] The notion of arming slaves was never seriously debated by the Confederacy until late in 1863, but after the military reverses of late 1864, the Confederacy edged closer to raising a black army. On March 13, 1865, the Confederate Congress, with the strong backing of Davis and Robert E. Lee, authorized the enlistment of 300,000 additional troops irrespective of color, but no more than 25 percent of any state's able-bodied slaves between the ages of 18 and 45. Litwack, *Storm*, pp. 42-44. (B.G.C.)

[57] The Tredegar Iron Works in Richmond. (J.M.W.)

Susan Emeline Jeffords Caldwell to Lycurgus Washington Caldwell

Undated, 1864

Dearest Papa

Feeling sick yesterday I wrote you a hurried note thinking Cash would leave to day—but he came to see us and told us he would not leave until Saturday—He dined with us yesterday. I told him I would write and tell you he had not been very sociable having been but twice to see us—He is a first rate fellow & my favorite. Alice Royston called yesterday and begged me to write and thank you in her Mother's name and the name of the family for your kindness to Tommy—that even in his delirium he calls for you and talks of you. She said Mr R. would return to me the $50 loaned him— He's very ill of typhoid fever—Aunt Martha has gone to Jefferson to be with him. Please send this pair of Mitts to Ma if you can fix them up—

We are all tolerably well—my head aches some this morning and my neck continues painful—but I could bear all pain of body if my spirits were not so much depressed—I feel too sad this morning—Frank made a remark a few moments ago about what had happened and what was done and oh! it seemed Papa as if I was about to pass through that dread trial of the month of September—the little fellow did not think how Mama's heart would ache over his remark—he was telling it all to Willie—oh! Papa language cannot express to you how much I every day miss my baby child—oh! I long so to have her near me—forgive me papa as I cannot refrain— Good bye—God bless you. Willie is much complaining to day—has a severe cold.

Undated, 1864

The Yankees are on the Manassas Rail Road at Salem & the Plains. We are expecting them here daily not to remain—but raiding parties. I dread their approach—for they steal all the horses and cattle. Willie brought a beautiful pony from the farm his Grandma gave him. Fielding gave it to her. I would be grieved to have the yankees take the pony. Mr F. has two horses also.

Do write me the particulars about Dr Helen's death and what his conduct was. We have never heard any thing of him[,] did not know he was dead.

Miss Lucy Jones is married. She married Capt. Barber lives near Stanton I think—has done well.

Do write us exactly what the army is about and the prospects of the Confederacy—Mr F. wants you to write all you know—for so many inquire what your views are when your letters arrive—

Mr. Bronough was glad of his letter[,] on the strength of it he sent me a basket of delicious fruit—

Frank wants me to write you a letter—well Papa I can tell you that Frank is a good boy and learns a lesson every day, can read short sentences, and oh Papa he tries so hard to comfort poor Mama[,] he sleeps in bed with her, because she has no Lee now—and puts his arms around her neck as baby used to and when Mama's heart aches he comes and stands by her, he is so troubled but oh Papa I cant find comfort any where I want so much to see and feel my lost baby near me.

Undated, 1864

Dearest Papa. Your letter of the 10th of October was received to day (Sunday 16th) my heart was made glad to learn you were well—but deeply grieved to hear your battallion has again been ordered out. Oh! may the Great God shield your defenseless head. I pray for your safety day and night. My dearest husband the bible states that afflictions are sent in mercy, tis not always as chastisements—this may be our case as you say—the loss of darling Lee may be the eternal gain of our souls. I feel too keenly how neglectful I have been of my duties as a professed follower of the Saviour, have neglected *even prayer* which is the Christian's safe guard. I try to feel humble, to feel submissive. I know and feel that God can send heavier afflications upon one[.] I have a dear husband and three precious treasures left me. I should be grateful and not repine. Jessie feels much sympathy for me—has been sleeping with me. Tells her Anty she thinks it comforts me some and makes me think when I *dress* and *undress* her—and hug her close to my bosom that Lee has come back to me[.] Darling child she does give me comfort, but oh! when I am doing all this for her, how my heart *pines* after my *lost loved one*. Oh! Papa you know not how I miss my baby—oh how I long to see her. I know she is happy—freed from this world of sin—but even that at times has no comfort for me. May God forgive my wickedness and help me to live nearer to Him—All are well[,] write as often as you can 'tis such a great relief.

Warrenton Via
Sunday Oct 30th 1864

Dearest Papa

Your most welcome letter of the 26th I received through Mr Fants. On first opening it I was rejoiced to see it dated from Richmond—but my joy was soon turned into sorrow on reading you were only detailed for business—oh! may you soon be relieved. Dearest Papa I wish you were with me—then we could talk more than I am able to write you—I have nothing these days to write that will prove interesting. I try to be cheerful but the effort is a great one—

I will try to do as you desire me. I am very anxious to do all in my power to promote the children's good. I need self control and pray for it daily—Our children are the same as the generality of children who have known little else than indulgence from all. Now I find they need to be properly disciplined and it is to me a very great responsibility. I want to do what is right. Willie is self ruled but is soon made to yield by strict positive means—Frank is a very good child[,] Jessie is very perverse—she has been so much indulged and petted since her sickness—but I hope by good advice and forbearance on my part to make her a good amiable child. The children are all very affectionate and very kind hearted. They have felt this affliction very deeply. It makes one's heart sadden to hear Jessie speak of her precious little Sister—oh! how she longs she says to go to Heaven where sweet baby Sister is gone. I am as lonesome she says—I miss Lee so much—but Mama she is so happy now singing praises to God.—

Willie can never speak of her, his heart grows so full, he loved her very fondly— Frank talks often about her[,] seems to want me to satisfy his mind with the idea that Lee can see him from Heaven—I believe it truly and feel she is ever near me in spirit. Am I right? Papa you wrote me to day saying thus—"It makes me apprehend that you may not be equal to the affliction put upon us." You speak the truth—I feel that it is at times more than I can bear—I need strength. I need support daily—and when I sit down to write Papa I can see, or hear of nothing but my own deep trouble. I can sit and talk about her—write about her, or think about her all day, every day—You loved her—and saw but little of her—then just stop and think—think how much she was with me—oh! Papa miss her—yes—more than I can tell you—oh! at times I feel as if I could scream my existence away I feel so depressed—time seems so long— longer now than in my childhood. I try to do my best. I try to be cheerful—but the effort is so great—that intense *longing to see my baby* and the *knowledge* of the *impossibility* of it takes such entire possession of my soul that my brain sickens & reels. You have never felt the deep keen anguish of a Mother's heart. You love & love truly— but not with a Mother's ...

Mrs. Tongue called in to see us this afternoon. She has been to Baltimore—says the city is guarded by *Negro* soldiers—I better not say guarded because really I paid so little attention I have forgotten, but at any rate the streets were filled with the *wretches* strutting about with their *shoulder straps*. She said most of the respectable citizens were southern in their feelings but were compelled to keep quiet. They seemed to be growing restless having been trodden under foot so long. You have seen by the papers how many stores have been closed through the aid of this detective, acting as Sutler to the people of Middleburg and it appears very strange to me that Mosby should have allowed him so many privileges and taken him to his Head Quarters—that was just the thing the villain wanted and he soon told on Mr Mosby for his kindness[.] I hope the Merchants will be released—

The rumour is this evening the Yankees are leaving the Railroad[58]—they have done all the mischief there they could—they will try some other field.—Edwards is captured again—it will go hard with him. Found at Mr Lake's[59]—Mr Lake was captured also. Have you seen Cash Cologne? Write us about him. The yankees keep us excited daily—every day such a running away in the woods to hide horses—They were in four miles of town last night. I dread their coming—they have been acting so outrageous

[58] This is probably Col. Henry Goonesvort, 13th N.Y. Cav., who had been operating along the Manasssas Gap R/R. He had burned the house of Joseph Blackwell which Mosby had used as a headquarters. (J.E.D.)

[59] Ludwell Lake lived near Atoka, where Mosby was wounded in December. (J.E.D.)

mean every where, stealing and taking off the Citizens. I hope you are comfortable—keep dry and warm feet as much as possible. I feel very unhappy about you.

I hope Mother's letter will come safely to hand[.] I seldom get a letter from home. I wish very much you had sent it by hand—but I will get it in some weeks to come. I am anxious to read it, I hope by this time you have received my letter through Mr Bartain. Please send me some *writing* paper by him if you can conveniently.

Willie enjoys his pony very much—it is a very beautiful little animal—

Frank is very anxious to see you—when he grows tired of waiting for you to come home—he wants us to send some one for you to come right now—he wanted you home—He is ever looking after my ease and comfort—will never leave me in a room alone, he will remain if all go out. If I look troubled or sad he will come to know what I am thinking about. He tries to comfort me[.] I should encourage him—but at such times my heart is aching and all around me fills me with sorrow—Oh! Papa how I long for peace, to be with you again, to have a home I long for—to know you are near me—but why should I repine when so many thousands are in a suffering condition bereft of their protectors—

I must close—night is closing in—I wish some times it could be always day—'tis so lonesome at night. I cant sleep, my thoughts disturb me, 'tis then I long for your society.

God bless & protect you—keep you in health. Love & kisses from all to dear Papa.

Your devoted daughter
S.E.C.

1865

Susan Emeline Jeffords Caldwell to Lycurgus Washington Caldwell

Warrenton Via
Jany 15th 1865

Dearest Papa

Your letter written since your arrival in Richmond was received yesterday per Dr J.G. Elhenny[1] (sic)—We have had no mail since you left. The Hazel river could not be crossed[,] it had risen so high from the recent heavy rains—The Misses Pollocks[2] crossed the River the Saturday following your departure and the driver on returning to Warrenton was drowned as is supposed—the horses were found drowned and the wagon was in the river—since that no one has attempted to cross coming or going—so we have had no mail—I wrote you a few days after you left but the letter remains in the Post Office—

I was truly grateful to learn you had arrived in safety at your *adopted home* and were heartily *greeted* by your officers—You can return him my most grateful thanks for his kindness manifested in your behalf—and I hope you will be in demand at the Office so that your presence there will be necessary to the business to be carried on—

I was much disturbed in mind at the loss of your *shoes*—I wish much you had worn them instead of the *boots*—but we must expect to meet with losses. I have much to tell you about a yankee raid made in our town last Friday morning about 7 O'clock or 8. We were not all up—I had suffered very much the night before with a sick head ache and was too sick to get up—but I attempted it and dressed. The cry of the Yankees coming up the *pike* did not even startle me—(you were out of danger). I went on down into Sister's room, she was not up—strange we did not feel alarmed. I went down into the dining room—(The yankees were in town all the time) and had break fast, did not *hide* any thing save the forks and spoons) we all eat [sic] break fast and I went on up to my room to fix it in order—Very soon Susa came running up stairs begging me to open the back door that the yankees threatened to break it down. I told her *no* she should not, go and find Mr F. While I was talking a yankee came up the kitchen steps and opened the door himself and 4 yanks walked into the parlor. Mr F. then came up. I inquired what the soldiers wished. They said they were searching for *arms*. I assured them we had nothing of the kind in the house—one of them went to my What-Not and tried to open it[,] finding it locked he ordered me to open it. I did so and he satisfied himself—there was nothing there he wished—and while I was putting back the articles they all went out into the upper rooms—three going up stairs and one into Sister's room—(Sister seeing them getting near

---

[1] John William McIlhany, M.D. (1835-1891), a graduate of the Richmond Medical College, was a surgeon in the Confederate Army and also saw active service as a private in Co. D, 43rd Batt'n, Mosby's Rangers. After the War he practiced medicine in Warrenton. (J.K.G.)

[2] Daughters of the Rev. Abraham D. Pollock, D.D., pastor of the Warrenton Presbyterian Church, and his wife, Elizabeth G. (Peyton) Pollock, of 'Leeton Forest.' Of his daughters, Margaret, Anne L., Elizabeth and Roberta, it was the latter who made the famous ride across View Tree Mountain in the cold of winter to inform Mosby of the Union presence at Warrenton in late December, 1864. Mrs. Caldwell does not mention the incident, if she knew about Bert Pollock's ride, which is told in some length in Alexander Hunter's *Women of the Debatable Land* (Washington, D.C.: Cobden Publishing Co., 1912). (J.K.G.)

the meat house before they came to the back door[,] she ran into the street to get an Officer[.] I was not aware of what was going on in the yard.) Mr F. followed the men up stairs and I had to protect Sister's room, unfortunately her wardrobe was unlocked and he was in it in an instant, took Mr F's *new cloth frock coat*, and Sister's *cloak.*—by the very hardest I got the cloak from him and Aunt Lucy took it and ran and hid it— he looked over every article in the wardrobe and I had to beg and plead with him not to take any thing more—he told me not to be rude to him[,] if so he would take all he saw. I remarked to him I had never behaved as unbecoming a lady—and he must behave as he should—he did not take another article—while he was stealing in Sister's room—the three men were *breaking* all the *locks* off from my *trunks* and *bureaus.* They went into my wardrobe and got Mr F's 4 *new hats* he had put there for safe keeping—then broke open *my* black *travelling trunk* that has 2 locks and stole out of it as much as they could carry away. I have no idea what they stole as I had placed things there that I would not want for some time to come—every drawer was searched and they took what they pleased—did not care for Mr F. Had I been up there they would not have stolen as much from me—because the man in Sister's room did not take small articles—and would put down when I would ask him kindly—he only took the *coat*, true[,] that was a very great loss to Mr F. and I did my utmost to save it—but had I not been in the room Sister's cloak and other valuable articles would have been stolen—but I am truly glad I protected her room—while she was up the street. (She could not find an officer.) While the man up stairs was ordering me to get the *closet* key—(I went up in my room when the man left Sister's room) fortunately for me another soldier made his appearance up stairs. I appealed to him for protection and begged him to get the *coat* and *hats*. He said he could not[,] they did not belong to his Regt. but he would try and get them out which he did—Mr. F. then offered to buy the hats from him—he said ... he would for $5. Mr F. offered him the money, but he wanted to get the money in his hand—Mr. F. would not do that whereupon this soldier that drove them out told Mr F. to hand him the money—he then ordered the man to give up the *hats* and the rascal held the hats (but not sufficiently in Mr F's reach as it proved to be afterwards) and the soldier handed him the money, he took the money instantly, cut his horse and away he went—*hats, money.* After all this had transpired Mr Ryan (a soldier we were acquainted with last winter) rode up—we were much surprised to see him among such a band of robbers—he said he wished much he had rode up sooner he would have protected us—and told Mr F. to go to the Col. and try and find the rascal[,] Mr F. did so—the Col sent his Adjutant with Mr F. Mr F. saw the man with the hats, pointed him out and the Adjutant did not as much as order him to dismount but walked off without opening his lips—Mr. F. returned to the Col.[,] told him he found the man but the Adjutant did nothing in his behalf— The Col. did not make a remark but turned off and left him standing, which proved at once that he had turned them loose on the town to rob and plunder—They were the 8th Illinoise [sic] Cavalry—commanded by Col. Clendenning [sic]—They came to Warrenton to bring a *pass* and a letter to *Mrs* Bartain[3] [sic] for her to go North—

_____

[3] Emma H. Barten, wife of the Rev. Otto S. Barten, Rector of St. James Episcopal Church, Warrenton, Va. Mrs. Barten, aged 28 years, was a native of New York. (J.K.G.)

Now we paid dearly for Mrs B's permit. The Col said W was very much out of his way but having this letter he wished to deliver it in person. They had never been here before—

While all this stealing was going on at *our* house, the same was going at the store. Dr H says they must have been told about the tobacco, for they went directly to where it was hid without going any where else and carried off 300 pounds—after that they took all the Castor oil and every article out of the show case[,] also all the *money* in the drawer. *Green backs* & confed. I think Dr H. had sufficient time to get the money from the drawer and to have hid the articles in show case[.] I am much astonished at his leaving money in the drawer. The wretches stole all of Mrs Smith's meat and much of her bed clothes—took 10 blankets from Mrs Daschielles[4] [sic] and meat from Mr Bragg—also took some articles from Rindsburg—from Boatwright's store and Jno. A. Spillmans. It was very singular *they did not disturb* a *house* on *any other street*—and only *our* house on this corner[.] Mrs White, Mrs Brooke, Mr Gaines[5] were not disturbed. Jessie said we must be the *baddest* people or God would [not] have let us have all our things stolen and saved the other neighbors things, she was much annoyed. I feel much tried myself and wished much that Sister had not gone up the street—for she would have protected her room—men will at all times have some respect for Ladies—and she might have enabled me to have saved the hats and other things up stairs—I feel very glad I was enabled to save her *cloak*.

My hand trembles for just as I commenced this letter the cry came the yankees are coming and Sister and I have been trying to hide several articles—and I feel tired out[,] I have but little fortitude. I cannot stand a great deal more. I long for quiet—my mind is in a miserable state[,] I am tired of living such a life—but oh! why should I complain when thousands are faring worse than I—God help me to be resigned. I long to be a true pious christian—to live for Heaven—to feel assured I shall reach there—to be at rest—but I find it hard. My heart is so *rebellious*.

I was truly glad to hear from my dear parents—may God preserve the life of my dear father and permit me to see him ere he dies and is no more—I long to see them both. The children were delighted with their books—Jessie has some one reading hers all day and all night, she knows very many of them by heart. Frank has learned some in his—We are all well—Mr. F. has come in with papers[,] no[,] a letter for me from Mrs Goodloe dated Dec 17th as the mail has arrived at last. I must answer it soon. Love & kisses from all hands—Your affec daughter

S E C

You must fix up the conduct of the yankee *Sargant* [sic] I wrote about and

---

[4] Eliza R. Deshields, widow of James Deshields, proprietor of the "Warrenton House," a hotel in Warrenton located on Main Street. (J.K.G.)

[5] Judge William H. Gaines (see pg. 105 n. 64) owned 67 Waterloo Street during the Civil War. After the war the house was the home of General Eppa Hunton and also Alexander Hunter, journalist and author of *Women of the Debatable Land.* The Brooke house was across Waterloo Street from Gaines, at the corner of what is now Waterloo and Pelham Streets; it is believed that the White's were immediate next-door neighbors of the Caldwells and Finks, on the corner of Smith and Waterloo Streets. (J.M.W.) (J.K.G.)

publish it in the "*Sentinel*" and send us a paper—the behaviour of the Col. and Adjutant is as bad I think.

It is too true a yankee has no shame[,] to think the *Sargant* would show his face to us again with one of the stolen *hats* on *his head*.

Please write by *mail*—

I forgot to mention in my letter that Uncle John stood by me all the time the yankees were stealing[,] tried his best to get them to stop meddling with "omans (womens) tings" [sic]—but they ordered him to shut up and begone—He was very faithful for once—

Willie Beckham arrived from Richmond last night—he says things look blue in R—just at present. We were grieved to hear of the death of Frank Beckham[.] He was an excellent officer and will be sadly missed.

Monday. Genl. Payne will leave in the morning and I will send my letter.

Pray dont waste your money again on *tobacco* and *dont think of buying Green backs* at such prices[,] I dont need any at present. I have now $10 and that will last me a long while for my purpose.

Sister *did not* succeed in getting a *guard*.

My pen is miserable.

Warrenton Fauquier
Friday night Jany 27th/65

My Dearest Papa

I received a letter from you to day dated the 20th. Mr Royston sent it to me from Jefferson. Tommy is with him. The weather has been so *intensely cold* that he could not travel on foot to Warrenton. I am truly glad he has been honorably discharged. I hope he will not be disturbed by the *yankees*. He is too young to be away from home. I wish I had some way of sending word to Aunt Martha to relieve her mind. Mr R begged me to try and write to her about him. I will do so by the first chance.

You write me you have not heard from me since the last yankee raid. 'Tis strange—I wrote by Col Payne on the 15th giving you a full and correct statement of all that took place. Thinking perhaps the letter may be miscarried I will give you some idea of their misdoings. The 8th Illinois Cavalry came in town very unexpectedly on the 13th early in the morning. After hiding the horses, we felt secure. I had suffered all night with the sick head ache and hearing of the arrival of the yankees I had break fast over and felt no more concerned (as you were not here) than if all had been quiet as usual. I left the dining room after Sister came down and had gone up to my room when Susa came running up to me to know if she must open the back door—the yankees were knocking at it to come in. I ran down, but told her not to open it[.] By the time I was on the last step Mr F. had opened it and in walked 4 yankees—they went into the parlor and had me open my *What Not*, looked into every thing and then they scattered into the bed rooms. The one in Sister['s] room stole Mr

F's new cloth coat, and did attempt to steal Sister's cloak, but I succeeded in getting it away from him—during the time he was searching Sister's room—3 of the wretches were in the upper rooms stealing all they could find. (When they first came in the yard they went to the *meat house* and tried to open the door—Sister seeing them feared her meat would go—ran out into the streets for a guard.) Mr F. was with them but could not prevent them from going into trunks & bureaus. They stole Mr F's 4 new felt hats from my wardrobe. My large black trunk was broken opened and various articles taken out of it—nearly all of my spool cotton. They would have stolen more, but a Sargant came in and sent them away—He would not make them give any of the articles up they had—said he had no orders to that effect—At the store Mr F lost every thing from the show case—all the money that was in the drawer—and 350 pounds of tobacco. We had no idea they would search houses or even stores—did not think it worth while to go to the trouble to hide even the *hats* as we had been doing—only a few houses were searched—Should you not have received my first letter when you write again—I will then write more about it, but I have almost forgotton how things were carried on.

We have had the coldest weather the past week I have ever experienced—a coat of ice has been over the ground the entire week making the walking very dangerous—Has it been as cold in R? I miss you very much these cold nights. I almost *freeze*. To night it is snowing—

I have just heard of the death of Churchill Diggs,[6] [sic] a member of the Black Horse—was found dead Thursday on the Road side—he was on his way home—cause of his death unknown—unless from the intense cold weather.

Jessie has enjoyed sleighing—she has a *plank* and she lays flat down and goes out like a Steam boat. She has worn the heels from her shoes—Every body is sleighing—*soldiers,* boys and girls—Mrs Brooke has a large company to night, cakes and ice cream in abundance—

Willie keep [sic] head in all his classes—Frank studies very well. Jessie is spelling in three letters. I must close 'tis 10 O'clock and Mr F. wants to retire—Please write by *mail*—it comes *twice a week*. There is much talk about *Peace commission*[.][7] Write us about them—God bless and protect you.

Good night all join you in love. Kisses from all[,] I hope to dream of you—(may you do the same of me)[.]

Your devoted & affec daughter
S E C

Mr. F. says the behaviour of the yankee in regard to his *"hats"* is worthy of a notice in the *Newspapers*. After stealing the 4 hats out of my wardrobe Mr. F. anxious to get

---

[6] Churchill G. Digges enlisted in the Black Horse Cavalry (Co. H, 4th Virginia Cavalry) July 20, 1861. He was captured at Stevensburg, June 9, 1863 and exchanged June 12, 1863. (J.K.G.)

[7] Peace Conference held Feb. 3, 1865 on board a steamer in Hampton Roads, Va. between Alexander H. Stephens, Vice President of the C.S.A., Robert M. T. Hunter and J. A. Campbell representing the Confederacy and Abraham Lincoln and William H. Seward representing the Union. The conference failed when the Confederates insisted on independence and the Federals refused, especially since slavery might continue in the South. (J.K.G.)

them back offered the rascal $5 for them. He agreed to the bargain but held on to the hats till he made sure of the Greenbacks—Mr F was afraid to trust him. A "*Sargant*" was near and offered Mr F. to see he got his hats if he gave him the $5. in his hand. Mr F. did so. The Sargant held the money to the man, the man held the hats to Mr F. and before Mr F. could take hold on the hats, the Sargant let go the $5 to the man, the man cut his horse & galloped off with hats and $5 to boot. The Sargant said 'tis too bad for him to have acted so and promised to pursue him and get them. In about half an hour the Sargant returned (much intoxicated) and met Mr F. by the gate— told he had tried to get the *hats*—but did not succeed. Mr F. says strange you should say so—when you have one of the hats on your head. 'Tis too bad he should act so.

Undated, 1865

Dearest Papa

Cash leaves in the morning and I must scribble you a few lines—I can scarcely bend my head *low* enough to see the lines to write well—suffering with a severe *pain* in my *neck* and *right arm*. I think it must be *rheumatism*. I have had it twice since you left. The people here seem to be in good spirits regarding *peace*. The paper of the 31st stated Commissioners had gone from Richmond to Washington—God grant it may end as we all most ardently desire. That we shall be an *Independent nation* and nothing else—We cannot go back into the *Union* no, no—the blood already shed in the cause would cry aloud for vengeance—Oh! I long for the glad tidings of peace throughout the confederacy—but even tho' peace should dawn upon us—it *will not gladden the hearts* of the *widow* and *orphan*—*sorrow* has *forever shut out* all *Sunshine* from their hearts. Oh! Papa I do *sympathize* with the *bereaved*. I know from better experience what the *heart ache* is. Papa why dont you write to me by *mail*, it comes twice a week—and Mr F. thinks hard of not getting *papers* by *mail*. Do attend to their coming if you possibly can—I wrote you of the death of Churchill Diggs by freezing—Another death has occurred in our town—a soldier from Salem by the name of Russel[8] [sic] started from Warrenton at dusk for home and furlough—(he was from Northern Neck, a member of Mosby's command) he was much intoxicated on starting and Mr Bragg insisted on his remaining at his house till morning—but he refused saying he had a *short furlough* and had much to attend to to make his family comfortable (he had a wife and 5 children). In the morning Mrs White's boy had occasion to go into Mrs John Smith's field and there found the unfortunate man frozen to death—near the branch—he was taken home to his family—what *sorrow*. I hope you keep well—God preserve your life to us—Frank is seated by me learning his lesson for to day—he *loves* his book—

---

[8] John W. Russell (1821-1864) married Mary F. Jeffries, December 17, 1849 in Fauquier County. Mr. Russell and his family lived at Marshall (then Salem) where he was a bricklayer. They were the parents of six children. He was a member of Co. C, 43rd Batt'n., Va. Cav. (Mosby's Rangers), commanded by Capt. William Chapman. At the time of his death, Feb. 1, 1864, Mosby's men were active in the Shenandoah Valley and the area of upper Loudoun and Charlestown, W. Va. The reason for the presence of Pvt. Russell in the Warrenton area has never been explained. (J.K.G.)

but loves out doors best—but I need not complain of the little fellow—he does very well—He is very good and thoughtful of me—keep me well supplied in wood and chips—I do better without Alice than with her. I get on first rate—Willie is not looking well—he has grown very thin. Sister thinks he studies too hard—he does apply himself very closely—and deserves much credit—he has the highest merit marks at school of all the boys in his class—and very many are much older than himself—you must write him of the good news you heard of him—Jessie tries to be good and sometimes is very studious. She wants to send you some *apples* by Cash— if he has room—we wanted to send something nice but Cash is going on *horse back.* Please fix up these *Mitts* and send them to Ma for me—I want her to have them.

Tommy Royston is very ill at Jefferson with typhoid fever—Aunt M is with him—she sends a thousand thanks to you, will never forget you.

Standing of Wm Caldwell for the quarter beginning Nov. 16th 1864, and ending Jan. 31st 1865.

Reading	38	0	3
Spelling	26	4	1
Geography	38	0	1
Arithmetic	18	0	
Eng: Grammar	30	0	1

Absences from roll call 1.

Jas R. Marr.[9]

Warrenton Fauquier
Monday Jan 30th 1865

Dearest Papa

I have written to you very often lately, but they must be miscarried as you say you have not heard from me since the Yankee raid. I wrote by Col. W. Payne. I have just heard that Mr Boothe leaves in the morning and altho there is company in—I beg them to excuse me so I could write you a short note—

The weather has been intensely cold the past ten days—I have heard that several soldiers were found frozen [to] death on their posts. Oh! I thought of the soldiers day and night and felt truly grateful that you were in comfortable quarters and I hope you will not be compelled to leave Richmond during the winter. But I pray your presence will ever be necessary to the business in the Office—

I hope you have on a necessary quantity of clothing during this severe weather—more than you usually wear I mean—you should wear a pair of *white* drawers with your *flannel drawers.* You must wear your *over flannel shirts* also. *Do keep warm.*

---

[9] James Ripon Marr (1822-1879), son of John and Catherine (Horner) Marr, and brother of Captain John Quincy Marr. Mr. Marr was a graduate of the University of Virginia (1852) and was a teacher. (J.K.G.)

Do write us about *your peace commissioners.* What does it mean? And what will it amount to? I cannot for my part place any reliance upon these peace makers—but from my heart I pray God it may end in good to the confederacy and peace be declared. I do long for families to be *reunited.* Mrs Brooke says Mr B. writes in good spirits about the state of the times—He will be home during the last of February—I received a letter by Tommy Royston—He has not yet arrived in W. is sick at Jefferson—I have had no opportunity to send word to Aunt Martha—but I am so glad he is so near his home—I wrote you that several ladies had started from Warrenton to Fairfax hoping to get to Alexandria—Mrs Souers[10] [sic] had received a permit from Genl. Gamble[11] to reach Fairfax unmolested—Mr Finks hired his horses and wagon to them—The ladies left and arrived safely at Fairfax Court H—and was politely entertained by Genl. Gamble—he fully intended to get them to Alexandria as he had promised Mrs Souers. (The Genl had felt under obligation to Mrs S's family during sickness) but the day the ladies arrived in Fairfax the Provost received orders to let neither man, woman or child go to Alexandria without taking the *oath.* Of course the ladies did not go—but they were able to purchase very many articles and all the groceries they needed at Fairfax—Mr. F. wrote a letter to Genl. Gamble informing him of the depridations [sic] committed by his soldiers—and asking permission to allow Mrs Souers to buy him in Alex. a coat and hats—Had they gone to A. he would have permitted them to have brought any articles they wished out. Mrs Souers says the General was much annoyed when he heard of the order—and went so far as to telegraph to the Provost in Alex—and asked of him as a *personal* favor to grant the ladies permission to pass in and out without the oath—but he was *refused.* They were disappointed—but felt satisfied to be able to buy groceries—brown sugar only 22 cts per pound—

I must tell you something on Frank—on going to bed last night I said Frank you have not said your *commandments* to day—what is the *first*—I dont know it[,] he said[,] I never heard of it—Why said I—Jessie does and you should, I have taught you well if you have—then 'tis *"Jesus Christ"*—I had to laugh out to think a Baptist Mother's son[12] did not know any better—he was thinking of *"who redeemed him."* I will try and do better.

Mr F. is much disappointed when the *mail* comes in to hear that there are neither *letters* or papers from you—he thinks you might write and see that the Sentinel sends papers—Mail here twice a week regularly—

Bettie Mullins has never received my letter—I would have heard from her before this, where did you mail it at?

---

[10] Mary Frances (Smith) Sowers (1844-1922), daughter of John and Ann D. (Adams) Smith of Warrenton and wife of James R. Sowers, M.D., a member of Mosby's Rangers. (J.K.G.)

[11] Brig. Gen. William Gamble (U.S.A.). After a short career in the U.S. Army, General Gamble became a successful civil engineer in Chicago. At the outbreak of the Civil War he became Lt. Col. of the 8th Illinois Cavalry; promoted to Colonel on Dec. 5, 1862. He was known to the residents of Warrenton by 1865, having seen his first war service in the vicinity in early 1862. In May 1864 he was assigned to the command of the cavalry division in the Department of Washington where he served until the end of the war. He died December 20, 1866 in Nicaragua on his way, with his regiment, to California and is buried there in Virgin Grove Cemetery. (J.K.G.)

[12] Frank Caldwell became a member of the Warrenton Baptist Church and served the church for many years as a Deacon. (J.K.G.)

Oh! what a long dreary month this has been—I am so tired of almost every thing—even the very sun shine seems to mock me—my sadness amounts to almost despair—but I know I am wrong—but really I cannot help myself—at times—

To day the sun is bright and the weather milder—and we may be on the lookout for the yankees—altho Genl Gamble called up the Officers after reading Mr F's letter and told them that if they had done their duty when in Warrenton they would not have permitted the *rebels* to have gotton [sic] out of town—and they would have had no time to spare for plundering & stealing. He ordered them to surround the town by day light at every point but they failed to obey orders—

Tis dinner time and I must close—

Children are all well and send much love & kisses—We want to see you oh! I cannot say how much.

Good bye—God bless and preserve you from all harm.

Your devoted & affec
daughter—S E C

Warrenton Fauquier Co.
Sunday March 26th 1865

My Dearest Papa

I have sent you letters by Jerry Cash and by Melville Withers. 'Tis a long time since you have heard from me, and you are anxiously awaiting the arrival of some friend from Warrenton to bring you a letter from home and loved ones there. Willie Foster I understand intends to make another attempt to go to Richmond to morrow. I hope he will be more successful this time—I am not altogether selfish in my wish for he is very desirous to return to his duties—and then again he has been much disturbed by the yankees—

All the good people have gone to Church to hear a sermon to be preached by Mr Fitzpatrick, a Methodist minister. I felt no desire to go—I feel as if I do wrong to encourage this wish of being in doors during the *sun* shine—oh! my dearest Papa since the spring has set in and we have had very many pleasant days my heart has ached so much the more—*my baby I miss all the day*—I try to feel that my hands should find enough to do in taking care of those left me—but oh! me I cannot fill up the void by either work or any thing else—Oh! why—why has the Good Lord thus punished me?—I know I merit punishment for my short comings—but oh! me this was so severe—may this heavy affliction prove an everlasting blessing to me—I do strive to live for Heaven—I want to meet again my precious darling—I know she is safely housed in Heaven and I long to go there to be with her, to be ready when my Saviour calls.

Papa write to me by the first opportunity and tell me if you will be compelled to go out on duty with your company[.] I am so much troubled about you. Time seems very long to me. When oh! when shall we meet again? When will this cruel

261

war end? Many years yet I fear, we are to endure these severe trials. Mr Pugh prays for the end to come this year—God grant and hear all prayer—Kate Withers has been spending some time with us—Mr. Bronaugh sent me some very nice apples—also some nice spring vegetables—he is kind and thoughtful. Miss Susan Jennings has arrived from Washington. She has seen Mrs Helen and Roberta—Roberta has been sick most of the winter with her old complaint *Erysipilis.* Mrs Helen saw her husband before he died—he was ill in New York—and she went on there to see him—his family have nothing to do with her.—I feel very sorry for her and Roberta—Mr Finks says Mr Marshall would have been elected, but the rumour got out he was in favor of *reconstruction.* I wonder if such a report is true of him? I want peace but I don't want to go back into the *union.* I want *Independence* and nothing else—I could not consent to go back with a people that has been bent upon exterminating us. Willie, Frank and Jessie are well—and send love and kisses to their dearest Papa—they all want you to come. The people have come from church and I will lay aside my writing. It is cold and looks stormy—March days come in bright but end in clouds—we do not look for settled weather till May—Good bye. God preserve and keep you from sickness and danger till we meet again.

Your devoted daughter
S E C

AFTERWORD

Upon the retreat from Petersburg and the burning of Richmond, Custis Lee's men moved toward Appomattox with the remainder of the Army of Northern Virginia, surrendering at Sailor's Creek on April 6. It is assumed that Lycurgus Caldwell was among them.

Following Lee's surrender, Lycurgus, at length, made his way home to Warrenton, his wife and his family.

And, on Saturday morning, Nov. 11, 1865, a new weekly newspaper for Fauquier County—published and edited by John W. Finks and Lycurgus W. Caldwell—was on the streets, eloquently assessing the South's post-war predicament:

"We see no path open to our people but that of honest, sincere and persistent effort to repair as far as possible the damages already sustained, and to avert those which a senseless adherence to exploded theories will most surely entail upon us," Lycurgus editorialized in Volume I, Number 1 of *The True Index.*

That same issue carried advertisements for Hamme & Finks Drug Store on Main Street; the ubiquitous Mr. Finks would continue to prosper.

Lycurgus published and edited *The True Index* through much of the remainder of the 19th century, and eventually sold it to his son, Frank, who in turn would sell it in 1899. The paper was sold again in 1905, and re-named *The Fauquier Democrat;* it continues to flourish as *The Fauquier Times-Democrat* today.

Susan Caldwell would live in relative peace and happiness after the war, bearing two more children—Charles and Harry—and would eventually enjoy a number of grandchildren.

The Caldwells would live, together with the Finks, in their home on Smith Street in Warrenton until their deaths. In 1879, John Finks died; in 1910, Lycurgus; in 1911, Lucy Finks; and in 1913, Susan Caldwell.

All rest today in the Warrenton Cemetery, a few blocks from their home.

Jessie Caldwell Walraven would live in her family home on Smith Street until her death in 1946; her daughters, Helen Walraven Edwards and Jessie (Finks) Walraven Welton, would also live in and look after the home until their respective deaths in 1977 and 1983.

Appendix

13 July 1860

1860 CENSUS—UNITED STATES

Town

State **Virginia**   County **Fauquier**   Township **Warrenton**   Call No.

Town of Warrenton, Fauquier County, Virginia

Number	Dwelling Number	Family Names	Age	Sex	Color	Occupation, etc.	Birthplace	Remarks
345	328	Charles Bragg	39	m		Carriage maker & Mayor of Warrenton	Virginia	*RE: 7,500 **PP: 25,895
		Mary A. "	36	f			Maryland	nee: PASOPE, dau. of Moses, m: 7-6-1837
		Wm. M. "	21	m		Coach trimmer		
		Charles P. "	19	m		Clerk		
		Henry C. "	10	m				
		Clayton "	8	m				
		Millard F. "	3	m				
		George Brown	25	m		Blacksmith	Maryland	
		James H. Stout	22	m		Coach painter		
		Elijah W. Fairbanks	59	m		Carriage maker	Maryland	
		Carr White	20	m	m	Blacksmith apprentice		
		Henry Tyler	14	m		Coach painter apprentice		
346	329	John Ross	44	m		Carriage maker	Cassell Hesse Germany	*RE: 1,000 **PP: 3,150
		Elizabeth C. "	32	f		Housekeeper		
		Charles P. "	11	m				
		Virginia Hudson	19	f		Seamstress		
347	330	William A. Caruth	51	m		Coach maker	Ireland	*RE: 600 *PP: 60
		Mary A. "	40	f		Housework		
		Alice A. "	14	f				
		James T. "	12	m				
		George S. "	10	m				
348	331	Jno. N. Grant	37	m		Machinist		RE: 800 PP: 1310

*   Real Estate
** Personal Property

265

Number	Dwelling Number	Family Names	Age	Sex	Color	Occupation, etc.	Birthplace	Remarks
		Lucy A. (Grant)	34	f		Housekeeper		nee: Latham m: 12-23-1844
		Cath. O. "	9	f				
		Elizabeth B. "	13					
		James H. "	11	m				
		John R. "	8	m				
		Mary W. "	5	f				
		Thomas "	3	m				
		Theodosia "	2	f				
		Lucy A. "	1	f				
349	332	John Smith	63	m		Farmer		RE: 21,275 PP: 29,162
		Ann D. "	59	f		Housekeeping		nee: Adams, dau. of Thomas; m: 12-15-1841
		Mary F. "	15	f				
		George S. "	11	m				
		Lucy J. Kerfoot	44	f		Sewing etc		PP: 1,500 nee: Adams, dau. of Turner; m: Geo. L. Kerfoot 5-5-1837
		Wm. T. "	16	m				
		Martha A. "	14	f				
		Kate S. "	23	f		Sewing etc		
350	333	Wm. Johnson	35	m		Confectioner		RE: 1500 PP: 2400
		Sarah C. "	33	f		Mantua maker		
		James W. "	11	m				
		Judith A. "	10	f				
		John C. "	8	m				
		Rosina L. "	2	f				
		Isabella Williams	13	f	m			
351	334	Thos. C. McLearen	40	m		Painter		RE: 1,000 PP: 156
		Mary F. "	31	f		Housekeeper		nee: Pattie m: 2-9-1848
		Mary M. "	11	f				
		Olivia A. "	6	f				
		John S. "	4	m				
		Frank L. "	2	m				
		Henry M. Daniels	30	m		Painter	Maryland	
352	335	Richard Cooper	60	m		Negro Trader	Virginia	RE: 13,000 PP: 6,500
		Almedia A. "	40	f		Housekeeper		
		Silas L. "	12	m				

Number	Dwelling Number	Family Names	Age	Sex	Color	Occupation, etc.	Birthplace	Remarks
		Emma S. " (Cooper)	10	f				
		Harriet F. "	8	f				
		John R. "	6	m				
		Wm. F. "	4	m				
		George S. "	2	m				
		Kate "	4/12	f				
353	336	John S. Byrne	49	m		Clerk, Circuit Court		PP: 1,250
334	337	Wm. A. Jennings	24	m		Clerk, County Court		PP: 200
335	338	A. M. Jennings	30	f		Housekeeping		nee: Ann Maria Corbin, m: Wm. H. Jennings 1-27-1848 4000 - 4000
		Francis W. "	11	m				
		Mary J. "	9	f				
		Elizabeth C. "	7	f				
		Lula	5	f				
		John C. "	3	m				
		Henry	30	m				
		Benjamin Williams	24	m	B	Gardener		
		Mary Brown	16	f	B	Housemaid		
		John Turner	21	m		Clerk		
		A. G. Embrey	23	m		do.		
336	339	James D. Triplett	37	m		Dry goods clerk		PP: 13,750
337	340	D. E. Graham	44	m		Tailor	Maryland	700 - 1400
		M. J. "	36	f		Seamstress	Virginia	nee: Mary Jane Cologne, dau. of Vincent; m: David E. Graham 4-16-1844
		Edgar C. "	15	m				
		Mary A. "	13	f				
		John V. "	12	m				
		D. E. " Jr.	10	m				
		Richard B. "	9	m				
		Herbert N. "	7	m				
		Horace A. "	5	m				
		Charles C. "	4	m				
		Sarah Putnam	17	f		Tailoress		
		Blanche E. Barker	16	f		Tailoress	Maryland	
		Margaret Castoff	33	f		Sewing, etc.	do	

Number	Dwelling Number	Family Names	Age	Sex	Color	Occupation, etc.	Birthplace	Remarks
358	341	John M. Abel	25	m		Jour. Tailor	Virginia	
359	342	Richard B. Mitchell	45	m		Jour. Tailor		
		Mary F. "	28	f		Tailoress		
		Richard T. "	9	m				
360	343	William Rolland	40	m		Jour. Baker	Scotland	
361	344	R. H. Ross	36	m		Confectioner	New Jersey	
		Abi "	34	f		Housekeeping	New Jersey	
		Violetta "	8	f				
		Minerva "	6	f				
		Alonzo H. "	1	m				
362	345	Mason Weaver	19	m		Confectioners Clerk		PP: 75
363	346	George Rabbitt	46	m		Shoemaker	Maryland	
364	347	Thos. E. Sanders	38	m		Boot & Shoemaker	Kentucky	4000 - 4437
		Mary E. "	37			Housekeeping		nee: Mary Eleanor Berry, dau. of Benj.; m. Thos. E. Saunders 5-2-1844
		Isabella Sanders	14	f				
		Wm. E. "	12	m				
		Richardson "	9	m				
		Lilly "	5	f				
365	348	James F. Martin	43	m		Plasterer		350 - 87
		Emily	36	f		Housework		
		George W."	3	m				
		Georgiana "	2	f				
		Sally "	11	f				
366	349	Rinaldo Brown	28	m		Tailor	Maryland	
		Daniel Sweeney	17	m			Ireland	
367	350	Wm. Lear	24	m		Dry goods clerk	Virginia	3500 - 25
368	351	L. E. Hamme	32	m		Druggist	Virginia	PP: 2300
		Thomas E. Frankland	31	m		R. Road conductor	Virginia	PP: 250

Number	Dwelling Number	Family Names	Age	Sex	Color	Occupation, etc.	Birthplace	Remarks
369	352	Jos. Seigert	32	m		Boot & shoemaker	Bavaria	PP: 650
		Christine "	30	f		Housework	Hesse Damstadt	
		Betty "	11/12	f			Virginia	
		Henry Strath	19	m		Appr. Shoemaker	Germany	
370	353	Jos. H. Watson	36	m		Jeweller & watchmaker		6000 - 7500
		Mary E. "	33	f		Housekeeping		nee: Mary E. English; m. Joseph H. Watson 4-27-1847
		Evelyn R. "	12	f				
		Mary J.	8	f				
		Ida E.	6	f				
		James H. "	3	m				
371	354	John W. McGee	39	m		Dentist	Pa.	4,000 - 600
		Elizabeth "	32	f		Housekeeping	New Jersey	
		Thomas F. "	10	m			Indiana	
		Rebecca E."	8	f			Virginia	
372	355	H. A. White	47	m		Merchant	Virginia	7000 - 27,350 m. Caroline B. Withers 6-3-1846, widow of Horatio Withers
		Meade F. "	13	m				
		Robb "	10	m				
373	356	M. J. Follin	51	m		Merchant	Virginia	7000 - 4700 nee: Bise; m. 3-17-?
		Eliza Ann "	43	f		Housekeeping		
		Cath. C. "	21	f		Schoolmistress		
		Mary Ann "	16	f		Sewing		
		John M. "	15	m		Dry goods clerk		
		James F. "	12	m				
		Charles R.	8	m				
		Wm. A. "	5	m				
		Emma F. "	4	f				
374	357	Ben. F. McConchie	32	m		Journeyman Shoemaker		1500 - 662
		Mary A. "	32	f		Seamstress		nee: Fletcher; m. 2-8-1849
		Mary E. "	10	f				
		Sarah J. "	6	f				
		James R. "	4	m				
		Frances S. "	2	f				

Number	Dwelling Number	Family Names	Age	Sex	Color	Occupation, etc.	Birthplace	Remarks
375	358	Robert H. Fletcher	31	m		Jour. Shoemaker		
		Mary E. "	26	f				
		Robt. H. ", Jr.	7	m				
		Marion "	2	m				
		Wm. A. "	9/12	m				
		Susan Allison	28	f		Seamstress		
		George W. Hughes	26	m		Saddler	Maryland	
376	359	Alexander Dodd Fletcher	50	m		Shoemaker	Virginia	PP: 125 father of Albert Fletcher, Family #361
		(Louisa) Lethe "	45	f		Housework		
		Agnes A. "	20	f		Seamstress		
		Lavinia "	18	f				
		Emma M. "	16	f				
		Virginia E. "	14	f				
		Delaware "	13	m				
		George Wm."	11	m				
		Charles R. "	9	m				
		Mary E. "	7	f				
377	360	Wm. B. Sinclair	59	m		Gun Smith	Virginia	2000 - 657
		Ann M. "	47	f		Milliner		nee: Ann Maria Johnson, ward of Eppa Hunton; m.9-22-1828
		Louisa "	29	f		School teacher		
		Cornelia "	22	f		Apt. Milliner		
		Alice "	18	f		School teacher		
		Albert "	17	m				
		James "	13	m				
		Cath. "	10	f				
		Charles "	8	m				
		Andrew J. "	6	m				
		Robt. "	4	m				
378	361	Elias Williams	50	m		Painter		
		Sarah M.	42	f		Housekeeping		nee: English, dau. of James & Elizabeth; m. 6-1-1841
		James T. "	14	m				
		Richard "	11	m				
		Edward "	7	m				
		Elizabeth "	3	f				
		Maria C. English	30	f		Sewing etc		
		Florence "	6	f				

Number	Dwelling Number	Family Names	Age	Sex	Color	Occupation, etc.	Birthplace	Remarks
		Albert Fletcher	19	m		Grocery clerk		PP: 25
379		Unoccupied						
380	362	John R. Tongue	50	m		Tanner		10,000 - 14,360
		Frances E. "	43	f		Housekeeping		nee: Yeatman, dau. of John; m. 7-8-1834
		John Z. "	17	m				
		Thomas W."	14	m				
		Addison Utterback	24	m		Merchant		Capt., CSA
		Virginia "	21	f		Sewing, etc.		
		Ann L. Tongue	61	f		Knitting, etc.		
381	363	John W. Tyler	62	m		Judge, Circuit Court		8000 - 88,250
		Gwynetta "	46	f		Housekeeping		nee: Dade; m. 12-2-1847
		Constance "	11	f				
		Gwynetta "	9	f				
		John W. " Jr.	7	m				
		Jane C. "	30	f		Sewing, etc.		
		Madison C.	26	m		Lawyer		
		Gwynetta Slye	23	f		Teacher		
		Marian Slye	25	f		Sewing, etc.		
		Estelle Washington	16	f				
382	364	Bushrod Jolly, Sr.	41	m		Bricklayer	Virginia	5000 - 16,850
		Lucinda "	33	f		Housekeeper		
		Eddy "	8	m				
		Anna "	6	f				
		Ada "	4	f				
		Bushrod " Jr.	1	m				
		Jacob "	83	m		Stonemason		
		Elizabeth "	75	f		Knitting, etc.		nee: Elizabeth Furr; m Jacob Jolly 1-4-1806
		Bushrod Pierce	19	m		Appr. bricklayer		
		Andrew Feddon	32	m		Jour. Do.		PP: 50
		Arthur Payne	21	m	B	Tender		
		Thomas White	16	m	B	"		
		Frederick Pinn	50	m	B	"		
383	365	Sally B. Edmonds	55	f		Housekeeping	Virginia	3000 - 10,750
		Nancy E. Lucas	43	f		Sewing, etc.	"	
		Fanny B. "	20	f		"	Mississippi	
		A. Thomas "	16	f		"	"	

Number	Dwelling Number	Family Names	Age	Sex	Color	Occupation, etc.	Birthplace	Remarks
		Elizabeth J."	15	f			Virginia	
		Robt.	13	m			"	
		Wyndham						
		Lucas						
		Courtney	15	m			"	
		Washington						
384	366	Alexander	71	m		Weigh master	Mass.	1200 - 950
		Richardson						
		Jane	55	f		Housekeeper	Pa.	
385		Unoccupied						$3,000
386	367	Robt. C. Newby	38	m		Produce & Comm'r Merchant	Virginia	6400 - 30,835
		George Anna "	37	f		Housekeeping		
		Henry Ward "	1	m				
		James O. Pemberton	19	m		Clerk		
387	368	Lucy Jennings	68	f		Housekeeping		3500 - 4400
		Fanny "	34	f		Sewing, etc.		
		Susan "	29	f		Do.		
388	369	John L. Fant	71	m		Farmer		36,880 - 13,600
		Lucy E. D. M."	69	f		Housekeeping		
		Narcissa B. Jones	80	f				
		Cecelia "	45	f		Sewing, etc.		
		Margaret A. Combs	45	f		"		
		Lucy Jones	40	f		"		
389	370	A. Rindsberg	50	m		Dry goods merchant	Bavaria	10,000 - 30,000
		Sarah "	40	f		Housekeeper	"	
		Caroline "	11	f			Virginia	m. Adolph Ullman
		Henrietta Einstein	21	f		Clerk	Bavaria	
		Sarah Dingfelder	16	f		Do.	"	
390	371	Wm. D. Brooks	32	m		Tinner	Maryland	700 - 825
		Mary C. "	31	f		Housework		
		Edwin "	10	m				
		Martha R. "	9	f				
		W. Franklin "	7	m				
		Joseph "	6	m				
		Oliver "	3	m				
		Mary C. "	1	f				

Number	Dwelling Number	Family Names	Age	Sex	Color	Occupation, etc.	Birthplace	Remarks
391	372	Wm. A. Pattie	39	m		Carpenter	Virginia	1300 - 1700
		Alice L. "	68	f		Housework		
		James S. "	17	m				
		O. H. W. "	15	m				
		Alice E.	13	f				
		Thomas E. "	8	m				
		Mariana "	6	f				
		F. Cordelia	4	f				
		Wm. B. "	1	m				
392	373	Jas. V. Brooke	35	m		Lawyer		10,800 - 28,825
		Mary E. "	36	f		Housekeeping		nee: Norris, dau. of
								Thaddeus;
								m. 5-22-1844
		Wm. T.	14	m				
		Richard N. "	12	m				
		Janie M. "	10	f				
		Jas. V. " Jr.	7	m				
		Francis C. "	5	m				
		Annie A. "	2	f				
393	374	Antoine	46	m		Founder	Alzes, France	5000 - 3425
		Manyett						
		Cath. C. "	41	f		Housekeeper	D.C.	
		Rebecca F."	15	f			D.C.	
		Antoine E."	13	m			D.C.	
		Mary V. "	10	f			Virginia	
		George W."	9	m				
		Cath. O. "	5	f				
		James	3	m				
		Buchanan						
		John L. "	1	m				
394	375	Jos. M.	36	m		Merchant	Virginia	
		Ricketts						
		Jane M. "	36	f		Housekeeper		
		Ida "	6	f				
		John T. "	2	m				
		Jos. E. Moore	17	m		Clerk		
395	376	Benjamin	47	m		Merchant		2000 - 11,560
		Sedwick						
		Cath. V. "	34	f		Housekeeper		
		John F. "	18	m		Clerk		
		Wm. B. "	16	m				
		Charles E. "	14	m				
		R. F. "	12	m				
		R. A. "	7	m				
		Edward A. "	5	m				
		Lizzy C. "	3	f				
		Samuel "	1	m				

Number	Dwelling Number	Family Names	Age	Sex	Color	Occupation, etc.	Birthplace	Remarks
396	377	Edgar N. Cologne	49	m		Town Sergeant		2000 - 280
		Susan F. "	37			Housekeeper		nee: Cash, dau. of Lucy Y.; m. 10-10-1838
		Jno. A. C. "	19	m		Clerk		
		Ed. M. "	18	m				
		Lizzy A. "	12	f				
		Leverite A."	10	m				
		Lucian B. "	7	m				
		Newton S. "	4	m				
		Florry "	2	m				
		Betty Moran	12	f	M			
397	378	Susan Evans	69	f		Housekeeper		3000 - 2650 nee: Shumate; wid. Elisha B. Evans
398	379	Susan C. Menifee	40	f		Housekeeper		1600 - 8300 nee: Evans; m. Banks S. Menefee 2-28-1839
		Laura V. "	15	f				
399	380	Sally Nickens	30	f	M	Seamstress		PP: 50
		Eliza "	26	f	M	Do.		
		Jno. C. "	10	m	M			
		James M. "	8	m	M			
		Charles F. "	6	m	M			
		Eugenie L. "	4	f	M			
		Morton White	25	m	B	Blacksmith		PP: 25
400	381	John G. Kirby	64	m		Wheelwright		PP: 390
		Cecelia "	58	f		Housekeeper		nee: Clagett; m. 6-30-1824
		James D. "	20	m		Wheelwright		
		Thos. L. "	16	m		"		
401	382	Richard A. Thompson	23	m		Overseer		433 - 1596
		Minny "	66	f		Knitting, etc.		
		Susan Fletcher	14	f		Housework		
402	383	B. W. Howard	30	m	M	Blacksmith		PP: 850
		Mary A. "	31	f	M	Washerwoman		
403	384	Lucy Jackson	55	f	B	Washerwoman		PP: 200
		Betsey "	14	f	B			
		Frances "	12	f	B			
		Lucy "	9	f	B			

Number	Dwelling Number	Family Names	Age	Sex	Color	Occupation, etc.	Birthplace	Remarks
404	385	Wm. Golway, Sr.	35	m		Grocer	Ireland	3000 - 750
		Christina "	30	f		Housekeeper	Virginia	
		Mary J. "	8	f				
		Wm. " Jr.	6	m				
		Charles "	4	m				
		Christina "	1	f				
405	386	Phil S. Johnson	69	m		Farmer		7500 - 10743
		Chas. McL. Johnson	28	m		Editor		3350 - 1750
406	387	Henry J. Tapp	24	m		Painter	Virginia	
		Ida J. "	21	f		Housekeeper	Pa.	
		Margaretta "	20	f		Seamstress		
407	388	Abby White	32	f	M	Seamstress		
		J. W. "	14	m	M			
		Jas. W. "	11	m	M			
		A. C. "	9	m	M			
408	389	Fred. Jeffries	27	m		Carpenter	Virginia	
		Elizabeth "	23	f		Housework	D.C.	
		Fred "	5	m				
		James H. "	1	m				
409	390	Cyrus Cross	40	m		Jailor	D.C.	1300 - 1310
		Columbia "	40	f		Housekeeper	Virginia	nee: Kemper, dau. of John P.; m. 4-29-1845
		Jos. H.	14	m				
		Ann Eliza "	12	f				
		Sally S. "	10	f				
		Salina "	8	f				
		L. Morgan	6	m				
		Molly "	4					
		Andrew S. "	2	m				
		Janet B. "	6/12	f				
		George H. Dudley	22	m		Printer (Fauquier County Jail)		
410	391	George W. Wells	63	m		Post & rail fencer		PP: 300
		Mary A. "	50	f		Housework		
		Pat. "	27	m		Farm laborer		
		Eveline "	25	f		Seamstress		
		James H. "	23	m		Fencer		
		Eliza Ann "	20	f		Seamstress		
		Mary Ann "	16	f				
		Jos. Evans "	15	m				

Number	Dwelling Number	Family Names	Age	Sex	Color	Occupation, etc.	Birthplace	Remarks
		Zera Washington (Wells)	12	m				
		Barbara "	10	f				
		Henry Allen	38	m		Fencer		
411	392	Chas. H. Tavenner	38	m		Hotel Keeper	Virginia	19,619 - 14,415
		Maria "	30	f		Housekeeper	D.C.	
		Lewis E. "	7	m				
		Phil. R. "	5	m				
		Wm. H. "	2	m				
		Elizabeth Burgess	26	f		Sewing, etc.		
		Thomas E. B. Collins	18	m		Dry goods clerk		
		Hugh T. Kemper	29	m		Office tender		
		Sally M. Kemper	29	f		Sewing		
		Hugh F. "	2	m				
		T. Howard "	6/12	m				
		Samuel Russell	60	m		Gentleman		PP: 8500
		Eliza J. "	51	f		Sewing, etc.		
		James H. Moffett	33	m		Head Gardener		PP: 200
		Frances "	25	f		Sewing, etc.		
		J. W. Pugh	29	m		O.S. Pres. Preacher		PP: 500
		Ada "	23	f		Sewing, etc.		
		Caroline "	1	f				
		Sam'l. B. Fisher	48	m		Physician	Virginia	4000 - 27,000 nee: Withers; m. 2-14-1837; dec. 4-25-1867
		Mary "	50	f		Sewing, etc.		
		Edward "	19	m				
		Henry Yates	16	m		Office tender		
		Edwin Smith	33	m		Merchant		2000 - 27,300
		Mary "	26	f		Sewing, etc.		nee: Mary M. Ward; m. 11-18-1851
		Carrie	8	f				
		Harriett "	2	f				
		Kate Pickett	25	f		Sewing, etc.	D.C.	
		Ellen	4	f				
		Theodore "	1	m				
		Jim Nickens	20	m	M	Hack driver		
		Henry Hudnall	12	m	M			
412	393	Charles Hughes	40	m	B	Ostler		
		Franky "	32	f	B	Washerwoman		

Number	Dwelling Number	Family Names	Age	Sex	Color	Occupation, etc.	Birthplace	Remarks
413	394	Ann McFelan	64	f		Housework		1000 - 100
		John B. Hendrick	38	m		Harness maker		
414	395	Laura Grayson	29	f	B	Washerwoman		
		Charles "	1	m	M			
415	396	Sarah Carter	34	f		Milliner		
		Willie Anna "	10	f				
		Josephine "	10/12	f				
416	397	Wm. M. Ward	45	m		South. Meth. Epis. Minister	Maryland	2500 - 13,050
		Frances "	40	f		Sewing, etc.	Maryland	
		Ellis C. "	19	m			"	
		Jno. E. "	17	m			"	
		Mary F. "	13	f			"	
		Emma "	11	f			"	
		Anna "	9	f			"	
		Laura "	7	f			"	
		Willie "	2	f			"	
417	398	J. W. Michie	37	m		Sporting	Virginia	PP: 300
		M. A. "	42	f		Housekeeper		
418	399	Sally B. Fitz Hugh	73	f		Knitting		
		Eliza W. Peace	29	f		Housekeeping		25,750 - 38,400
		Washington "	2	m				
		A. M. Goodwin	51	f		Sewing, etc.		PP: 12,500
		Belle R. Vass	20	f		Teaching		
		Elizabeth "	14	f				
419	400	F.C.R. Ludewig	32	m		Grocer	Hanover, Germany	PP: 2900
		M. F. "	32	f		Housework	"	
		Anna "	3	f			Virginia	
		Theo. A. "	1	m			"	
420	401	J. H. Stephens	46	m		Druggist		6000 - 12,400
		Elizabeth "	26	f		Housekeeping		
		Albert "	7	m				
		Susan "	4	f				
		Lewis H. "	1	m				
		Lydia "	60	f		Knitting, etc.	Pa.	
		Jos. A. Jeffries	20	m		Clerk	Virginia	
		Alex'r. G. Day	16	m		Carpenter		
421	402	Freeman Harris	40	m		Carpenter		RE: 750

Number	Dwelling Number	Family Names	Age	Sex	Color	Occupation, etc.	Birthplace	Remarks
		Margaret S. (Harris)	34	f		Seamstress		
		Martha Pinn	13	f	B			
422	403	Thos. B. Finks	35	m		Carpenter		RE: 750
		Lucy E. "	29	f		Housekeeper		nee: Pattie; m. 12-19-1848
		Virginia A. "	1	f				
		Elizabeth Pattie	10	f				
		Maria "	9	f				
423	404	L. H. Reynolds	38	m		Merchant	N.Y.	4,000 - 30,000
		Lucy "	39	f		Housekeeper	Virginia	
		Alvile "	7	m			"	
		Birdie "	3	f			"	
		Macarta Thornton	19	m		Dry good clerk	"	
424	405	Wm. C. Norriss	53	m		Distiller		2800 -
		Ann E. "	49	f		Housekeeping		
		Sarah A. "	55	f		Sewing, etc.		
		Annie E. "	17	f				
425	406	A. H. Spilman	54	m		Post Master		PP: 100
		A. G. "	52	f		Housekeeper		
		Maria "	18	f		Sewing, etc.		
		Samuel B."	13	m				
		George L. Markell	32	m		Tanner & Currier		PP: 200
		Ellen E. "	31	f		Sewing, etc.		
		Henry H. "	5	m				
		Ida "	2	f				
		Theodosia "	1	f				
426	407	Jno. W. Finks	42	m		Druggist	Virginia	8,000 - 3,500
		Lucy A. "	36	f		Housekeeper	"	nee: Caldwell; m. 1-8-1840
		Frances Caldwell	55	f		Knitting etc.	"	nee: Pattie
		Wm. "	5	m			"	
		Pendleton Triplett	14	m		Store boy	"	
		Elcon Jones	18	m		Clerk	"	
427	408	Mordicai Stewart	47	m		Coachmaker	Maryland	PP: 50
428	409	Samuel Biays	50	m		Tinner	Delaware	400 - 500
429	410	Ann P. Brooke	57	f		Housekeeping	Virginia	12,000 - 51,000

Number	Dwelling Number	Family Names	Age	Sex	Color	Occupation, etc.	Birthplace	Remarks
		Alex. J. Marshall	59	m				
		Elizabeth	36	f		Sewing, etc.		
		Lucy P. "	5	f				
		Agnes R. "	1	f				
		Elizabeth R."	23	f		Sewing, etc.		
		Markham "	17	m				
		Harriett Blackwell	27	f		Sewing, etc.		
		William Marshall	5	m				
430	411	Mary Porter	58	f		Housekeeping		
431	412	Thornton Withers	54	m		Hotel Keeper		17,000 - 10,845
		Agnes "	40	f		Housekeeper (Farmers Hotel)		nee: Nelson; m. 10-21-1841; she m. (2) George G. Booth; he had m. 1st Katherine Nelson
		George A. "	12	m				
		Betty "	11	f				
		Samuel Phillips	45	m		Daguerrean Artist	N.Y.	PP: 800
		Mary C. "	19	f			Maryland	
		Charlie "	10	m			Pa.	
		Elizabeth Nelson	65	f		Knitting, etc.	Virginia	
		Sarah B. Weaver	30	f		Sewing, etc.	"	
		Cath. Nelson	20	f		Sewing, etc.		
		Thomas Martin	43	m		Plasterer		PP: 30
432	413	Tom Coram	65	m	M	Carpenter		PP: 50
		Sophy "	50	f	B	Cook, etc.		
433	414	Lucretia Day	54	f		Housekeeper		10,000 - 3690
		Virginia "	22	f		Sewing etc.		
		Josephine "	14	f				
		Henry "	21	m		Copying clerk		
434	415	Mary Gordon	65	f		Housekeeper	England	1300 - 350
		Ann Milburn	62	f		Sewing etc.	do.	nee: Mary Milbourn; m. 12-1-1826 Robt. Gordon
		Robt. W. Gordon	36	m		Printer	Virginia	
435	416	Wm. Helm	62	m		Prosecuting government claims	Kentucky	40,000 - 9,600

Number	Dwelling Number	Family Names	Age	Sex	Color	Occupation, etc.	Birthplace	Remarks
436	417	John H. Davenport	40	m		Brickmason	Kentucky	2500 - 1200
		Eliza F. "	38	f		Housekeeper	Virginia	
		Ira E. "	11	m				
		James B. "	8	m				
		Henry A. "	2	m				
		George S. "	1	m				
		Susan "	75	f		Knitting etc.		
		Ben Tyra	15	m	M	Appr. brk. mason		
437	418	John Ward	33	m		Physician	Virginia	3700 - 600M
		M. G. D. "	26	f		Housekeeper	Maryland	
		Robt. H. "	8	m			Virginia	
		Mary A. "	6	f				
		John S. "	4	m			"	
		Mary A. Hamilton	62	f		Knitting etc.	"	PP: 12,000
438	419	Rice W. Payne	41	m		Lawyer	Virginia	28,800 - 13,470 "Mecca"
		America "	32	f		Housekeeping	D.C.	nee: Semmes; m. 1-4-1848; he m. 2nd Virginia Semmes 4-4-1864
		Bessie W. "	9	f			"	
		Cora "	7	f			"	
		John Carroll "	4	m			"	
		Wm. Gaston "	2	m			"	
		Raphael S. "	1/12	m			"	
		Matilda Semmes	60	f		Sewing etc.	D.C.	
		Virginia "	39	f		Do.	"	
439	420	Wm. H. Gaines, Sr.	53	m		Retired merchant	Virginia	97,700 - 189,875
		Mary F. "	29	f		Housekeeping		nee: Mary Mildred Foster; m. 1-24-1850
		Lizzie F. "	8	f				
		Grenville "	6	m				
		Wm. H. " Jr.	4	m				
		Lena "	2	f				
		Susan Foster	23	f		Sewing etc.		PP: 2200
		Thomas Foster	68	m		Merchant		
440	421	Wm. J. Risdon	29	m		Carpenter		PP: 100
		Mary "	27	f		Housework		nee: Mary Kirby; m. 7-9-1851
		Frank P. "	8	m				
		Wm. N. "	6	m				

Number	Dwelling Number	Family Names	Age	Sex	Color	Occupation, etc.	Birthplace	Remarks
		Jno. R. Risdon	5	m				
		Joseph "	3	m				
		Cora C. "	1	f				
441	422	Judy Malvin	55	f	M	Washerwoman		PP: 50
		Sarah "	30	f	M	Seamstress		PP: 25
442	423	Richard Payne	50	m		Presiding Justice		55,300 - 32,940
		Alice "	47	f		Housekeeping		nee: Alice Fitzhugh Dixon; m. 9-4-1834
		Alex. "	22	m		Lawyer		
		Lillie "	11	f				
		Agnes "	6	f				
		Mary "	4	f				
443	424	Robt. Randolph	23	m		Lawyer		PP: 300
		Charles T. Green	39	m		Do.		PP: 13,000
		P. Bell Smith	22	m		Do.		PP: 495
444	425	Jane Craig	30	f	B	Washerwoman		PP: 50
445	426	Jane Williams	35	f	M	Seamstress		PP: 30
446	427	Cath. J. Marr	62	f		Housekeeping		2500 - 12,425 nee: Horner; m. John Marr
		Sally "	43	f		Sewing, etc.		
		Margaret M."	30	f		Do.		
		Fanny H. "	26	f		Do.		
		Jane B. "	20	f		Do.		
		John Q. "	35	m		Pub. buildings & lots; Ex. High Sheriff		25,000 11,600 - 23,312
447	428	Fred'k Horner "	53	m		Physician		9000 - 4300
		Ann M. "	43	f		Housekeeping		
		Gus. B. "	18	m				
		Severe L. "	15	m				
		Robt. C. "	13	m				
		John G. "	11	m				
		Richard B. "	9	m				
		Mariana "	7	f				
448	429	Wm. H. Payne	30	m		Laywer		17,100 - 13,800 as ex'r & trustee 12,000 - 12,000 nee: Mary Elizabeth Winston Payne; m. 9-29-1852
		Mary "	28	f		Housekeeping		

Number	Dwelling Number	Family Names	Age	Sex	Color	Occupation, etc.	Birthplace	Remarks
		Wm. W. Payne	7	m				
		Arthur M. "	5	m				
		Henry F. "	3	m				
		John W. "	2	m				
		Richard "	6/12	m				
449	430	Wm. B. Brawner	46	m		Negro Trader		PP: 6200
		Fanny "	22	f		Housekeeper		
		Chas. Wm. "	1	m				
		Sarah E. French	35	f		Sewing, etc.		
		Mary M. "	13	f				
		Eugenia B."	11	f				
		Lucinda "	9	f				
450	431	Peter Dolin	68	m		Well Digger	Ireland	600 - 90
		Malinda "	45	f		Housework		
		Mary Pickle	40	f		Do.		
		Anne Gordon	5	f				
451	432	Lucy Baker	68	f				
		Susan "	30	f				
		Mary E. "	28	f				
		Lucy "	10	f				
		Dillard "	20	m		Segar maker		
		Jacob "	17	m				
452	433	Nat. Proctor	45	m		Well Digger		PP: 75
		Susan "	40	f		Housework		
		John (Proctor)	5	m				
		William "	3	m				
		Lucy "	1	f				
453	434	Otto S.Barten	29	m		Prot. Epis. minister	Hamburg, Germany	4500 - 2028
		Emma H. "	23	f		Housekeeping	N.Y.	
454	435	Sally Glassell	60	f		Housekeeping		10,000 - 8500
455	436	Wm. Smith	62	m		M C [Member of Congress]		19,000 - 9155
		Elizabeth A."	58	f		Housekeeping		
		Mary A. "	28	f		Sewing etc.		4000 - 1500
		Fred. W. "	16	m				
589	544	John A. Spilman	41			Merchant	Virginia	11,600 - 55,000
		Susan R. "	40					
		Wm. H. "	16					
		Mary A. "	13					

Number	Dwelling Number	Family Names	Age	Sex	Color	Occupation, etc.	Birthplace	Remarks
		Annie F. Spilman	11					
		Hugh C. "	9					
		Clara F. "	6					
590	545	Erasmus Helm	56			Merchant & farmer	Virginia	53,000 - 45,411
		Mary A. "	46					
		Agnes P. "	16					
		Edward "	14					
		R. Henry "	12					
		Francis M. "	10	m				
		Littleton "	9					
591	546	Geo. H. Whitescarver	54			Teacher		1000 - 450
		Geo. H. " Jr.	21					
		Matilda N. Oliver	19					
		Frances C. Whitescarver	17	f				
		William H. Oliver	22					
592	547	John A. Chilton	43			M.D.		PP: 11,283
		Catherine "	30					
		John A. "	2					
		Nannie "	2/12					
593	548	Edward M. Spilman	32			Lawyer	Virginia	11,750 - 12,250
		Eliza C. "	28					
		Jennie D. "	9					
		Baldwin D. "	7					
		Edward G. "	5					
		Mary M. "	1					
		Henry E.	23/30					
594	549	Benj. H. Shackleford	40			Lawyer & farmer		10,940 - 25,190
		Rebecca B. "	29					
		Jones G. "	7					
		John H. "	5					
		George S. "	3					
		Lucy "	11/12					
		Fannie L. Green	21					
		Arthur Payne	21	m	B	Laborer		

Number	Dwelling Number	Family Names	Age	Sex	Color	Occupation, etc.	Birthplace	Remarks
		Wm. H. Payne	18	m	B	Cook		
		Salina Payne	16	f	B			
595	550	Alexander Brodie	30			Taylor	Edinburg, Scotland	1200 - 300
		Jennett "	27			Tayloress	Virginia	
		Margaret "	6					
		Josephine "	4					
		Charles "	2					
		Margaret "	51				Edinburg, Scotland	
		Eliza Prettiman	18			Tayloress	Virginia	
596	551	Matilda Howard	61				Virginia	3500 - 100
597	552	Israel Schwap	31			Merchant	Bavaria	PP: 3300
		Rosa "	28				"	
		Fannie "	3				Va	
		Seina "	1					
		J. M. English	34			Merchant	Virginia	PP: 5500
598	553	Fanny P. Digges	34			Principal of female school	Virginia	PP: 6050
		Octavia "	16					
		Ludwell "	14					
		Lelia "	12					
		Henrietta "	10					
		Sallie G. "	8					
		Wm. E. "	6					
		Julia Parker	21					
		Harriet A. Hillery	30					
		Richard "	7					
		Worthington "	5					
		Annie "	2					
		Mollie Renoe	25					
		James M. Hope	18			Clerk & boards with Spilman & James _____		
		Bond Collins	18			"		
		Hugh W. Davis	17			"		
		Eliza Longane	86			Boards with Spilman		
599	554	Jacob Mytinger	63			Silversmith	Virginia	1700 - 5650
		Evaline "	58					
600	555	George Deatherage	33			Merchant		PP: 9250
		Mary E. "	28					

Number	Dwelling Number	Family Names	Age	Sex	Color	Occupation, etc.	Birthplace	Remarks
		Mary Geo. Deatherage	1	f				
601	556	James Deshields	53	m		Hotel Keeper (Warrenton House)	Maryland	4600 - 6500
		Eliza R. "	36				Virginia	PP: 2250
		Roberta "	18					
		Martha "	17					
		Eliza C. "	12					
		J. D. "	14	m				
		William "	6					
602	557	G. W. Jackson	30			Lawyer	Virginia	
		William Wall	32			Clerk		
		William D. Scott	28			Reads the newspapers		
		Horace C. Withers	19			Hunts & fishes		RE: 3000
		Wm. McCarty, Jr.	21			Studying law		
		E. M. Mureh	30			Teacher	Missouri	
		John W. McIlhany	25			Doctor of Medicine		
		Robert Lear	25			Merchant		
		B. Cerf	27			Watchmaker	N.Y.	
		Marion English	29			Merchant		
		Kemp B. Grigsley	53			Lawyer		
		T. R. Lunsford	35			Discounts paper		
		Nelson Thornton	60	m	B	Servant		
		James Allan	45	m	B	"		
		James White	13	m	B	"		
603	558	Geo. G. Booth	39			Journeyman Coachmaker	Maryland	PP: 150
		Cynthia A. "	32					
		Mary E. "	11					
		Barbary L. "	8					
		Emily J. "	4					
		Elizabet Grant	60					
		William D. Fletcher	45			Journeyman Coachmaker		
		Frederick Feige	28			Journeyman Coachsmith	Maryland	
		Mary A. "	22					
		Mary A. "	5/12					
		John Minter	17			Apprentice to coachsmith		
		Emma L. Feige	6				Maryland	

Number	Dwelling Number	Family Names	Age	Sex	Color	Occupation, etc.	Birthplace	Remarks
		Virginia Ann Williams	22	f	B			
604	559	John R. Spilman	36	m		Carpenter & builder		4000 - 4000
		Sarah A. "	33					
		Wm. Field	19			Apprentice to carpenters trade		
		John M.Henne	20			"		
		Henry Thomas	19			"		
		James Kaynor	18			"		
		George F. Jenkins	22			Journeyman carpenter		
		Robert H. Grones	25			"		
		George B. Kaynor	25			"		
605	560	Charles A. Smith	27			Carpenter & Joiner		850 - 1200
		Margaret G. "	27					
		Wm. "	4					
		James "	2					
606	561	Flora E. Suddoth	33			Widow		PP: 50
		Edlow "	4	m				
		Jeremiah "	2					
607	562	John Leary	62			Supervisor of his own affairs	Ireland	2500 - 23,560
		John B. Leary	26				Virginia	
608	563	Ann D. Baylor	80			Widow		2200 - 12,000
609	564	Geo. E. Yeatman	62			Farmer		10,000 - 10,321
		Chloe A. "	57					
		Mary E. "	20					
		Sophronia "	17					
610	565	Daniel Warner	65		M			1000 - 75
		Jonnie "	16		M			
		Wm. Patterson	27	m	M			
		Cornelia	22	m	M			
611	566	Romulus Hudnal	30	m	M			
		Ada "	22	f	M			
		Dodridge "	10	m	M			
		Albert "	8	m	M			
		James "	1	m	M			

Number	Dwelling Number	Family Names	Age	Sex	Color	Occupation, etc.	Birthplace	Remarks
612	567	Abraham D. Klotz	54			Deputy Post Master		1000 - 1900
		Lucinda "	53					
		Eliza "	25					
613	568	Wm. Smith	17	m	B	Laborer		
		Octavia "	36	f	B			
		Tom "	5	m	B			
		Martha "	1	f	B			
		Frank Gaskins	25	m	M			
614	569	Charles Hughs	38	m	M	Laborer		PP: 30
		Frances "	33	f	B			
615	570	Ann Bragg	72	f		Widow		1000 - 3200
		Eliza "	50					
		Margaret E. "	31			Mantua maker		PP: 175
		Lewis Bragg	64					
616	571	Mildred Rinn	26	f	M			
		Sophie	4/12	f	M			
617	572	Robert Coons	35			Auctioneer		PP: 75
		Lucy "	27					
		Catharine Pinn	12	f	B			
618	573	Horace Pattie	36			Carpenter		PP: 200
		Josephine "	23					
		Annie M. "	3					
		Cora A. "	2					
		Estelle "	3/12					
		Ann Samarque	44					
619	574	Thomas Hudnal	40	m	M	Butcher		1050 - 50
		Eliza "	31	f	M			
		Posey "	11	m	M			
		Scott "	8	m	M			
		Aquilla "	6	m	M			
		Bell "	2	f	M			
620	575	Wm. Martin	21			Plasterer		PP: 75
		Lucy A. "	21					
621	576	Horace Page	40	m	M	Livery stable keeper		PP: 865
		Thos. Gaskins	23	m	M	Hack Driver		
		Eliza "	21	f	M			
		Wm. H. "	3	m	M			

Number	Dwelling Number	Family Names	Age	Sex	Color	Occupation, etc.	Birthplace	Remarks
622	577	John E. Scruggs	34	m		Editor of Warrenton Whig; also Col.-85th Regt. Va. Militia		8000 - 3500
		Susan C. "	35					4000 - 10,400
		John H. Alexander	13					5000 - 9000
		Wm. R. "	11					5000 - 9000
		Chas. E. Shearer	23			Publisher Warrenton Whig		
		Nathan "	17			Asst. Publisher Warrenton Whig		
		Edward Walden	17			"		
623	578	Alfred Saunders	46					
		Ann "	30					
		Thomas "	22					
		Mary "	19					
		John A.	16					
		Martha E. "	14					
		Eliza J. "	10					
624	579	E. D. Owen	41	m		Minister of M. E. Church	Pa.	RE: 2000
		H. L. "	30	f				PP: 1750
		S. H. Hall	25	f				
625	580	John T. Bronaugh	53	m		Farmer		25,110 - 14,818
		Mary G. "	33					
		Mary A. Stone	21					
626		Unoccupied						J. T. Bronaugh
627		Unoccupied						A. M. Brodie
628	581	Thomas Wood	29	m		Confectioner	Virginia	PP: 300
		Keziah "	27	f				
		Willie "	1	m				
		Fanny "	10	f	M			

INDEX

Marr, Catherine H. 259n.9
  James Ripon 259, 259n.9
  John 259n.9
  John Q. 19n.2, 26n.18, 72n.10, 94n.43,
    135, 135n.104, 259n.9
Marshall, Charles 244
  John 15
Martin, Robert E. 217, 217n.16
Mason, James 68n.3
McCafferty, Mary 231
McClearan, Mary F. 155, 155n.134
  Thomas C. 155n.134
McClellan, George B. 7, 34n.27, 83n.27,
    90n.34, 97, 98n.51, 106, 110, 115,
    116, 119, 121, 122, 123, 126, 132, 134,
    134n.103, 135, 141, 143, 148, 173,
    238
McCormick, Robert E. 136, 136n.105
McDowell, Irvin 35, 90n.35, 127n.94,
    141n.119, 144n.123
McIlhany, John W. 253, 253n.1
McLane, Louis 78n.21
McMillan, William 60, 60n.50
McNeil, John H. 213, 213n.9
Meade, George G. 7, 196n.44, 211
Melville, Malcolm L. 24n.13, 118n.82
Miller, Brent 101n.57
  Greene 101n.57
  Middleton 101n.57
  Paul 63
Mitchell, Frank 28
Moncure, R. C. L. 19n.2
Moore, Ellen 43n.39
  Samuel P. 43, 43n.39, 47, 238
  Susan 43n.39
Morgan, John H. 230, 230n.30
Morse, Samuel F. B. 10, 15, 62, 62n.54
Mosby, John S. 5, 7, 23n.9, 141n.118,
    175n.7, 182n.14, 184n.18, 185n.20,
    186n.24, 186n.25, 187, 187n.27, 188,
    213, 213n.9, 218n.17, 219, 219n.19,
    221, 223, 226, 240n.49, 248, 248n.58,
    248n.59, 253n.1, 253n.2, 258, 258n.8,
    260n.10
Muir, Portus 29
Mullins, Bettie 260
Munford, Thomas T. 80, 80n.23, 88n.32,
    92, 105, 120, 122
Murray, Edward 36, 36n.31
Neal, Willa 40
Nelson, Agnes A. 205n.54
  Katherine 205n.54

Newhouse, John P. 136, 136n.105
Norris, Ann C. 19n.2
  Mary E. 19n.2
  Thaddeus 19n.2
  William 190, 190n.36
Norriss, William C. 190n.36
Norton, George H. 187n.28
Oxlade, Elvira 102n.58
  Thomas 102n.58, 137
Palmerston, Lord 68n.3, 139n.116
Patterson, Billy 124, 124n.90
Pattie, Dudley 205, 217, 227
  Frances 14
  Horace 61
  James S. 85, 85n.30
  Tom 216, 216n.14
  William A. 72, 72n.9, 85n.30, 133, 165,
    171, 176, 216
  William, Sr. 14
Payne, Alban S. 124n.90
  Alexander D. 184, 184n.19, 185, 233
  Billy 142
  Brook 124n.90
  Inman 188
  Mary 107n.69
  Raphael S. 141n.119
  Rice W. H. 141, 141n.119, 142, 188
  William 117
  William H. 100n.55, 130n.98, 184,
    184n.17, 256, 259
  Winter (W. R. H. W.) 107, 107n.69, 184
Pelham, John 176n.8
Pemberton, John C. 193n.42
Penn, William 62n.55
Peyton, Henry E. 85, 85n.29
Phillips, Roberta 168, 172
Phillips, Stanley S. 36n.31
Pickett, George E. 31n.20, 245, 245n.54
Pollock, Abraham D. 253n.2
  Anne L. 253n.2
  Elizabeth 253n.2
  Elizabeth G. 253n.2
  Margaret 253n.2
  Roberta 253n.2
Pope, John 7, 144, 144n.123, 146,
    146n.124, 147, 147n.125, 148, 149,
    149n.127
Porter, John M. 136, 136n.105
Pugh, John W. 190, 190n.37
Quarles, James 28
Radford, Richard C. 93, 93n.40, 121, 144
Randolph, Robert 232n.38

Rindsburg, Abraham 52, 52n.44, 56, 58, 176, 179
Roberts, John 227
Robertson, B. H. 147n.125
Rogers, Asa 90, 90n.36
    Hugh 97n.49
    Mary C. 97n.49
    Susan 97n.49
Rosecrans, William S. 171n.1, 200, 200n.50
Royston, Alice 246
    Marshall R. 81, 81n.24, 114
    Martha 166
    Tommy 260
Russell, John W. 258, 258n.8
    L. W. 203n.52
    T. Triplett 5
Samson, George W. 74n.18, 221
Saunders, Alfred 186n.25
    Ann 186n.25
    John A. 186, 186n.25
    Jordan 133, 133n.102
    Ned 71
    Thomas B. 136, 136n.106, 231
Scott, John 73n.12
    Martin P. 124n.90
    R. Taylor 19n.2, 31, 31n.20, 46, 120, 121
    Robert E. 31n.20, 107, 107n.68, 109, 111, 114
    Winfield 34, 34n.27, 37, 39, 70n.6
Screven, William 11, 62n.55
Scruggs, John E. 32, 32n.22, 33, 34, 35, 89, 90
Sedgwick, John 196n.44
Sedwick, Benjamin 33n.23, 56
    Charles 33, 33n.23, 35, 126, 131, 143, 161, 162, 171, 172, 173
Semmes, America 141n.119
    Virginia 141n.119
Shackleford, Benjamin H. 24n.13, 35, 142n.120
    Rebecca 142, 142n.120, 174
Sheridan, Philip 230n.35, 232n.37, 240n.48, 245
Sherman, Thomas W. 60n.49
    William T. 229, 230, 230n.29
Shields, James 7, 90, 90n.35, 90n.36, 90n.37, 101n.57, 120, 121, 130, 132n.100
Shumate, George H. 143, 143n.122, 144
Sickles, Daniel E. 189n.33

Sigel, Franz 149, 149n.127, 150, 150n.129, 151n.131, 229n.27
Sinclair, Louisa 104
Skinker, Howard 209, 209n.2
    Sarah G. 26n.17
Slidell, John 68n.3
Slye, Gwynetta 111, 111n.72
Smallwood, Emma 74n.19
Smith, Ann D. 260n.10
    Anne Brooke 20n.5
    Elizabeth B. 94n.43
    Frank 107, 111
    G. W. 182n.14
    John 260n.10
    John (Mrs.) 191, 191n.39, 258
    Kirby E. 230, 230n.34, 233
    Lucy S. 19n.1
    Mary A. 94, 94n.43
    Peter B. 185, 185n.22
    Richard M. 19, 19n.1, 24, 80, 90, 93, 150, 154, 179, 236
    William ('Extra Billy') 20, 20n.5, 36n.31, 87, 94n.43, 185n.22, 229
    William R. 19n.1
Smoot, Samuel C. 74, 74n.19
Sowers, James R. 260n.10
    Mary F. 260, 260n.10
Spilman, Alexander H. 118, 118n.82, 121
    Cud 136
    Edward M. 24, 24n.13, 38, 97n.49, 158
    John A. 97, 97n.49, 149, 191, 216
    John R. 24, 24n.12, 116
    Lucretia 24n.13
    Luther M. 22n.8, 233
    Mary A. 97n.49
Stephens, James H. 33, 33n.25, 46, 73, 97, 128
Stofer, Alfred J. 231, 231n.36, 232, 237
    Rebecca A. 10
Stoneman, George 233, 233n.41
Stoughton, Edwin H. 175n.7, 182, 182n.14
Straight, A. D. 211, 211n.5
Strother, Gaines 97
Stuart, J. E. B. 7, 87, 88, 134, 134n.103, 147, 147n.125, 148, 149, 164, 164n.144, 167, 187n.27, 189, 190n.35, 196n.44
Suares, Anna 40n.36, 102n.60, 164n.145
    Basil 40n.36, 137, 137n.112, 171n.2
    Benjamin 40n.36, 102n.59, 102
    Benjamin C. 40n.36, 137n.112, 164n.145, 243n.50

Carry 40n.36, 102n.60, 164n.145

Ellen 40n.36, 102n.60, 164n.145, 180, 180n.12

Elvira 40n.36

Harriet 40, 40n.36, 101, 113, 119, 137n.112, 164, 164n.145, 243n.50

Julia 40n.36, 102n.60, 243n.50

Sullivan, Jeremiah 121, 121n.85

Tavenner, Charles H. 33, 33n.24, 35, 78, 227, 233, 234

Taylor, Richard 193n.42

Tharpe, Tom 101n.57

Thomas, D. W. 22n.8

Thompson, Lila J. 43n.39, 62n.55, 62n.56

Tiffany, C. Hunton 5

Tongue, Frances Y. 23, 23n.9

John R. 23n.9, 23n.10

Johnsie 23n.9, 184, 185

Virginia P. 23n.10, 38, 95

Willa 107

Willie 95

Tourison, Ashton S. 96, 96n.47, 142

Towles, Dick 136, 136n.109

Trenholm, George A. 233, 233n.42

Triplett, Alice 233, 233n.43

Carrie B. 233n.43

Daniel 15

Edwin M. 233n.43

Elizabeth 233n.43

James D. 35n.29, 39

James P. 35n.29, 178, 233n.43

Mary P. 233n.43

Thomas H. 35n.29, 233, 233n.43

William B. 35n.29, 178, 233n.43

William H. 35n.29, 233, 233n.43

Trumbo, Gertrude 6

Tulloss, Joseph D. 127, 127n.96, 128

Tyler, Charles E. 189, 189n.32

Gwynetta 111n.73

John W. 73, 73n.12, 111n.72, 111n.73

Utterback, Addison W. 23, 23n.10, 59, 84, 236

John A. 23n.10

James T. 23n.10, 53, 55, 156, 158

Mary C. 23n.10

Virginia P. T. 23, 23n.10, 34, 59, 68, 165

Walraven, Edgar 11

Jessie 11

Ward, Berkeley 48n.42

Berkeley (Mrs.) 128

Clay 36

John 48n.42, 118, 119, 120, 121

John (Mrs.) 48

Warner, Daniel 133

Warren, Joseph 13

Watson, Henry E. 38n.34, 131

John 38n.34, 131

Joseph H. 38n.34, 155n.135, 175, 176, 177

Mary E. 38, 38n.34, 109, 131, 155n.135, 156, 175, 176, 177, 180

Mary J. 155n.135, 156, 158

Weaver, Tilman 136, 136n.109

Westcoat, Preston 55, 70, 153

Thomas 49

Westmore, William 43

Wheeler, Joseph 230, 230n.32

White, Billy 38

Elijah 123, 123n.88

Frank 122

Ham 97, 188

Harriet C. 89n.33, 255, 255n.5

John 142

Mary A. 99, 99n.54, 148

Octavia 48, 89n.33, 96, 191, 200

Thomas 200

Wilkes, Charles 68n.3

Williamson, James J 184n.18

Willis, Charles B. 136, 136n.105

Wilson, Calla 112

Willis 30

Winston, Minerva W. 107n.69

Wise, Henry A. 74n.13, 74n.15, 91n.38

O. Jennings 74n.15

Withers, B. L. 24

Frances E. C. 57n.47, 129n.97

Jesse H. 57n.47, 67n.1, 129n. 97

Katherine E. 129, 129n.97, 135, 148, 262

Melville 261

Sally 10, 54, 57n.47, 57, 129n.97, 67n.1

Samuel M. 57n.47

Thornton 205, 205n.54, 210

Wonham, Harry 6

Wood, Emily A. 233n.43

Wyndham, Percy 175, 175n.7, 176, 180, 182n.14

Yeatman, Chloe A. 71n.8

George 71n.8

John 23n.9

Martha 22

Sophronia 71, 71n.8